Saint Alphonsus and His Brothers

SAINT ALPHONSUS AND HIS BROTHERS

A Study of the Lives and Works of Seven Redemptorists

Hamish F. G. Swanston

Liguori
LIGUORI, MISSOURI

Published by Liguori Publications
Liguori, Missouri
http://www.liguori.org

Library of Congress Cataloging-in-Publication Data

Swanston, Hamish F. G., 1933–
Saint Alphonsus and his brothers : a study of the lives and works of seven redemptorists / Hamish F. G. Swanston.—1st ed.
p. cm.
Includes bibliographical references and index.
ISBN 0-7648-0578-9
1. Redemptorists—Italy—Biography. 2. Liguori, Alfonso Maria de', Saint, 1696–1787. 3. Redemptorists—Italy—History—18th century. I. Title.

BX4020.Z7 S93 2000
271'.64022—dc21
[B] 99–057764

Printed in the United States of America
04 03 02 01 00 5 4 3 2 1
First Edition

I am one of the Brothers of the
Congregation of the Most Holy Redeemer
to whom you have most graciously granted
Apostolic authorization.

Alphonsus de' Liguori, 1696–1788,
Dedicatory letter to Pope Benedict XIV,
Theologia Moralis, vol. I, 2nd ed., 1753

Acknowledgments

Commissioned by the Very Reverend Thomas M. Santa to "do something on the Brothers" which should complement what I had written about Saint Alphonsus, *Celebrating Eternity Now,* and Celeste Crostarosa, *Singing a New Song,* I looked about for helpers. I found them everywhere I looked. This was just the time I was moving from England back to Scotland, and I could not have managed to shift my books, research papers, file boxes, typewriter, without the van-driving of Dr. Philip Cattermole, once one of my graduate students at Canterbury University, who obtained gracious leave of his wife Zuzana to go off on this removals weekend. In Scotland, Mrs. Pamela Gilchrist, Librarian of New College, Edinburgh, has been several times willing to dusty her hands in the book-cellarage for me. I had equally personal assistance from Librarian Colin Bovaird at St Mary's College, St. Andrews University. And while I went off to foreign parts to track down some sprightly Brother's past, Mr. Bob Jardine at Scone relieved me of a worry by storing my papers in his fireproof box. In those foreign parts, Brother John Condon, the Capuchin Provincial in England, at the end of a lecture I'd given at the Franciscan Study Centre, Canterbury, brought, for one grand e-mail moment, both Brother Charles Serignat at the Collegio San Lorenzo and Brother Servus Gieben of the Capuchin Historical Institute onto my research team. Getting to Italy, books and manuscripts were brought out for me by Signora Marielle in the Biblioteca Teatrale de Burcado, Rome, Dottore Rocise in the Archivio di Stato, Naples, and Revdo P. Giovanni Ferrara, the superintendent of the Naples Oratory archives, who went through their "book of the dead" with me. The Reverend Master of the Collegio of the Lady of Consolation, the eager young women and young men of his Community of Peace, and his stray dogs, together ensured that I had a lively time at d'Iliceto. Down in the little crypt, touching each Redemptorist skull in turn, I said my prayers that Antonio Maria Tannoia and the rest of them would oversee my researches in the house. I had a splendid day being shown Muro Lucano by Monsignore Don Antonio Barbieri, the enthusiastic guardian of all things Majellan. And, further afield yet, I was given a stupendous welcoming hug by S. E. Mario Paciello, lately Alphonsus' successor as bishop of Sant' Agata dei Goti, and now bishop of Altamura-Gravina and of Acquaviva delle Fonti, Vito Curzio's hometown.

"Something on the Brothers" turned out to be rather larger than an essay on "Gerard and companions," for as I worked it became apparent that a range of distinguished men had made their ways through a Brother's vocation among the eighteenth-century Redemptorists and, at the same time, that whatever scope any one of them had for his vocation depended from Alphonsus' understanding of his experiences. How he assessed his relationships with others as eldest brother in a family, as active member of charitable confraternities, and then as "one of the Brothers of the Congregation." In coming to some estimate of Alphonsus' converting these experiences for the exercise of authority as Rector Major, for a cooperative ministry with other priests in a missioner Congregation, and for their all persevering with the lay Brothers until they should be saints together, I have needed a variety of Redemptorist helpers.

I am grateful for the encouraging gestures of the Very Reverend Juan Lasso de la Vega Miranda, Superior General of the Congregation when I began this piece of work in 1996, and of the Most Reverend Joseph Tobin, Superior General now.

A great number of priests in the Congregation have tried to prevent my making too many gross mistakes about life within "our customs," chief among them the Very Reverend Padraig Gallagher, the director who invited me to be Scholar in Residence at the Alphonsian Institute, Kinnoull, under the favor of the Very Reverend Fathers Provincial James McManus and John Trenchard. In the London Province, Fathers Beverley Ahearn, Charles Corrigan, Paul Douthwaite, Denis McBride, and many others have shown themselves to be on my side. In Rome, the Very Reverend Emilio Lage Martinez has, during my twice or thrice yearly visits to the General Archives, made the Alphonsianum house a most welcoming place in which to work and grin. There were many in his Community willing to give time and energy to answer niggling questions, notably Professor Giuseppe Orlandi who knows so much about the Kingdom of Naples in Alphonsus' lifetime that what he doesn't know isn't knowledge, and Professor Sante Raponi, whose grand inquiry into every aspect of Brothers' experience is as delightfully daunting, and along with them, in the Historical Institute, Fathers Hernan Arboleda Valencia, Raul Campos, and Adam Owczarski have each one taken attention from his own research in order to help. But then, a host of good Fathers came hurrying to be kind and useful, Professors Dennis Billy, Sabatino Majorano, and Francesco Lage Martinez; the computer whiz John Charles Vargas; Marian Brudzisz and Paul Sindermann in the Library; Hans-Adolf Niesen and Josef Wimmer in the Curia offices. The Very Reverend Fathers Rector at Pagani and Ciorani were attentive hosts, letting me wander at my ease along the aisles of their grand libraries. At Materdomini I was equally graciously received, and there Revdo P. Raffaelo Martino guided me through the records of house history and allowed me a moment to reverence the bones of Paolo Cafaro in a box at the back of his parish office. In the Naples provincial house, I was happy to coincide with Dottore Francesco Chiovaro, the busy editor of *Storia della Congregazione*, who, by then proving so willing to talk about my work, found he had made himself even busier later as my further queries came in the mail. A similar graciousness had the same tiresome result at Madrid for Fathers Fabriciano Ferrero and Marciano Vidal. And, at Liguori, the Very Reverend Henry Grile has taken presidential care of the work from proofreading to publication.

There are two ways of uncovering what it is to be a Brother in the Congregation; the better is to live the life, the other is to pester those who are living the life. My questions have been answered with exemplary patience by many Brothers: Alban Ivess at Edmonton; Alessandro Lopez Castillo, and his colleague at Madrid, the garage manager Eliseo Vide; Anthony McGrave at Belfast; Anthony McKell and Willie McDermott in London; Daniel Korn, the spiritual director at Liguori, and Gerard Clark, his convivial chum; Dermot McDonagh, Richard Costello and Tommy Walsh at Dundalk; and Jarleth O'Neill in Dublin, who has several times done a little approving skip on my risking an odd opinion; Gaudenzio de Jong the bookstore supremo and soccer coach in Rome; Kevin Garvey, who during a few weeks at his house proved a most charitable friend, along with Edgar Hoffman and Raymond Pierce in

Toronto; Matteo Ergoli, the elegant controller of the Naples community; Michael Duxbury, the enthusiastic prison chaplain at Plymouth, Richard Golding and his amiable collie dog Meg at Hawkstone; William Roberts, the poet at Seattle. I have been especially aided by Brother Pius Carmichael at Kinnoull, who typed a rough draft of my work, and by Brother Malachy Kelly, who read through versions of a couple of chapters, smiled, and found something encouraging to say each morning on his way to work. But at the close of my review of their seven predecessor Brothers, I expect, presuming again on the Brothers' habitual modesty, that they will all approve my dedicating this storybook to those many others, like Giuseppe Sereno who died at Ciorani in 1789, about whom the official chroniclers say only "of this Brother we know nothing."

HAMISH F. G. SWANSTON,
OBLATE OF THE CONGREGATION,
ALFONSIAN INSTITUTE, KINNOULL, PERTH, SCOTLAND
OCTOBER 16, 1999

Contents

Brother Alphonsus

Alphonsus liked to sign his letters to members of the Redemptorist Congregation as "Brother Alphonsus" and "Brother Alphonsus Maria," even, when hurrying to catch the mailman, "Br. Alphonsus."[1] They were all to recognize themselves as "my Brothers," "my dearly loved Brothers," "my dearly loved Brothers in Jesus Christ."[2] He would make this affirmation of fraternity when writing to a likely candidate. Francesco Margotta, 1699–1764, still dithering at home, was already "my dear Brother." As Alphonsus explains, "I use the title "my dear brother" because I receive you today into our Congregation as a brother."[3] He would immediately cease to acknowledge fraternity when some treacherous man abandoned the Congregation. Giuseppe Muscari, 1710–1793, who had until a few days before been a well-approved General Consultor, found on his leaving the Congregation in mid October 1751 that Alphonsus at once began subscribing his letters "Yours most respectfully, etc."[4]

The precision of Alphonsus' use of "Brother" is nicely demonstrated in the sequence of increasingly distanced signatures to his correspondence with Francesc' Antonio de Paola, 1736–1814, who was, from 1780, effecting a separation of the Redemptorist houses in the Papal States from those holding to Alphonsus in the Kingdom of Naples: "Brother Alphonsus Maria, bishop" being succeeded by "Alphonsus Maria de Liguori, bishop," and "Your very devoted servant and brother" by "Your very devoted servant."[5] That this sequence was interrupted by the simple "Brother Alphonsus Maria" on January 4, 1781, more exhibits Alphonsus' personal carefulness in such matters, for that letter had been dictated to Brother Francesc' Antonio Romito, 1722–1807, who had unthinkingly appended Alphonsus' usual signature for correspondence within the Congregation. Antonio Maria Tannoia, 1727–1808, Alphonsus' fussily devoted hagiographer, was more sensitive to the purposefulness of their saint's use of "Brother." He observed tartly that Alphonsus, at the close of his final letter to the Very Reverend President de Paola on this sad business, June 21, 1782, having made his prayer that "Jesus Christ will bless all those in your Houses," signed off simply as "Alphonsus Maria," not adding, as Tannoia wanted the readers of his great *Life* to note, any protestation of his remaining "Your most affectionate and most obliged Brother."[6]

Alphonsus was as consistent in his correspondence with loyal men within the Congregation, signing himself "Brother Alphonsus" at the close of letters to individual Fathers, Tannoia cherished a packet of these,[7] and to them collectively as a House community, or as members of a mission team.[8] He was "Brother Alphonsus" again to individual Students, and "Your very affectionate Brother" to the whole Student body when, for example, he was asking, in August 1779, that they should "as a great sacrifice for Jesus Christ" be prepared to work in Sicily.[9] And "Brother Alphonsus" to an individual novice, warning Vincenzo Buonopane, 1743–1764, that he should not expect to feel good and cheerful while he's praying, more likely he'll be "dry and weary" like the rest of them,[10] and telling "My very dear Brothers," the novices at d'Iliceto, how much he envies them, "Had I only had in my youth, your happiness of living retired in God's house in the midst of so many virtuous companions, exciting one another to love our Lord more and more."[11] He is "Brother Alphonsus Maria" to Brother Michele Ilardo, 1745–1795, when he wants a letter delivered to his brother, Don Ercole de' Liguori, 1706–1780,[12] and the lay Brothers are all always "My Brothers," "My dear Brothers."[13]

One might suppose, reading these letters, that Alphonsus had in mind some revival of primitive practice among Franciscans, all Brothers together in communities of clerical brothers with lay brothers, every one of them deemed capable of holding office, distinguished only by the clerics' being tonsured and razored "on account of reverence for the Sacrament of the Eucharist."[14] Certainly, the Congregation had its origin in the experience of Celeste Crostarosa, 1696–1755, on the vigil of Saint Francis' feast, October 3, 1731.[15] And there seemed to several distinguished men among the early Redemptorists something sympathetic in Franciscan ways of living. The writings of the Capuchin, Antonio da Olivadi, d. 1720, excited Brother Gerard Majella, 1726–1755, to bloodiest reenactments of Christ's Passion.[16] Domenico Blasucci, 1722–1752, the ideal Student, had first thought himself called to be a Conventual Friar at Matera.[17] Rector Tannoia had, in what spare time he found at d'Iliceto, written a *Life* of the blessed Minorite, Benevenuto of Gubbio, d. 1231.[18] And elements in Alphonsus' own early characterization of his Institute led some to speculate that he must have sometime been a member of a Franciscan "Third Order."[19] Any quick paralleling would, however, be delusive. The prospect of Brother officers was somewhat overcast generally by the particular Franciscan experience of the great Elias, who had died in 1253, unhonored, no one's Brother.[20] Alphonsus would come to a eucharistic description of clerical and lay sharings in the Congregation, but not until late in life when he was no longer determining the Redemptorists' self-image. And he was, all his life, notoriously unconcerned for the cut of his beard. He was never a member of a Franciscan confraternity.[21]

Alphonsus' understanding of himself as "Brother" was realized in a peculiar structural relation which he had with each member of the Congregation and with them all together.

He did make a short attempt to establish some similar sense of himself as Brother, when he was consecrated bishop of Sant' Agata in 1762, with the diocesan clergy. He wrote to his "Very Reverend and Dear Brothers," the rural Deans.[22] But nothing could come of this project. They did not believe in it. Nor, indeed, did he. Therefore, he never addressed the secular priests of the diocese, in personal correspondence or in his many Pastoral Letters to the lot of them, as "My Brothers" or "Dear Brothers." They very soon became "Very Revd. and Excellent Sirs."[23]

Within the structure of the Congregation, Alphonsus was very aware of his holding a singular office, "like the Pope in the Church," for life. Aware of his being thereby a singular Brother among these Brothers. His usage of "Brother" and "Brothers" could not be taken as an encouragement to any individual Redemptorist's slipping into the reciprocities of a personal relationship with him.[24] There could be no question of Tannoia's writing to the Rector Major as "Brother Alphonsus Maria," or of his signing himself to Alphonsus as "Brother Antonio Maria." He should always be "Your most unworthy Servant and Son." It was with a precise sense of his office's being coresponsibly sustained in the Congregation by successive Vicars General, Andrea Villani, 1706–1792, and Bartolomeo Mattia Corrado, 1733-1797, that Alphonsus acknowledged each, during his term of office, as "Revd Brother in Christ" and "Most Revd Father and Brother in J. C." Neither of these Vicars, knowing how uncomfortable Alphonsus was with such power-sharing, was so indelicate as to insist on his right to address him in turn as "Brother." Or to write as "Brother" to the Fathers. At the most, Villani would risk signing himself their "*confrater*" at the close of a circular letter to Rectors.[25] They all understood the distinction.

They were sensitive, on ordinary occasions, to other unstated distinctions. When their Brother Alphonsus has finished his letter to Gaspare Caione, 1722–1809, the Father Rector at Materdomini, about the declining health of Brother Pietrangelo Picone, 1733–1754, who was being prepared for ordination, and about Brother Gerard Majella, 1726–1755, who seemed to Alphonsus a likely Bursar for the house, there's no mistaking the three different uses of "Brother."[26]

If it is plain that there are these differences, it is not always easy to catch at what remains the same through all Alphonsus' uses of "Brother."

There must always be something awkward in any leader's attempt to express his relations with others in the group in a language of family. Though they do not all seem to notice this awkwardness. And most assume that the leader is "Father" rather than "Brother." In Alphonsus' time, the kings of Naples and Sicily, whether Hapsburg or Bourbon, were still happy with the language of *Paterfamilias* when reviewing their relations with their subjects.[27] Father Abbots equally, had long been accustomed, in Naples monasteries as everywhere, to address the monks as "dear sons of our family."[28] So, at the very start of the Congregation, while Alphonsus was still feeling his way to the exercise of "my will" among them, Bishop Tommaso Falcoia, 1663–1743,[29] was happy to be recognized by Alphonsus and all the Brothers as "the Father."[30] Each of the first batch of Redemptorists had been, in some fashion, his "Servant and Son."[31] On Falcoia's death, Alphonsus was accepted as the Brother who had become their Father. He was heir to certain notions of decent family order. He meant to maintain these decencies. Those expressing difference within the family as forcefully, at least, as those expressing likeness. "You tell me in your letter," he wrote to murmuring lay Brothers in 1773, "that the Rule orders all to live in a uniform manner: that is to be understood only in reference to the Fathers and not in reference to the Brothers; thus it was decided by our founder, Bishop Falcoia, and thus it has been practiced these forty-one years."[32] Concomitantly, Alphonsus' use of "Brother" in letters to Fathers, though it must imply some equalities in their relationship, is not implying every equality. Even between Fathers. And they knew it.

Cesare Sportelli, 1701–1750, wrote in December 1747 to let "our most Reverend Father" have news of Father Francesco Garzillo, 1690–1786, of "our brother Margotta" who, though ordained six years before Sportelli, was, as their novice now, not to be reckoned among the Fathers, and of Brother Gaspare Corvino, 1722–1805 who, as a lay Brother, was not to be reckoned "our brother."[33] As distinguishingly, surely, Sportelli told Alphonsus that Gaspare, the very model of a pious Brother, was anxious to get hold of Jannielli's *Holy Quarry*, while in his next-day letter to Villani he could hint that this Brother would be pleased to get a packet of snuff for Christmas.[34] For letters to Villani and fellow priests of the Congregation, the exact Sportelli could employ the forms of courteous fraternity, signing himself "your Servant and Brother."[35] Or at least to most of his fellows. He remained "servant and Son" not only in letters to Falcoia, and to Alphonsus after Falcoia's death, but to the stiff Rector of Pagni, Giovanni Mazzini, 1704–1792,[36] and to Paolo Cafaro, 1707–1753, perhaps because he could never be quite at his ease with a man whose in-House nickname was "The Anger of God."[37] Sportelli could, however, enlarge his courtesies into "your affectionate Brother" at the close of letters to Giulio Marocco, 1714—at least 1763.[38] It was a nasty shock for him when this pleasant priest left them to be pastor of his hometown parish at Piano di Caiazzo.

Whatever the significances of Sportelli's courtesies, Alphonsus' acknowledgments of difference between his Brothers were related to differences of function on the mission: Fathers preaching, hearing confessions, celebrating the Eucharist; Reverend Students coming along for the experience, listening, watching, taking kiddies' catechism class, leading the women's rosary recitations, presenting good examples to the men by kneeling purposefully in the pews; lay Brothers scouting for fresh straw to plump the palliasses, keeping the thin soup hot on the hearth, sweeping the yard, ringing the bell for mission services, saying their prayers for mission success. But status and function may not be always congruent. What if a Father, depressed by the response to his alarming sermon or to his merry quip in the recreation room, turn to a lay Brother for some encouragement?[39] What if a good Student find that none of his classmates is as cheerfully intelligent as the Brother in the tailor's shop, and goes regularly to talk theology there?[40] What if a Brother, mistaken for a Father on the street, discover that he can actually preach a converting sermon?[41] Or what if a Brother, tired of the whole community, Fathers, Students, even Brothers, suddenly decide on giving them all a penance as if he were their Rector, and very much oversalt the soup? What if a Brother were *de facto* acknowledged to be, even by Alphonsus, "the head of my household?"[42] These things happen. Happened. How were status and function to be re-related then, among all those whom Alphonsus called "my Brothers"?[43]

Some matters can be fast settled by an efficient Rector. The depressed Father can be sent straight along to his spiritual director. The tailor's shop can be put out of bounds to Students. And there need be no mistaking a lay Brother for a Father when the Brother's habit is of a regulation shorter length.[44] The salt-in-the-soup may be a mite trickier to sort out. But they all managed to find their ways of dealing with the situation when the widower lay Brother Giuseppe Caputo, 1707(?)–1765, presented his son, Domenico, 1732–1767, to be trained as a Reverend Brother up to ordination as a Father who would, with sometimes a wry grin it is to be hoped, address his old father as "Brother." It was another nasty shock when, the year after his father died the death of a persevering saint, this young Father had to be let go on account of his uncertain health.[45]

Settling such matters of status and function "on the hoof" may be well enough for a while, but in the long trek there must be some shared principles of living if activities are to be shared amicably, fraternally. Otherwise, what seems to be gratuitously asserted as "right" and "just" and "brotherly" may be as gratuitously contested. "Be on your guard," Alphonsus found himself having to write to a Rector in 1756, "these lay Brothers are claiming some *ius*."[46] Some right in law.[47] They were, in fact, alleging some likenesses with Franciscan Brothers. He was much hurt and, indeed, alarmed, by talk which could so readily translate into the horrid impertinences of Tom Paine and Rousseau.[48] He found it abhorrent that anyone should attempt in a Christian community to place fraternity with equality. Or with liberty. The proper study of these Brothers must be "to do what they are told."[49]

"I love you as brothers, but I wish you to become saints; what is the use of entering the Congregation if you do not wish to become saints?[50] They had all to learn from one another the developing meaning of their vocation to be saints together. That this was surely a learning process by which he and they, many of them, could discern possibilities of human fulfillment may be concluded from Alphonsus' retaining the lifetime loyalty not only of the squirelike Vito Curzio, 1707–1745, the first Brother, but of a range of others, vastly different in temperament, upbringing, talent, through to Alessio Pollio, 1742–1813, "once his servant but now our Brother," the last of them to know him intimately.[51] "No man is a hero to his valet," said Napoleon, and that, as Wilde commented, is "because he is a valet." But Alphonsus and Alessio are both shown to fine advantage as Alessio gives evidence at the 1796 preliminary beatification Process of Alphonsus' "heroic virtue."[52]

The history of Alphonsus' relations with these Brothers is, therefore, a history of the interactions of his presumptions, expressed in a language of family, realized in the structural conventions of a Rule, with the vaguely apprehended, roughly articulated, sense of their vocation which living in the Congregation suggested to Brothers.

Within that grand range of happenings which Alphonsus experienced during just more than ninety years of living, 1696–1787, I have taken it that those who hope to appreciate his presumptions about both "brother" and "saint," and his developing sense of what a brotherliness towards saintliness might mean for him and his men, have to make a start by looking at his experience as eldest among the Liguori blood sisters and brothers, then at his cooperative work within the institutional structures of contemporary charitable Confraternities, and then, without much preliminary hypothesizing as to how they should all have been conducting themselves, at his living so long in community with some distinguished Redemptorists to whom the Fathers were variously referring as "Brothers," "lay Brothers," "serving Brothers," and whom Alphonsus himself once in a moment of irritation called "these blessed Brothers."[53]

Saint Alphonsus and His Brothers

I

THE BLOOD BROTHER

Tannoia, at his immediate ease with the Congregation's use of "Father" and "Brother," could take it for granted that it was in the structures of the family that Alphonsus had found his model for their living together.

Not all families are alike, however. Not all of them are likeable. In any society. In any class of society. The peasant children's stories collected by Giambattista Basile, 1575–1632, for his posthumously published *Story of Stories,* declare that in homes throughout the countryside of the old Kingdom of Naples, as in homes everywhere and everywhen, there was a readiness to believe in wolf-grannies, wicked uncles, tyrannical fathers, witch step-mothers, ugly sisters, and hungry babes abandoned to their cold fates in the wood.[1] Family life in the Naples tenements was no better. And if Celeste Crostarosa were able to rely on the loving interest of her brothers, Giorgio the Jesuit as consistently as Francesco the junior partner in the family law firm, the astoundment of bishop, vicar general, and mother prioress in 1733 that these bourgeois brothers should intervene on her side during the crisis in the Scala convent suggests that such family tenderness was not commonplace in middle-class families.[2] And Alphonsus could readily discern that not all was well with the upper-class family. Those with whom he was best acquainted seemed to value only success in the struggle, generally amoral, sometimes immoral, to increase clan wealth and power.

That the conventions of contemporary family life opened up a way for uncontrolled land greed and money greed, and at last for such families to eat up themselves in wolfish enmity across the generation gap, came climactically within Alphonsus' horrified understanding at the collapse of the 1723 Amatrice lawsuit.[3] That landed squireling caste to which Don Giuseppe de' Liguori, 1670–1745, hoped his eldest son would ascend was habitually in debt, and, since there could be no question of such persons stooping to earn their living, as habitually looking about for some excuse to prosecute a claim on a neighbor's estate. The dispute over the ownership of the lakeside fiefdom of Amatrice, involving three sets of aristocratic litigants and their attendant lawyers, Alphonsus among them, had its origins in an impatient Orsini heir's making a grab for the family property while his father, the Duke, was in prison awaiting trial for the murder of the wife whom he had suspected of adultery. The settlement of the case, which recessitated some bribing of the judge with a pair of bear cubs, some disregard of relevant documents, some ignoring of pertinent legislation, allowed a carve-up of the estate by the two more powerful families. Alphonsus came to an open-eyed astonishment at the ways of such families, at the ways of "the world."[4]

Alphonsus came to see, too, that these aristocratic conventions opened the way for sexual unrestraint. Husbands of that class generally, if not the Orsini Duke, were very free with their wives. They were, in order to be left unrebuked themselves, prepared to tolerate, even approve, a system of "*Cicisbeo*" by which a wife consorted with a recognized gentleman caller. The custom had begun in husbands' relief that some other gentlemen would undertake to escort their wives to church while raunchy French soldiers were occupying the city streets. But it had little to do with church-going when Alphonsus was working in Naples. "Only with great difficulty can married ladies nowadays save their souls," he thought, "for the great majority of them live in sin on account of the numerous cicisbeos who collect around them to lure them into sin."[5]

Those who were not aristocrats imitated their betters. It was a matter of real frustration to Alphonsus when bishop of Sant' Agata de' Goti that so many local farmers connived at their wives' misconduct on account of their thus gaining a complementary freedom to strut among the women of the next village. One wife in San Maria a Vico was entertaining, Alphonsus complained to her parish priest, no less that three of the young men while her husband was making his regular trips to see another farmer's wife in Cimentara.[6] Such loose conduct was, it seems, quite usual. The previous bishop, Flaminio Danza, 1691-1762, had not thought it worth his while to attempt any reform. Even Alphonsus was not confident of accomplishing much. Nevertheless, he must put up some opposition to such family misconduct. It would be best, of course, if the parish priest should send the whole pack of them to the bishop's palace for a reprimand. "But I fear it will be difficult to get them to come." The priest will have to employ a little equivocation. He must at least suggest to them that "if the bishop were to hear of their behavior" he would be sure to make it a police station matter.

Alphonsus next turned his unpleased attention to the San Stefano parish where he had heard a father was putting two of his daughters out to prostitution. Alphonsus sent for the parish priest. Don Felice Nuzzo, however, forewarned of the summons, had shepherded these black sheep across the parish line into Sant' Agnese. Alphonsus sent for the Sant' Agnese priest. But Don Francesco Ferrara had already instructed his curate, Don Angelo Sgambati, to move them all on to San Felice. So Don Simone Lucia was instructed to deal with this father and, as Alphonsus had meantime discovered, his four errant daughters. Something must be done. But everything cost money. Alphonsus had to provide dowries large enough to get the men to marry the girls.[7] "These marriages," Tannoia recorded, "were happy ones, generally."[8] After all, Alphonsus was, generally, in such cases, generous enough to forego his matrimony fees. Still, not all parents were pleased to see their bishop marry their sons off in this way. Alphonsus was himself not quite easy in his mind about it. "It is true," he allowed, "that there are certain kinds of forced union of which I do not really approve, but of two evils one must choose the less."[9]

Not all clergy were so unconcerned as those country parish priests at the incidence of the greater evil. His old acquaintance at the Incurabili told him of a girl who, to escape her parents, had run away to Naples, had caught a venereal disease, and had come to die in their ward. She proved, astonishingly, curable. So Alphonsus authorized Don Salvadore Tramontana to consult with Brother Francesco Tartaglione, 1715–1774, and lay out money so that the girl had a serge petticoat, a hard-wearing dress, a warm mantle, and some thick stockings and sensible shoes from one of the secondhand clothes stalls where, he knew from shopping for a clerical cassock, "such things may be found in good condition."[10] He warned the Incurabili priest, again from sad experience, against false economies. "If one were to take the really old goods, everything would have to be done over again the next day." That time, on being told that the girl thought it worth another try at family life, Alphonsus sent the girl's mother the coach-ride money to collect her errant daughter. There was a suggestion of a young man's being ready to marry her, even now. Such a restoration of family relations was not, however, his preferred solution to problems of this sort. "What caused Alfonso the greatest consolation was to be able to get one of these penitents to shut herself in a convent."[11] That would be so very much better for her, as it was so much better for any woman, than getting married.

Alphonsus was certainly not consistently in favor of getting those who were living in sin to make what the bourgeoisie would think honest women and men of themselves. Or of getting married persons back together after a separation. But he knew that for many women separation from the husband meant separation not only from her children, but from the very necessities of food, clothing, and a roof. One of the most telling examples of the uses of equivocation in his *Moral Theology* textbook is that of the adulterous wife who is in terror of her violent husband.[12] No quick appeal to the values of hearth and home there. Rather, a compassionate recognition that the woman should not be blamed if she manage, without a lie, to keep the man in ignorance of her infidelity. And at other times a recognition of family breakdown. Discovering that a woman from his diocese had left her bullying husband at Frasso and taken her little boy to live with a paramour in Ferrazzano, Alphonsus made no attempt to get the family back together, but arranged that the wife be found a place in the refuge of Santa Chiara in Naples.[13] Those who put their trust in saints are not disappointed. On her man's most conveniently dying, Alphonsus this time helped the woman to secure another, quieter, husband.

There were other unions not so easily discussed in polite society. It is significant that, in the *Moral Theology,* when considering how detailedly a penitent should confess his sins, Alphonsus takes for his example the requirement that he specify the degree of incest he has committed, whether it was between son and mother, father and daughter, brother and sister, stepson and stepmother, father-in-law and daughter-in-law.[14] These things were well-known to be occurring in the Kingdom—in all classes of society. The desire of her brother for the Duchess of Malfi had been played upon the stage. And the fulfillment of the like desire had, perforce, been for some time common among the poorest Neapolitans. Those who could not afford to marry. Could not, for a start, afford the marriage fees which their priests, generally, would not forego. Brothers and sisters slept together in tenement corners. Gerard Majella knew that such things happened in the countryside too. Coming upon a peasant boy at play outside his father's cottage, he foresaw a terrible future for the family which was nurturing "this monster." So it proved, on the boy's growing into adolescence. Being reprimanded by his father at the discovery of his incestuous dealings with his sister, the youngster seized a gun and would have killed his father if the old man had not wrested the weapon from his hand and, in self-defense, shot him dead.[15] The likelihood of such a family row, within such economic pressures, led to an increase of back-street abortions, as brothers and sisters made frantic efforts to avoid the fury of their fathers.[16]

Then again, the abandonment of newborn babies was also a terrible commonplace on city streets. Those who survived long enough to be found were taken to the children's hospital of the Holy House Confraternity or to the orphanage of the Holy Spirit Confraternity. But by the middle of the eighteenth century, these institutions had proved quite unable to manage this increasing problem. In 1759, Alphonsus took a hand at reforming a foundling hospital at Gaeta where at least another four hundred children of unknown parentage were ill-brought up. It was years of work for the Congregation to bring the place to a satisfactory condition,[17] and thenceforward an unending work to keep the hospital going, for the number of babies placed on convent doorsteps did not decrease during Alphonsus' lifetime.

Working in such a society, Alphonsus thought it entirely relevant to tell his mission congregations, those parish assemblies of "the rough and the cultured" sitting together in the pews, some frightful stories of what happens in families.[18] He would expect them to recognize a reference to their own relationships in a story of a son's dragging his father by the heels down the road out of town and of the father's suffering unprotestingly until they came to a turn in the road at which he insisted that the son cease his abuse; "Why should I stop here?" the son asked, "Because this is the place," replies his father, "to which I dragged my father years ago."[19] They were to recognize their own relationships in another story of a daughter-in-law who nags her husband until he first persuades his father to transfer the family property to his control and then puts the old man out of the family house, even at last turning him away when he comes to the back-door begging for food; seeing this, Alphonsus told the congregation, even the toad on the doorstep was shocked at the course of family life.[20] There's no great surprise then that, being told tales of relaxed observance of the Congregation's Rule by his Brothers in some of the houses, he should envisage a terrible justice that might put them all back again among such sons and fathers and daughters-in-law: "We are in danger of being sent home to our families, which would be the worst punishment that we could receive from God."[21]

The son who so shocked the toad's sense of natural order was evidently eldest in the family, the heir who had some rights of primogeniture to the father's property. None of his brothers could have managed such a thing. They could not have made any significant move without the heir's say-so. Not at any rate in any family that had a place in society to protect. "At sixteen years of age," Brother Paolo Amato, 1729-1785, the younger brother of an Aversa civil servant, wrote in his autobiographical sketch for the Prefect of Brothers, "I wanted to be a monk of S Antony of Padua. And because he was the head of the house, *capo di casa,* I meant to do nothing without his consent. I waited for my brother to return from a business trip."[22] While Gerard Majella, who came to the Congregation in 1749, the same year as Paolo, had felt himself quite at liberty to run away from his mother, the male head of the Amato house was an altogether more impressive person. Confident in his knowing what was best for this younger brother, "he ordered me back to Aversa." Paolo should go back to school.[23] Alphonsus' place in his own and others' estimate had, likewise, been secured by his being the Captain's heir in the family. In the social tradition of Don Giuseppe and his friends, Alphonsus occupied a position of real privilege.

Not that the Captain supposed that this is a world in which a firstborn son could come effortlessly into happiness. God has not ordered things so. Don Giuseppe knew the histories of Cain, Esau, Amnon. He knew the history of Jesus. Don Giuseppe had four statuettes on a shelf in his cabin representing Jesus in Gethsemane, Jesus at the flogging post of the Roman barracks, Jesus presented all bloody to the people, and Jesus taking up his Cross. Coming onto the deck of his trireme, seeing innocent press-ganged men chained to oars alongside rapists, murderers, prisoners of war, all being lashed with the same lash, Don Giuseppe understood that he was made in the image of the God who looked on as his innocent Son was lashed.[24] Looked on as his Son died. What he had been made to learn on board the *Padrona,* the Captain told his highly favored son. Told him that these horrors were a reflection of what happens universally. His son, shudderingly, accepted the truth of what his father told him. Accepted that there was a frightful correspondence in human and divine judgments of the innocent along with the guilty. "On earth Pilate says, 'Let Jesus die,' and the Eternal Father in just the same way says from heaven, 'Let my Son die.'"[25] This was the way things were. But Don Giuseppe did not intend Alphonsus to be content with the way things were. He was not content himself. Of course, the Captain knew as well as Prince Hamlet that no man is wholly innocent—"Use every man after his desert and who shall scape whipping?"—but he was determined that his son should never come under the lash. Alphonsus should be protected.

For a start, a fine list of protectors' names was provided for his godparents to declare when they presented this firstborn son at the font on September 29, 1696: Alphonsus, Maria, Antonio, Giovanni, Francesco, Cosimo, Damiano, Michelangelo, and Gasparo.[26] The Captain's son would be covered two ways. Saints and grandees would be his guardians. He was given the name of Mary, Frederick Jones said in his painstaking biography, on account of "the quite remarkable love of his mother for the blessed Virgin."[27] The baptismal naming of Gennaro Maria Sarnelli, Antonio Maria Tannoia, Bernardo Maria Apice, and others among the first Fathers of the Congregation suggests that there was not much remarkable in a boy's being named after the Lady. Quite as usually, some of these holy patrons were invoked by Don Giuseppe in a gesture of courtesy from one gentleman to others of his sort. The martyrs Cosmos and Damian, patrons of medical men and the Medici, had their feast on September 27, Alphonsus' birthday, and he was being baptized on the feast of Saint Michael the Archangel. More programmatically, the baby was declared to be inheriting the grandeurs of Don Antonio, his great-great-grandfather, and of that revered ancestor's brother, Don Giovanni, the Co-Rector of the Incurabili hospital and of the even ancienter dignities of Don Francesco their grandfather, and of Don Gaspare, the founder of the Liguori line. Most particularly, Alphonsus was to be recognized, by himself as by others, as the inheritor of Don Alphonsus de' Liguori,

1593(?)–1652, the first member of the family to be enrolled as a magistrate on the *sedile* of Portanova.

The rhetoric of this baptismal genealogy would be translated into practical arrangements for Alphonsus' safety in the frightful world. The largest part of his Captain's pay should be spent on whatever the city might offer against the rough forces menacing Don Giuseppe's eldest son. Tutors were hired to equip Alphonsus for entry on politest society.[28] A small sword was made so that the youngster might hand it over to the doorkeeper of a great man's house as he went in to the party.[29] Calls were made at the grandest palaces to which the Captain could procure an invitation. And, at home, Alphonsus was ever being reminded of the privileges of the firstborn.

These privileges were oftentimes stupendous. No human being can be brought to play a keyboard instrument well,[30] to read the *Aeneid*,[31] to hear the first performance of a Handel opera,[32] to attend the Law School where Giambattista Vico, 1668–1744, was lecturing,[33] to stand in a box at the San Bartolomeo opera as the whole cast of *Siface* sings Metastasio's *finale* phrase in praise of the largest mercy, *generosa perdona*,[34] no human being, surely, can experience such civilizing moments and not be the better.

The eldest son's privileged youth was intended to be prologue to an even more privileged middle age among the local aristocrats. Between whiles, Alphonsus was to secure a money-making reputation as a fiefdom lawyer. But at the climactic moment, when Alphonsus stood in court as attorney of the Orsini Duke, arguing his claim to that Amatrice fiefdom, he discovered that Virgil, Handel, Vico, Metastasio, were ineffective there. "*O Mondo*. . . ."[35] Within a very short while the privileged firstborn son had rejected the comfortable future projected by Don Giuseppe. Imitating "the firstborn among many Brothers," "the firstborn of every creature," "the firstborn from the dead," Alphonsus left home when he was thirty years old, collected a company of like-minded men about him, and set out to preach the Good News to the poor.

It was an essential element of that *imitatio Christi* to which Alphonsus and his companions were called that each should make his own that radical rejection of family exhibited in the Gospel. Their families understood that very well. And would, commonly, not acquiesce in such a rejection. There was a famous story of Gerard Majella's being locked in his room by his mother and escaping to join the Congregation by climbing out of a window.[36] Complementarily, Gerardo Grasso, 1719-1760, was expelled from the Congregation account of his petitioning Alphonsus to keep him at the Pagani house so that he might coach his younger brother for a Salerno University examination.[37] In Alphonsus' admiring obituary notice of Paolo Cafaro, it is noted praisingly that this Redemptorist was "as detached from his relatives as he was from the goods of this world," particularly when, having been informed that his sister was seriously ill and longing for him to visit her, he returned only the one-sentence messages, "I wish that her pains may grow greater yet so that she may the better conform to the suffering of Jesus Christ."[38] Each postulant was undertaking to set a like distance between himself and his family. "Sometimes," Alphonsus admitted to Gasparo Caione, "it is unavoidable that young people be allowed to speak to their relatives."[39] But it must always be against the spirit of the Redemptorist vocation. So, in the autumn of 1755, when it was evident that Donna Anna Caterina was dying, Alphonsus left her in Naples and continued to Benevento where he was to conduct a mission.[40] He and each of his companions had been called to make the imitative declaration as he looked about him in the refectory or on the mission journey, "Here are my mother and my brothers, for whoever does the will of my Father in heaven is my brother and sister and mother."

They were to be Brothers who know that "Jesus loves you more than any relative loves you," "more than your brother," and that they must imitate him in this loving;[41] it was without irony, without, certainly, any sense of an impertinence, that Alphonsus wrote to the brother of Francesco Pentamelli, 1714-1761, on the missioner's sudden death, "I do not know whether my sorrow has been greater than yours...."[42]

If what he is saying about loving them more than brothers, and about his expectations of their so loving one another, is to be of any real help in their working out the future shape of their relations as Redemptorists, he surely has to be talking from a good experience of relevant forms of a brother's love. He must know what it means to love a brother. Or, if it be unfair to require that Alphonsus, along with so many other virtues, be more adept than most others in his fraternal relations, at least he must be talking from experiences which made him longingly aware of some better form of brotherly living.

There's a need, therefore, to review the history of Alphonsus as a brother among brothers and sisters at home.[43] For whether Alphonsus' life among the Liguori was a realization of fraternity as happiness or as disappointment, that intimate experience in ball-game disputes, dinner-table winks, lights-out confidences, and talebearing betrayals must color all his grownup uses of "Brother."

Antonio, 1698–1739

Alphonsus was older than his nearest brother by a couple of years, and had always been where Antonio came. Except perhaps at the Oratory of Saint Joseph which the Naples Oratory organized for "young noblemen."[44] In the sodality's register, Antonio is more than once listed as a fine singer. Alphonsus never made Cantor, though his administrative talents were recognized by his being chosen as Secretary and as Master of Novices.[45] That capacity to hold a tune and keep others with him as they sang a psalm might gain Antonio some standing with their musical father. But Don Giuseppe had fixed his entire hope on his brilliant eldest son, so, singing apart, Antonio must have found a good number of opportunities to practice self-effacement in the home.

In 1713, when he was fifteen years old, Antonio got truly out from under Alphonsus' shadow and, making the very most of his talent as a chanter, became a novice at the local Cassinese monastery of San Severino.[46] He was professed as Dom Benedict Maria three years later, March 21, 1716. "The second son," Frederick Jones remarked in a quick dismissal, "apparently posed no problems." Anyway, these Benedictines had a nice way with problems.[47] "At the monastery of San Severino," Alphonsus told a Prioress bothered by overzealous nuns in 1764, "the Office was first said at midnight, but because few of the monks attended, and for other good reasons, the Abbot some years ago changed the hour and arranged that the Office should be said an hour after sunset, or thereabouts."[48]

Among these civilized monks, Antonio began to flourish, becoming himself Master of Novices while still a young man.[49] Seven years on, Don Giuseppe, perhaps supposing that a man who could so sensibly alter the time of Matins would give decent gentlemanly advice, enlisted the aid of the Abbot, Giambattista di Miro, 1666–1731, in persuading Alphonsus to surrender the notion of becoming a priest.[50] The abbot could point to the example of his own brother, Don Vincenzo, a member of the Royal Council, as demonstrating that a man may remain a lawyer, increase his family's influence and prestige, and find ways of doing a great deal of good.[51]

On Alphonsus' climbing the grand staircase to the cloistered upper garden where the Benedictines took their pleasant evening walks, Dom Giambattista, making his dignified objections to any eldest son's surrendering his primogeniture responsibilities, did indeed quietly allege that the whole notion was a temptation from a demon. Not an inspiration from God. But Alphonsus was convinced of his power to discern spirits. "I am not persuadable, Father Abbot. God does not wish me to stay in the World. He wishes me to get ordained. I ought and wish to correspond with the call of God rather than the will of my father."[52] Alphonsus may have been rather a young man to withstand such a personage, but he proved more unbiddable than those who had argued against changing the time of Matins.

The Abbot's successor proved equally unable to manage Antonio. Along with Don Giuseppe's musicality, Antonio had, it appears, inherited his poor mother's unrelenting dread that she was not doing all that God required of her. Antonio became, Tannoia recorded, "a martyr in his penances," treating himself with anxious severity, taking too little to eat in the refectory, whipping himself too hard in his cell, staying up too late at his prayers.[53]

Antonio was just forty-one years old when he died. Whatever was Ophelia-like in his death as he chanted snatches of old Lauds, Tannoia was a trifle too ready to make his obituary observation that this monk "drowned in self-denial."[54] To his contemporaries at San Severino, Antonio seemed to have perfectly fulfilled the demands of their Benedictine life. He had assuredly fulfilled one demand that Alphonsus so insistently made on every religious, for Antonio made no call at all on his brother's time, energy, love. There's no reference in the Abbey journals to Alphonsus' visiting his brother to take a turn around that upper garden. No letters from him have survived. Or to him.

Barbara, 1700–(?)

Alphonsus never forgot that interview with the San Severino Abbot, along with the similar interviews Don Giuseppe had insisted that he endure with Don Vincenzo Cutica, Superior of the Congregation of Missions, with their kinsman Canon Pietro Gizzio, and the senior jurist of the Naples Bar, Don Muzio di Maio.[55] For the rest of his life, these things rankled. At the drop of a hat, he would go raging against parents who used such means to stop a child's becoming a priest or a monk or a nun. "When a young man, in obedience to the will of God, wishes to become a religious, what efforts do not his parents make on account either of their own undisciplined emotions or their thinking only of the interest of the family, to dissuade him from following his vocation."[56] Such dissuaders, Alphonsus was certain, "cannot be excused from mortal sin," such parents "are cooperating in grievous evil," and those clergy who tell a child that he should obey his parents are ignoring the teaching of Aquinas and following the condemned opinion of Luther. "See what I have written on this subject in my *Moral Theology*."[57]

Alphonsus did not feel any complementary doubt himself about his Christian duty of advising girls and boys, but especially girls, that they should "enter religion." If at the convent door, they hesitated, or if, having once become religious, some afterwards began to doubt their vocation, Alphonsus was ready to assure them that they were being assailed by the temptations of a demon:

> I see you are now placed in the house of God and made, willingly or unwillingly, the bride of Jesus Christ: for my part I cannot pity you any more than I could pity a person who had been transported, even against his will, from a place infected by pestilence and surrounded by enemies, to a healthful country, to be placed there for life, secure against every foe.[58]

He has Saint Francis de Sales with him on this, he knows. The example of Blessed Hyacinth Marescotti. And there's the nearer instance of the local nun, Maria Bonaventura in Torre dei Specchi. But he hardly needs their backing. He has the tone of a man who, whatever his opinions on this or any other matter, has long had the freedom to express them. And to act on his opinions. "Alphonsus has a stubborn streak," Don Giuseppe had remarked to his nervous wife in the midst of a family row, "and it's a mighty job to get him to come about."[59] But the captain and the captain's son were of a mind when it came to dealing with the womenfolk of their family.

Something of Alphonsus' understanding of the proper office of a brother with his sisters may be gauged from the admiring account he gave of young Paolo Cafaro's conduct when his mother was out of the house and he was left, therefore, in charge of his sisters:

> He watched over them sedulously, especially securing that they did not leave the house and if any of them did step out, he punished her, not by hitting her, but by shutting her up in her room, keeping her there for a time calculated according to the length of her absence and the distance she'd covered.

And Paolo Cafaro was not even the eldest of the children.[60]

Whatever Barbara overheard Alphonsus say about convent life, whatever she may have understood of the supper-table arguments of a guest who opposed his view of things, she may well have thought that nothing could be worse than life in a house where she might be locked in the attic for taking two steps along the street. At any rate, when she was nine years old, Barbara went off to be a boarder at San Girolamo, the convent of a local Franciscan community. Alphonsus was then already, at thirteen years old, a Law student, an avid opera-goer, a regular man about town.[61] So the little girl's departure from the family house at such an early age and her entering an enclosed community must now make her almost a stranger to her elder brothers.

Founded in 1434, the San Girolamo convent was one of the most respectable of the religious houses of the city, and one of the richest, decorated "like an earthly Paradise" as a local guide book declared a few years later.[62] The Prioress, Maria Felice di Costanzo, 1677–1743, was another of the Liguori clan.[63] Barbara was likely, such was Don Giuseppe's will to keep his money and the charm of his sailor smile, to have been taken at reduced fees. After six years as a boarder, not living with the nuns but, along with other girls between the ages of seven and twenty-five, observing the rules of enclosure and silence with the community, getting to know well the ways of these nuns, Barbara announced to the Prioress, to her God-mother, Virginia Reitano, Princess of Presicce, and to her father and mother, that she wished to be admitted to the community.

There could be no grumbling, at the formal scrutiny of her application, about Barbara's not being of gentle birth.[64] But it was only after some unseemly scroungings by Don Giuseppe for contributions to his daughter's dowry, pleading poverty to a charitable fund in the very month that he put down a large deposit on a palazzo in the Supportico Lopez, that he and the nuns agreed on terms.[65] Having next completed the requisite few weeks' stay at home, "in the world," so that the girl might, if she wished, reconsider her choice, Barbara entered the San Girolamo novitiate in 1715, taking Maria Luisa as her name "in religion." She was professed on April 17 the next year, the feast of the martyr Pope Anicletus who, the antiphon for Vespers that day declared, "remained steadfast unto death, taking no heed of the words of the ungodly." But before she could set about being steadfast like her patron, Maria Luisa had to have words with the ungodly. Or so it must have seemed to her. Very soon after the acceptance of her sister, Maria Anna, as a novice, two years later, Barbara found herself taking Don Giuseppe to the courts to enforce his agreement to hand over that portion of her dower which would come from family funds.[66] Perhaps the community did not find such a law suit that odd. Squirelings were often, in their experience, financially retentive.[67] Their relatives were often having to appeal to the courts.

After this rather distressing incident, not much more is known of Barbara's individual pursuit of saintliness in the community. Again no letters from Alphonsus. Again no letters to him. And Barbara seems to have been almost as unvisited as Antonio.[68] She would not have expected Alphonsus to come. Not, anyway, after reading his recommendation to the *True Bride*. There was a use for equivocation in the convent as well as in the bully's household:

> Never seek a visit from your relatives. When they come, endeavor to withdraw from them as soon as possible, excuse your withdraw-

> ing by saying that you must attend to the duties of your office, that you must assist some person who is sick, make some apology of that sort. If you set your mind to it, some reason for leaving your relatives will occur to you.[69]

Perhaps Barbara was indeed the perfect enough nun to accept this direction for herself as she worked her way through the chapters of her famous brother's book. For she, like every nun in the Kingdom must have been given copy after copy by unimaginative well-wishers on feast day after feast day. She seems to have retired, self-obscuring, into an anonymous life of prayer beyond the convent grill. And an anonymous dying. There's no record of the date of her death. That death, too, was what Alphonsus would have wished for her:

> Imagine you see, on the one hand, a princess dying in a splendid palace, attended by a retinue of servants, surrounded by her husband, her children, her relatives, and then represent to yourself a nun expiring in her convent in a poor cell, mortified, humble, far from her relatives, stripped of property and self-will. Tell me, which of these, the rich princess or the poor nun, dies happier?[70]

Maddalena, 1700

Barbara had been early acquainted with death. Her twin died in infancy.

However statistically ordinary such infant mortality at this time, and a long whiles after, the pain of this sudden infant death could not be ordinary for Donna Anna and Don Giuseppe. How little either of them allowed their other children to be aware of their grieving may be gathered from the stark insensitivity of Alphonsus' asking his brother, years later, as Ercole's little boys played at their feet, "Would you be displeased if you were to lose one of them?"[71]

Gaetano, 1701–1784

The third of the brothers, born September 4, 1701, was named after Saint Gaetano da Thiene, the patron of a lay confraternity at the Liguori parish church.[72] As pleasing a singer as Antonio, Gaetano came near to being as longevitous as Alphonsus, dying at the family house in 1784, eighty-three years old. Gaetano was when a youngster, Don Domenico Buonaccia, the Liguori childrens' tutor, declared hand on heart, "of all the boys I have had under me," the cleverest and the most given to Study.[73] Gaetano, however, when he recalled his childhood, returned not to the schoolroom and his books, but rather to those evenings when Don Giuseppe was away at sea and he, his brothers, and his sisters, gathered at their mother's knee for family prayers.[74]

Donna Anna's kindred had a devotion to Saint Philip Neri and in the years since 1676, when the Naples Oratorians founded their sodality of Saint Joseph, the young men of the clan, Donna Anna's brothers Emilio Cavalieri, 1663–1726, and Giuseppe, 1666–1728, prominent among them, with their cousins Lellio Gizzio, 1661–1729, and his careerist brother Pietro, 1662–1741, had been enrolled as "Young Nobles of the Oratory." Alphonsus and Antonio had followed them. Don Giuseppe would have approved, though not perhaps for the reasons that commended it to his wife, of this upper class boys' club. Gaetano was put on the register of probationers, September 29, 1712, having been proposed immediately on his reaching the qualifying age, and, February 24, 1713, he joined his brothers among the elected nobility.[75]

On a more than usually lengthy shore leave in 1715,[76] Don Giuseppe, noticing this academic and devotional strain in the boy, decided that Gaetano should also be ordained, but not as an unprofitable monk like Antonio. Gaetano would be a stay-at-home collector of a few fat livings. He had, with all the other Young Nobles, attended the first Mass of Don

Mondillo Orsini, 1690–1750, on July 1713, and, hopeful of getting Gaetano's rewarding clerical career started, Don Giuseppe now presented his fourteen-year-old son to the Oratorian's brother, Don Filippo Orsini, 1689–1740, Duke of Gravina, as a fit candidate for the sinecure and income of the cathedral chaplaincy of San Matteo de Ferilli. The Duke was willing enough to settle the benefice on the boy. He further assigned the rents of his house on the Via Toledo to Don Giuseppe, to be passed to Gaetano as he should have need of money to maintain his clerical dignity.[77] Gaetano was, thereupon, tonsured, and took immediate possession of the first annual stipend of twenty-five ducats and thirty grains. He was then sent back to his books and his prayers, impressing Don Buonaccia the more with his endeavors in *litterae humaniores* and Don Casimiro Sicola, 1687–1720, the Prefect of the Oratory sodality, with his devotion to practices of piety.[78] On All Saints' Day, 1718, the exemplary Gaetano was promoted to be Master of Novices in the sodality. All seemed ready for his going forward, under Orsini patronage, to ordination and a succession of benefices.

But in 1723, Alphonsus lost that Amatrice lawsuit in which he had been retained by the Orsini Duke and announced his intention of getting ordained. This threw everything into confusion for Gaetano. The Orsini were unlikely to promote their failed advocate's brother not for some time anyway. Don Giuseppe was no likelier to be content that his first, second, and third sons should all become priests. But Alphonsus could not be dissuaded. Gaetano had long ago learned that it was a brother's part to stand aside when Alphonsus was following up one of his notions. He was now in his usual hurry. "When he thinks of something he has to get it done at once," Gaetano remarked. So, after less than a total of three years' studying with Don Giulo Torno, 1672–1756, Alphonsus leapfrogged over Gaetano into the priesthood.[79] It was not until the house had quieted and the future shape of things had been accepted by their father that Gaetano could resume his career and proceed to the subdiaconate, December 18, 1728. This time his sponsor was that Don Vincenzo Cutica who had before been striving to persuade Alphonsus to abandon his design for ordination.[80] Made a deacon by Bishop Domenico Invitti, 1667–1732, on December 17, 1729, Gaetano followed Alphonsus as assistant in the city parish of Sant'Angelo a Segno.[81] He was ordained priest in September 1730 and settled back into the Liguori household.

Alphonsus, meanwhile, had moved out of the house to live at the "Chinese College" of the Holy Family. Gaetano and Matteo Ripa, 1682–1746, the amateur naturalist at the head of the College became good friends, supper companions after a short para-liturgical service with the trainee missionaries.[82] But Gaetano, unlike the romantically imaginative Alphonsus, was not the sort of priest to fancy himself as a China missionary. No dream of converting the Orient for him. Nor even of doing something about southern Africa.[83] He would just stay quietly at home, looking after their mother during their father's absences, eking out a little life on the proceeds of a chaplaincy in Sant' Anna dei Lombardi which he had acquired to top up the inconsiderable income from the San Matteo altar and the Via Toledo house. Don Giuseppe had not been regular in paying those house rents over. Probably Gaetano had not expected him to observe that part of the arrangement. But Don Giuseppe was certainly on the outlook for some further opportunity to use the family's connections for Gaetano's greater comfort.

Francesco de Liguoro, 1660–1734, prince of Presicce and duke of Puzzomauro, the second husband of Barbara's godmother, Donna Virginia, had more than once deigned to take an interest in Don Giuseppe and his family. He had, in May 1701, secured Don Giuseppe a place alongside him in the honor guard for the State Entry of King Philip of Spain upon his Naples demesne.[84] There had been, in 1710, some serious talk between the two men of Alphonsus' marrying the prince's daughter, Teresa, 1704–1724.[85] On the death of his sixteen-year-old son, Cesare, in 1727, and both his daughters becoming nuns, Teresa at the Holy Sacrament convent and Antonia Clara, 1707–1783(?), at San Marcellino with Barbara, the Prince redrew his will.[86] He now bequeathed an annuity to Gaetano to pay for a daily Mass at the family altar in the Monte Oliveto church.[87] Gaetano had a seven-year wait before coming into this legacy. But once he had established himself in the benefice, there was no need for him to walk half across town each day to say the Mass. He could well afford to pay a stipend to some substituting priest of the Monte Oliveto community.[88]

On Gaetano's being preferred by the Porta Nova magistrates, in 1736, to the richly endowed cathedral Treasury of an Gennaro, Alphonsus suggested that his brother should transfer his Presicce chaplaincy to him. Alphonsus was always a skilled manager of Mass stipends and arranger of chaplaincy proceeds. But no Liguori ever willingly surrendered a hold on capital. Gaetano was ready with an answer. "Dearest brother: concerning the renunciation of the chaplaincy that your Lordship asks from me: I've thought about it and determined that it would be better if I keep it united to the Treasury rather than renounce it in your favor."[89] There may have been a touch of mockery in Gaetano's addressing his brother, who had resigned all family claims to title, as "Lordship," but he was perfectly serious in his explaining how it was that he would not resign his own claim to the funds. If he were to relinquish the chaplaincy, the patrons would certainly appoint Alphonsus in his place, but very likely not in the same unconditional manner that the Prince had appointed Gaetano to the benefice. "It was assigned to me in perpetuity, but you would receive it on a temporary appointment, revocably." So, "I've resolved to keep both chaplaincies." However, he continued quickly, not wishing Alphonsus to think him parsimonious, "I'm making you a donation of fifty ducats a year." However, again, he could not be so generous all at once. "Not this year, because of the expenses I've had in procuring the document of appointment, the manteletta, and all the other trappings." There was nothing left this year. Less than nothing. "I have got myself into debt to our brother Don Ercole, to the tune of thirty ducats."[90] On the outside of this letter, which he kept very carefully as proof of the offer, Alphonsus made a note of the promised income: "D. Gaetano, fifty ducats," and then added laconically, "He is not able to resign the chaplaincy."

Gaetano was, despite the Treasury benefice, never able to live within his income. Their mother, writing in September 1737 to let Alphonsus know how things were with them all in the Naples house, for she had never got used to his claims to be indifferent to the family's interest, warned him that because of the expenses of a little trip Gaetano was planning to Portici, there'd be no money for Alphonsus until December.[91] But Gaetano's debts and his perpetual want of cash were not the results of any reckless self-indulgence. That he could not put his hand on enough ducats and grains for a little country excursion and still keep up his promised payments to Alphonsus was, though his mother did not declare this, the result of Gaetano's being persuaded to make substantial contributions to the household running costs, even while Ercole was proving no readier than their papa to hand over the Via Toledo rents. After all, Ercole argued, it was all in the family.

Even more important to the brothers than keeping hold of family money was keeping up family appearances. This is plain from the affair of Alphonsus' coach. In the terrible winter of 1762–1763, Bishop Alphonsus had decided that if the poor were to have the bread to which their hunger gave them a right, he must raise the money by dismissing his coachman and selling his carriage. He asked Ercole to organize the sale in the city.[92] But his brother was entirely opposed to the suggestion. A bishop, a Liguori bishop, must maintain a certain dignity. He'd spoken to Monsignore Testa about this and he agreed with Ercole.[93] Alphonsus must keep his coach with the coat-of-arms on the door and keep his liveried coachman, too. Alphonsus returned an unnuanced declaration that Ercole had certainly succumbed to "a temptation from some demon." It was very wicked of him to add to the worries of a man who was about to die. "I beg you therefore not to trouble me any more about this affair, or, if you do, I shall not answer your letters." Alphonsus would find someone else to do the business for him.[94] He would send the coach to Naples to be sold on the open market, coat-of-arms and all. There being no other way of avoiding this shame, Gaetano bought the coach himself. He paid, Tannoia recorded marvelingly, "far too high a price" for it.[95] Ercole, having agreed that the coach should be parked in the Marianella stables, wrote assuring Alphonsus that there would thus always be a coach for him to use on his visits to Naples, "all at my expense."[96] But, on the brothers' taking a closer look at the bishop's vehicle, it was apparent that it needed to go to the menders. The repairs took some time. So it happened that when Alphonsus was next in Naples and had need of a coach to get him to a Novena at the Congregation of the Missions, he was compelled, embarrassedly, to make use of the household's much more splendid equipage.[97]

Alphonsus would have noted that whatever he said about "at my expense," it was again Gaetano's chaplaincy money that Ercole had channeled to his own purposes in this matter of the coach. The quiet chaplain was generally resigned to his younger brother's presuming that, as legal head of the family, he could dispose of any income any member of the family received. But even Gaetano objected in 1776 when Ercole started to raid the endowment fund of the Presicce chaplaincy. Their brother, the appalled Gaetano told Alphonsus, had taken a thousand ducats out of the capital and, despite the chaplain's remonstrations, was not willing to put the books right.[98] Alphonsus, too, was scandalized. He wrote at once to Ercole in severe terms. But Ercole could not deem this a matter of any great urgency. Alphonsus wrote again. "You've not yet informed me what you are doing about this." And again. "This delay is making me, I assure you, very uneasy." At last, after further denouncements of "this act of injustice," and after further warnings about "the prejudice to your conscience,"[99] Ercole was persuaded to repay thirty-seven ducats a year to the fund. Gaetano expressed himself content with this minimalist gesture.[100]

Gaetano was never a grabber. Like Alphonsus hoping that their nephew, Alfonsino, Ercole's eleven-year-old son by his second marriage, would be ordained, and remembering perhaps his own teenager delight at being given a benefice by the Ordini Duke, Gaetano took steps in 1778 to surrender to Alfonsino that little San Matteo chaplaincy he'd held since 1715.[101] He had always taken an interest in this boy. Had even bestirred himself to do some tutoring. "I am pleased," Alphonsus had written to Ercole in 1770, "that Don Gaetano is engaged with little Alfonsino."[102] But the lad had really no aptitude for books. Nor, it appeared, for prayers. It was a great disappointment to both uncles that Alfonsino withdrew from the clerisy in 1783.[103]

By then, Gaetano had given a life time's service as a conscientious functionary. Going each morning to say Mass in the Treasury chapel. Except when he was rather poorly in December 1770. Attending the great ceremonies of the cathedral in his rochetto and manteletta with regular decorum. Keeping the books of Treasury incomings and outgoings in neat order. Nothing is recorded against him for the rest of his long life. He was buried among his Proto-Notarial fellows in the vault of the Arch-Confraternity of Priests on the Via Toledo.[104] A Liguori to the last, his will ensured that his savings and his movables remained in the family, inherited not by the disappointing Alfonsino but by his other nephew, Don Peppino.[105]

Alphonsus' relations with Antonio and, even more exiguous, his relations with Barbara, suggest that he had come very early to his conviction that those who enjoy a religious vocation should expect nothing from their kindred.[106] And that they must take no part in family affairs. Have no interest in them.[107] Secular priests, however, may very well find themselves drawn back into their families' business. And they should not be surprised if these affairs are often distasteful, acrimonious even. Alphonsus accepted this for himself. He accepted it for Gaetano. His relations with Gaetano, as they discussed the distributing of the chaplaincy income, the buying of the manteletta, the selling of the coach, and the complaint about Ercole's raid on the capital fund, instance Alphonsus' career-long worries about getting finances straight and his equally career-long reluctance to entrust these matters to "my Brothers": "How often have I forbidden the incurring of extraordinary expenses, and now you want to buy planks on credit. On credit!"[108]

Anna Maria, "Annella," 1702–(?)

Annella, too, when she came in her turn to require some of the family money for her future security, experienced Don Giuseppe's meanness at firsthand.

Nearly two years younger than Barbara, Annella seems to have had a keener sense of self-preservation than her sister. Or perhaps she was just more unbiddable. The Brief of Pope Clement XI, Albani, 1649–1719, approving the little girl's being received as a border at San Girolamo suggests that the four-year-old Annella may have possessed a livelier appreciation of what was going on about her than most children of that age and what was due to her sense of herself, "her honor."[109]

At first, Don Giuseppe appeared surprisingly ready to pay out the thirty ducats for Annella to lodge in the boarders' wing of the convent.[110] Perhaps this daughter was even then proving difficult for him to manage at home. That was in September 1707. A full two years before her elder sister arrived at the convent school.

That papal brief insisted on the girl's total freedom to choose, in her own good time, whether to leave the convent at the end of her school days or apply to stay as a member of the community. Barbara took her first opportunity, immediately after her fifteenth birthday in 1715, to be clothed as a novice. Annella did not yet have to fix on a way of living. She was just happy to be out of the home. But after another two years, when Anna Maria also reached her fifteenth birthday in 1717, she, too, applied and was accepted by the community as a novice.[111] After another year, she was professed and received her religious name, Maria Anna.[112]

The nuns of San Girolamo were generally daughters of well-placed and well-moneyed fathers. There was an assumption that an aspirant would put a substantial sum at the disposal of the convent business managers, so that she could eat her bread and sleep in her cell during the rest of her life without ever having a sense of being a cost to her sisters. Maria Anna soon discovered that her father, who had not made any difficulty about paying her school fees, nor about her joining her sister in San Girolamo, supposing perhaps that this girl was rather too self-minded to please a husband, was not eager to hand over the one thousand ducats of the promised dower.[113] And that he had not yet handed over Barbara's dower.[114]

It had been evident to Don Giuseppe that his pay as the *Padrona* Captain could not, however well-managed, prove equal to supporting all his children in his ambitious style. He had thought it best to spend what he had on the promotion of his eldest son, the up-and-coming fiefdom lawyer and opera-goer. It was now apparent to his daughter that their father was attempting to cheat her as he had been cheating Barbara. The San Girolamo nuns, as the Captain had doubtless told himself, could well afford to keep the two Liguori women without their bringing any dowers. Perhaps they had not thought it worthwhile instructing their attorneys to recover one dower. Barbara had, it seems, not felt pressured to get the money from her father. She had simply gone on with her prayers. Annella was made of sprightlier stuff. Upon her entry among the novices, the nun's lawyers were instructed to dun Don Giuseppe on behalf of both his daughters. This novice had, it seems, persuaded them all into something like her own sense of honor.

The nuns' resort to law may have surprised no one.[115] Not even Don Giuseppe.[116] Nor would it have made his daughters notorious. Maria Anna's fame, such as it was, derived from another, sadder, cause.

She began to be ill, frequently unable to lift herself out of bed on account of the pain and, therefore, as she wrote to the cardinal's office in 1741, requiring that her confessor, Don Giunno from the Seminary for Nobles, come into her cell. By 1766, the convent was employing an outside helper to look after the sick woman.[117] Such physical decline was becoming almost an overwhelming problem for the convent. In 1767, the Abbess, Maria Gabriella Borgia, calculated that the community had been reduced to nineteen Choir nuns, too many of them infirm, four just about able to recite the Office in choir, three unable to do anything at all.[118] Among them, along with her physical infirmities, Maria Anna was having to endure trials of the spirit.

That sense of her own honor which had carried her through so many difficult situations when she was young had now been transmitted into the ordinary affliction of the self-regarding. She had become very scrupulous. Notoriously so. The honorable girl found herself the talk of the gossiping classes. The Jesuit biographer, Saverio Santagata, 1714–1771(?), writing in 1751, took it to be known all over the city, and more widely in the Kingdom, that "Donna Maria Anna di Liguori, a nun in the San Girolamo convent, before going to communion suffers from such scrupulousness that she is constrained not to go to communion at all or, if she communicates, to do so in a most disturbed state of mind."[119] There was nothing Don Giunno could say, nor any of those tale-bearing Jesuit retreat-givers could say,[120] to bring her to a more comfortable mind.

Anyone who had lived for any time under the Captain's roof, his wife, his children, his daughter-in-law, was likely to become prey to such exhausting scruples. Don Giuseppe was assured that in laying down a law for total submission a father was offering his children a perfect image of the rule of God their Father. So he brought the conventions of the trireme home. And they knew just what he was doing. And hated it. "A man should chastise his children," Alphonsus observed in his *Instructions for the People,* more than fifty years after, "with the tenderness of a parent and not with the harshness of a galley-sergeant."[121] But the image of God as galley-master, waiting to punish each jot and tittle, dram and scruple, of their failures in his service, was naturally received by the household more vividly than any image of the redeeming Christ. And, more vividly yet, they would see themselves in the foreground of their lives, would concentrate not on Christ but on themselves and the likelihood of their having committed some offense which would attract the attention of their task-master Father.

Alphonsus could very well see what was happening to his sister. Tannoia records, in connection with Bishop Alphonsus' stay in Naples during 1767, when he was seeking patrons for his several lawsuits, that he found time for a visit to the San Girolamo convent to talk with the scrupulous Maria Anna.[122] It is clear what Alphonsus would have told her. He had spelled out his views in his *True Bride.* "Scruples are very well and useful," he had written, "for the soul that has but a short time since renounced sin." Such a soul, he'd said, stands in need of repeated purgations, and scruples clean out the soul most effectively, making it careful to avoid real sins and humble enough, self-distrustful enough, to place itself in the hands of its spiritual Father to be directed as he pleases."[123] However, he had observed that scruples are hurtful to those who have for some length of time given themselves to God. Too delicate of conscience, not trained to discern what is lawful from what is not, they are shaken by unreal fears. At the suggestion of demons, they throw themselves out of windows. Down wells.[124] Or at the very least stop going to Communion. Again, the only resource for such a scrupulous person, for his sister, is to place herself in the hands of a spiritual Father "and obey him blindly."[125]

Alphonsus has, most significantly, turned himself from a brother into a father in his relation with any nun beset by such troubles, with his sister. A father like Don Giuseppe in his demand for total obedience from the womenfolk. Appalled by his sister's refusal to accept his fatherly guidance, Alphonsus says terribly, "You will die mad." And, says Tannoia sharply, rather pleased to have so neat an exemplar of prophecy and fulfillment, "Mad she died."[126]

There's no further word, in Tannoia's account or anywhere else, of the tormented Maria Anna. It would be too awful to suppose that her mother, who lived until 1755,[127] had been as rare a visitor at San Girolamo as Alphonsus, or that her brother, Gaetano, who survived until 1784,[128] did not sometime make his way to the convent. Perhaps her married sister, Teresa Maria came quite regularly to exchange commiserations. But Alphonsus frowned on that sort of visiting:

> When your parents and friends come to the grate, they certainly cannot make you a partaker of their worldly amusements, for you cannot go beyond the limits of your enclosure. In their visits, then, they only recount their misfortunes, their infirmities, and their wants. Surely such narratives only serve to fill your head and heart with so much inquietude, with so many distractions and defects, that after each visit you will be for several days disturbed and distracted in your meditations and communions by the remembrance of what you have heard.[129]

But it might have been all to the good now and again for poor Maria Anna to be thinking about someone other than her inoffensive self.

Teresa Maria, 1704–(?)

"To become a saint in the world," Alphonsus wrote encouragingly in the first chapter of the *True Bride,* "it is necessary for the married woman to resort to the means of sanctification":[130] she must, just like a nun, go often to the sacraments, have long and frequent recourse to mental prayer, practice interior and exterior mortifications, welcome humiliation, love poverty. She must, like the nun, be perfectly detached from the world, its good, its human ties. This is a counsel of despair. For how should she fit such practices with her married life? How find time for such prayer? How reconcile her place in society with a desire for humiliation? Her care for the children with a love of poverty? How be so detached? There's no way. "The married woman must provide for her family, educate her children, pleasure her husband, his parents, brothers, the whole clan, who can be the cause of many irritations to her." Alphonsus' memories of his mother in the Liguori household suggest to him that the husband can be a cause of enough irritations all by himself. "If his directions be neglected, or his commands be not immediately executed, he breaks out into complaints and reproaches."[131] He's evidently talking to communities which accept the rather moneyed sort of postulant when he reminds them that servants are another trouble to disturb the married woman, making their noise, quarreling, demanding higher wages, time off. But nuns from every sort of home will recognize the distraction that children create. At every age. When small, they seem always to be screaming; when toddlers, they are always pestering for attention; when teenagers, they are always going about with the wrong sort of companion. And there's always a worry that they'll catch some illness or fall into some accident. "How," he asks again, "in the midst of so many occupations and difficulties can a married woman attend to prayer, preserve recollection?" She'll not even be able to get to Communion more than once a week. While, on the other hand, most dangerously, she "must keep up appearances, visiting, talking with all sorts of people, her husband's friends. "Oh how great, on such occasions, is the danger of losing God." He can only conclude, "How unhappy, truly miserable, is the life of all married women."[132] If then, a woman is to become a saint in the world, it will be as a martyr. A martyr who longs to be like a nun. That is, he adds, if she does not die young in childbirth.[133]

Alphonsus cannot, therefore, have looked on too pleasedly when a Baron came calling for the sixteen-year-old Teresa Maria and his proposal was accepted by Don Giuseppe. But, indeed, most observers would have prophesied the unlikelihood of happiness for this poor princess. Domenico del Balzo was a man of some rank and more fortune. His profitable estates were scattered across the Kingdom as far as Acquaviva in the east. There, he was patron of several rich benefices, including a few sinecure canonries at the beautiful rose-windowed cathedral.[134] His sister Anna had been another of those ladies considered by Don Giuseppe as a suitable wife for Alphonsus himself.[135] But the bridegroom was, in 1720, already a late-middle-aged man. A widower. He had been the second husband of the bride's aunt Ippolyta[136] and there was a squad of teenage children to confront the teenage bride. Neither her husband nor any of these stepchildren was as fond of music as her father or of books as Gaetano or of paintings as the young Ercole. A little boar hunting through their own woods with others of their class was quite enough amusement for one year.[137] For the rest, Teresa Maria's life back in the city palazzo del Balzo had nothing so cheerful about it as to alter Alphonsus' view of the unhappiness of wives. However, "emulating the virtue of her mother," she "became herself a saint in the fulfillment of the duties of her position."[138]

Something may yet have interrupted Teresa Maria's progress. On page twenty-four of Alphonsus' notebook for 1729(?), recording private "matters of conscience," there is a curiously clipped reference to "Barb." and "Ter.," and the possibility that they had somehow incurred excommunication.[139] If this refer, as seems wholly likely, to his sisters, Alphonsus was taking one short way with two women who were leading quite diverse lives. Barbara had by then been a professed religious for almost a decade and a half, Teresa Maria, a wife for near a decade. "Take care, above all things," Alphonsus warned the True Bride, "not to get interested in the temporal affairs of your relatives," for "if you do, you will lose all peace and recollection and it may be you will lose your immortal soul."[140] Perhaps Alphonsus supposed that Teresa Maria, on a sisterly visit to Barbara, had somehow led her sister into some unseemly gossip, into a foolish joke perhaps about the convent chaplain, even into a disrespectful laugh against Alphonsus himself. There'd be a risk of excommunication for both sisters, surely, in that merriment.

Teresa Maria, such was the gap of years between them, may have always seemed to Alphonsus a charming little creature.[141] Perhaps the only one of the children unaware enough of his primogeniture rights to laugh with him and, disturbingly, at him. Certainly Alphonsus had had opportunities of knowing and liking her which he did not have with the other sisters. Teresa grew up in the family home. But still there is no sign of any closeness between eldest brother and youngest sister, either when she was a child or when both were adults, any more than between Alphonsus and his other sisters. And no sign of any closeness when they were boys between Alphonsus and Antonio, or between Alphonsus and Gaetano. There's not much in any of these relationships to inform any sense of "Brother" as an affectionate, complex, sharing in family ways of life, putting up with one another's characters, grimacing at the memory of shared fun, embarrassment, or distress, looking at the rest of the world together. Indeed, on these evidences, it might well be concluded that Alphonsus' understanding of the relations of a brother with the others in the family, and therefore his ordinary meaning for "Brother" in the Congregation, was entirely lacking in affection, being concerned only with the distribution of money within the clan and the claims of clannish honor. Such a distancing version of "Brother" could not have brought Alphonsus to sign himself "Brother Alphonsus" with any sense of convivial nearness. But that his appreciation of what it might mean to be an elder brother was more complex than this is manifest in his awkward expressions of interest in his youngest brother, Ercole, and Ercole's three surviving children.

Ercole Maria, 1706–1780

Though Alphonsus would always start a letter with either "My dear Brother" or "My dear Don Ercole," sometimes continuing with both modes of address in the body of his letter,[142] he could sign off with something from a much larger repertory, "Your affectionate brother, Alphonsus," "Your very affectionate brother, Alphonsus, Bishop-elect of Sant' Agata," and, almost as he signed himself in the Congregation, "Brother Alphonsus de Liguori of the Most Holy Redeemer," or quite simply "Brother Alphonsus Maria" which may well have seemed to Ercole the most distancing of all.[143] The oscillation between "brother" as sibling in the family at the start of a letter and "Brother" as member of the Congregation at a close,[144] suggests that whatever experimentation with versions of identity Alphonsus is trying, he is yet aware of his abiding need to sustain a fraternal relation. So, Ercole is still "my dear brother" for Alphonsus in the very sentence that "Brother Alphonsus Maria" is complaining that Ercole is treating him "like a bastard."[145]

Alphonsus' relation with Ercole is better documented than any he sustained with his other sisters and brothers. Most attractively, the very first evidence which is preserved of that relation is of Alphonsus' coming, a tenderly protective elder brother, to the defense of the grown-up Ercole. Against their Father's abuse. "For pity's sake, have a little more charity for your son," he wrote to Don Giuseppe in October 1737(?), "this morning he came to see me at Naples and there in front of me began to weep, quite unable to stop, from sheer unhappiness: My God! do you mean to make him suicidal and throw himself down the well?"[146] Don Giuseppe had been giving Ercole the silent treatment through family meals, just when Ercole was needing his support in dealing with his new in-laws,[147] and then on a sudden bursting into fitful abuse of his thoroughly nervous son. Taking it for granted that Don Giuseppe will always treat ensigns and midshipmen and ship's cat, ostlers and kennel keepers, horses and hounds, badly, Alphonsus protests, "Remember that he is your son, not a dog." He even makes an attempt to put the highest value of all on the pitiful Ercole: "He should be dearer to you than money."

Don Giuseppe died in November 1745. Within three months, Alphonsus was discovering his own reasons for being furious with Ercole. Money reasons. Their father had some years before settled 150 ducats a year on Alphonsus. He had also, in the will brought out of the lawyer's box, bequeathed a lump sum of 200 ducats for the work of the Congregation. Ercole, on taking charge of the family funds, decided that this legacy could not possibly have been intended as an addition to the annuity. The 200 ducats must rather constitute its once for all substitute. Alphonsus protested. Ercole professed himself much surprised. He assured Alphonsus that he'd never let him go penniless. Alphonsus wrote back, this time employing all his old lawyer language: "litigation," "court appearance," "legacy," "testatory disposition," "anterior notarial act." All his devotional language: "Now that I am rereading your letters I do nothing but make the sign of the Cross, I offer to God what you write to me, and the way that you treat me." All his family language: is Ercole acting like this because he's confident that Alphonsus will not provoke a repetition of the unpleasantness when their sisters took their father to court? Ercole had written to him in terms of injured brotherly affection, making a specious appeal to "fraternal charity," but his actions were those of a barbarian outsider, of an enemy, not of a brother. So now, "if you do not mean to treat me as a bastard," let them negotiate like brothers. Alphonsus will be content to take one hundred twenty ducats a year out of the family fund. One hundred eight ducats, even. "Is this acceptable?" Or is Ercole's "fraternal charity" mere talk? "I treat you with brotherly charity" but "You convince me that none but God truly loves us."[148]

This was quite enough for Ercole. He prepared an arrangement for the payment of legacy and annuity, only asking, as he would ask Gaetano after his hand had been discovered in the Presicce till, for some present delay in paying the full amount agreed. He would pay seventy-two ducats a year for now. Alphonsus, February 22, 1746, conceded, "I make you that allowance."[149] Having sent off this final message, Alphonsus made his own will, stating plainly that the Congregation inherited his rights to whatever arrears remained unpaid of that one-hundred-fifty–ducat annuity, "due to me from my family since December 1745 on the death of my Father," together with whatever remained of the capital sum he had reserved for his use on renouncing his primogeniture rights. Recollecting himself, Alphonsus added a codicil further securing to the Congregation that legacy he'd had by Don Giuseppe's will.[150]

No letters from Ercole to Alphonsus or Alphonsus to Ercole survive from the next decade. Perhaps Alphonsus did not need to write because he could get Brother Francesco Tartaglione, who was stationed at Naples, to relay any message. In November 1755, he let Ercole know that the Brother would come to the palazzo and help in the general running of things while their mother was dying. It may be a sign of continuing awkwardness between the brothers that Alphonsus can think of nothing he wants to say to Ercole at this sad time. He offers only the bare intelligence that he was then leading a mission team of eighteen Fathers in Benevento. "There's no other news." But the brothers have evidently been discussing what they should do with their mother's jewelry. Alphonsus is rather prematurely suggesting that Ercole now send "that ornament you promised," so that it may be placed in the crown of the Blessed Virgin.[151]

Alphonsus did not, it seems, see a need to write to Ercole for the next six years. But on May 24, 1761, it is back to the old complaint. Brother Francesco had told him that his brother was late again in paying the annuity. "According to what he keeps marked down in his books, there are fifty ducats due." The community needed all the ducats it could lay hands on. "We must buy grain and cannot see how to do so." This is just the situation in which Ercole had said Alphonsus could apply to him and he would be generous, and now he was not even being just. Of course, all this talk of paying out money must, Alphonsus understood, irritate Ercole as it had irritated Don Giuseppe. "Have patience with me; I am trying to get our account settled because I am in such need."[152]

The next May, however, Alphonsus felt quite confident in asking Ercole to use his credit in Naples so that he should have the use of something between fifty-five hundred and four thousand ducats. He required such a huge sum so that he might cover the expenses of going to Rome and being made a bishop. Rather ungraciously, but not uncharacteristically, Alphonsus managed to turn Ercole's willingness to pledge his credit to a money lender into cause for complaint: "Had you not expressed a wish to do this, I had already thought of writing to the Pope, as a last resort, to tell him I had no money to pay for the Bulls and the rest of the necessary expenses, and who knows whether he might not, on account of my inability, have let me off the episcopate."[153] Ercole had, therefore, better be clear about the largeness of the sum required, about the arrangements for Alphonsus' paying the interest, and about the length of time it would take him to pay off the capital sum they were borrowing, The diocese should be able to put about fifteen hundred ducats a year towards reducing the debt. Ercole had better be clear, too, about Alphonsus' needing the money in a hurry. At least money can be saved by his living in the family house when he's in Naples. "It will be sufficient for me to have one or two rooms on your first floor where I can receive persons of quality, the upper floor will do for my companions, as it would not suit me or the persons who will call on me." And then there's the question of a coach....

At the close of these tiresome arrangements, the brothers were still on good enough terms.[154] Ercole was a distinguised guest at the supper after Alphonsus' installation at Sant' Agata,[155] and, for a while, their correspondence flourished. Ercole was best pleased to have his brother a bishop. He wrote to Alphonsus about torches for the out-runners if he drove out at night. Alphonsus wrote to Ercole about planting white mulberry for a cash crop.[156] Ercole wrote to tell him of his wife's death.[157] Alphonsus wrote back with advice about choosing a second wife, especially noting the dangers of marrying too young or too grand a lady who would want to go gallivanting every evening. "If you do not take my advice," the clerical bachelor told him, "you will have a disturbed mind and a troubled conscience for the rest of your days."[158] Ercole was rather pleased to inform his brother that he had only to sit back and receive a great number of handsome proposals from eager parents. Alphonsus observed deflatingly that the girls themselves might not be so pleased with a husband of advanced age, "as you are."[159] Meanwhile, to maintain their honorable name, Ercole had better sack the younger housemaids. And, oh, yes, about that borrowed money which Ercole now wanted back so that he could plan for this second wedding, Alphonsus was hoping not only that the loan could be extended, but that he could be advanced a further sum. "At present you would have to put me in prison to wrest even a carlin from me." It was, he allowed, a real difficulty that the episcopate and the marriage should come at the same time, or rather that they should both be marrying, and that, as it now seemed to him when he took a look at the pair of them, Alphonsus should be entering the more demanding union, "I also am married but to a spouse that does not give me a moment's rest." And, to speak plainly, Ercole is still aiming too high. After all, the social position of the Liguori is not what it was "when our father was alive."[160]

Don Ercole found himself a bride. In March 1763, he married Donna Marianna Capano, the daughter, more importantly, the only child, bringing money and title with her, of the Prince of Pollica, another of the Orsini clan. He brought his bride to meet his brother, the bishop. Rather to Alphonsus' irritation, since he had no intention of turning this visit into "an occasion," the local Redemptoristines sent in a few extra delicacies for the luncheon table.[161]

Not everyone had food that year. There was another poor harvest. By November, Alphonsus was writing to Ercole, as one of the Regents of the City, for help in organizing relief for the starving of his diocese.[162] It must have seemed to Ercole an attempt to rub his nose in that reduction in their status since their parents' time when Alphonsus wrote to ask him about selling the coach. Ercole could not bear the deep disgrace of a coachless brother. Alphonsus could not understand him. "Your letter has caused me pain."[163]

Donna Marianna had her pain, too. In March 1764, Ercole had to tell Alphonsus of his wife's enduring a miscarriage. "My very dear Brother," Alphonsus wrote back in a stiff attempt to say something affectionate, "I have received your letter in which you inform me of the accident that has befallen Signora Donna Marianna." But he could not get the properly sympathetic, human, tone into his note. "Since God has permitted it, we must," he tells the unhappy wife and husband, as if their miserableness were no harder to bear than his own, "be resigned to his holy will."[164] Inappropriately self-regarding, irritatingly pious, Alphonsus shifts at once to discuss the high price of corn in the marketplace. "This pains me greatly, but as God wills it, may his holy will be done." The citizens have only themselves to blame. "I say that God is especially chastising Naples because there are so many there that do not believe in Him; God grant that they may now be converted." At least he does not suggest that his sister-in-law and brother have only themselves to blame for the loss of their child. But he does make an unfeeling connection between the miscarriage and the corn prices. "In a word, we are all in distress, you at Naples, we here."

Whatever the distance such a letter might have put between them, when, later that year, Alphonsus became ill at Sant' Agata, Ercole was quick to send a pair of grand doctors from Naples to relieve his brother from the attentions of the local barber and blood-letter.[165] He did not, thereby, obtain influence enough at the bishop's palace for his letter of recommendation to secure confessor's faculties for a Dominican Prior of his acquaintance.[166]

Rather to the chagrin of Don Ercole, who was looking anxiously for this second wife to produce a male heir, Alphonsus presenting a statue of the Lady to the newly pregnant Donna Marianna, prophesied, "This will not be a boy, but a girl" and, he added, exacting full payment for this piece of fortune-telling, "I want her to be called Maria Teresa." And so, as Tannoia faithfully recorded again, it was.[167] Teresa was born in 1765. The next year, however, when the couple visited Alphonsus at Airola, he gave Donna Marianna two little statues of Saint Aloysius Gonzaga, telling his sister-in-law to be confident of God's care for her. "The two figurines worked a mystery."[168] Donna Marianna became pregnant again. This time with twin boys. Giuseppe and Carlo were born in 1766. She had another boy, Alfonsino, in 1767. The bishop baptized Teresa. Alfonsino too. Perhaps the twins as well.[169] He certainly confirmed all three boys. But already things were going wrong in his brother's family.

Ercole had written, soon after his wedding visit to Sant' Agata, that his future happiness was guaranteed not only by the prayers of his brother and his brother's companions, but by the piety of his new wife, which was increasing daily. "She was always devout and now she is a saint."[170] Donna Marianna was making the time for prayer, meditation, and daily Communion that Alphonsus had said was necessary for the woman in the world to become a saint. She was, alas, beginning to be entirely occupied with the perfectest fulfillment of these devotions, and soon the whole household was feeling the baneful effects of her scrupulosity. The Liguori clan consulted about the chief's wife. Antonia at San Marcellino,[171] on being told all the details, decided that the lady was possessed by a demon and had best be sent to Alphonsus for exorcism. Alphonsus was much alarmed by this suggestion. "Donna Marianna is not possessed," he declared authoritatively, "she is out of her mind." He could not be expected to do anything. "For pity's sake don't let Antonia send Donna Marianna here; that would be just an added bother for me."[172]

The little boys went on, however, filling Ercole's life with happy expectations. Not that he was left to look forward cheerfully. There was that terrible question in the parlor: Would you be very much distressed if you were to lose one of them?"[173] Carlo died in 1770. Ercole besought his brother never to speak of such a thing again. So the others grew up to be the representatives of the family in whom uncles Alphonsus and Gaetano, as well as their parents, invested a deal of interest.

Alphonsus' expectation, "I hope that they wish to become saints," may seem somewhat previous when applied to toddlers. But he felt it to be his right and responsibility to fix just what prayers they should be saying. He wrote out a set for them. Ercole reported that these had been well received. "I am happy," Alphonsus wrote back, "that the children are practicing the devotions I sent them."[174] Perhaps Ercole raised an eyebrow as he passed on to Don Domenico Pedicino di Vitulano, the boys' tutor, that strict "rule of life" his brother had also sent, with the plain warning that only if the boys kept up the practices he recommended would they become saints.[175] Alphonsus might seem to be thinking in ways nearer our own in his protesting against Ercole's determination to send the boys, then aged five and six, off to boarding school. "It is not good for boys to go away to school before they are at least ten or twelve."[176] It was not the loss of the give and take of family affection which Alphonsus had in mind, but their escaping paternal discipline, "To preserve their early boyhood from vice, it would be better if they stayed at home. And, anyway, Alphonsus remarked reprovingly, the choice of school for his nephews was his business. "I'll have to think further where to send them." Ercole had plans for them to attend the Nunziatella de Pizzofalcone, once a Jesuit novitiate house but, after 1767, converted to a lay-run school for gentlemen's sons, popularly known as the "College of Nobles."[177] This would be the place to start the boys on their ways to careers at court. Alphonsus was horrified. "I have no good opinion of this College."[178] The boys should stay at home for a while and then sent to board with the Fathers of the Pious Schools for three years. Perhaps Alphonsus had heard a rumor that the Greek master at the Nunziatella was suspected of being a clandestine Mason.[179] Ercole, still thinking of giving his sons a social shove, counter-proposed that the pair of them be sent immediately to the Royal School for Pages. Alphonsus, who had heard a cautionary tale of one such young gentleman's declining into a highwayman, was again appalled.[180] "It takes only one bad boy to ruin a hundred."[181] So Ercole, with some skill returned, as if compromisingly, to his original suggestion about the College. "Well, you are their father," Alphonsus remarked in a huff, "do whatever you want."[182] But, having let Ercole have his way about the education of his own children, Alphonsus could not refrain from another of his doomful prophesyings. "The day will come when you will regret this and not be able to remedy some evil consequence." However, he'd content himself with writing one of his letters to the Rector which Ercole would take with him when he brought the boys to their new school. Pushing his luck, Ercole let slip that he would soon be presenting them at Court. "You do just the opposite of what I tell you to do," Alphonsus grumbled.[183]

The Father in the Congregation

Ercole's notion of his parental rights and responsibilities was irksomely surprising to Alphonsus. It had seemed quite the usual way of things that the adult, house-owning, married, Ercole should come to him in tears, asking for advice and protection.[184] It was, therefore, the more extraordinary that he should now be thinking himself the person to settle the future of his boys. There was in this the puzzling suggestion that Alphonsus might do well to limit his responsibilities to a caring for "the sons of this Institute."[185]

Certainly, his relations with the Students, those Reverend Brothers of the Congregation, seemed to offer him the chance to be a good father. They were so evidently "my dearest children" when they arrived at the Congregation's door and would be his dearest children always.[186] He wanted them to know this. To know that they were members now of a family ruled by love.

"No father's tenderness," Tannoia observed, "could equal the tenderness that Alphonsus felt for our Students."[187] He might even, on occasion, give one of them some little tweak of affection. Falcoia rather disapproved of such demonstrativeness.[188] So warned, Alphonsus accepted that he should limit his expressions of tenderness, contenting himself with the more usual head of family's enquiries about the Students' prayers, "I hear that they go to excess," their classroom studies, "Physics is not an absolutely necessary topic: it is ornamental," their recreations, "what do they do after dinner?"[189] Thus, the reports he had required from his nephews' College tutors, and from the fellow-boarders, school-mistresses, and convent-Prioress of his niece, were parallelled in the tales that he demanded watchful Fathers and Brothers send him of each Student's conduct.[190] He was simply being the good father. Don Giuseppe had expected him to make such reports on his returning from convoy duty. Paolo Cafaro's father had expected a like tale-bearing.[191] Very probably, each bourgeois Student would expect this Father to be, in this and other ways, just like his father at home.

There was scriptural warrant for such an expectation of likeness between their families; "every family in heaven and on earth," the author of Ephesians 3:14f had declared, derives from the fatherliness of God. Bishop Falcoia was fond of representing his will for others as a reflection of the will of "the great Father of family."[192] So was almost anyone then who called himself "Father in God." But while Alphonsus, the rightful heir succeeding, was ready to exploit a psychological advantage that the death of Don Giuseppe on November 10, 1745, gave him in the clan, along with that advantage which the death of the bishop, April 20, 1743, had given him in the estimate of most Fathers, Students, Brothers, he had never been comfortable with the image of "the great Father." Always at his back he hears that terrible echo: "Let my Son die."[193] Alphonsus is keenly aware of the need for that awful sentence. "I love Thee, O Eternal Father, who dost condemn thine innocent Son to free me."[194] But in "the horrible theater of Calvary" he identifies with the Son.[195] His sense of himself as rightful enjoyer of a father's authority in the Congregation derived from a peculiarly christological perception of his place.

Writing to the troubled novice, Ludovico Capuano, 1739–after 1781, intent on showing him the difference of the Congregation from his family back in Cava dei Tirreni, Alphonsus began with a rhetorical question of some subtlety: "If you're worrying about your relatives, well, along with Jesus, most holy Mary, and the Saints, who are assuredly more to you than father, mother, and brothers, are not we also your brothers?"[196] Capuano has left his blood kin. He has made his own the Congregation's familiar prayer: "Thou O Jesus art my Father, and thou Mary art my Mother."[197] He has recognized that, as Alphonsus is affirming through his parallels, the Saints are his brothers. He has now only to give real assent to its being among his new Brothers in the Congregation that he will himself become one of those brother Saints. Alphonsus well understands how persuasively attractive for the novice, for anyone, is this promise of fraternity here, now, and in the Kingdom, eternally. For himself, however, when he recites that prayer, when he meditates upon those parallels, it is most significant that he can identify Jesus, the firstborn Son, as the fulfiller of the Isaiah prophecy: "He shall be called the Father of the world to come," "*Pater futuri saeculi.*"[198]

"Not through any generative act," Thomas à Kempis had written in "that golden book," the *Imitation of Christ*, "but through his doing the work of a father,"[199] Christ has paternal authority among us. He comes from his Cross to upbraid each one of us as his ungrateful child. "What are you saying, son? Stop complaining. Just think of my Passion."[200]

Such a relation of fatherly work and fatherly authority is inherent in our world's order. Joseph in Egypt, after his years of being on the outlook for the people's economic future, could say, "God has made me a father to Pharaoh." Micah, wanting to be liturgically correct, invited the young Levite, who was "like one of his sons," to stay on his homestead "and be to me a father."[201] Contrariwise, it is a sign of chaos coming when a father has to do the work of a son. From his tutorials with good old Don Buonaccia, Alphonsus knows that painful Homeric story of King Priam's carrying his son's body from the tent of Achilles for burial. The fall of Troy cannot be long delayed after such a reversal of due order.[202] He seems to know, too, from conversations with some theatergoing Spaniard, the terrors of Shakespeare's *Lear*. That old king's having to seek raiment, bed, and food, from his daughters shows that chaos has already come.[203]

Jesus on the cross, as the demons of chaos waited for him to die in the dark, was renewing order. "Reconciling us with God," Alphonsus tells the meditator working through his *Glories of Mary*, "he made himself the Father of souls in the new law of grace," "*padre dell'anime nella nuova lege di grazia.*"[204]

This gracious new law is a law of Life, Liberty and Happiness. It is for living. Living in freedom. Confidently. Alphonsus was well acquainted with the confident tradition of those who recognize the Christ as their Father. "My paternal mercy will protect you," Christ had said to Saint

Gertrude of Helfta, 1256–1302(?), whom Alphonsus so often cited as a reliable exponent of Christian experience.[205] That Sicilian nun, Maria Crocifissa dei Tomasi, 1645–1699, had, as Falcoia enjoyed telling Sportelli, recommended that the worried Christian run to Jesus "as a child runs after its father, calling out at the top of its voice."[206] The novice Capuano, dutifully reading the suggested *Theology of the Mind and Heart* of Vincent Contenson, 1641–1674, would have come across, in the chapter on mariological devotion, an incidental warning from Jesus that "it is no use invoking me as your Father, if you are not venerating Mary as your Mother."[207] Most immediately for Alphonsus, the Lord of their own Rule, the early *Regole Grandi,* tells them all, "See how I am a father to you, better than any father on earth."[208] Alphonsus himself, appreciating that Christ is paternally protective not only of members of the Congregation, "My sons, my dear Sons,"[209] but of all Christians, bids his mission congregation look confidently towards the crucifix, to the open-armed Jesus: "Be assured, you children of so good a Father."[210]

Christ should always be the paradigm. What Christ is and does, Alphonsus takes as what he is to be and do. He looked to Christ in order that he might understand his own human nature and talent and the gracious use to which he should be putting himself. Imitating Christ, Alphonsus would come from being the son, the firstborn, the heir, into being a father. Brother Alphonsus is "the Father of the whole family," "the common Father."[211] He is properly addressed as "Your Paternity."

Father and Brother

Alphonsus was not proud. He would follow directions if the director seemed good and intelligent and to be throughly sensitive to Alphonsus' needs. There were quite a number of good and intelligent men, besides Bishop Falcoia, to tell him how he might be a Christlike Father. Mostly in terms suited to the education of bishops and abbots. Alphonsus read the foundational description in the *Cura Pastoralis* of Saint Gregory, the exposition in the second chapter of the Rule of Saint Benedict of what it means to be both *dominus* and *abbas,* the suaver *Exhortacion* of the Jesuit expert, Francisco Arias, 1533–1605, and the *Letters* of Saint Francis de Sales to a range of religious superiors. The consistent line of understanding in these writings, was most plainly expressed in the sober instructions of St. Bernard's *De Consideratione* to which Alphonsus' own 1745 *Reflections Useful to Bishops* was itself compared.[212] His tract was intended as a practical guide, with hints on how to manage seminary Rectors, Vicars General, and contemplative nuns. He had sent a copy to every bishop in the Kingdom. But for himself, to know how he should be "the Superior as Father," he reckoned that he should take the pattern of a Christian fatherhood presented in the life and writings of Paul. This was a consistent theme in his plannings for the Institute.

In the early statement of the *Idea and Purpose* of their Institute, put together with Falcoia during the summer of 1733, Alphonsus is demanding that any who would join them "make their own what the Apostle said to his disciples, "Imitate me as I imitate Christ," 1 Corinthians 11:1."[213] Presenting his *Compendio* of their self-description to the bishop of Bovino in 1745, Alphonsus assured Antonio Lucci, 1690(?)–1752, that he and his helpers were aiming at a conformity with their Lord Jesus Christ, manifesting the Lord's death and life in their mission work, "as the Apostle says."[214] Working with Sportelli and Villani on a Rule to be presented at the Chapter of the Congregation in 1747, Alphonsus returned to 1 Corinthians 11:1 for a starting text.[215] Even in the legalist Pontifical Rule text of February 1749, there remains a hint of this Corinthian *imitatio* at the Redemptorists' promising to find their pleasure in humiliations suffered for Christ's sake, "like the Apostle."[216] In these accounts of his hopes in the Institute, Alphonsus was offering a Pauline meaning for all their lives, but the paradigm was most personally significant for his estimate of his own vocation as Rector Major.

He had, as a student reading the *Commentary on the Pauline Epistles* of Willem Estius, 1542–1613,[217] been made aware, at Estius' exposition of 1 Corinthians 11:1, that Paul esteemed himself "the father in Christ" of the Corinthian community, teaching them that to be faithful proclaimers of the Christ "who gave himself as a redemption for all," they should imitate Paul himself "as sons imitate a father."[218] It was precisely within a context of announcing how "I became your father in Christ Jesus" that Paul had sent Timothy, "my beloved and faithful son in the the Lord" to be a missioner. Alphonsus, sending them to preach "redemption for all," took it that each of his missioner helpers was to be "like a son with a father."[219] That he was to be "like a father with his children."[220]

There was more for him. As he had gone on studying the Corinthian epistle with Torno, Estius on the desk, he had been made aware that Paul had not thought to express the fullness of Christ's gracious relation with our race within the categories of "father" and "son" only. Immediately next, in the Vulgate, Paul was telling his sons in Christ Jesus, "I praise you, brothers," *Laudo autem vos fratres.*[221] To imitate Christ, as the Apostle imitates Christ, is to be both father and brother.

Evidence of this mystery came crowding back to Alphonsus' mind on his recollecting the climax of Torno's reading of these New Testament epistles. "Here I am," the suffering Christ of the epistle to the Hebrews had said to him "with my children," and at the same place, the editor of Paul's notes for this epistle, who Estius suggested was either Clement of Rome or Luke the Evangelist, avers that "in bringing many sons into glory" Christ is not ashamed to call them "brothers."[222] They are, at Hebrews 2:11 and 2:12, "My brothers in the midst of the congregation," giving proper praise to the Lord.[223] Arriving at these verses, Torno handed Alphonsus his copy of Bellarmine *On the Psalms* down from the shelf.[224] There is in this Hebrews pericope, Bellarmine assured them, an early Christian accommodation of verse 22 of Psalm 21, the great Passion psalm, "My God, my God, why hast thou forsaken me?" Every Christian knows this psalm. Knows, too, as Alphonsus said in his own translation and commentary on the *Psalms and Canticles of the Divine Office,* 1774,[225] that "this psalm is to be understood, in the literal sense, of Jesus Christ, and especially of the prayer which he said before his death from the height of the Cross, and especially also of his glorious resurrection."[226] That's plain. "Bellarmine says it would be temerious to turn it to any other sense." Alphonsus, as he recited this psalm at Prime each Friday, was, on coming to verse 22, very ready to take his lead from Hebrews and identify these "brothers" who are "in the midst of the congregation" as the first Christian missionaries in the midst of churches in the Levant. More, in making that call from the Cross, Christ himself declares the value of every apostolic preaching in his Church. "He says, 'I will publish the glory of Thy name by means of my brothers the Apostles,' etc."[227] Alphonsus is, therefore, emboldened to make a further accommodation of that "etc." The members of this least of Congregations have their present share in this publishing of the Lord's glory. As then Paul had recognized an enlargement of his paternal relation with his missioners so that he should talk of them fraternally in the congregation, "Titus, my brother," "Quartus, our brother, Timothy, our brother,"[228] so Alphonsus now is enabled to recognize the missioner sons around him in the Congregation, "the children whom God has given me," as also "my brothers."

In being both Father and Brother, he was manifesting Christ to the Congregation in ways which he discerned in a continuous tradition of the Church from those Apostolic times. Reading the Passion meditations of the loquacious Franciscan Bernardino de Busti, d. 1513, for instance. Reimagining the moment of Christ's dying, those who took Bernardino's *Mariale* as bedtime reading would hear, certainly Alphonsus heard with him, the Mother of Jesus lament all she had lost in losing him; "Ah, my Son," he heard her cry, "You were my Father, my Brother."[229] Alphonsus' filial devotion to Mamma Mary would thus come together with his reading of the New Testament and the mystical tradition of the community to encourage his sense of Jesus as Father and Brother, of Jesus' being imitated by the Apostle with his sons and brothers on the mission, and of himself, imitating Paul imitating Jesus, as Father and Brother in the Congregation.

So it is in imitation of Christ that he writes to "My Brothers and Children" or, better, for this declares more plainly the sustaining value of their relations, "My Brothers and Children in Jesus Christ."[230]

Alphonsus had had impressive exemplars of what it was to be a contemporary father. Neither Don Giuseppe nor Bishop Falcoia, "the Father," had been much given to self-doubt in their relations with sons. These had been compelling exponents of paternity. "Depend in everything," Alphonsus had written to himself, "on Falcoia who has accepted you as his son....Right....Obedience not to doubt any more."[231] Alphonsus would become such a compelling Father himself. There had not, however, been comparable exemplars of congenial fraternity in his experience down home. "The longer we live familiarly with those we love," he had noted, "the colder love must become, since the closer men look at one another, the more defects they discern."[232]

However he'd missed his opportunities for easy comradeship with Antonio and Gaetano, whatever the causes of his understanding Barbara and Annella so little, wherever he was going wrong in his relations with Ercole and Ercole's children, Alphonsus was determined that none of the Brothers in the Congregation should doubt his care for them. "God knows how much I love each of you more than my brothers."[233] It was not without some little irony, therefore, that just when Alphonsus was deciding that he could no longer sign himself "Brother" in letters to Francesco de Paola, he was willing to allow, as he told him, that "we should continue to treat each other as brothers."[234]

But how was he, in the house with Brothers, to express this love which was beyond the love of brothers? Alphonsus could never feel quite at his ease with Villani: "I shall *act* as you say; I thank you for having freed me from these troubles; I bless your Reverence."[235] Never relax with the nervously devoted Tannoia: "You know, my dear Father Antonio, that I esteem you, but this time I must speak to you plainly."[236] There is something awkward even in the sincere pieties of his letter to the sickly Donato Melaccio, 1732–1764, telling "my dear son" to rejoice that he is about to die in the Congregation, and sending him the interim good wishes of "Brother Alphonsus" until they meet in blessed eternity.[237] There was about as much informal brotherliness in most of these encounters as when Pope Clement XI was writing to Cardinal Francesco Pignatelli, 1660–1734, letting him know that he had sanctioned the four-year-old Annella's entering San Girolamo, "*Venerabilis frater noster….*"[238] Considerably less brotherliness than when the *Padrona* gun-crew drilled together, "serving brothers," "*fratelli servienti.*"

But Alphonsus was eager to talk as Brother with brothers. So where should he go looking for the right language? Not in the curial formalities, evidently. And he had not been expensively tutored in order that he should lapse into the oaths of those rough sailors. Nor even into the raffish language in which his father's brother officers told tales of those "Brothers of the Coast" against whose piracies the *Padrona* patrolled the busy shipping route between Naples and Spain.[239] There was not much for him, either, in the lawyer's clerks' jargon as they got out those rolled parchments stacked in the cupboards of Don Luigi Perrone's office and in the metal clientboxes at the even more prestigious chambers of Don Andrea Giovene,[240] anticipating a neat deflation of the rhetoric of "my brother for the defense" or "my brother for the prosecution," as the case might be. Though each and all of these experiences offered a few helpful hints, helpfuller, certainly, than anything he'd known at home, none showed him enough of brotherhoods, of the egalitarian loyalties they promote, the comradely obligations they impose, to sustain Alphonsus' mature sense of himself as "Brother," or to inform his conversation with brothers. His father had presented him with other opportunities, however, for just that necessary appreciation of what it is to be a Brother.

Don Giuseppe on home-leave would have seen that Alphonsus did not find his brothers at all interesting. He would not have spent much time regretting that. He couldn't much bother with them himself. He could appreciate how it was that Alphonsus preferred to spend his evenings at the opera or the card table rather than at home. The Captain would certainly have rather gone to some palazzo music than sit with Donna Anna as she read her Office. Once he'd gained that Law degree, Alphonsus should be freer to enjoy himself. And in the opera box or between hands of "basset," Alphonsus could be forming a few of those friendships which are so useful to the professional man. Don Giuseppe had himself, perhaps, played a few games of "primero" with an elderly admiral when he was an ensign. Meanwhile, his heir should become acquainted with other brotherhoods at least as useful.

Don Giuseppe, this time at least knowing Donna Anna would approve his plan for their son, placed the young Alphonsus with the squirelings of the Naples Oratory sodality. Later, he brought him into those socially influential Confraternities of do-gooding gentlemen which he himself had joined as an ambitious junior officer aboard the *Capitana.*

The Captain had learnt at these Confraternities, as he advanced in his naval career, to practice some more systematic charity than those impulsive responses any decent man made to the abandoned babies down by the arsenal or to the old salt's appeal on the wharf, "Brother, can you spare a dime?" Once enrolled in these admirable Confraternities, his son would do a little good, recommend himself to persons of the right sort, and be authorized to employ their usual style, signing himself "D. Alfonso di Liguoro, Brother."[241]

But all in good time. All in decent order. "Ship-shape and Naples fashion." First, Alphonsus must be presented to his hereditary fellows on the magistrate's bench.

II

BROTHERHOODS

Of the six magistracies into which the city was divided,[1] seats on five benches were reserved for the "one hundred and thirty first families" of Naples.[2] These urban aristocrats ran the most ancient of the *sedile* districts, the Capuano and the di Nilo, and the quite old Porto and Arcangelo a Segno and the Portanova in which the Liguori were among the senior men.[3] The influence, power indeed, of these magistrates had increased steadily since the abolition of the Parliament in 1642. Together they formed an assembly, nominating representatives to treat of city-wide interests with the King's Ministers. Correspondingly, the privilege of membership of these *sedile* benches had been the more jealously hugged by those families who had already secured their places.

When Alphonsus was thirteen years old, Domenico Liguori, 1674-1752, one of his father's clan, was deputed by the Portanova' gentry to take responsibility for their celebration of the feast of Saint Gennaro, September 19.[4] This was a grand responsibility, one that demonstrated the magistrates' confidence in the family. Next year, 1710, Alphonsus was formally presented to the *sedile*, and, having not blotted his copy-book in the meantime, was on his eighteenth birthday officially aggregated to the rota of serving magistrates and took his first turn carrying one of the *sedile* crosses in the Holy Week processions.[5] He remained sedulous in his attendance at court sittings and supper celebrations until he was made a cleric in 1723.[6]

This was a society dedicated to the defense of local privilege which, as the gentlemen talked together after settling some public business, about taxation, highways and their cleaning, and saints' festivities, very easily shifted into an old-boy network for their mutual advantage. Alphonsus, who in 1722 presented the *sedile* loyal address to the newly arrived Cardinal Michel Friedrich Althann, 1682–1734, Austrian viceroy, 1722–1728,[7] was able to use his continuing membership to obtain a *sedile* grant towards the building of the Ciorani house twenty years later.[8] All this was very acceptable. But Alphonsus must have become uneasy at the magistrates' short way with poor vagrants shunted across the bounds of neighboring jurisdictions.

There had been in the Kingdom of Naples, for at least a century, a problem of rural unemployment, on account of frequent failures of the wheat crop and associated attempts by a refeudalizing gentry to displace their vassal laborers.[9] Cleared off land which was required for a good day's boar hunt, a homeless peasant would necessarily take up begging along the highway. And if honest begging failed, become a molester of travelers, or an enticer at the entry to a city side-alley. Highwaymen and prostitutes figure largely in the stories Alphonsus tells of the men and women he encounters on his mission travels.[10] Gerard Majella got a fright when, as he was going through a darkening wood one late night, a man sprang out and seized his horse's reins.[11] In Naples he had at least as unpleasant an experience when he was stopped by a pair of unblest sirens in a narrow street.[12] Ever-increasing numbers of these unemployed and often unemployable women and men threatened to disrupt the civil order of the city. Neapolitan property owners, viewing these incomers, would likely remember with a shudder the popular revolt led by Masaniello in 1647.[13] This was a time for all good men to band together for one another's betterment here.[14] And hereafter. Existing Confraternities revised their Rules to accommodate increased numbers of Brothers and moved to larger chapels for their meetings. New Confraternities were founded.[15]

Some, a majority even, of Neapolitan men who grouped themselves in Confraternities may have joined primarily in order that they might advance an individual prospect of salvation. But the social effect of such an increase of volunteer charity workers was immense. While, as late as 1667, the Naples government was attempting the forcible deportation and enclosure of city beggars, the Confraternities founded in the sixteenth and seventeenth centuries were putting their energies to organizing bread distributions, pauper schooling, prison visiting, hospital nursing, and the burying of the dead, making together a socially effective response of lay Christians to the degradation of their countrywomen and men.

These coworkers, sisters and brothers in Consororities and Confraternities, were assuming, just as the charitable Naples jurist Giovanni Maria Novario, fl. 1627, had declared in his influential 1623 tract *On the Privileges of the Poor,* that the Church not the State must take primary responsibility for poor relief.[16] The Church was "Mother of the Poor" and, as the Church in action, the Christian sodality must take responsible care of the vagrant, the refugee, the dismissed cleric, the lunatic. The confraternities, as they achieved social and political influence in towns across the Kingdom, were, in the middle decades of the century, effective in restraining that sort of violence against the structures of civil administration which Alphonsus himself witnessed during the wheat famine of 1764.[17] If there had been such a socially-conscious confraternity at Arienzo, the scarified Mayor might not have been forced to run to the bishop's palace for sanctuary from a lynch mob.[18]

Usually organized about a shrine in a city church, at whose altar the Brothers stood for their devotions, there were over three hundred sodalities in Naples run either by laymen or by a conspiracy of lay and clerical officers.[19] They were generally societies of men since they, unlike the women, had evenings free. Anyway, husbands did not care for their womenfolk to be out of the house at night. Even if it were for some form of self-improvement.[20]

Alphonsus, not by temperament a team player, but alert to the effectiveness of the Portanova network, seems from early youth to have been made Christianly aware that nothing can be done solitarily in the family of God. It was vice that was solitary. He knew about that. Took precautions when a teenager. Later, he had stories to tell of other sorts of danger in solitariness:

> There was this solitary, in a desert, spending night and day in prayer, leading a most austere life, and honored, therefore, by many. The unhappy man began to think well of himself and, on account of his virtues, regarded himself sure of perseverance and salvation. But then a demon appeared to him in the form of a lovely woman and tempted him to sin. The solitary was unable to resist the temptation, and fell. Immediately after his fall, the demon burst into loud laughs and disappeared.[21]

The solitary afterwards, Alphonsus says, fell into one horrid vice after another. "Thus he became a warning to show how dangerous it is to trust in your own strength." Contrariwise, it is by enlisting in companies of cooperators, putting talents to gracious use, persevering in service, that a man may learn what it is to be a good Brother.

Alphonsus became an enthusiastic joiner. In the Associations, Colleges, Companies, Confraternities,[22] that he joined as a young man, Alphonsus shared a range of experiences which would give content to his later idea of imitating Paul's *imitatio* with "My Brothers in Jesus Christ."

Young Nobility

Francesco Maria Tarugi, 1525–1608, the most charming of the disciples of Saint Philip Neri, had come from Rome to Naples for his health's sake in 1583 and again in 1584 and then, in 1585, his friends, determining on the foundation of an Oratory in their city, had, for five thousand ducats, bought the splendid Seripandi palace directly opposite the cathedral.[23] To make space for a church fit for such a house, the Oratorians pulled down three chapels in the area, including that of Saints Cosmas and Damian where the Barbers' Confraternity had been meeting for at least a century. By 1592 the Oratorians had laid the foundations of a great church to the design of the Florentine Giovanni Antonio Dosio, 1533–1609, and his pushy assistant Dionisio Nencioni, 1570–1623. Dionisio Lazzari, 1615–1690, had his facade in place in 1655. Statues were being niched, chapel ceilings painted, masterpieces hung above altars, all through the eighteenth century. The very sight of such a place must be a wondrously enlarging experience for any sensitive youngster in the Oratory congregation.

Along with employing the Florentines, the Oratory Fathers had put a local architect and local painters, Arcangelo Guglielmelli and Francesco Malerba and Cristiano Russo, to work on the three-stories-high Library, to house their increasingly splendid collection of books and manuscripts and musical scores. The Oratory house and parish very fast became a center of academic influence in the city. In Alphonsus' time, Giambattista Vico, 1668–1744, the greatest intellectual of contemporary Europe, was one of several Law School professors who were regular members of the congregation.

Perhaps intent on attracting such clever men to join their Brothers of the Little Oratory, the Provosts made over to this sodality a pleasantly decorated chapel for their Sunday afternoon meetings. There, after a short sermon, prayer, and hymn-singing, they could plan their week's good works. This chapel was also used, on Wednesdays usually, by the Oratory of Young Noblemen, instituted by the Fathers in 1676 for rather a different sort of client, and placed under Saint Joseph's patronage on his feast day, May 1.[24]

The first ten members of this select confraternity had proceeded, under license from the Father Prefect, to elect from their number a Rector, two Consultors, a Secretary, a Master of Novices, a Master of Ceremonies, a Sacristan, two Cantors, and an Infirmarian. Evidently each of the boys had a job. As the Young Nobility flourished and the number of Brothers increased so, of course, must the number of offices. In 1706, when Alphonsus was elected a member, there were two Masters of Novices, four, possibly six, Sacristans, four Cantors, and two Infirmarians, as well as two Readers and three doorkeepers, under the supervision of Padre Filippo Pisani, 1668–1747. Alphonsus enjoyed clerical as well as gentry connections to promote his application for membership. Provost Filippo Mastrillo, 1656–1716, at the Oratory was a near kinsman of Donna Andreana Mastrillo, Don Giuseppe's mother.[25]

At the start, Alphonsus seems to have been esteemed a most pleasing Brother. Within a year of his election, on the feast of the Assumption, 1707, he was chosen to be one of the Sacristans. For whatever reason, he was not elected even to a Doorkeeper's job at either of the two polls of 1708. He'd recovered popularity in the Confraternity by Epiphany 1709 and was then elected one of the Masters of Ceremony and got himself reelected to this office in August that year and again in January 1710. At the Epiphany vote of 1711, when the Young Nobity was being supervised by Tommaso Pagani's pupil, the newly ordained Casimiro Sicola, 1687–1720, Alphonsus was voted Secretary and Master of Novices. He lost the Secretary's job in the summer election that year but was retained as Master of Novices and was again reelected in 1712 when first Don Antonio and then Don Gaetano were received among his novices.[26] By that time their Cavalieri cousins, Francesco and Federico, had followed the three Liguori boys into the Young Nobility.[27] Within a year both Antonio and Gaetano were Cantors. Within two years, while Gaetano was still a perfectly treble Cantor, Antonio's voice had cracked a little and he was Master of Novices.[28] Alphonsus was back to doorkeeping. Federico Cavalieri, already surprising his parents with talk of becoming a Dominican, was elected one of the Sacristans at that same January 28, 1714, vote. Elections, once held only at Epiphany and Assumption, seem now to occur quite irregularly. Francesco Cavalieri, Alphonsus' fellow candidate for Law School, was elected a Reader, May 20, 1714. It must have been dawning upon Alphonsus that if he were to retain a leadership among this clutch of clan members it could not be by any assertion of a right of the eldest son.

Don Pisani, and after him Don Sicola, encouraged the boys, on their confraternity outings, to play those team games whose fond remembrance in later life should prompt the grown nobility to sustain the friendships begun at the Oratory. They'd be nostalgic friends and benefactors of the Fathers. And, now that the Confraternity had been going for nearly forty years, that one generation of alumni should further the careers of the next was beginning to seem quite the ordinary thing with them. Alphonsus' being hired by Duke Filippo Orsini to make his family's case in the Amatrice lawsuit is likely to have owed something to this connection. Don Mondillo Orsini at the Oratory was a solicitous forwarder of the alumni. Though Alphonsus would have been benefitting, too, from uncle Giuseppe Cavalieri's being by then the Minister for War and a regular supper guest of the Orsini.

Alphonsus' experience of the young noblemen had not been uniformly happy. There was a particular unpleasantness on one of Don Sicola's expeditions. A ball game's being started in the statued gardens on Capo di Monte, Alphonsus declared himself too much the duffer to join a team.[29] Being prevailed upon, he proved, it may be just luckily, so good a throwing to the mark that one boy, who perhaps had lost a few coins betting against this beginner, could not restrain an ostler's oath. Something about "the hustler," perhaps. Young aristocrats have ever learnt their vocabulary from stable lads and boot boys, but in this matter of swearing Alphonsus was not quite the aristocrat. Maybe even his father would suppress a nautical oath in the presence of his mother. At any rate, it was remembered for some long time that Alphonsus had at once retired from the gamesters, to be discovered much later in another part of the garden, making a filial prayer of reparation to the Blessed Lady.[30]

There were happier memories for him of Girolamini music-making. If, as appears from those office lists, Alphonsus was never judged a good enough singer to be their Cantor, his voice was thought dramatic enough for him to be allotted a role when Don Sicola decided in 1712(?) that the Young Nobility would present a little opera, a holy opera, of course. They would perform the life and virtues of Saint Alessio.

Over the altar of the first chapel on the epistle side in the great Oratory church there was—and still is—a stupendous early Baroque painting of the dying Alessio by Pietro da Cortona, 1596–1669, all curly-haired angels and curvaceous clouds above and elegantly disposed draperies about the handsome saint below. Don Sicola, looking at this fine picture, would see that Alessio was just the saint for his boys. The son of a rich patrician of the fifth century, Alessio had, as he reached manhood, become convinced that his goods, his talents, his time, should be given to the most miserable of the poor. Abandoning at the altar the betrothed his parents had chosen for him, Alessio traveled to the furthest reaches of Christendom, working his way as a hospital orderly from town to town until he came round again to his parents' home in Italy. Being received graciously as a beggar whose remnants of handsomeness reminded them of their son, he was given a mattress in a corner under the stair. It was after seventeen years, only a little while before his death, that he discovered himself to his parents. Pietro da Cortona's painting shows the saint with the letter ready to be delivered. Then, amid their joy and sadness, Alessio died a truly Baroque death.

The story of Alessio's hospitaler stay at Edessa was already being told in Syriac in the fifth century, and had been quickly translated into greek and then, with some nice elaborations, into Latin. He was the hero of a rather tiring eleventh-century epic. And, just before Alphonsus' time, his legend had been turned into a couple of operas.[31] The *Sant' Alessio* of Stefano Landi, 1590–1685, had a verse libretto written by Pope Clement IX, Rospigliosi, 1667–1669, while he had been papal nuncio in Madrid. This was long before he inquired about the determination of Annella to become a nun.[32] Pietro da Cortona had designed backdrops of earth, hell, and heaven for the first performance at the palazzo Barbarini, March 2, 1631. If Don Sicola were planning to present this papal piece, he could have taken a copy of the upper background of their chapel painting for his scenic "heaven." But, having decided to show off their Young Nobility as capable of dealing with *avant-garde* music, the Oratorians would probably have selected the more modern piece of Bernardo Pasquini, 1637–1710. He had been the Roman Oratory's organist at the Chiesa Nuova from

1661, making there a wide reputation for himself, writing, as he said, "in today's fashion with bizarre and spirited ariettas," but having the cautious sense to set a shortened version of the workmanlike Rospigliosi libretto.[33] So, like the Landi opera, this entertainment had a couple of good scenes for the Demon who is trying to tempt Alessio out of his beggarly disguise and back into domestic comfortableness with his parents and his patiently waiting betrothed. Alphonsus was evidently thought a good actor, for the Demon appears in several disguises. And well able to raise the necessary grins. But it was not his comic acting which got him the part. On the Demon's suddenly sitting down at the gravocembalo keyboard, there is an erruption of gleeful tunes hardly to be resisted by an audience who must, as they applaud the player's skill, be the more astonished at the saint's steadfastness.[34] It was on account of his having paid proper attention during those expensive lessons with Gaetano Greco, 1675–1728, at the Conservatorio de' Poveri and thus his being accounted the best keyboard player among the Young Nobility, that Alphonsus had secured the Demon's part.[35] He made the most of his moment, seeming to the admiring company at the two performances Don Sicola's young nobles gave of their opera, one for the gentlemen of their clans, the other for their mothers and sisters, to be indeed a demon at the keyboard.[36]

Antonio and Gaetano, as new novices were, doubtless, unremarkable among Alphonsus' supporting chorus of "little demons." Doubling in the other chorus of "little angels." Not at all disgracing their papa. Or we should have heard of it. But Alphonsus had made just the sort of bright noise among the nobility that Don Giuseppe was wanting.

Looking back on his life at home, Alphonsus could recollect only once refusing to obey Don Giuseppe. Sometime after this Oratory performance, there was a proposal that Alphonsus take part in a palazzo melodrama. But even though the Captain made it a matter of filial obedience, so important were such things in the round of aristocratic entertainments, Alphonsus could not bring himself to appear again. He was irritated to think that this opera should so occupy his mind and imagination during those rehearsal weeks. And for the weeks afterward. Disturbing memories of this *Alessio* experience remained with him for the rest of life. "If you are invited to take part in any little opera," he warned, "avoid it as far as you can, for it will distract you for a month or two at the least."[37]

Those Young Nobility rehearsals, however, and the two performances, had given Alphonsus an opportunity of discovering what could be managed by a company of fellows intent on putting their talents to common purpose, and his personal success in the *Alessio* suggested that he was able to take a lead among Brothers.[38]

It is not surprising, therefore, that while, from 1710 onward, Alphonsus was often engaged in *sedile* business with the Conservatorio della Pieta dei Turchini, he did not take any part in the performances there of Leonardo Leo's 1713 *Sant' Alessio* opera.[39] Anyway Don Giuseppe would not have thought it proper for his son to play with the scholarship boys. So Alphonsus could sit comfortably with his papa in the best seats. And take an untroubled delight in the performance.[40]

What he had first glimpsed at the Young Nobility *Alessio* performances was made glaringly, excitingly, obvious in the course of an evening at the San Bartolomeo *opera seria.* Whatever any aristocratic gentleman told him at the palazzo reception about "effortless superiority," Alphonsus was being better instructed at the public theater. At each performance, the opera-mad Alphonsus was made ever more keenly sensitive to the possibilities of a leadership, an authority, which was not founded on the position of a family in society or of a son in the family. The thrill of the achieved high note established a performer, most especially a great *castrato,* in unchallenged control even of a San Bartolomeo audience of preening bigwigs.[41] And the singer was likely to have been one of those scholarship boys at the Turchini of whom Alphonsus' father was snobbishly wary. By a combination of talent, hard work and luck, a *primo uomo* might get as high in society as any of Don Giuseppe's acquaintance. Higher. Farinelli, who made his debut in the *Angelica e Medoro* of Pietro Metastasio, 1698–1782,[42] and Nicola Porpora, 1686–1768,[43] in 1720, and was the idol of metropolitan audiences during the last three years of Alphonsus' opera-going, came afterwards, by the fine power of his singing and the delicate wisdom of his conversation, to be the trusted adviser of Kings Philip V and Ferdinand VI of Spain.[44] This great castrato and the rest of the applauded opera stars offered fine proof of what a man might manage by a prudent exercise of talent. And of talent exercised in a cooperative venture. Indeed, in a fraternal venture. Farinelli and Metastasio, after their shared triumph with *Angelica,* habitually addressed letters to each other as "my dear twin brother."[45] There was a significance in all this for Alphonsus as, in the summer of 1715 at the end of his three years of study in the university, with a fast developing confidence in his own talent, he proceeded into the College of Doctors.

The College of Doctors

The Naples Law School was state-funded and did not expect students to pay tuition fees, but lodging, eating, drinking, and every sort of student entertainment were expensive. So were private tutorials from the university professors. Vico's main source of income was the out-of-school teaching he gave backward boys so that they'd have Latin enough to get through the final *disputatio.*[46] There was some pressure from their families, therefore, on poorer students to submit themselves for examination as soon as they thought they had done enough studying to get themselves a passing mark. It may be that Don Giuseppe's continual fretfulness about money was a like persuasive to Alphonsus' forming in these Law School years that rather unaristocratic habit of putting in the hard work required to get a job done. At any rate, he was among those who early declared themselves ready for examination. The candidates were handed a list of topics, two from Pontifical, two from Imperial law, with their attendant mass of commentary, for elucidation at the disputation before the Grand Chancellor or his Deputy, which would take place the next morning. The examination might not have scared the citified Alphonsus as greatly as it did that majority of candidates, the lads from small country towns.[47] Aggregation to the College of Doctors opened upon a fine life for these young men, conferring privileges which all other commoner subjects of the King would envy: a Doctor was exempt from provincial taxes, could not be imprisoned for debt, could not be put to the torture by the police without the warrant of a *sedile* magistrate, and, more positively, could reckon himself a member of the nobility "second grade."[48]

Alphonsus was assigned topics at his doctorate examination from the canon law dealing with married clergy, *Decretales* III, Lib. iii, 3, and from the civil law regulating the second marriages of gentle folk, *Codex, Lib.*

v,9. The disputation was set for January 18, 1713. His not being yet of the stipulated age had entailed that Prince Marino Francesco of Avellino, "*ex Hispaniarum primae Classis Magnatibus*" and "*perpetuus Magnus Cancellarius,*" should, on January 17, issue a royal dispensation for Alphonsus' taking his place before the examiners. Thus sanctioned, he presented himself to the Vice-Chancellor, Andrea Botteglieri, and was cross-questioned by the magnificoes Giuseppe Porpora and Hyacinto de Baucio.

Those in charge of the College required, along with the university Registrar's written assurance of the candidate's learning and good moral standing, his parish priest's certification of his baptism, and the witness of two respectable referees to his leading an orderly life off-campus, the Secretary of the Portanova *sedile's* formal avowal of Alphonsus' being a legitimate son, born within the bounds of their city. The Secretary had added helpfully that Alphonsus was the son of a nobleman and that he himself enjoyed all the privileges of the knights of the *sedile.* This was a customary hint, suggesting that in reviewing his performance at the examination, the College might like to make its usual indulgent assessment of a noble candidate.[49] His passing the examination was posted on January 20. He returned for the graduation ceremony on January 26.

Considering the moral implications of Swearing and Oath, Alphonsus asked, nearly forty years after his graduation, "whether in progressing to the doctorate, formally unqualified students may employ some equivocation when swearing that they have fulfilled all the requirements for the degree?."[50] He answered that it now seemed to him, as it had seemed to Torno and his other tutors then, that the graduand was not actually swearing an oath when he set his hand to the formal declaration: "I take my oath...." No official of the university would suppose him to be doing much more than going through the formalities. But then, for the most of its recent history, the College had been rather careless of all its own regulations. Successive Spanish viceroys had hoped to raise standards of matriculation, they had especially attempted to suppress the convention which allowed a candidate for a fee, either to avoid the disputation altogether or at least to have some longer private notice of the topics to be assigned.[51] The viceroys had also been asking questions about the convention which allowed so many underage candidates, for a fee, to proceed to graduation. There was a suggestion that the age-hurdle had been deliberately fixed so that each year several otherwise qualified candidates would have to pay the dispensation fee to the college secretary.[52]

As well as being those three years under age for the conferring of a doctorate in canon and civil law, for which he had, with a couple of equally precocious friends, obtained the Vice-Chancellor's dispensation, Alphonsus had been short by a term of the regulation attendance. But he did not then hesitate to repeat the oath "which all who receive their degrees are obliged to swear," to defend the doctrine of Mary's Immaculate Conception with his life's blood, "*usque ad effusionem sanguinis.*"[53]

The Congregation of the Visitation

Along with most of the other graduates who were clients of the Oratorians, Alphonsus, armed with his doctorate diploma, which he'd collected from the official scrivener on March 19, 1713, applied for admission to their Congregation of the Visitation.[54]

The Visitation Congregation recruited graduates from the College, almost exclusively, and chiefly Doctors of Law, "*in jure Pontificio et Cesareo*" as the official register phrased the qualification of those who had passed in canon and civil law, though there were also a few medical doctors in the Visitation membership list. Since the Visitation was a confraternity of laymen it did not include those priests anxious to qualify for episcopal consecration on whom the College, for a fee, would at times confer doctorates in theology.[55]

If there were, as Don Giuseppe would recognize, some social prestige associated with membership of this Confraternity, there was, too, some personal discomfort. Alphonsus in making this application to the Visitation was volunteering to work as an unskilled, unpaid, helper in the Hospital of Santa Maria del Popolo, generally called, from the sad condition of those who came to die on the wards, the "*casa degli Incurabili,*" the House of the Incurables. This was a depressing place. When Alponsus' Moorish servant became seriously ill in May 1715, Filippo Mastrillo at the Oratory suggested that Abdalla had better die with the fee-charging Brothers of Saint John of God at the Ospedale della Pace.[56] There, knowing himself to be on his deathbed, loving Alphonsus, wanting to be like him, Abdalla asked for baptism. Gaetano and Ercole agreed that they could not remember any other "among so many slaves in the house" having been persuaded to become a Christian. Perhaps these two Liguori had sent all other sick body-servants to the cheaper hospitals. But none of the brothers would have needed Mastrillo to warn him against sending a man to the Incurabili. No servant would have admired the Christian charity of a master who placed him on those wards.

There had been an Oratory interest in this local hospital ever since the Girolamini, in clearing their church's great forecourt frontage on the Via Tribunali, had pulled down that chapel of SS. Cosmas and Damian. These saints had, in Naples as in other cities, been the patrons of barbers and blood-letters and early modern surgeons. In Naples these had formed themselves into a professional guild, the Collegio di SS. Cosmo e Damiano dall'arte de Barbieri, which included the full range of medical men: elegant university professors, like Nicola Cirillo, 1671–1735, who wrote a new *opera seria* libretto for each theater season,[57] grand gentlemen specialists, like Don Francesco Dolce who was summoned to supervise the country doctor's treatment of Bishop Alphonsus at Arienzo in August 1768,[58] general practitioners like Gerard's last physician, Nicola Santorelli,[59] curiously skilled men like Alessandro di Liguoro to whom the Nuncio had granted the monopoly of castrating boys destined for city church choirs,[60] hospital assistants like Pietro Sant Agata, 1736–1794, who took off his surgeon's apron on hearing Andre Villani preach a grand mission sermon, applied to the Congregation, and was duly placed among the Brothers, finding himself working alongside the blood-letting barber, Saverio Schiavino, 1729–1779.[61] Each of these sorts of medical men, except perhaps the university professors, might have given a few hours a week to work in the hospital up the road, and when the Oratorians took over the chapel they accepted the ward responsibilities of the ancient Guild of Barbers, allotting this form of good works to their own new Confraternity of the Visitation.

The hospital had been the project of Maria Lorenza Longo, 1463–1542.[62] She, though settled into middle-aged comfort in her Catalan home, had, in 1508, married a Neapolitan bureaucrat and very soon became his widow. She was on the outlook for some good work to employ her energies and wealth. Ettore Vernazza, 1480–1540, the saintly promoter of the Company of Divine Love in Genoa and Rome, having founded his Neapolitan Company of the Bianchi in April 1519 and restored the hospital at San Nicola al Molo, persuaded the widow Longo to take responsibility for the funding and running of a new larger hospital that the Neapolitans were to build to confront the widespreadedness of syphilis.[63] The disease had taken such notorious hold on all classes in the city that it was vulgarly known in England as "the Neapolitan bone-ache,[64] though Neapolitan medical men persisted in naming it "*Morbus gallicus*" and, in the vulgar, "*mal fanciosati*," on account of their patriotic conviction that the infection had been spread among them at the garrisoning of Louis XII's French infantrymen in the city from 1501 to 1503.[65]

Maria Longo's hands-on matronage at the hospital was an element in the citizens' larger effort to relieve what they were all recognizing as the dangerous condition of the poor. Dangerous, that is, for the property-owning classes.[66] The Incurabili was not the best established provider of free care in Naples. The richer Confraternity of the Holy House managed a hospital with five hundred beds and at times of severe pressure, when the fleet was in port, for example, looked after another one thousand out-patients.[67] Bishop Gilbert Burnet, visiting the city in 1686, wrote home to England about the Holy House as "the greatest hospital in the world."[68] Nevertheless, the Incurabili provided, by its specific care for the dying poor, a particular, much appreciated, service in the community. And the general sorrow of the indigent at the death of their Spanish protectrice prompted Neapolitans to subscribe moneys in order that so socially helpful an enterprise should continue among them.

The interest on Maria Longo's legacy, even when eked out by capital bequests made by citizens anxious to secure a remembrance at the hospital chaplain's annual Mass for benefactors, proved wholly insufficient to cope with the sad numbers of the dying poor who were being deposited at the hospital steps. The Incurabili finances had been set on a more auspicious footing by Alphonsus' great-great-grandfather's brother, Don Giovanni de Ligorio, 1589(?)–1650(?), one of several outstanding seventeenth century Co-Rectors of the hospital, after whom Alphonsus had been named at his baptism. Don Giovanni had been responsible for obtaining from the Spanish authorities an indult linking the hospital's finances to music-theater performances in the city."[69] Their share of a night's box-office takings of an opera which had caught the fancy of a larger than usual crowd would enable the trustees to provide beds, nurses, ointments, for a larger than usual number of the dying. A flop at the San Bartolomeo, and a ward might have to be shut. By Alphonsus' time the fashion for *opera seria* among the members of polite society and the popular taste for vernacular *buffa,* first at the teatro di li Shiorentine and then at the Nuovo sopra Montecalvario and the della Pace houses,[70] ensured a continuous enlargement of the hospital's bed capacity.[71] But if the opera management endured a season of failures, the hospital's work had yet to be continued. True to the responsibilities they had taken over from the Guild of Barbers, the Oratorians subscribed suffient annual funds for 48 beds and undertook an indirect care for many more.[72] Up to 510 patients were being supported by members of the various sodalities who took the Oratorians' suggestions for Christian living: by the Brothers of the Oratory from the lower classes, by the provincial lawyers of the Vistation, even by collections taken between hymn-singings and ball-throwings by the Young Nobles.

The lawyers who were accepted as serving members of the Visitation were expected to do the work of general orderlies rather than any specialized nursing. The alert, observant, Alphonsus could not but gain a little knowledge of drugs and their uses, distempers and their causes. In later life, he was very ready with advice about the ways Redemptorists should take to preserve health and energies. "I think you should use quinine," he wrote to Villani in that letter about the uses to which his College pension might be put, "and it will be a satisfaction to me if you do so as soon as possible," adding with a sort of bow to the expert he had learned was expected on the Incurabili wards, "provided the doctors should so advise," and then offering the complacent assurance of the experienced orderly, "as I am sure they will."[73] But generally during their time at the Incurabili, rather than measuring out medicines in the famous apothecary's room, Alphonsus, Gennaro Maria Sarnelli, and the others were set to empty bedpans, change sheets, and wash patients. Not much had changed on the wards from the holy foundress' time. Poor, moaning, patients lay all day, all night, on their straw mattresses, waiting in long rows to die. The largest number of the patients, at least fifteen out of every twenty, women and men, were suffering from venereal diseases, and confraternity members were quite usually employed in preparing these poor patients for treatment. The dying Alphonsus' horror at the Brothers' efforts to change his underclothes resulted, likely, from an unwanted recollection of the condition of the Incurabili patients whom he had himself undressed and washed. There were, possibly, even more distressing memories of his ward duties. Sometimes, the lawyers might find themselves called to assist at the daily application, in the special closed hot-room or by the ward stove, of the paste of quick-silver, pork fat, turpentine, myrrh and helibor which contemporary medicos were still recommending to be smeared on the affected parts.[74]

The services of the Visitation graduates, however amateur, were essential for the continued running of the Incurabili where beds were provided at no cost to the patients' relatives. Indeed, a good many of these disfigured sufferers, "offensive to eye and nose," as Pope Leo X, Medici, 1475–1521, remarked, had been turned out of the family home to die.[75] The hospital was taking over the duties of the Neapolitan family. Caring for the sick until death, arranging burial, securing that a chaplain said a requiem Mass. In their twice-weekly attendances, middle class and aristocratic Visitation members were, often clumsily no doubt but always well-meaningly, attempting to be as much brothers of these poor as any Brothers of Saint John of God at the Ospidale della Pace.

Within this hospital community which, as a substitute for the less than caring family, was demonstrating the inadequacies of blood kin at a moment of human need, Alphonsus was learning how obedience might be expected of every brother who had pledged himself to live and love with others. His acceptance of the distasteful directives of Incurabili doctors and nurses would make it quite natural for him to expect others later to do just what he told them to do in the common enterprise, however their sensibilities revolted against the job he had appointed them. What he learned for himself as an orderly in the Visitation confraternity would be expressed as a peremptoriness in his ordering members of the Congregation.[76]

What he learned would be expressed, for some while, in rigorist judgments on disputed moral questions. He had gone straight to the Incurabili after the collapse of the Amatrice lawsuit in the summer of 1723. Getting away from the disorder of the courtroom. It must have seemed to him then that there was a stark opposition of the venal pretenses at justice in the human assize and the reality of divine justice so immediately discernible on the venereal wards. There was a plain relation between offense and punishment in the dyings of those women and men. They were suffering terrible pains on account of their sinnings against the promulgated Law of God. For Alphonsus, in that unsettling moment, there was within this awful justice a reassurance that human beings were still living within an intelligible order.[77]

Alphonsus had left the courtroom muttering, "*O Mondo*...," "O World,

I've found you out."[78] In the Incurabili, he heard a call, "*Lascia il mondo!*" "Leave that world!"[79] He was still young enough to make a simple response. He would become an announcer of good order. He would present himself for priestly ordination.

In the pulpit he could point to the inexorable connection of crime and punishment. In the confessional, next, he could administer clear justice, pronounce the appropriate divine sentence. Set women and men in the way of making restitution. So, against the shouted will of his father, he put himself to school with Don Giulio Torno, 1672–1756, just the sort of rigorist to keep him in this mind. "During the course of my ecclesiastical studies, my masters from the start were all of the Rigorist School; the first book of Moral Theology they placed in my hands was Genet, the prince of Probabiliorists, and for a long time I was an active defender of my masters' teachings."[80]

Torno would always be "the most learned Torno" for him,[81] but Alphonsus could not remain that sort of rigorist. Always at his back he heard the Incurabili patients crying out for divine pity. He could not, as he grew through acquaintance with the lives of those to whom he was preaching, of those whose confessions he was hearing, halt at that declaration of divine justice. He came to recognize a wondrous relation of wounded flesh and punishment and pity in the Cross of Christ. He came to appreciate what the Brother in the Visitition Confraternity was doing at the Incurabili to be a sharing in that "remembrance of His mercy" celebrated in Mary's *Magnificat.* And to find an image of that hospital in the personal care of the Lady as she handed on the effective pity of her Son:

> We may say that our Lord has given us Mary as a public hospital in which all who are sick, destitute, poor, may be received—and I would now ask who, in hospitals founded expressly for the poor, have the greatest claim to be admitted? Why, the most infirm.

So the worst of us may say to her

> Lady, you are the refuge of the sick poor, take me in for I am the poorest and most infirm of all, so I have the greatest claim to be welcomed by thee.[82]

This was a petition and claim to be sustained through his life.

Coming from Rome at the very end of June 1762, after his Minerva consecration as bishop, he went to the Oratory on the feast of the Visitation, July 2, for the celebration of the festival of his "Brother Doctors."[83] Alphonsus, with all those learned, influential, prosperous Brothers, as they sang the *Magnificat* full-throatedly, was acknowledging his need, along with the lowly and the hungry and the diseased, of the mercy of God their Savior.

The Congregation of Nobles of Our Lady of Mercy: The *Misericordiella*

By that 1762 festivity, Alphonsus' sensitivity to the Cross as *locus* of the Son's fulfillment of the demands of Divine Justice within the Father's will for mercy, and, complementarily, his sensitivity to each Christian's being now called to hand on this mercy, had been finely developed. The beginnings of this humane appreciation of the quality of mercy may be divined at his joining his father, sometime during 1715, or perhaps early 1716, in the Theatine Misericordiella, a flourishing Confraternity of laymen with their chapel in the Liguori's parish, "*in suburbio Virginium.*" The Confraternity's taking the Lady of Mercy as their protectress directs these men to that moment when she became their Mother at the Cross, handing on her Son's mercy to his brothers, and, therefore, to their vocation as sons and brothers.[84]

The Confraternity had been founded in 1533 by the glorious Saint Gaetano da Theine, 1480–1547, immediately on his arriving in Naples and seeing the need for such a pastoral care. He meant to give practical outlet for any aristocratic impulse to charity.

Gaetano and his newly founded Theatines had set up house at San Paolo Maggiore and begun working at the Incurabili. Their community gained, from the steady drudgery of Gaetano himself, of Blessed Giovanni Marinoni, 1490–1562, and Blessed Paolo Burali, 1511–1578, a reputation for hardworking holiness. And for using donations prudently.[85] Most importantly for their acceptance by Neapolitans, they were seen to have identified with the citizens and their aspirations. Neapolitans, at moments of civic crisis, still repeat Gaetano's prayer of Christian fraternity:

> Hear the voice of the blood of our brother Jesus cry out to You from the cross: "Hear, forgive, attend, and act; do not delay, for Your honor's sake, O my God, because Your name has been invoked upon this city and this people."

and they still give Gaetano's own emphasis to his final characteristic plea:

> Deal with us according to Your mercy.[86]

So there were city-wide celebrations in 1712 at the canonization of Andrea Avellino, 1521–1608, who had joined the Naples community in 1556. This was a community with which a good Neapolitan gentleman could be confident of doing something useful for his city.

Like the Young Nobility, like, indeed, most lay women and men of that time and others, the Misericordiella Brothers took it that they would be the more likely to become good persons as they conformed themselves to the paradigm of a religious community. So they, also, along with the Father Co-Rector, had their lay Co-Rector and Consultors and Master of Novices, with his novitiate of youngsters, and Sacristan, and Porter to keep temporary cloister for the Brothers in the chapel, preventing outsiders from disturbing their prayer meetings.[87] They also, in a city where the monsignors were almost as litigious as the dukes, retained their firm of attorneys who knew their way through Canon Law. There would be less risk, that way, of loosing their lay hold on lands and funds bequested to the Confraternity in Brothers' wills. And, again, like monks and nuns and canons, these Brothers had their special patronal feasts: the Lady's wedding day, January 23, Low Sunday, the Beheading of John the Baptist, the parish protector, August 29, the Stigmata of Saint Francis of Assisi, September 17, and Saint Michael, September 29, when the year's accounts were settled. On these great days, the Father Co-Rector would preach what the Brothers called their "Family Sermon," and they would form a little procession through the streets round their chapel. Their white habit and scarlet cape may have seemed to onlookers a little ostentatious for men who had enrolled to assist poor prisoners. But they were reminded, at their confraternity Mass before setting off, of a symbolism in their robes of an innocence won by the shedding of the blood of Christ. Lorenzo Cupoli, c. 1530–1610, the great Neapolitan Theatine and shaper of the Brother's devotions, had taught them a post-Communion conversation; they are to say:

> Most High King of Heaven, who has led you to come to me, a miserable, poor, blind, naked, man?

and the Lord will answer simply:

> Love.[88]

After this, the good gentry must feel a Christian compulsion to give practical sense to their clothing ceremonies.

The Brothers had began by asking what they could be doing to assist the clergy. So, on the last Sunday of every month, they still went to attend the clerics immured in the two ecclesiastical jails of the city, one for the archbishop's prisoners, the other for those the nuncio had taken off the street. On the other Sundays, in the earliest years of the Confraternity, the Misericordiella Brothers would gather at the hostel which they had established for clerical visitors to their city, especially those who came to pray at the shrine of San Gennaro, and feed, lodge, and wash the feet of these pilgrims. Their being popularly called "*Bianchi*" derived not from their white habit, which may not have been worn then, but from their original task of laundering the linen, "*biancheria,*" of these dusty clergy.[89] However, in Alphonsus' time, no one in Naples who undertook to do some charitable work could restrict his social service to the washing of priests' small clothes. So, about 1700, the good Misericordiella Brothers had further widened their remit, and taken on the duty of burying the poor of the parish.[90] Don Giuseppe was a member when this decision was taken. They took care, too, of their own dead, establishing a cemetery for the servants of the gentlemen of the Confraternity, and another Terrasanta for the gentlemen themselves.[91] There, wrapped in his white confraternity habit of innocence, Don Giuseppe was buried in 1745.[92] The Brothers' charity persisted after the grave. They undertook the protection of poor orphans in the city, recognizing them as "our brothers and sisters," all sharers with them in "the blood of our brother Jesus."[93]

Individual Brothers were assigned to these corporal works of mercy at the weekly gatherings of the confraternity at their chapel at the Porta

San Gaenaro.[94] There, having laid aside their swords in the vestibule, they recited the Five Psalms of the Most Holy Name of Mary "to praise her, bless her, and pray to her as their special Protectrice." Alphonsus learned these "Psalms" and their caudated invocations by heart. He was delighted by their simple cadences and cheerful piety and made a vow at this time, from which he never sought a dispensation, that he would recite them every day of the rest of his life.[95] Hearing him recite them at Sant' Agata, Brother Teodosio Flumeri, 1727–1798, supposed that Alphonsus had composed the prayers himself.[96] If he'd asked, Alphonsus would have told him that this chaplet of Marian verses had its beginnings in the devotions of Saint Bonaventure. That's what the Misericordiella chaplain had told him.[97]

After the *Magnificat,* which is the first "psalm" of this *Corona B. Mariae Virginis,* the sequence of "In my distress I cry to thee," "Deal bountifully with thy servant," "When the Lord restored the fortunes of Zion," and the climactic "To thee I lift up my eyes"[98] is recited as a commentary on the Lady's song of the Lord's unseating the rich, feeding the hungry, raising the servant. What the Lord has done for Israel, what he has done for Mary herself, he will do for those who recite Israel's verses within the Lady's cloak. Divine Justice will be manifest as liberating Mercy. The five prayers of the *Corona* declared to the young lawyer that, whatever the constrictive power of Medici and Hasburgs the Christian who meditates "upon Your Statutes," enters his plea in the court of the Lord, will come into perfecting freedom.[99] Through the seconding prayer of the Lady, who is neatly invoked by an acrostic of the five letters of MARIA, each will be freed from whatever oppresses.[100] This is all in accord with that Law of Love manifest in the five wounds of her Son. Reciting this *Corona,* the Brother is brought from "Rejoice dear Virgin" through "the shining mercy of our Lord" into "a share in his Resurrection now through grace and in the future through glory."[101]

It was as a coda to their reciting these psalms together that the Brothers received from the Rector and Consultors of the Confraternity their uncomfortable assignments. While there might be some pious self-satisfaction for a nobleman in donating his money for charitable purposes, it went against every instinct of upper-class self-preservation for a gentleman Brother to accept his assigned place in the roster of street collectors, rattling his poor box like one of the poor themselves. The great

Scupoli had anticipated such human self-regard and provided his knock-down counter image:

> Placing before the eyes of your mind the dishonors and bitter shames that He tasted because of you, and His perseverance and endurance, you should be ashamed to recognize that your willingness to put up with such things is a mere shadow, for yours are not real afflictions and disgraces.[102]

Nevertheless, standing in the cell, waiting at the grave, counting the quarter-hours for the collecting time to be over, it cannot have been easy for the Brother of the Misericordiella to forget that he was a member of a "Congregation of Noblemen." There could not but be, sometimes, a patronizing element in his do-gooding. And on a Sunday procession, wearing the perfectly laundered habit and cape, he might find notions of class distinction crowding his mind. And the most decent of noblemen would not deem such notions inappropriate. Indeed, Pope Innocent XIII, dei Conti, 1655–1724, having granted a plenary indulgence to observant Brothers in 1722, the arrival of the illuminated vellum rescript two years later prompted a properly elevative rethinking of their Confraternity statutes. These were given a more aristocratic tone, suggesting that the Brothers belonged to some knightly Order of high romance. An emphasis was now put on what an honor it was to sport the Confraternity's coat-of-arms, in which the Redeemer shone in glory between their Lady and the Baptist patron of the parish. This was a badge no decent family would care to surrender. So it was that when Alphonsus resigned in March 1726, he was careful to arrange that the youngest of the Liguori brothers should fill the vacant place. He described himself to the Rector of "this venerable Congregation of Pilgrims" as "an unworthy Brother who had, in the recent past, on account of so many occupations, neglected the exercises," and who was now prevented, on account of his becoming a cleric, nearing ordination to the diaconate, from taking part in this laymen's Confraternity. He had, therefore, to ask permission to withdraw in Ercole's favor.[103] Alphonsus was evidently intending that the Governors should agree at once to Ercole's replacing him and thus render the postulancy, oral examination, novitiate, endured by other hopefuls, mere formalities. He pledged, in his letter applying for such an indulgent transfer of membership, that shuffles of this unedifying sort should not be repeated. Ercole, he assured the Brothers, would be an observant Brother to the day of his funeral. The Liguori were a family no one in the parish would wish to irritate. Certainly not any one who knew the Captain's temper. Rector and Consultors readily agreed to this youngest Liguori's being aggregated to their Confraternity. Ercole was just the sort of person to join the Brotherhood. And he succeeded among them. The Misericordiella Brothers were pleased to form, in their splendid robes, an honor guard for Ercole's wedding to Donna Rachele da Liguoro in June 1732.[104] No resigning for him. Ercole was still a practicing Brother when, in the new climate of 1753, the Misericordiella along with other confraternities, having been inspected by the royal officials, received a reinstating grant of approval from the King.[105]

Alphonsus did not approve this or any other confraternity's obtaining the royal license. A decade later, it seemed to him, as a responsible diocesan bishop, that too many of these Brothers were wanting to get themselves out from under episcopal jurisdiction. Perhaps they were. Still, Alphonsus' disapproving their alteration of character in this one matter cannot have seemed to Ercole and his pals justification for his choosing their pulpit, in 1761, for a extraordinarily fierce attack on city manners. Ercole would be as unlikely as any of the Brothers to make the connection of the *Magnificat* prayer for the Lord to fill the hungry with good things and Alphonsus' high-pitched cry: "Beware! Beware! God will punish your crimes with a terrible famine." These well-fed citizens must have looked somewhat surprised. "Yes, I repeat, God will punish you with a great famine."[106] That Alphonsus was not here being wholly driven by the impulse of his own excited rhetoric is suggested by the wheat failure three years later. Don Nicolo Rotando, who was in the Misericordiella chapel that day, certainly thought Alphonsus had been yet again proved a prophet. So did Tannoia.[107] Though, of course, it was not the well-to-do Brothers who died of starvation. The dearth killed off many of the Kingdom's poor.

The chief interest of this homily is not, however, in whatever literal fulfillment Alphonsus' contemporaries may have marveled to discern, but its evidencing Alphonsus' willingness to talk of self-respecting folk as "criminals" and of their lifestyle as "punishable." When, as so often in his mission addresses to mixed congregations, he tells stories of the bandit, the runaway nun, the rowdy student, the battered wife, there is no trace of the wrathfulness of this Misericordiella sermon. There was, evidently, something to irk him in the Misericordiella pretension that their Redeemer, His Mother and His Baptizer, were to be well contented by the display of an embroidered coat-of-arms. And in their insisting so much on membership of the Confraternity's being a matter of special social privilege. These men were becoming, too, like the mighty in their seats. This was not the understanding he had come to expect in those he would call "Brothers."

Bianchi della Giustizia, the *Fraternita e Compagnia di Santa Maria succerre miseris*

As he made his way from the Oratory, opposite the cathedral, past the palazzo on the Via dell'Anticaglia in which the College of Doctors met, and along the Via Luciano Armani to the Incurabili, Alphonsus would be walking within quite a small area of the city, and as he turned into the Via Maria Longo, he would come upon the small Lady Chapel of the *Bianchi della Giustizia.* That there had been many distinguished Bianchi was made impressively clear when, in 1720, Paolo de Matteis, 1622–1728, decorated their headquarters with a series of crowded frescoes portraying the many popes, cardinals, and other grand personages who had been associate members of the confraternity. All very impressive.

In 1725, Alphonsus' learned relative Canon Gizzio was Governor of the confraternity, and so in February that year Alphonsus made a confident application, supported by the august Pagano, to be one of "this holy Brotherhood." He was duly admitted on April 15, nine days after being deaconed. He would, it was understood by the Brothers, within a year or so become one of the twelve priests of their confraternity.

Though the Neapolitans and their chroniclers showed and still show some reluctance to acknowledge the originating impulse of Ettore Vernazza in the foundation of the Incurabili hospital, they have been content to allow his being, along with the Piacenzan priest, Don Callisto de' Fornari, co-restorer in April 1519 of a moribund confraternity originally established, it was said, by San Giacomo della Marca in 1473.[108] These two foreigners speedily organized their *Bianchi della Giustizia* for the material and spiritual comfort of those "under the condemnation of justice."[109]

There were to be a hundred Brothers, each at least twenty-five years of age, able to make an annual subscription of at least two but not more than twenty carlini, and to pay any fine the Governor of the Confraternity might impose for a fault against their Statutes. No more than twelve of them were to be priests.[110] One of these would undertake the spiritual directorship of the hundred Brothers. This not underworked chaplain was, at the religious exercises of the confraternity, to preach a series of renewing sermons to the assembled Brothers, encouraging them to confession and Communion.[111] But the northern founders were not primarily concerned with the Brothers' individual spiritual development. They had it in mind to found a working group which should express the corporate interest of Christians, concentrating energies on the corporal welfare of those who were not able to help themselves.

In 1525 the *Capituli di Fraternita* were reworked: the Confraternity had found itself a motto from Scripture, *Qui timet Deum faciet bona,* and was drawing out its meaning by pointing to an universal agreement that honest good manners are "the complete behavior of the moral Life" and thus the only true definition of "how the Brothers of our Congregation ought to live" in a contemporary society.[112] This was no premodern expression of secular respectability. Without this decent attention to the proper expectations of good mannered people in the wider community, "we must find ourselves in hell." Paying attention, "we live in a Paradise on earth."[113] These Brothers were intending to regain paradise for every citizen.

Their meetings were now overseen by a Governor and two Counsellors elected each year on Assumption Day, the proceedings at this election being, like all other business of the confraternity, covered by an oath of secrecy binding under pain of committing mortal sin.[114] Alphonsus would have thought this a nice regulation. He always liked to be told a secret. Almost as much as he liked to be telling a secret, with the usual injunction "don't tell anyone else."[115] All that was to be known of the Bianchi by outsiders was what they could see almost any day in the streets of their city: the white-robed Brothers making their way to the viceroy's prison to call on the "*giustizie*" in their dirty cells, supplying their last meals, walking with them to the marketplace gibbet, collecting heads and bodies after executions, ensuring decent burial, providing for surviving dependants.[116]

That Alphonsus well appreciated the work of the priest among these Bianchi is suggested at those passages of the *Pratica del Confessore* and the *Homo Apostolicus* in which he proposes ways of bringing the life of a criminal to a graceful close. It is clear, splendidly, in the tract he devoted to just this pastoral concern, "Notes for the Priest who is to assist those Condemned to Death," 1775. "The unfortunate man," Alphonsus wrote feelingly, "in the depths of his prison, has been abandoned by his relatives and friends."[117] He had observed a reciprocity of abandonment. The prisoner imagines what the remains of life will be like for those he must himself abandon, his old parents, his incomeless wife and children. He is very conscious of his failure to be the good son, husband, father. His shame is greater than any shame they are feeling on account of a member of their family's dying "in public," "as a criminal," "reviled." There is no escape from his nagging shame. And no escape from the shudders of his fear. He is closely guarded. Kept alive in order to be put to death, he who, like the most of us, had thought to live a long life. In the darkening cell, his shame and his fear of physical pain lead him to contemplate the horrider terrors of the punishment that waits beyond the gibbet. At this moment the *Bianchi della Giustizie* must exercise that love for which Jesus looks, visiting the least of his brethren in his cell; it is the Bianchi priest's happiness to be visiting this brother along with Jesus:

> What consolation it is to a poor prisoner that he has an affectionate friend, who keeps him company, consoles him, gives him hope, looks after him, thinks of relieving him in his misery. Behold our good friend Jesus Christ who in this Sacrament encourages us, saying, "I am with you always." Look at me, he tells us, I am all yours. I am come from heaven into your prison expressly to console you, to help you, to deliver you. Welcome me, welcome me always. Hold onto me. Thus you will never feel your miseries, and afterwards you will come with me to my Kingdom.[118]

So the good priest will take an appointment by the Bianchi Governor to attend the condemned man's cell as a call to be his effective consoler. "Above all he should be careful not to speak of the rigors of Divine Justice or anything of the sort to inspire terror; he should put before him the image of the Divine Mercy." Later, from experience of what worked, Alphonsus offered some simple guidelines to the priest attempting to be the true consoler. He is to make the man feel his membership of the ecclesial community, "call him by his Christian name," his membership of the company of the redeemable, "greet him with 'God wishes to save you,'" his being so very nearly in the company of the saved, "tell him that God wishes to take him out of this misery into eternal happiness." The man has only to be sorry for his sin, make his confession, and go gratefully from Paradise here into the Paradise hereafter.

Not everything will be sweetness and light, not every time. Alphonsus learned what it is to be rejected by the unrepentant prisoner. Many of these men, some of them, doubtless, innocent of the crime for which they were about to die, but as many entirely guilty, horrified him by refusing to pardon their accusers. And made it plain that they could not forgive God for letting things come to this. Faced by such a man in his cell, the good Christian will not leave him to his own devices. "We must do what we can for him." He must be made aware that he is guilty if not of this crime then of some other of those sins which blot men's lives: "You have condemned yourself to hell." But, even though "at this moment you hate God," it is still true that "He wishes you well." Each criminal's death may be that of the bad or the good thief crucified with the Lord. So the Bianchi priest must bring the condemned man to a personal sense of present Calvary: "How can you say that He hates you when He died on the Cross because of His love for you?" And, "if he continue obstinate," the priest "must insist the more that the thought of Calvary supplant all others in his consciousness. He need not fear divine justice. The cross is the sign of divine mercy. For him. For them both. The priest "must get the man's imagination working. He must see the Lady at the foot of the cross. See himself as that disciple whom she has accepted as her son. "Make him say to her, 'Mary, Mother of God, see how close I am to damning myself; help me with your prayers!'" Even this representation of Calvary may not be converting. But the Bianchi priest is not to be just another abandoner. The condemned man is still his brother.

They are all brothers now. The priest must be aware of himself as a sharer in liability to a divine condemnation and of the condemned man as a sharer in an expectation of mercy. If the condemned man does not realize this for himself that cannot relieve his brothers of their shareful responsibility, "the priest should get the others to pray for him." Alphonsus is coming, as he works in the Confraternity, to an enlarged and enlarging appreciation of confraternity. They must all come to the Lord together.

That confraternity in human need for mercy is to be manifest in the Bianchi priest's staying alongside the condemned man to the very utmost of his time. He must walk with him, however shamed he feels to be in the man's company, into the marketplace. Step with him onto the gibbet platform. Pray with him as the rope is placed about his neck. Be with him to that moment when he is flung off the ladder. See himself and all judged humanity in this man:

> If a criminal condemned to death were already standing at the gibbet with the rope round his neck, and a friend were to come and take the rope and put it round his own neck, and die in the place of the guilty man, how great would be his obligation to love him. That is what Jesus Christ has done.[119]

That is what the Brother who has been enabled to appreciate the painful wonder of this rescue must tell his brothers, not in the prison cell only, but anywhere women and men are feeling abandoned. "There are many confines, wards, dungeons." Many gibbets.[120]

In Alphonsus' society, the only course he could take, if he were to be acceptable as an announcer of the redeeming Passion of our Lord, was to get himself ordained. Then he could be fully a Brother among his brothers.

Apostolic Missions

In 1721, Cardinal Francesco Pignatelli issued an *ad cleram* decree requiring candidates for the priesthood in his archdiocese to enroll in one of three stipulated confraternities of priests: they could ally themselves with the Jesuits in the Assumption Confraternity,[121] founded by Giuseppe Pavone, 1569–1637, with the Pious Workers at San Giorgio Maggiore on the Via del Duomo,[122] or with the grander Propaganda Congregation of the Apostolic Missions, up at the cathedral.[123] This was a confraternity replete with upper-class clergy. The Cavalieri's ubiquitous relative, Pietro Marco Gizzio, and Alphonsus' theology tutor, Giulio Torno, canons of the cathedral, were prominent in Propaganda. They each had a hand in the training of the young priests. Gizzio was one of the two Novice Masters, Torno one of the two Student Masters. It was, as Don Giuseppe would know, from this group of secular priests that both the cardinal and Cappellano Maggiore, the government minister for religious affairs, were likely to choose their bishops. Alphonsus applied to join the Propaganda confraternity in November 1724 and was provisionally accepted into a novitiate comprising twenty-eight priests, deacons, sub-deacons, clerics, and lay hopefuls.

The Congregation had been erected by Sampson Carnevale, vicar of the cathedral parish, and his friend Francesco Staybuono, with an idea of training some of the superfluity of Naples clergy for work in the foreign missions. That was in 1646. Cardinal Ascanio Filomarino, 1588–1666, assigned them a fine chapel for their services in the cathedral. The Congregation was evidently going to be a great success. There were thirty-seven candidates admitted in the first year of the Congregation. These were at once set to study the languages of Araby and Illyrica.[124] However, once the time came for them to go out on the foreign mission, it proved too difficult persuade them to leave "Mamma." The Propaganda authorities were realists. They had their deeds of incorporation altered so that their men should be put to work at home.[125] Nevertheless they could not bring themselves to surrender their Propaganda title.

The training that the candidates endured under the governance of Gizzio, Torno, and their co-masters was quite rigorous. Taking special example from the lifestyle of Saint Francis de Sales, to whom they had a special devotion,[126] and on whose feast they had been granted a seven-year and forty-days' indulgence, the Propaganda authorities insisted that the younger Brothers thoroughly prepare themselves for questioning at their regular Monday theological seminar, even if the trainees had but recently returned from taking their dogsbody share in the springtime countryside revival or in the October annual general mission to the city.[127]

On those missions, the Propaganda Brothers did not, as other missioner societies thought advisable, separate a parish congregation into socially or educationally or sexually distinct groups. Their sermons, in city and country parishes, were delivered to the entire people.[128] Alphonsus recognized an ecclesiological wisdom in this gathering of "the rough and the civilized" in a common celebration of their redemption.[129] He maintained the practice in his later missioner enterprise. As he retold the stories told by poor farmers alongside those he had discovered during his readings of the Fathers, all those who sat under the high pulpit were being brought to a larger appreciation of what they shared as Church. He maintained, too, the Propaganda use of a "*zelator*" to keep a watch on the conduct of other priests on the mission, most especially the style of their sermons, and to report back.[130]

Though Alphonsus' own record at the weekly study groups, 1724–1725, was not as consistent as might be expected of an ideal trainee, the zelator seems to have allowed that this novice had good enough excuses to absent himself.[131] Alphonsus was, at the election on October 1, 1725, the only candidate to get through without a single black ball.[132] But again, it must have been a test of his elders' patience that Alphonsus was absent for three of the eight days of retreat which followed this election.

Alphonsus certainly recognized a value in that regimen of the Propaganda novitiate from which he had just been released. He maintained the practice of this straddling existence all his days. Theological reading, seminar discussion, creative inquiry into scriptural, dogmatic, and moral questions were, he assumed, the usual and necessary employments of the relaxing missioner.[133] Others, anxious to be good priests "in these deboshed times," recognized their value, too. By 1724 there were 107 Brothers in Propaganda.[134] And this despite their authorities' maintaining a determined policy of expelling the unworthy. No shirker need apply.

However constrained by their ordinary duties, the intelligent priests of Propaganda, by a careful management of their times and energies, were capable of organizing a very complex program of missions. They generally aimed to put a dozen men in the field, at times twenty men, and now and again twenty-five, each with his precisely determined share in the conduct of the time-tabled day of meditation, liturgy, sermons at street corners, catechesis, rosary recitations, sodality meetings, penitential processions, confessions through the day, and the climactic Great Preaching.

Alphonsus preached his first sermon, after his ordination as deacon in April 1726, in the little church of San Giovanni in Porta for the Forty Hours devotions of the Blessed Sacrament confraternity to which his Cavalieri relatives belonged.[135] Though this sermon, if rather too lengthy, was well put together, the witnesses of scripture and liturgical practice leading into declarations of doctrinal truth and the moral demand to conversion, it was not at once as a preacher that Alphonsus was employed by the Apostolic Missioners.[136]

He was now often absent from those Monday seminars and from the confraternity spiritual exercises on account of his being employed by elder Brothers as all-round humble gofer. In 1727, for example, he was sent in February as a member of the mission team to Posillipo, in March he was at Teslizzi near Bari, in April at Compagna, south of Salerno. He was off again as one of the "second assistants" for the whole of May, and again for missions in early and late June. In the last week of October, the start of the new mission season, he was an attendant priest, "fit to swell a scene or two," at the tail end of the missioners' procession through the capital. He was now ninety-sixth in a listing of a hundred and nine Brothers. In November, he was assisting at the Bosco mission, and on Boxing Day he was working with another set of missioners at Pollena,[137] entrusted with such simpler tasks as taking the village children through questions and answers of the shorter catechism and leading the evening congregation of their parents in recitation of the rosary. Not until January 16, 1728, was he thought ready to preach a little meditation. Then not until late October 1729 was he put up to preach a morning sermon at the city mission to which not many persons were expected.[138]

Alphonsus admitted later that during these years he was preaching in far too monotonous a tone. It was an added cause of his gratitude to "the Father" that Falcoia had cured him of that flatness.[139] But the sermon he preached for the city mission cannot have sounded too badly since he was brought to preach in the Congregation Retreat at Santo Spirito in December and was sent to repeat his sermons at Casoria in January 1730. Then, on April 22 that year, at Capodimonte, keeping him under their close supervision, the elders took the risk of permitting Alphonsus to make an attempt at the Great Preaching itself.

After that, Alphonsus was almost uncontrollable in his eagerness to climb into the pulpit and tell people, for an hour or two, the exciting truth about Christ and His Mother. He was off again next week to the large Naples church of the Annunziata. And then, when he was supposed to be taking a bit of a rest in the hills, he found himself conducting an unofficial mission to the goatherds above Amalfi. In the Octave of Corpus Christi, he was preaching in the cathedral at Scala. Immediately after, giving a conference to the nuns of the Visitation convent up the road. There he met Celeste Crostarosa for the very first time.[140] She was quick to recognize his missioner talent. Others were slower. But at the end of 1731, his old tutor Torno having been elected Superior in July, Alphonsus was entrusted with leadership of a January mission being planned to Nardo and Polignano a Mari, south of Bari.[141] He was now esteemed a good enough homilist to be regularly allotted the Great Preaching, and a good enough moralist to be the senior Confessor of the group. Alphonsus rejoiced in these responsibilities. He was ready for more.

Passing through Foggia on his way home, he called on Bishop Giampietro Faccolli, successor of uncle Emilio Cavalieri, and readily agreed to preach in honor of the Lady of the Seven Veils. Her icon had recently protected the Foggians during an earthquake. The sermon made a fine impression on the Foggians.[142] So the impetuous Alphonsus, thinking only of an evening's having been well-spent in speaking of the Lady to her clients, was astonished to be met by unpleased seniors of the Congregation on his return to Naples. Their tight schedule had been ignored.

Their careful planning thrown into confusion. On March 3 and again on March 10, 1732, the brothers pointedly renewed an order that members of Propaganda were never to preach extraneous sermons without specific permission from the Superior.[143]

Alphonsus had made a bad mistake. He had assumed an authority to be the arranger of his own times and activities; recognizing an opportunity to do something, he'd taken it. This is the characteristic mistake of the woman or man of talent and good will who has not come to appreciate what is required of a team player, of a Brother.

The possibilities for further conflict between the time-tablers of the Apostolic Mission and their spontaneous preacher were obvious, but in the immediate future Alphonsus had, with the rest of the Brothers, to respond to the request of the Duke of Termoli that they conduct a street collection for the Incurabili of which the Duke was now Co-Rector. The collectors, led by Gennaro Maria Sarnelli, were reminded, first, that they were not to bother ladies in their carriages, and, second, that they must themselves keep the keys of the collecting boxes and not entrust them to the hospital's staff.[144] Then Alphonsus had to be off on another mission assignment. This time on the island of Procida.[145]

The Turquoise Laity

The sea crossing to Procida takes just over an hour from Naples on a modern steamer. Rather longer, and riskier, if the Bay were under storm, in the fisherman's boat hired by Propaganda. But the islanders were absolutely first-class seamen. And if a traveler required a glass of refreshment on landing at their wharf, they could prove that they were absolutely first-class vinedressers, too.

The mission sermons were chiefly to be given in the parish church of San Michele on the Terra Murata at the highest point of the island. There the missioners' rhetoric might be much encouraged by the flighty ceiling of Luca Giordano, 1632–1705, celebrating the victory of the Archangel in his sky battle against Lucifer. Other mission exercises could be more cosily accommodated. The church was built into a hill honeycombed with cellar chapels which offered various sized meeting places for the several missioners to conduct their catechetical classes to groups of women, men, boys, girls. It was in these cellars that Alphonsus had been first allowed by the Propaganda elders to give a little instruction to a small group, while the senior Father's Great Preaching was still rattling in their ears. That was in 1725.

The Missioners earned some lasting respect during that island mission.[146] Gizzio and Torno were recalled to Procida in 1729 to settle a dispute between the clergy of San Michele and the local Dominican Priory. They had returned, at the request of the still-disputing parties, for a resettlement in 1731.[147] They took Alphonsus with them again when, at the request of Cardinal Francesco Pignatelli, the missioners were to preach the mission in June 1732.[148] This time Alphonsus was a senior member of the mission team. He was appointed to preach an evening sermon on the Lady.[149]

The religious imagination of the islanders had, from at least the medieval performances of their locally boasted Passion Play, been shaped according to a dramatic appreciation of the Gospel. Alphonsus could well sympathize with such devotion. His own enthusiasm for San Bartolomeo and Shiorentine operas enabled him to present the Passion of Jesus in his imagined "theater of divine love."[150] To reimagine the Lady at the foot of the Cross as the Procida islanders had seen her in their play. And then to get fishermen and their wives, vine-dressers and their husbands, to turn to one another at the end of the mission sermon, as at the close of an affecting presentation of their play in the wharfside piazza, asking what meaning these scenes in his theater of love had for them.[151]

But how keep them in this gracious self-questioning? Alphonsus' experience in the Visitation, Misericordiella and Bianchi brotherhoods had convinced him that it might be as combining members of a confraternity that these Christians would encourage one another in charitable service. So, on the mere hint of Torno, the freshman missioner began reorganizing a local *Congregazione dei Laici Torchini,* first noticed in the pastoral visitation records of Innico d'Avalos, the cardinal of Aragon, in 1593, described more fully in the 1601 visitation of Cardinal Alphonsus Gesualdo, 1540–1603, and known to have been put into better order by the Jesuits in 1627, when the Society was sponsoring sodalities of this sort all over the Kingdom.[152] Then, the elders of this ancient Congregation not taking to the changes he was suggesting, Alphonsus encouraged the younger men to gather themselves in a new "congregation of the secret."

These young islanders had first to be persuaded, like the Young Nobles of the Oratory, that this secret of good living was best known to those who enjoyed offices in a religious community. Their Congregation of our Lady of Sorrows should, therefore, have Consultors, and a Sacristan, a Master of Novices, a Master of Ceremonies, Cantors, and a Porter.[153] But there was always something of a bachelors' club about their evening meetings. They would receive as novices only "those who have not engaged their word to marry."[154] They would be lads together for a while. Alphonsus insisted, however, on their promising not to take part in the sort of water sport offensive to God.[155]

He had other promises for them to make. "All Brothers of the Congregation shall take the Blessed Virgin for their own Mother, conceiving for her a strong affection and demonstrating a child's confidence in their perfect observance of all our Rules and Constitutions." As true sons of their heavenly Mother, these young men shall "attend to a life devoted to increasing in our souls the Christian virtue so necessary for the gaining of Paradise."[156] It is clear enough what sort of life this is to be: after an initial general Confession, they are to proceed to daily meditation for at least half an hour, regular examination of conscience, attendance at Mass, weekly Communion, and frequent visits to the Blessed Sacrament. They are, as her particular sons, to keep the Saturday fast in honor of their Mother, to recite each day the *Stabat Mater,* that grand hymn recalling the motherly sorrows of Mary under the cross and her present care for Christians, or, instead, the Litany of Loreto, or at least seven Hail Marys.[157]

He can slip for a moment into addressing these Brothers as servants rather than as sons. "All her domestics," he quoted from Proverbs' description of the good lady of the house, "are clothed in double garments,"[158] so it was to be hoped that, if any Brothers were tempted to slacken their devotions, the habit and cape which they wore to Confraternity meetings would bring them back to an appraisal of themselves as the Lady's bound servants in her livery.[159] They were like those trireme oarsmen sent to work in his mother's kitchen. Men without rights who are to be grateful that their slackness does not get them sent back into slavery. "Now all good things," they should acknowledge, "come to me with her."[160] But Alphonsus is quick to return to their greater vocation. They are called to be Brothers in the family of the Firstborn. They are her secondborn sons.[161]

There was a sensible recognition of the realities of fiancé and fiancée relations in the Brothers' putting that stop to a boy's continuing membership. A regimen so consistently directing attention away from her to her young man's Immaculate Mother would not have long survived a charming girl's engaging a Brother's word to marry her. But to secure that most of these bachelors continued good sons after the mission, the missioners appointed Leonardo Scotto di Galletta, the parish priest of San Michele, to be the Brothers' first overseeing Father.[162]

The Procida confraternity was Alphonsus' trial experiment for a lifetime enterprise. "It would be of very great benefit," he advised the Fathers in his 1760 *Instructions for the Missions,* codifying his quarter-of-a-century practice, if they were everywhere to establish "a confraternity of the secret in honor of the Mother of God." The setting up and encouraging of congregations of craftsmen, of squires, of boys, of unmarried girls, had by then become an ordinary part of every Redemptorist's mission work.[163]

Alphonsus sustained an enthusiasm for founding and refounding such confraternities right through the time he was bishop. Taking a first look round his diocese in 1762, he was quick to notice the dilapidated condition of a Confraternity founded in 1608. Once Don Tommaso Talia's company had numbered 150 men for the Monday, Wednesday, Friday discipline, but now the confraternity was not much more than a barroom meeting for a gossip and a drink while the women got the Sunday meal ready.[164] Alphonsus therefore replaced it, establishing a new Confraternity of Gentlemen at the Arienzo church of Our Lady of Mount Carmel. He also set up a Consorority for girls, first at Mount Carmel and then, to keep them quite apart from the gentlemen, at Monte Vergine.[165] Other confraternities were established at Airola, Durazzano, and Frasso, as well as at Sant' Agata, where two of his Redemptoristines were recruited to train "these children" in virtue and domestic science.[166]

These Redemptorist foundations were put in deliberate contrast with the usual brotherhoods of select men in a parish which were designed to help the members achieve greater economic success. The reformed confraternities that the missioners left behind them had "no commercial interest in view," the members, taken from every class in town, were enrolled on account only of their having "the motive of serving God with a true heart."[167] The practice of setting up such a confraternity during the parish mission was settled into the Redemptorist Constitutions of 1764, with two unalterable rules, that no money subscription be taken and that the appointed priest chaplain have absolute control of the Brothers of the Confraternity. From the observance of these two rules all else, prayer, sacramental practice, charity towards the poor, would flow in orderly fashion.[168] So it was, as Alphonsus liked to retell the little local history of the Duke of Popoli, that this nobleman was moved to speak some fine final words to his son: "Know that the little good I have done in this life I attribute to my belonging to the Confraternity, hence I have no greater treasure to leave you than membership of the Confraternity of Blessed Mary: I value more having belonged to this than being Duke of Popoli."[169]

Towards a New Missioner Institute

His Propaganda Brothers in "this Illustrious Congregation" had no wish to press their complaint against Alphonsus after that Foggia escapade.[170] They could not long hold a grievance against so eager a missioner and, in perhaps too lavish a fling of reconciliation, they conferred their richest benefice on the young man, and appointed him to preach their 1732 autumn Retreat.

The cardinal's most exceptionally attending this Retreat, on three evenings, must have increased the elder Brothers' willingness to grant Alphonsus scope.[171] And after the Retreat, Alphonsus stayed in the city to do his part as a morning preacher in the annual city mission. By this time, he had discovered, in his conversations with Celeste Crostarosa, a particular vocation which could not be fulfilled within the confines of Propaganda. And it was flattering that the suavely rhetorical Falcoia, from the Pious Workers, should profess himself interested in Alphonsus' future. On November 3, 1732, Alphonsus was off again to Scala, staying this time for almost a month. The Brothers of Propaganda were by now discerning that, with or without their approval, Alphonsus would give himself scope. On February 23, 1733, their Scrutineer reported, among a range of Brothers' delinquincies, Alphonsus' unsanctioned activities at the convent. This time there could be no ignoring the report of their spies. Or, indeed, the general sacristy gossip in the city about him and Falcoia. Alphonsus had evidently been secretly plotting with a representative of one of Propaganda's keenest rivals in the evangelization of the Kingdom. Both of them were, it now appeared, engaged with some nun in a scheme to found another missioner congregation. There was a general sense that Alphonsus ought in decency to surrender that benefice.[172] He appeared to have no sense of what it meant for them to be Brothers, to be going on together in shared aim, shared work, shared set-back and achievement. But, on the indulgent cardinal's suggestion,[173] Torno decided that they must simply go on favoring him; he even brought himself to tell Alphonsus, our Congregation regards you as one of its most esteemed members.[174] He could keep the benefice.

It was by then too late for Alphonsus to be reintegrated into regular service.[175] Alphonsus was still a member of Propaganda. Would remain a member all his life. But, he was already the leader of his own troop of friends. A company of envangelizers like and not like themselves. In his family, among brothers, Alphonsus had been brought to appreciate that he was to endure singular responsibilities in any society he would join. He had been rather better prepared than others for life as Rector Major. But whatever he had learned within those diverse Confraternities which he had joined as an earnest layman and enthusiastic young priest, Visitation, Misericordiella, Bianchi, whatever he had learned about reliance on others and others relying on him, about cooperation, even about comradeship, fellow-feeling, had been brought into missioner focus at Propaganda. He had come at their city and countryside preaching of the Gospel, to some appreciation of what it might mean to be a priest among priests, Brother among Brothers. This appreciation of missioner fraternity shaped the demands he would make, in the new Institute, on the Fathers.

It was in confident expectation of Propaganda's approving his general procedure that, as late as 1746, making his first attempt at writing about contemporary moral problems, Alphonsus sent his paper for discussion at one of the missioners' study days. They did approve and voted to second his efforts to get the local episcopate to recognize what was actually happening when Neopolitans lost their tempers and began "cursing the dead" who mouldered in their opponents' family grave-plots. They were all experienced enough missioners to recognize, once he'd pointed it out, that poor uneducated folk should not be classed as mortal sinners on account of their using a common cuss. "Your memorandum was read out at a general meeting and all judged your argument unanswerable."[176]

If a continuity between Propaganda and the Institute of the Most Holy Savior were discernible in the general tone, purpose and program of the mission enterprise, the discontinuities were chiefly to be seen in the organization of the missioners. The number and length of Propaganda missions being constrained by the missioner's being university professors, cathedral canons, diocesan administrators, occupied for a good part of the year in these other works, suggested to Alphonsus that he should have only full-time workers in his Institute. Full time but less influential in the decision-making of the company. Alphonsus did not at all care for the democratic structure of Propaganda by which each and every Brother might have a say at a company meeting, even combining with others to outvote their Rector. He did not care either for that unsettling custom by which every Propaganda officer, including the Rector, tendered his resignation at each June close of the mission year. In his Institute there should be no question of resignations. The Rector Major would be elected for life. He would exercise a central, divinely approved, permanent, authority—just like the Pope. Alphonsus could, however, very well recognize a Christian sense in all others being entirely moveable as the Rector Major should dispose them.

That he had fast become used to having his own will was demonstrated when, having been favorably impressed by Alphonsus' pamphlet "On Cursing the Dead," the Propaganda authorities invited him in September 1747 to give a couple of lectures on "How to Preach a Mission Sermon."[177] His whole tone, during the first of these, was offensive to their ears. Most especially, they objected to his denunciations of the elegant preaching of the Capuchin master of Baroque rhetoric, Bernardo Maria Giacchi. Alphonsus had seemed to them almost skittish in his dismissal of the recently deceased homelist: "I hope to God that he does not have to lament his vanity in Purgatory right up to the Day of Judgment." Alphonsus was not, of course, being at all skittish. He was deadly serious. And his response to their increasing distaste for what he was saying and how he was saying it nicely exemplifies the difference of his mode of governing his Institute from what they were used to at Propaganda. No bothering to take their majority nonsense into account. The following week, he repeated his assessment of Giacchi, at least as forcefully, putting an immediate end to any general discussion they might have been intending. "I have no purpose of amendment."[178] Nor, he saw in pained surprise, had they. They had not been reconverted to that style of preaching which Alphonsus knew for sure was "apostolic."[179] These new men at Propaganda had, it was plain to him now, surrendered their claim to be "the Mission of Apostolic secular priests under the patronage of Mary, Queen of Apostles."[180]

Alphonsus said as much to Cardinal Antonio Sersale, 1702–1775, immediately on his appointment as archbishop of Naples. Their old Propaganda was not what it had been when the two of them were young missioners. "You will find a falling off in the spirit of those who are coming to ordination and, what is worse in all the Congregations of priests as well."[181] But, as he had told Pope Benedict XIV immediately after his unfortunate experience as a Propaganda lecturer, his new Institute was ready and willing to take over the work: "Having for many years given missions as a member of the Congregation of the Apostolic Missions erected at the cathedral of Naples, and having observed the great neglect in which poor people found themselves, especially in the country districts of vast areas of the Kingdom, he, beginning in 1732, had formed a Congregation to…."[182]

III

SEVEN BROTHERS

The manner of his upbringing within the Liguori household, readying him to be the heir, had shown Alphonsus how a man might come naturally to the exercise of authority. There were difficulties for him in converting this natural authority into the gracious *imitatio Christi* of the Rector Major. But he had few, if any, questions about the status in the decent family of an eldest among brothers. As it had been at home, so it should be in the "*Familia Alphonsiana.*"[1]

His Confraternity experience of working with others under God to do good for their fellow citizens was as determinedly significant for Alphonsus' understanding of what he was wanting from the Fathers of his Congregation. They were to be his cooperators. They would be known as "Alphonsus and Company."[2]

But if, at the setting up of the Congregation of the Most Holy Savior, Alphonsus had formed ideas of the status of a Rector Major and the function of the Fathers, he had almost no pre-Congregation experience by which he might judge the proper character and function of a lay Brother in their Institute.

Not every Father could be contented by a likening of the priest in the Congregation to a member of some Confraternity. Rather, it sounded as if the Confraternity Brothers offered the paradigm for the Brothers serving them. These were, both sets of them, laymen. The Theatine tradition which was manifesting itself in the organization and work of the confraternity of the Visitation at the Incurabili, in the Misericordiella and in the Bianchi, and those other sodalities in which these Fathers had almost all been enrolled, offered them a ready set of guidelines for their treatment of all lay helpers. Marcantonio del Tufo's forty-two rules for the governance of confraternity Brothers might be more numerous than they needed right now, but this Theatine bishop's suggestions that such

Brothers be forbidden to wear the same habit as a Father, engage in preaching like a Father, or gorge themselves in the refectory, could be as useful in 1732 as in 1587.[3] That the vocation of their Brothers in the Institute was being quite uncomplicatedly assimilated to that of the Confraternity Brothers is suggested by its being common to appoint the same Father as Prefect of the local Confraternity and as Prefect of Brothers in the community. And by its being commonly assumed that this Father would be ministering to these two sets of men in the same way. Thus, in Tannoia's *memoire* of the old priest, it is remarked how well Angelo Latessa, 1686–1754, exercised responsibility for the three hundred men of the Confraternity of Artisans, collecting them for a regular series of addresses on the mysteries of the Faith, hearing their confessions, "never dismissing them without having added ardour to their piety" and, equally, how well he had exercised responsibility for the Brothers of the Materdomini house, collecting them for regular instruction in the mysteries of the Faith, hearing their confessions, "always urging them to greater love of Jesus and piety towards the blessed Mother."[4]

There were differences, Latessa, Tannoia, and the other Fathers recognized, between the Sunday and Wednesday evening Brothers and those who were making their everyday commitment to Christian service as their Brothers for life. But they were more impressed by the likeness. Alphonsus, however, compelled at several moments of his community life to consider carefully who Fathers and Brothers were, what they were doing, did not shift from his understanding of the Confraternities' offering a paradigm for cooperating Fathers in "a new Congregation of Priests." He had to look again at his experience to find some helpful paradigm for their joint appreciation of the Brothers.

Reconsidering Paul and Philemon and Onesimus

Their new Institute's being defined as a grouping of "secular priests living together"[5] entailed that Alphonsus would not be looking to have men about him who should enjoy the status and self-estimate of tonsured clerics, on the pattern of Brothers in some religious Order, the Franciscans, say. These Brothers of his were to be, by definition, lay Brothers. They were, by description, to be doing a range of jobs about the house which someone or other, not Alphonsus, of course, nor any of his brothers, had had to do about his father's house. Alphonsus was looking for men whose contribution to the Congregation's work would be expressible in the language of domestic service.

Alphonsus' notion of a fit household arrangement included, along with father, heir, siblings, and assorted toddlers, a range of servants to hold the flambeaux for their master's departing guests, to attend the heir when he went a-visiting, to coach those siblings in the management of horse and hounds. And a range of young housemaids, up and down stairs, to nanny the toddlers, to scrub, launder, do the dishes. Dangerous flirts, these. Or so Alphonsus found them.[6] Still, Gaetano bequeathed thirty carlins to his maid-of-all-work, Geronima, "whom everyone calls 'Ciomma.'" Perhaps she was a comfortably older person. Or was so by the time Gaetano was a-dying.

Alphonsus might be wary of the younger housemaids, but he was always interested in the status, condition, and treatment of servants. At home, he was remembered as the defender of a nervous torch-bearer during a family row.[7] He kept up a more general interest as priest and bishop. It was one of the very few specific recommendations he made in 1774 to Cardinal Giuseppe Maria Castelli, 1705–1780, touching the need for the renewal of Christian living in the episcopal palaces of the Church, that the next pope should determine for bishops "the number of persons whom they may have as servants, according to a prelate's rank: so many valets, and not more; so many housemen, and not more; so many ostlers...." "This would be the way," Alphonsus assured the cardinal, "to silence the heretics."[8] It is a remainder from life with his own many-servanted family that in his *Theologia Moralis* Alphonsus can ask and discuss quite seriously whether a domestic who had been taken prisoner in "a just war" battle, could be morally excusable if he attempt to make his escape from his master.[9] It depends, said the Dominican Prierio Silvester, d. 1523, and the Jesuit Ludovico Molina, 1535–1600, whether the man were a Christian or not. No one could trouble much about a Muslim pressed-man, "*schiavio,*" about Abdalla, for example. But it might be a worry that some of those *servi* working in the Marianella yard were Christians, Don Giuseppe had, therefore, better pick carefully when compelling the more presentable of his oarsmen into unpaid service ashore.

Alphonsus could not remain contented by such categorizing of Christian serving men and pagan slaves. He would, whatever the restraining conventions of the Captain's household, have to start converting the pagan slaves into Christian servants. And then their case in Naples would be just that of those held by the Turks. He would be brought, only gradually it may be, to appreciate how incongruous was the trireme relation between Christian master and Christian slave with the freedom won by Christ. *Copiosa apud eum redemptio.*

Whatever the divisions that careful moralists were making, out of respect for the social conventions of their times, Alphonsus had been shown something more generously unitive as he progressed through the Pauline letters with tutor Torno. They had taken old Estius as their guide to the complexities of the apostle's language and thought on this as on other topics. Coming penultimately to the Epistle to Philemon, Alphonsus would have encountered that peculiar Christian version of *servus* which Silvester and Molina had been invoking as they made their distinctions between baptized and unbaptized servants and slaves. Alphonsus would also have encountered a relation of this *servus* to *redemptio* which reached to a Christian version of *frater.* For Estius had drawn out the Pauline sense of Onesimus as both the bound *servus* of his master Philemon and his freed brother in Christ.[10] That elucidation of the dichotomy would prove very helpful for the later development of Alphonsus' understanding of a Brother in the Congregation.

More immediately, Alphonsus found something to his purpose in Estius' exegesis of the name Onesimus as "usefulness." Paul, in telling Philemon that he wanted very much to keep Onesimus with him "so that he might be of service to me," is making one of those puns that he and Alphonsus both enjoy. Onesimus is, as Estius paraphrases the apostle, "*et mihi et tibi utilis.*"[11] Paul's punning reaches into Alphonsus' life. As he endured with Fathers and Brothers, it would at times seem to him that he was experiencing precisely what Paul was experiencing in his relations with Philemon and Onesimus. "I am doubly obliged to you," he wrote to Rector Tannoia at one such moment about his keeping Brother Rafaele Daniele, 1754–1833, to tend him when he should have been sent back, "for the good offices for which I am indebted to that Brother. You will please excuse him for delaying his return to you."[12] Alphonsus, imitating the imitator of Christ, was making just the apostle's acknowledgment of "usefulness."

To acknowledge "usefulness" may be to make a start at recognizing value in the *servus*. It may lead into talk of "helpfulness." Of "cooperation," even. But it is only a start. Alphonsus had been quicker to recognize the bounden duty of the Brothers. Most particularly, he had his idea of what was being established at that vow of perseverance each one of them had taken. Such a bound *servus*, if he were to run away from his master, Estius had explained, would simply compound that original fault for which he had been bound at first.[13] The runaway Onesimus is in mortal jeopardy. So Alphonsus will be unyielding in his demand upon any who run away from the Congregation once having made the vow of perseverance. All are free. All are bound. All freely bound. Under pain of mortal sin. "Whence should dispensation come? I, for my part, will never give it if he that leaves without dispensation does not return to the Congregation. When he returns and has received due penance, then I will reflect on what more needs to be done."[14] None of them should complain. None of them was a prisoner of war. "Good God! It was they who bound themselves to Jesus Christ, and now they accuse me of keeping them by force!"[15] He would not like to guess what will happen to these "*fugantes*," run-aways, traitors. "God knows where they will end."[16]

There were in Estius' Commentaries suggestions for a language of "*socius*," "fellow worker" in relation to "*frater*" which might have been taken up by the Fathers.[17] But your mission preacher was your only "*socius*."[18] The Fathers preferred to refer to a Brother as "*operario*," "workman,"[19] even then distinguishing him from the "*operai*," those who do the real work, themselves or the Pii Operai fellows of Falcoia.[20] They were, some of them, sometimes, tempted to call for the services of a "*garzone*," "errand boy." But Alphonsus forbade it.[21] He'd got at least that far in his meditations on what those Paul classes with Torno had suggested for their lives together.[22]

The ordinary engagements of a man running a household took Alphonsus another step in his progress from Liguori assumptions about the oarsman *servus* into a Pauline appreciation of the freedman *frater*. When he was hiring a packman to convey a portmanteau, a special messenger to carry a letter, or, significantly, when he was hiring Alessio Pollio, 1742–1813, to be his Sant' Agata manservant, he would have to reconsider not only the status and function of the unpaid *servus* in the household but the claims of the paid *famulus*.[23]

It was an interesting clutch of questions for the ex-attorney, raised by quite a number of Neapolitan employers, not only bishops, what rights these *famuli* had in Canon Law. What claim could the hired man about the house maintain against his master if he were bitten by one of the family's boar-hounds?[24] Or were dismissed on account of his catching syphilis?[25] Alphonsus generally advised that employers should exercise a modicum of enlightened self-interest in such crises. He had the reputation of being such an enlightened employer himself. Irritatingly so. When Tannoia went gathering information about Alphonsus' working a miracle cure for a servant of a local bishop, he rather too pointedly turned their talk to how good a master Alphonsus had been. "That's very true," the grandly servanted prelate interrupted, "Mgr. Liguori's household, *famiglia*, was treated just like mine." Reporting this impertinence, Tannoia remarked that "that prelate prided himself on his fine coach and horses," and then added ironically "he was quite indifferent to the miracle done for his servant."[26]

Tannoia had, of course, read Alphonsus' pamphlet on the *Fidelity of Vassals,* in which he had, in 1776, assured every sort of king, bishop, knight, that they would be entirely safe from rebellion if they dealt Christianly with their people.[27] Cardinal Castelli had most obligingly distributed the pamphlet to the king's ambassadors in Rome.[28] But Tannoia would recognize that, with these monarchs, Alphonsus had in mind the wider readership of country boar-hunters and city merchants. As he described them, feudal *vassali* were very like domestic *famuli.*[29] And *famuli* were in some ways like their masters' children.

Even as early as 1746, Alphonsus had come to speak of the relation of *famulus* to employer as being like that of a son to a father within the family, a relation of love, reverence, and obedience, since the master is "*in loco parentis.*" In suggesting this likeness, Alphonsus was, he very well knew, going against Aristotle and Aquinas and the great casuist Valerie Raynauld, 1543–1623, who had drawn careful distinctions between the services to be offered to a King, a father, and an employer.[30] Alphonsus was thus unusually emboldened by the memory of a university discussion of *famulus.*

The Law School curriculum included, as an examinable topic, the status and responsibilities of such servants. Vico's course actually contained a lecture on their rights. If it is only a likelihood that Alphonsus himself attended Vico's lecture, it would be most surprising if some fellow student had not relayed the great man's innovative history of domestic service and its vocabulary:

> Philologians and philosophers have commonly supposed that the families in a so-called "state of nature" included children only, whereas in fact they comprised *famuli* also, and that was the original reason for their being called "families."[31]

Don Giuseppe would have been well enough pleased to hear his learned son report Vico's suggestion that these *famuli* had originally come to the head of the clan with petitions that they be accepted into his service, hoping that under the protection of the hero's *fama* they might find relief from life in the wild world outside his family palisade:

> Refugees were received by the heroes under the just law of protection by which they would be kept alive under the obligation, in exchange, of serving the heroes as day laborers.[32]

The *famuli,* on Vico's reconstruction of that long gone time, were slavekin. Housed, fed, protected, as if each were "one of the family," set to do the meanest chores as if he were not.

Vico was describing a society before an exchange of coin for services had entered the calculations of hero or *famulus.* This was a premoney equity. The *famulus* was, in those prime times, being offered food, lodging, protection. If he abandoned the hero's compound, he went away empty-handed. So Alphonsus ruled that the Brother who defected should not be given money for any past years' service. He was assuming, at this and other junctures, that the relation of hero to *famulus* might be sustained in the modern Congregation.

The *famulus* had, evidently, something of the *servus* about him and something of the *frater.* The reference of this vichian sociological analysis enabled Alphonsus to describe for himself and for others, the Fathers, the Brothers, what was being demanded in their lives together in terms of a renewal of the lives of Paul, Philemon, and Onesimus together. As Estius put Onesimus's case, "He is to be received not as *servus* but as *frater* because all servitude ends with this life, but Christian fraternity lasts into eternity."[33] This was the peculiar Christian status of the *famulus,* coming from *servus* in the world towards *frater* in the Kingdom, which Alphonsus would have each Brother enjoy with the Fathers. That was the good possibility announced at each one's making the vow of perseverance.

There might not be any precise congruence of Vico's etymological thesis about *famulus* with Paul's evangelical presentation of Onesimus to Philemon, but Alphonsus could respond to likenesses. He understood more after the work of founding and sustaining the Institute than he had when an undergraduate in Torno's study. Even to the point of refiguring what Estius had been telling him of Paul's meaning.[34] So, in his *Theologia Moralis,* Alphonsus began his *dubium* on the relations of *famulus* with the head of the *familia* with a citation of 1 Timothy 5:8: "If anyone does not take care of his people, and especially those of his house, he's denying the faith." In a lengthy passage of his commentary, "*in cap. V Epistolae I ad Timotheum,*" a confident Estius had expounded "*domesticorum*" as referring only to "those close in blood," such as parents, brothers, children, nephews. Alphonsus would have his readers understand that Paul's usage requires that "domestic servants" are included with "family members." He can, thus, carry Paul with him as, with vichian intent, he constructs another of those pleasing parallels, this time of Paul, the community's "father in God," Timothy, "our brother," and Onesimus, the *famulus,* the three of them, being in apposition with himself, Rector Major, received as "His Paternity," his fellow priests in the Congregation, "my Brothers," and the lay Brother whom Alphonsus understands as, in Estius' decription, "more than a servant," as "in a way his son, in a way his brother."[35]

The development of Alphonsus' sense of what it might be for a man who is "more than a servant" to sustain the character, if not of "son," then of "brother," would take some time. In order that he should appreciate the reference of this Pauline reassessment of the relation of Christian master and Christian servant within the mission to the demands of his own missioner vocation, Alphonsus had to endure the experiences of living with a few good Brothers. There was no likelihood that he would at the start of his enterprise, forming "Alphonsus and Company," have energy or interest enough to criticize his family's notion of servants and slaves. But Alphonsus was always wanting to understand himself in Pauline terms, and he would come, through his encounters with these

Brothers at crisis moments for his own Christian life, to be aware of a need to reevaluate the witness of his Brothers as they shifted out of *servi* into *fratres* for eternity. He would have to reevaluate them as Paul had reevaluated Onesimus.

Meanwhile, he was just looking around for pointers to what he should be doing in the Christian community. His sense of himself, his situation in the Kingdom, and his vocation, was given a push towards practical realization by what he observed during his time at the Chinese College. So was his sense that he would be needing some home-help. On that, as on many matters, he would be agreed with those *congregati* at the College with whom he was talking about all their futures, Vincenzo Mannarini, Gennaro Sarnelli, and Nicolo Vinaccia from Sant' Agata. All of them used to having a few servants in the house.

The College of the Holy Family

The "Chinese College" was the creation of Matteo Ripa, 1682–1746, not a Naples citizen by birth or family connection, born at Eboli, a ramparted town near Salerno, clustered about what was then a ruined castle and a church which even now retains some lively medieval frescoes of San Biagio.

At fifteen years of age, Ripa was sent to Naples by his father, Baron Gianfilipo of Planchetella, to finish his education. There he fell into "a thousand vices" from which he was suddenly withdrawn by a providential encounter with a Franciscan preaching at a street corner near the viceroy's palace. Ripa quickly determined to get himself ordained and, on his next questioning what especial good he might do with his talents, was encouraged by the great Torres, in May 1701, to join the missioner Congregation of Santa Maria della Purita. Ripa did as this famous spiritual director suggested but was not satisfied that he had found his vocation until he heard a voice "not bodily but clear," declare that he must go to Rome and establish there a group of missionary priests. These would place their inheritances in the hands of the Superior, like Pious Workers, put themselves at the immediate service of the Curia, like Oratorians, and settle a new sort of hat on their heads like no one else.[36]

Though the voice was clear enough, Ripa thought that the whole experience might have been a daydream. Still, this was a good time to go on his travels. Gemelli Careri, 1651–1725, had lately shown that a Neapolitan could circumnavigate the globe and come to no harm. The library of Giuseppe Valletta, 1636–1714, another city lawyer, contained shelves full of books about Christians in distant lands. Vico had been borrowing them.[37] So, probably had Ripa. And the example of the Jesuit missionaries setting out from Naples in emulation of Francis Xavier was another encouragement for him to think of the Orient. Torres, proving once more the soundness of his intuitions, gave him the final prod, "Off you go and get ready for China."[38]

Ripa noted in his autobiographical *Storia* that, upon this prompting, he danced all the way home. Though his first efforts to persuade the Roman Curia to sanction the project were unsuccessful,[39] on January 4, he and another of Torres' proteges, Gennar' Amodei from San Marco in Calabria, were on the packet-boat from Brill to London and, by mid-February 1708, had got themselves China-berths on the East India Company's ship *Donegal.*

Ripa began to make copious notes about the strange birds and fish they were encountering on the southerly voyage. He made sketches of them in his journal. He even chanced a queasy stomach by tasting them. The sailors for their part proved not to object to a few prayers to the Star of the Sea for an uneventful voyage. And the young missionaries were happy enough to pay their respects to King Neptune in rough and tumble games at the Crossing of the Equator.[40]

They arrived in China in February 1712.[41] By 1715, Amodei was dead. The new foods had not agreed with him. It was evident to Ripa that the pair of them had been ill-prepared for the enterprise. Their ignorance of this society and its customs ensured that they should often, very often, appear to the Chinese as intolerable boors. Ripa understood that if Neapolitans were ever to be effective in China they would have to present themselves as the modest assistants of Chinese evangelists. He determined to return home and found a seminary in which Chinese students should be trained alongside Neapolitans willing to work with them in the East. This was not quite a new notion. At the beginning of the century Luigi Fan, 1682–1753, had been brought to the Roman College by the Jesuit Giuseppe Antonio Provana, 1662–1720, and in 1740, Pierre Foureau, 1700–1749, brought five Chinese to study at the College Louis le Grand. But Ripa was the first to recognize the need for some special institute in which such students could be trained.

He returned to Italy, again via London, where this time he and his Chinese boys were received by George I. They were all in Naples by late November 1724. The Curia let it be known that he should have come at once to Rome before going south. He could only apologize and outline his plans.[42]

Negotiations for establishing the new Institute having begun so badly, it was not surprising that it was only on April 7, 1731, that Ripa was granted permission to open his College. But he had long before acquired a property and started classes.[43]

Ripa's hope was that his Chinese students would retain their own cultural ethos while gaining a thoroughly Neapolitan sense of Catholicism. His persisting in this hope was appreciated by the best of his fellow citizens as representing something akin to their own patriotic determination to maintain Neapolitan customs within the universal Church. The College prospered. By June 1729, the Congregation of the Holy Family included, besides the four Chinese boys who had been tonsured at speed, five Neapolitan priests, a deacon, another tonsured local youngster, and another Chinese boy who had decided that he needed time to look round Naples before he surrendered his lay status. Perhaps he was glancing at the conditions under which the three lay Brothers were living at the College. This was the month that Alphonsus, finally abandoning his attempt to live peaceably with his father in the family home, took up Ripa's offer of a room in College. He had probably been enrolled as one of the clerical "*fratelli,*" helpful Brothers of the new College, that Ripa was recruiting in the city. Alphonsus was now received as a "*convictor,*" a sort of holy lodger, almost indeed an oblate of the Holy Family Congregation.[44]

Whatever the training method of Torno's tutorials, Alphonsus' habit of thought and expression reflects a temperamental sympathy with Ripa's response to the "Chinese Rites" controversies and the rows about ancestor honoring. He would always want to ask contextualizing questions. His first try at a problem in moral theology would be that exploration of what women and men in Neapolitan society actually thought of "all your ancestors."[45] Later, in 1784, when Tannoia was making a little fun of both President de Paola and his protege Clement Hofbauer, 1751–1820, and the project of Redemptorist missions beyond the Alps, Alphonsus put a stop to the mockery: "Those countries are half abandoned. So the missions will have to be different from ours. There, in the midst of Lutherans and Calvinists, instructions will be more useful than sermons."[46] This was a most Ripa-like judgment of others in other places.

Alphonsus was also observing carefully the practical arrangements Ripa made for the good running of the College. He was becoming aware of the calls made on a Rector's energies by a daily oversight of both kitchen and lecture hall. And by the necessary engagement with civil authorities. He was learning something, too, of the practical difficulties in getting men to live together for a missionary ministry in which Rector, Fathers, Students, and lay Brothers were to take different responsibilities. All in all, he was beginning to think that the houses of his Institute should have something of this collegiate character. There was nothing much to attract him in the self-preserving corporations of clergy who sat so comfortably in the stalls of Collegiate churches at Arienzo, at Avella, Frasso, d'Iliceto, and other of the prosperous townships of the Kingdom.[47] But ever after his time with Ripa, Alphonsus liked the sound of "College." So did the Fathers. It quickly became ordinary with his men to speak of "the College of the Fathers of the Most Holy Savior at Ciorani," "the College of Saint Michael" at Pagani, "the College of Caposele."[48] Such a community would be structured along the lines of Master of the College, aggregated Fellows, Students, and, as at the Chinese College, men willing to serve them. Alphonsus had taken careful watch of the Brothers at the College as they kept house for Rector, Fathers, and Students. These were men whose constant application impressed him. He wanted such men.

Complementarily, Ripa thought Alphonsus was a very good catch. He was full of praise for this new man's energy in preaching, in hearing confessions, and every sort of pastoral work, "to the great profit of souls." He'd preached a very fine sermon for the Collegers and their guests on the feast of the Holy Family.[49] Ripa was already, it is plain, planning that Alphonsus should succeed him as Rector at the College. Though, reminding him of poor Amodei, this convictor's constitution was proving delicate. And there were soon other causes for worry within the house. Of the boys Ripa had brought from China, only two had allowed themselves to be turned into docile seminarians who would go quietly back to China. Three of them now fancied their chances of staying in Naples.

And of the clergy who'd joined him, Ripa discovered that some were "good priests" but "no good for this community."[50] Most provokingly, Alphonsus was proving to be one of these misfits. Ripa was as unhappy as Torno that Alphonsus had gotten himself mixed up with the spiritually imperialist Falcoia. Worse, if anything could be worse, Alphonsus had been chatting with some Scala nun, "who was said to have had a vision of God." He was always going off to Scala, "to give a Retreat," "to conduct a Novena," "to hear Confessions."[51] And Celeste Crostarosa was now saying that she had had another message from the Lord, commanding that there be a new Congregation of men, twelve preachers to a house, who were to live "the Apostolic life" under Alphonsus' leadership. Falcoia had taken it upon himself to tell Alphonsus to obey "these alleged visions" and quit the College. "All this time," Ripa grumbled as he wrote his memoir, "I was in Rome trying to speed up the granting of the Brief."[52] There was no one to warn Alphonsus against this distracting project. So he took seriously all that talk of visions and an institute and his having leadership qualities. He even began making overtures to other Collegers, suggesting that they abandon Ripa's enterprise. Still, among them all, only Vincenzo Mannarini, ever susceptible to the charms of novelty, had been persuaded away.

On July 25, 1732, the first day of a Triduum for the opening of the College, Don Gaetano, safely out of his brother's hearing,[53] told Ripa what had been happening while he had been waiting for the Brief in Rome. Immediately confronted by Ripa, "those gentlemen, Don Alphonsus and Don Vincenzo, confessed the whole truth." They were indeed planning to abandon the certain good to be done at the College, which needed their help, which had only just been approved by the Pope, for some quite uncertain good. "If Monsignore Falcoia wished to found a new Congregation," Ripa told them, "he could do it without disturbing us."[54] But they were not to be moved. Nor was Falcoia when Ripa remonstrated with him. They had all been seduced by that nun and her visions.

In the quarrelsome summer of 1732, Ripa had been particularly aggrieved that Alphonsus should have told his plans to the College lay Brothers. It was obvious that this troublesome convictor had been hoping to take them with him when he quit the College. Baltassare Zerla, Giuseppe Scotto, a relative of the parish priest left in charge of the Confraternity on Procida, and Giacomo Corcione were, however, men who proved loyal to their vocations as Brothers at the College, "even though," as Ripa remarked, "an Angel of God would suggest something else."[55]

Apostles and Deacons

It took some little time for Alphonsus to get his Pauline and Vichian understandings of *servus* and *famulus* and *frater* into intelligible order, longer to achieve their realization in the day to day working of the Congregation. It had for the moment, at the setting up of the Institute, appeared that he might manage well enough with some simpler reference to the Acts relationship of Apostle and deacon. They could all of them in various degrees, find encouragement for this equation of deacon with Brother in the citation Estius made of Ignatius of Antioch's appreciation of deacons as "imitators of Christ" precisely by being "ministers" in the household of a bishop, and Estius' own declaration that it is "beyond dispute" that deacons were "subservient" to priests.[56]

So it is with Acts very much in mind that the Comprehensive Presentation of their Rules, which he prepared with Falcoia in 1733 or a little earlier, starts with the plain announcement of an Apostle- and deacon-structure: "In each house there shall be at most, never more than, the number of twelve Fathers and the Superior," and, Constitution I continues, "there shall be seven lay Brothers."[57] In the preliminary version of the Rule taken to Rome in 1748, Alphonsus again makes a structural bid for the imitation of Christ, his faithful apostles, and their seven deacons: "In every house or College, besides the Rector, it shall not be allowed to have more than eleven priests and seven serving Brothers."[58] The 1749 Pontifical Rule's first reference to Brothers occurs in a paragraph about running costs and financial rectitude which is somehow brought back to the Acts model: "The income of each house cannot be increased beyond the sum of fifteen hundred ducats, an income sufficient to maintain church, house, twelve priests and seven lay Brothers."[59] There was at first a pleasing simplicity in the parallelling of apostles with Fathers "preaching the word of God" and of deacons with Brothers "serving at table," ignoring for a while that the Brothers were laymen. This could not last.[60]

Even when stipulating these numbers in the Pontifical Rule, it had been appreciated that their correspondence with the Acts model might be somewhat notional. Alphonsus had been careful to add the liberating clause, "in the novitiate house, the house of studies, or where the Rector major is residing, there can be a larger number." Somehow these things would work themselves out as Fathers and Brothers went on living together.

Where there was no definition of what it was to be a Redemptorist Brother, the description must depend on the personal qualities of the first Brothers, and the scope they were allowed or created for themselves in the Colleges.

It was significant for them all that the very first Brother to join the Congregation was a peculiarly distinguished man.

Vito Curzio

Vito Curzio was, as Tannoia introduces this Brother in his *Life* of Alphonsus, a gentleman.[1] Born in 1706 at Acquaviva, on the heel of Italy, a provincial town which could not even boast the presence of a bishop, Vito had, nevertheless, a grand sense of himself and what was due to him as a man of honor.[2] Perhaps his elder brother, the doctor, was not easily distinguishable from a blood-letting barber, but his younger brother was a Canon of the town's collegiate church. Neither of these respectable, educated, men nor their worthy father, could be content that Vito's only study was the management of "pistols, cutlasses, and every other sort of weapon."[3] They certainly would not have wanted him to disgrace the family by becoming a professional soldier. So Vito walked the streets, spoiling for a fight. Surprisingly, perhaps, there were sufficient men of similar honor in the town for the keen-tempered Vito, alive to the smallest insult, to take his pistols to several duels. Frederick Jones remarks, with his usual delicacy, that Vito's early years "are fortunately shrouded in mystery," but some things are too clearly known.[4] He had, most notoriously, taken a dawn pot-shot at the local attorney for some quickly perceived offense.

Vito was, evidently, in his mid twenties a man of real charm. Seeming at times quite tameable. His widower father was doubtless much relieved when Vito became the great friend of the entirely respectable Don Cesare Sportelli, and was regularly welcomed into the drawing room of Cesare's pious mother, Donna Maria Anna.[5] Her conversation must surely do him good. There came the time, however, when Vito's readiness to recognize an affront got him into a quite serious scrape. He took it into his head that he'd been insulted by a swaggering corporal from the local army barracks. There was a puzzle in this for Vito. The man was not his social equal. He could not challenge him to a duel. But there had certainly been an insult. The corporal must be shown his mistake. So Vito took his arquebus, a sort of sawn off shotgun, and tried to pick off the scalliwag as he came round a street corner.[6] Happily, he missed his mark.

These things happen. Gerard Majella knew a man who was shot down in the public square at Muro, dying on the cobbles without a moment to repent. Cesare Sportelli himself had got into something of such an escapade, but survived to tell his mother his side of the story. That time neither sparkish duellist had had a good aim with a pistol. There are soldiers out on the spree in every garrison town. And local lads ready to resent them.[7] But Vito's adventures were, it seemed to the barracks officers, of so unruly a sort that the police must do something. However excellent his social connections. However loud his protestations of offended honor. Vito had to skip town. He traveled, indeed, as far to the other side of the Kingdom as he could. His father and brothers, eager to have Vito out of their way, must have been entirely contented to hear that a job had been found for him on the Procida estate of the Marquis del Vasto. Sportelli was the Marquis' attorney in Naples.[8]

Tannoia suggests that Vito was the Marquis' agent for the practical management of all island affairs. Alphonsus thought he had been the Marquis' tax collector.[9] Either way, Vito does not seem to have held the job down for very long. His quixotic sense of his own honor made him seem "a bizarre chap" among the fishermen, "a braggart" among the vineyard dressers. Certainly he was not to be braved by any of these locals. There was again talk of a pistol. Of Vito's finger lingering on the trigger of his carbine. Even of some menacing play with a cutlass. There was a general murmur.[10] By October 1732, the Marquis had decided that his estates would be the quieter if this wild man were to resign. Vito was quite ready for some new adventure. He went to stay with Sportelli in Naples.

It was impossible for anyone to remain vexed long with so charming a swashbuckler. The Marquis' lawyer, whatever part he'd had in getting Vito the Procida job, could receive the dismissed agent without fear of offending his grand client. In Sportelli's house, Vito was, indeed, able to pay part of his way from the moneys that the Marquis was now giving him for some regular bookkeeping and document-copying work. His handwriting was better than that of most pistol-packers.[11] Meanwhile, he was looking around for something to do with his life. It would have to be something with a smack of honor to it, of course, worthy of a man who still carried a weapon. Coincidentally, his host was considering the reordering of his own life. Sportelli was wondering whether he should not join Alphonsus and Gennaro Maria Sarnelli in the new Institute. Like them, a member of a prestigious city law firm, he had come, like them, to think this not the way to spend the rest of life. But Sportelli had said nothing of his thoughts on the matter to his impetuous guest.

Donna Maria Anna, however, had not been an idle listener while Vito went self-questioningly through her house. She set about praying for him in earnest. And, in the drastic manner usual with him, Vito had his conversion.[12] He enthusiastically embraced a life of repentant tears, bread and water meals, and violent self-flagellation. He raced ahead of her son. For, just as Sportelli was ready to declare his determination to join Alphonsus' group, Vito came bursting into his room to relate the dream he'd had the night before: "It seemed to me that I was at the base of a high mountain, very steep, and many priests were climbing up, and I started to climb after them, But I couldn't manage it. My feet kept slipping. And I soon found myself at the bottom again." A man of parts could not be comfortable with such a failure. "I tried again. And again. But to my great irritation, I always slipped down again." In his dream, however, one of the mountaineering priests had seen what was happening and reached down to him. Vito, as his lodging with the Sportelli family shows, was never too proud to accept assistance from another gentleman. "Thus helped, I clambered up with the others."[13] What should such a dream mean?

Sportelli admitted that it was all very strange, but said nothing helpful in the way of dream interpretation as they walked out together. On the way to the Chinese College, they caught up with a cassocked man whom Vito had never met before, but in amazed recognition he turned immediately to his companion: "Cesare, that is the priest who held out his hand to me in my dream." So Sportelli introduced him to Don Alphonsus de' Liguori.[14]

Vito at once understood his dream to have been sent by God to show him what he should do with his life. This man of aristocratic mien, who had put his knightly sword to the service of their Lady, setting out on such a perilous enterprise, would surely require a squire. Vito determined to offer himself as Alphonsus' companion. Tannoia gets Vito's drastic tone just right. "As he said, so he did."[15]

His offer overtook Alphonsus' planning. After that setback at the Chinese College, he had not yet got round to recruiting this sort of helper. But no one could ignore the worth of such a man. Alphonsus agreed to take Vito as the first lay Brother of the Congregation. As yet, though, there was no Congregation. Vito's impatience to have his share in this fine quest was balked by the slowness of the others. He was told to wait in Naples for further orders. "He had, indeed, some time to wait," Alphonsus admitted later, "and this delay as to his definite reception among us was a great pain to him."[16] He was not used to waiting. Vito fretted, pacing about the house, until one morning he again bounded into Sportelli's room, this time announcing that he heard a voice in a dream telling him, most satisfyingly, that he should pack his bags. "You will soon be setting out." Within a week of the foundation of the Congregation, he was on his way to Scala.

The impetuous Vito had rushed into the Congregation without asking any of those ordinary questions which occur to a careful man about the duties required of him. "And it did seem to some that he was rather too sensitive of his own honor to undertake the menial offices of a lay Brother."[17] However, upon arriving at Scala, he was not given a moment to ask those ordinary questions, let alone consider their answers. "On his very first day," Alphonsus remembered with a chuckle, "he was told to wait at the dinner table." The trigger-happy Vito was appalled. This was not what he had expected when he offered himself as companion squire to the knight. This was not it at all.

Vito's original vision had been of Alphonsus' giving him a hand into heaven. Reciprocally, Vito would be putting his talents and energies at Alphonsus' disposal. That was the agreement between them. As gentlemen both. Belonging to the same class in society. Don Vito was, after all, as easy in his conversation as any of Don Cesare's acquaintance.[18] As chivalric in his manner as Don Alphonsus himself. It was entirely in character that Vito should scratch the Institute's coat-of-arms on the wall of the Scala kitchen.[19] This apron service among the pots and pans should be his way to investiture as the King's true knight. There was storybook precedent for such royal acceptance of a kitchen worker. Young Prince Gareth, leaving his home, wanting only to be a knight of Arthur's table, had undertaken to serve "among scullions and kitchen knaves" and at last had had his petition granted by the King:

> Make thee my knight? my knights are sworn to vows
> Of utter hardihood, utter gentleness,
> And, loving, utter faithfulness in love,
> And uttermost obedience to the King.[20]

Vito undertook a like kitchen service and made a like vow of perseverance, and hoped for a like acceptance by his King.

Vito would always be Alphonsus' squire even as he was doing a servant's work. He would make it a matter of honor, of his integrity, to undertake the most menial jobs about the house. Seek them out. Not considering anything of Vito's reasons, Alphonsus simply saw that what he wanted done was being done.

Brother or Servant?

Alphonsus really hadn't the time to think about the Brother. He was too busy prospecting for Fathers. He found Vincenzo Mannarini, 1700–1755, at the Chinese College, the unsettled and unsettling Gian Battista de Donato from Calabria, the dull young Canon Pietro Romano at Scala, and the gallant gentleman not yet ordained, Don Silvestro Tosques, 1701-1769(?), who proved, troublesomely, to be Celeste Crostarosa's faithful champion. These required his tender attention. So it was that in the busy time of getting the Congregation going, quite unthinkingly, Alphonsus drifted into acting as if Vito were indeed his personal manservant. He took the *frater* as the present substitute for that *servus* that Don Giuseppe had found for him among the galley slaves. It may have seemed to him a nice coincidence that Saint Alessio, whom he had been imitating among the patients at the Incurabili, had had, in that little Oratory opera, a page named Curzio.[21]

Others could not be so easy in their minds at this domestic arrangement. Even Falocia thought it worth asking Alphonsus to think the matter through more thoroughly. "Under what title ought he to remain with you? As a Brother of the Congregation, or as your servant?[22]

Alphonsus had not the leisure at this time for sorting out *servus* and *famulus* and *frater*. It would be some time before he could attend to the question Falcoia was asking. None of the other Fathers seems to have thought it demanded any urgent attention. They believed that a man could be both Brother and servant. The unpaid *servus* was a quite generally accepted model among them for the Brother. Tannoia, wanting an image for Alphonsus' own attitude, thought of his saint as another Captain Liguori on his trireme with the press-ganged men, not the skilled gun-crew, "*fratelli servienti*" but the poor slaves *servi*: "He considered them as the seamen laboring at the oars while the captain is working with others in his cabin."[23] Vito did not complain, after that first evening's shock, at least not to the Fathers. Sometimes to himself, perhaps. Perhaps sometimes to God. He kept his word. He kept on working.

Whatever value Vito was recognizing in that work, it was plain that the Fathers did not require a squire. They were looking for someone who could make an eatable meal. "Their cook was Vito Curzio who had laid aside the sword and put on a torn habit and," Tannoia remarks, rather laughing at the man's cack-handedness with condiments and herbs than admiring his willingness to make a stab at some unaccustomed service, "who had no knowledge of cooking." So, of course, the poor Fathers suffered at the dinner table.[24]

Treated as a servant by the others, Vito proved to be the only decent gentleman among the lot of them. In the spring of 1733, one by one Alphonsus' first companions, Donato, Mannarini, Tosquez, left the new Institute. Sportelli and Mazzini were, Alphonsus knew, getting themselves ready to join him. But on Good Friday, April 3, Vito alone remained with him. Whatever those others might do, a man of honor does not bow out of his commitments. A Christian does not give up his hope of heaven. Vito stayed faithful to his vision of what Alphonsus was to accomplish.

Vito's visionary commitment turned Alphonsus' notion of an Institute into a reality. Without him, Alphonsus would have been, what the gossipy Naples clergy were already calling him, a fantasist, an obstinate dreamer, living in a delusion of pious grandeur, the Founder of a one-man Empire.[25] And Vito knew precisely how to make the Institute more real by the hour, even when Alphonsus was off preaching. Left by himself at Scala, he rang the hospice bell for the Community recitation of the Office, for the Community rising, eating, going to bed.[26] This was a creative bell-ringing. Where there was observance of a Rule, there was the Community. As the local people, hearing him ring out the hospice order of the day, were gradually brought to recognize.

Others were not at all sensitive to their need of a Brother and his regular prayer. In July 1733, Falcoia wrote to Alphonsus declaring himself entirely happy with "the summary of observances" submitted for his approval.[27] This summary, probably a redraft of Celeste Crostarosa's Rule for the Scala nuns, which became the *Complesso* text instances portering, tailoring, gardening, "and so forth," as jobs for the Brothers. The Fathers would not have either time or energy for such work, and so that they shall have needful times and energies for these jobs, "the lay brothers shall never undertake work for outsiders."[28] While the practice of the Fathers' vocation is quite detailedly described in thirteen Constitutions, it was evidently agreed that there was no necessity to say anything more about the Brothers once they'd been wholly secured for the Fathers' service. When Falcoia and Alphonsus presented their 1736 memorial to Jose Joaquin Guzman de Montealegre, 1698–1771, marquis of Salas, describing to King Carlo's Secretary of State for Foreign Affairs the structure and working program of their new Institute, they began by offering a short history of how, four years before at Scala, "many priests formed a community," and managed to get to the end without making any mention of Brothers.[29] Nor did the Fathers suppose that these good Brothers would make any mention of themselves at any time, any where. They should entirely forget themselves.

It seemed to Alphonsus that Vito had surrendered all memory of what he had been. He had "ceased to think of his home and his old friends."[30] Well, not entirely. Not while Tommaso Falcoia, who rather fancied his talent for "spiritual direction," was advising him. Alphonsus had, perhaps, seemed always to be off on a mission or busy with rectorial worries at home, too busy for Vito to have some quiet time with him. So he was writing in March 1737 for guidance on how he might come to "Union with the blessed God." Falcoia was essentially a timid man, and Vito might appear to be making a request to stagger any ordinary director. Touching the inwardest purpose of both their lives. But Falcoia knew how to handle it. He enjoyed a fine command of the appropriate rhetoric. He recommended that Vito undertake a thorough deconstruction of his past, put himself self-accusingly in the presence of "HDM," His Divine Majesty:

> For the holy fire of love of HDM purifies better than the fire of Purgatory. The continual sorrow at having offended the infinite goodness of God, purges the soul of its faults, especially the sorrow of knowing that one has never loved God, that one has not, for so many years, done the Divine Will, and the good that could have been done for His glory, and the graces lost.[31]

But Falcoia assures him, proving by this assurance that he has not understood what Vito was saying or why he has written, everything will be better, "everything will come right," as soon as Vito gets back to work:

> For this reason: the love of Jesus Christ, who has undergone such trouble for us, gives great good value to the humiliations, the works, that we have to do in the world, and you, by a special grace of the Lord, have occasions of doing and keeping on doing good for Him, so do and keep on doing, cheerfully, rendering thanks, when these occasions of penance come.[32]

Whatever this Brother's hopes of experiencing that wondrous Union, Falcoia is sure that they can be realized only by hardworking observance under the Superior's scrutiny. But that was nothing to Vito's question. He quite understood, as well and better than Falcoia, the relation which his entering the Congregation had established between duty and integrity in his life. He had been hoping that the bishop might help him discern what further demands, beyond those of duty, that the blessed God was making on him. And what further offer of integrity God was making in those demands. Vito knew that there is always the offer of intenser union.

Probably, they both supposed that Union to be a divine reward for human work. Vito, eager to please, was ready to work harder, longer. But Falcoia had at least recognized that a Brother's day was making demands enough of Christian virtue without his enthusiasm for a converted life leading to penances over and above those suggested by the Superiors. Besides, it was not helpful to the business of the Congregation if a Brother were tiring himself in works of supererrogation. Those flagellations which Vito had begun in the Sportelli house had better stop:

> Put away for now the discipline during the day and those iron chains in the morning.

So, having added this energetic coda to a rather languid piece of pious prosing, Falcoia put a quick end to this correspondence:

> I am too hurried to write more. A thousand blessings.....

Thus unadvised, Vito could only continue along the way his Superiors had first indicated, responding with alacrity to their instructions, accepting the daily occasion they would find for his humiliation.

He had very fast, Alphonsus remarked satisfiedly, come to understand his place in the Institute, "always keeping his eyes on the ground."[33] Indeed, even in letters, Vito began to sign himself as "bending the head low in sign of profound humility."[34] Thus he became "the model" of a modern Brother. Putting his total reliance on that agreement by which the Fathers had promised to make him a saint. Rather like the Gideonites who had made a treaty with Joshua and the Israelites, but quite lacking Gideonite guile, Vito hewed logs, drew water. He accepted that he was the gofer in the house. "He did not disdain to be seen carrying our dung to the garden."[35]

He did not disdain doing the shopping for them. But he did disdain walking behind the porters that he'd been told to hire to carry the shopping up from Amalfi to Scala. "If he saw that they were overcome by the weight of their burden and by the difficulty of the ascent, he would say, "Now you must rest, and I will help you," and he would take their loads from them and carry them up the mountain himself." He was *famulus* enough to find it difficult to deal with a situation in which service was done for money. "When he gave us goods to carry," the porters remembered later, "he paid us for doing it, and then carried them himself."[36] There was an inherent tension between others' expectations of their servant and his self-knowledge as the squire. He did not disdain going up "the steep mount of Scala" to fill a heavy pitcher of drinking water for the Fathers, but he did disdain complaining how exhausted he was after this unaccustomed labor. Vito became more and more sensitive to a meaning for him in Christ's service to his Father. "When he arrived back at our house, he used to kneel down before the large crucifix at the entrance porch before he had deposited his burden so that he could offer up the fatigue it had cost him to God."[37]

Taken out of the house, he was as ready to make his service on the mission an offering to God. He was ready to be summoned by a Father at any moment to hold a little catechism class or recite the rosary with a clutch of village children in the middle of a day, which had begun with his heating water at the hearth in the earliest morning and would end late at night when he gave a last sweep to the dining-room tiles.

Vito, the Brother doing the work of the *famulus,* even the menial tasks of the *servus,* remained ever the squire; he never dwindled into a poor uncritical retainer. He kept his own sharpness about him still. Once, when he was cleaning the dung out of the house latrine, a passing Father could not resist stating the obvious: "Fah! What a dreadful stench Brother!" From the rhetoric of the Fathers' sermons, Vito at once dredged up the appropriate piety. "There's a worse smell in hell, Father," he barked out, and turned back to his digging.[38] And Vito was surely doing an imitation of some reproving Father when he was overheard muttering to himself, "You may be as fussed and tired as you please, but you must do it all the same."[39] Alphonsus assumed that the good Brother must have been administering a deserved self-reproof just in case the Fathers had not administered quite enough of such things.

Fathers seem to have been regularly inept in their management of Vito. There was the time when a Rector told him to put more fruit on the refectory table, and while he was piling the bowl with oranges, the Father Minister came into the room and told him to put less fruit on the table. In this awkward situation, Vito could not think it right to offer an excusing explanation. He simply judged it better to obey his and the Minister's Superior. Next day, he was again caught putting out fruit and got himself into the Minister's bad books as a disobedient Brother who should be punished. The Minister did not think it necessary to inquire how he came to be laying out the fruit. The Brother kept his hold on his integrity and said nothing. So he was punished. Like the honorable man, like Jesus, he did not complain. At last, the Minister heard of the Rector's order. So he stopped punishing Vito. No apology, of course. The Father Minister was not perhaps quite a gentleman. Not a man of honor. "But he did admire his patience in bearing reprimands he had not merited."[40]

Another time, when a Rector could not find an important document, he asked Vito what had become of it. He, knowing that a Father had destroyed the paper in error, was not going to sneak. That was not his way. But he must tell the truth. So he said, "It must have been burnt accidentally." The Rector at once assumed that Vito was trying to conceal his own misconduct and was, as he would be with a Brother, very severe in his reprimand.[41] A Brother was expected to take such reprimands as aids to holiness.

That Vito had nothing about him of the sneak, neither reporting another's fault nor putting the blame on another when he was himself accused, must have puzzled Alphonsus. Especially when it turned out that he was being wrongly accused. Don Giuseppe's servants had evidently carried tales all the time to their irascible master and always been ready to blame one another for each domestic disaster. That was how *servi* should behave. It was how everyone should behave. "Those that are really zealous, when they perceive some disorderly conduct or want of observance, should tell it privately to the Admonitor of the house, or inform the Rector Major."[42] "I beg each one of you to make known to me all serious faults…I shall find out a remedy."[43] "I beg each and all of you to write and tell me sincerely the faults you may have remarked in any of our young men."[44] "Brother Cesare should be careful to note who murmurs and complains and then report the matter."[45]

Vito's disinclination to squeal was, therefore, rather irritating to Alphonsus' mind. He would have to take him in hand, it seemed. Show him what was expected of a Brother.

The Helpful Mystic of Helfta

Just as Alphonsus fixed on Aloysius as the paradigm student and expected the young men of the Congregation to observe and imitate his particular virtues, so he fixed on Paschal Baylon, 1540–1592, the Alcantarine Friar, as paradigm Brother. "God wills that a Brother should be sanctified like a Saint Paschal."[46] The Franciscan had been beatified in 1618 by Paul V, canonized in 1690 by Alexander VIII, and had a rather greater fame in the next seventy-five years than later. Alphonsus was forever talking about this saint, recommending others, including his own father, to read his exemplary *Life*.[47] It was this talk which encouraged Giuseppe and Angiolo, two of the men at his Chapel Evenings, to become Brothers in the Alcantarine friary at Saint Lucia del Monte, down by the old fisheries of Lucullus.[48] And, it is to be noted, his recommendation of the saint was not on account of any exemplary eagerness for manual labor but of Paschal's intense self-forgetting response to the mystery of Christ's Passion. "At the thought of the death of Jesus, each of us should be, as it were, foolish for the love of Him, and should exclaim with S Paschal "My love has been crucified for me; my love has died for me."[49]

Vito made that cry very much his own. And later, when other Brothers came into the Congregation, he encouraged them to make it their own also. When he talked of the Passion, the Blood, the Death of Christ, "they had to listen." When he talked of the infinite Mercy of God manifest in Christ's death, "it was amazing to hear."[50] The Brothers knew that Vito was a great reader. But the Fathers, hearing a rumor of such conversations on such topics among the Brothers, agreed that Vito, if the rumor were true at all, must have been granted some "supernatural knowledge" by "divine infusion," since no Brother could have the natural intelligence to understand these deep matters.[51]

Vito was as capable of writing as of reading for himself. He wrote to Falcoia for advice on how he should deal with his resentments against a couple of difficult Fathers. Not thinking it to be at all impertinent thus to approach a bishop, though acknowledging what politeness demanded between gentlemen. Falcoia was as courteous as ever in his reply. And rather more direct than was his custom:

> Your letters do not trouble me, on the contrary they are a great consolation; so write freely to me whenever you have the opportunity.
>
> Concerning this doubt about which you have written to me, I answer: it does not please me that you should be put in a tizzy by these tiresome irritations, and I wish that you would accustom yourself in all things to the Divine Will, and I desire you to be at peace under the Divine Eyes; that will be, I want you to know, practically, what pleases Him.

Whoever was getting to him, about the fruit, the latrines, the eucharistic conversations, Falcoia, who was always at his best and sensible when advising good worried men, required Vito to remain calmly assured that God loved him:

> You should know that when works are done with the good aim of blessing God you have been well inspired: so do stay at peace.[52]

This time, Falcoia was not in such a hurry to bless him and be off. He was ready to take an interest in Vito:

> I wish, however, to know all the Devotions that you practice, and I will lay down how you are to order them more certainly.

It was a couple of months before Vito could find time and energy at the end of a Brother's working day to collect his thoughts, obtain paper and pen, and respond to Falcoia's invitation. As one gentleman to another he begins his letter with a nice deployment of Falcoia's ceremonious language:

> May God be blessed always for the kind charity that your Most Illustrious Lordship uses with me despite my disturbing your peace with my pesterings. I hope in the Lord that HD Majesty in his mercy will grant you His Holy Blessings in all that tends to His Glory and to the good of Your Most Illustrious Lordship;

but then he means that they should get down to business:

> I want to know if the method that I use at present will assist my going forward in the Spirit.

Vito is keeping the Rule, to the letter, doing exactly what he is told, and yet…

> I do not progress as I ought, but seem still to be full of passions, giving way to a love of self, and….

He's finding it surprisingly difficult to express the sort of struggle he is having with himself, but he knows from those old pistol-packing days, that he's truly got a fight on:

> I see things clearly which I cannot say.[53]

He's actually saying loud and clear that he doesn't want to be told that doing good works will get him as far forward in the Spirit as he is called to go.

Vito wants to fulfill his potential. To be that saint that Alphonsus had said he could be. He knows just what such a saint is like. He's been talking to saints. Perhaps Falcoia will be able to make better sense of him if he simply set out his personal litany. This list of the saints Vito is keeping in his morning, noon, and night prayers should convey something of both his experience and his aspirations, for it comprises both those saints who have been helpful to him in the past and those whom he now hopes will help him as he struggles to emulate their peculiar virtues.

In the morning, after kneeling arms at the outstretch, to recite *Pater Noster, Ave Maria,* and *Gloria Patri,* five times each, Vito seeks the protection of Saint Vito, his Guardian Angel, Saints John of the Cross and Teresa of Ávila, Saint Gertrude, and the saints whose feasts fall that month. In the evening, after the rosary, he is thanking Saint Joseph, Saint Michael the Archangel and his colleague Saint Raphael, Saint Benedict, Saints Gioacchino and Anna, Saint Paschal Baylon, Saints Mary Magdalene and Martha, Saint Francesco de Paola, and all the saints.[54]

Expectedly, Vito puts Saint Vito in first place among those morning saints. His baptismal exemplar had, as a boy, fled from Sicily to Italy. This was at the start of the fourth century. Vito would have known that his saint was heir to a respectable, educated, family. That he had an angry father who was ready enough to take a whip to him. That it was only by his nurse's prayerful care that he was kept from worse treatment.[55] So far, not unlike himself, his irritated father, and Donna Maria Anna Sportelli at Acquaviva. Alphonsus is likely, when they were alone together at Scala, the pair of them constituting the Congregation, to have reminisced not only about that Curzio in the *S Alessio* opera of the Oratory Young Nobility but also about that patronal Saint Vito whose affecting martyrdom had been the subject of another of Pasquini's Oratory melodramas. This had told, in thrilling baroque periods, the story of Vito's saint's Christian adventures in Lucania, the Emperor Diocletian's order for his racking on the iron horse, and the spectacular descent of an *angelus ex machina* to carry him to heaven.[56] Vito would have this theatrical anecdote as well as the local history to encourage his devotion. He would be happy, too, at the widespread celebration of his saint's special power to quieten those afflicted with Saint Vito's Dance. Such a saint was assuredly capable of quieting him when some disturbing thought of injured honor crossed his mind.

Along with his baptismal saint and his Guardian Angel, who had got him out of several nasty scrapes in Acquaviva, and with the Lady and Saint Joseph to whom all Catholics are praying, Vito puts patrons whom he has accumulated at significant moments of his Christian life. Every member of the Congregation would have been made aware very soon after meeting Alphonsus that he was exuberantly devoted to Saint Teresa of Ávila and eager that they should enjoy this devotion themselves. But Vito's keeping up his prayers to Saint John of the Cross along with Saint Teresa is a sign of his personal delight in the poetry of mysticism, a taste he shared with Falcoia and Sportelli rather than with Alphonsus.[57]

With Alphonsus' patroness in the morning, Vito gives proper place to Falcoia's chief patron, Saint Michael the Archangel, in his night prayers. The bishop would have expected everyone in the Institute to put himself under his own saint, but Vito's devotion is most likely to have begun as a child at Acquaviva on visits to the neighbor shrine of the warrior angel at San Michele di Bari. Vito's experience on Procida might well also have encouraged him to keep Saint Michael on his side in later life. He evidently had good enough memories of the Abbey on the island's hill to bring Saint Benedict along as well. His praying to Saint Raphael alongside Saint Michael may suggest that Vito was remembering the story of that great angel's care for Tobias on his journey. A Brother might well feel, as he shook the mattresses, bought the vegetables, cooked the meal, swept the rooms, when he was accompanying a troop of missioners, that he had taken on Saint Raphael's guarding role for the traveling Fathers, and that it would, therefore, be sensible to ask for his experienced assistance.

With these Archangels, Vito gives his devotion to Saints Gioacchino and Anna, the Lady's parents, each bringing the other along, doubtless, in married companionableness, but each also having a singular claim on his prayers. Anna as not only the popular patroness of everyone in his home district but as the saint so often invoked to protect him by Maria Anna Sportelli. Gioacchino as the patron of the latest Brother to whom Vito must be a decent Christian dragoman. And both together, again, as the protectors of Paschal who, entering a sickroom, would say, "May Jesus, Mary, and Joseph, Joachim and Anna, and Catherine cure you of every ill and deliver you from all pain."[58] Saint Paschal, 1540–1592, himself is, of course, included in the litany primarily on account of Alphonsus' so emphatically proposing him to the Brothers.[59] But Vito had come to value for himself this Brother's loving exposition of eucharistic faith. Paschal is a night-prayers saint because Vito was usually making his meditation on some element of Paschal's devotions the evening before those mornings that the Brother Master set for Brothers to go to Communion.

He would be taking the repentant Magdalene to be his proper protectress, not simply on his self-estimate of his sinfulness but in recognition of the enjoyable times he'd had at home and in Naples later with Cesare Sportelli. She was Sportelli's chosen saint.[60] Vito would assume that this Mary Magdalene was the sister of Saints Martha and Lazarus of Bethany, and his putting the two sisters together represents the general assumption that their dual care would be most appropriate for the Brother who, from sitting in the chapel in meditative attendance on the Lord, comes into the kitchen to be busy about many things.

That pairing of patronesses was a commonplace of the Brother Masters' addresses.[61] From Vito's devotion to Saint Francesco de Paola, 1416–1483, and to Saint Gertrude, 1253–1302, we may learn something of his personal appreciation of the Brothers' vocation. It is most especially in his establishing them among the saints of this personal litany that Vito manifests his Christian freedom within the Congregation.[62]

Alphonsus does not seem to have had any special devotion to Saint Francesco. Indeed, it appears that he and Falcoia quite deliberately removed this saint's name from Celeste Crostarosa's litany when they were revising the Redemptoristine Rule for men's use.[63] Nevertheless, anyone in the kingdom, and certainly those whom Vito met when he came to the western coast, would have been ready to tell him the story of the young hermit from Paola, a smallish town in Calabria, halfway from Naples to Reggio. The solitary had found himself, at nineteen years of age, the founder of a religious order which, in accord with his petition to the Pope in 1474, took the quaintly humbling title of "Minims." Thus Alphonsus' continual reference to the Redemptorists as "this least" of Orders was forestalled. Forestalled and quite conclusively undercut. For this was an Order consisting mainly of lay Brothers. Among the first Minims very few enjoyed the distinction of the priest. One, perhaps two, in each group would be, Francesco knew, enough to enable a liturgy. He himself, Corrector General of over four hundred houses in Italy, Spain, France, and Germany, had not been ordained.[64] This, together with his championing the eremitical life, must make him and his Rule irrelevant to Alphonsus' plannings for a company of secular priest missioners. But it was as a Brother among Brothers that Francesco made his appeal to Vito.

Vito had been a lawless gunman, taking potshots up and down main street whenever the fancy took him. But he was now signed up as a regular soldier under Christ's discipline. Francesco de Paola spoke to Vito as a fellow serviceman.[65] In the saint's cry "Love! Love! Love!"[66] Vito heard a colonel's rallying cry, calling his men to love their sovereign. "We live," Saint Francesco declared to his Brothers, "in the midst of military combat" against the world and its notion of honor, "all the Brothers, cleric and lay alike, are fighting men, under the flag of poverty."[67] There were fine soldierly examples for Vito in the brave history of Brother Andrea Pepoli, 1536–1621, "the glory of Naples," and, into his own time, in the stories he'd hear of the Calabrese Brother Nicola Saggio, 1650–1709. These were Brothers in arms.

It was as a man with more than a touch of the soldier about him that Vito had come to appreciate Saint Gertrude in her Helfta abbey fortress, near Eisleben in Saxony.[68] There was something of the "cutting edge" in his invoking a saint to whom modern writers were only just beginning to refer. It was only in 1677 that the uncanonized Gertrude had been put into the Roman Martyrology and given a proper feast day. It was only in 1710 that her sayings had been republished in Italian translation. Her local cult had not been extended to the whole Church until 1738, a year after Vito forwarded his litany to Falcoia.

Alphonsus has quotations from the Italian translation of Gertrude's sayings at a great many significant places in his writing, not only in the expectable *True Bride,* 1760, but in the *Love of Souls,* 1751, the *Brief Tract on the Necessity of Prayer,* 1757, *The Great Means of Prayer,* 1759, the *Practice of the Love of Jesus Christ,* 1768, the *Reflections on the Passion,* 1773, and the *Way of Salvation,* 1776.[69] These suggest in their variousness and in their plentifulness that his conversation in community room for over a quarter a century was peppered with references to Gertrude. Over half a century, perhaps, since there had been a knowing reference to the saint in Alphonsus' very first sermon as a deacon in April 1726.[70] There's a likelihood, therefore, that he was mentioning her to his Procida confraternity as he explained, in just Gertrude's language, how it was that through being brothers of the firstborn Jesus Christ they were all of them secondborn sons of Mary.

Modest chaplains may have repeated the great man's sermon in later years. Vito may have been enrolled as a member of the Confraternity while he was on the island. But he did not need a sermon from Alphonsus, then or later, to introduce him to Gertrude's writing. He was quite capable of picking up her *Life* and her *Messenger of Divine Duty* on one of the many Naples bookstalls.[71]

On his turning the opening pages, he would have been at once attracted by Gertrude's autobiographical relation of a dream, very much like his own, of wanting to come to the Lord and finding her way blocked. In Gertrude's dream, a high hedge keeps her apart from Christ. "Then I paused to weep over my faults and offenses which were plainly figured by this thorn hedge which divided us."[72] But the Lord reaches out his hand to her and lifts her over and she is with him. Only then does she see the bloody wound on his hand. He has had to push through thorns to reach her and bring her to him. The Passion of the Lord is here being appreciated as community-forming. Gertrude is to take her place in a chain of human reachers, hand holding onto hand, from the Lord who holds her hand, through each Helfta nun, Very Reverend Mother Abbess to the newest postulant, As community-forming beyond their abbey walls. Each nun's vocation has its reference into the wide world. All at Helfta are to hold out hands, sometimes deeply wounded hands to those on the other side of every hedge. To those on the other side of the hedge between living and dead. Making her prayers for one of those Brothers who had died while working on the Abbey building, she had a kind conversation with him. Brother Hermann was assuring her that he was very happy to have her join hands in prayer with him. Living and dead, in the convent and without, we are all one company. In a vision of the heavenly fellowship, Gertrude perceived that "those who had humbly recommended themselves to the prayers of others took hands as they were all going along together."[73]

As he read, Vito would recognize, too, that Gertrude was talking of that company of Christians as a troop of those same fighting men who figured in Saint Francesco de Paola's account of the Brothers militant. This is always the language to help him as he puts his energies to discipline himself, disabuse himself of every remnant of the tendency to freebooter rowdiness, place himself wholly under the command of the King of Glory along with the other Brothers, "*fratelli servienti.*"

Gertrude was using a language natural to the Helfta nun. The community was in continual apprehension of some local baron's plundering their property, some traveling brigand's burning down their walls. Gertrude and the others put a high value on the protection offered by the Abbess' brothers, whose seigneurial authority made it possible for good order to be maintained outside the walls and good praise, therefore, to be sung within to the Lord, "our most lovable brother."

So Gertrude's sense of Christ's love is gracefully expressed in the military forms of everything she says about the Lord's Crucifix at the head of a convent procession being the Standard "behind which marches a whole army," about the Lord's appointing his Mother as Commander of an angelic task force and the Lady's "setting a choir of Powers to surround the abbey as a guard battalion," and about these angels "obeying orders and shutting their shields together to form a barricade on all sides." She writes of her prayers as a campaign to bring women and men to the Lord's camp and of his receiving these converts from her "as a king would receive a prince who brought his enemies to his feet to swear obedience and inviolable fidelity to him."[74] She writes of those reliable Brothers who were doing the heavy work on the Abbey estate as the community's first line of defense. There was much in her meditations to excite Vito and much to steady him as others were packing their bags.

Like Francesco de Paola, Gertrude, as he read, was letting Vito know more about his Brothers in arms along the whole front of the Church. About their army record. Their final parade. She was again and again allowed to see Brothers at the very gates of their King. She'd seen war-weary Brother John, who had been the Abbey estate manager, stumbling on the step of heaven and being steadied by the prayers of those yet living in the Abbey.[75] More human still is Gertrude's eagerness to do something fast for old Brother Theobald "who had labored faithfully for the community for so many years" and had died in their herb garden, bent double as if carrying too heavy a pack. She understood from the Lord that if the community persevered earnestly in their prayers for him, he'd soon be standing up straight. Able to do press-ups even. "When the nuns prostrated themselves on the stone floor, he in spirit prostrated himself with the community, thanking God for having given him the privilege of living in so holy a place, where his labors had been specially blessed."[76] And then there was the veteran Brother Sequentus, who had died all forgotten when she was busy about other matters. She reproached herself for her neglect, and prayed the more strongly that the Lord would reward "one who had always served the community faithfully and affectionately as a lay Brother." And the Lord told her that he had already cheered this Brother by the remembrances of having so often done good, and of the pleasures he given to others, "when handing a toy to a child, a penny to a beggar, an apple to a peckish nun," and, climactically, "I have made him rejoice exceedingly in my approval of what he has done." At last, Gertrude shifts into a celebration of the lay Brother's life as leading to that wondrous Union with the divine for which Vito was longing. The Lord tells her simply: "I will supply all he needs, he will be perfectly happy, he will be with me."[77]

Gertrude has that same desire to be dissolved and to be with God. A trooper cannot, of course, choose the battle in which she shall die. It must be enough, it is enough that her commander-in-chief is with her in all battles. Every one of us is to be experiencing "this union of sweetness this sweetness of union" which the Lord is offering. She points out to us all how we may come into this union:

> Neither all my defects nor all my unworthiness prevented You from honoring me with Your Presence nearly every day, when I received the life-giving nourishment of Your Body and Your Blood.
>
> You were endeavoring by this kind easiness to attract my soul so that I might be wholly united to You, that I might know You better and enjoy You more fully.[78]

Nothing should come between them now that Christ has reached out so wonderfully. When the Helfta confessor was delayed in deep snowdrifts, Gertrude said that they should all, confident in Christ's forgiving love, receive Communion. And afterwards, the Lord came and told her that she had done just what he would have her do. More, the Lord told Gertrude, as she tells the nuns, to "pray with confidence," "doing me such violence that I cannot but heed you in all that you seek." Alphonsus had been made a little nervous by Gertrude's talk of "such violence." He had, when quoting the passage, thought it best to add a parenthetical diminution of the nun's too forceful language: "(in a certain sense)."[79]

Then he hurried on. But Vito could see in her account of the Lord a suggestion of how he might convert that element in his nature which had erupted at the duel with the lawyer and the potshot at the noncommissioned officer. Doing Christ such violence in his prayer for perfecting Union, Vito came to appreciate what violence he must do himself.

Not the physical violence of those iron chains which still figured in his correspondence with Falcoia. Vito was learning, as he read Gertrude's account of her experience with the Lord, that, if he were ever to come into that Union which would realize his true integrity, he must surrender not only those noisy "*Passioni*" against which Falcoia had conventionally warned him,[80] but that gallant "*amor proprio*" by which he had preserved some silent self-respect when others in the house were exercising their own passions for knowing better and giving orders. "I require nothing other from you," the Lord had said to Gertrude, "than that you should come to me empty of yourself."[81] So it was, taking this to heart, that that tension in his vocation as squire and as servant was brought to a shuddering halt at the eucharistic celebration. He was, in his meditations, made violently aware that, as he emptied himself of whatever was self-regarding in the squire, he was redeemed from whatever was servile in the servant; he had, as already frater, a communion in the Lord.

"He was so enlightened during meditation," Alphonsus recorded, "and his feelings so sensibly affected that he could not help bursting into tears and sobbing to such a degree that it seemed as if the violence of his love for God would suffocate him."[82] Serving at a Father's Mass, Vito shook with devotion, "especially when he was to receive Holy Communion," so that the priest "would have to wait some time before he could receive the Sacred Host."[83]

That shaking, at which the Fathers marveled, might have been a merely momentary response, an expression of passing passion. But, held within that Union all day long, Vito was being brought into that desirable integrity. He was enabled to respond unifiedly to the great call, "Love! Love! Love!" in devotion to his eucharistic King, in persevering kitchen service within the Congregation, and in eagerness to reach his helping hand to any who could not help themselves.

His old Acquaviva friend, Cesare Sportelli, falling into a dangerous fever, Vito felt an irresistible urge to do something, anything; he placed his own mattress under the patient's own, doubling what comfort the thin palliasse afforded. He from that time slept on the bare wooden floorboards.[84] That was an act of kindness for a friend. Everyone, says Jesus rather exaggeratingly, would be ready to do such a thing for a friend. Vito came to have equal care for the stranger in the house. He once offered to suck the pus from a dirty beggar's wound and had to be restrained by a more health-conscious Father. He learned to discipline even these impulses. Alphonsus made a note of "the attentiveness of Brother Vito to a secular priest who was taken ill in the guts at our Ciorani house," remarking that he had not once had to censure him for any over-enthusiasm. This stranger, like the beggar, was not naturally attractive. He suffered from an offensive malady. He stank. Yet Vito stayed in the sickroom day and night. For twenty days and nights. Feeding him, lifting him from the bed, cleaning him. Praying with him.[85] That he remained with "his dear invalid" even though the rest of them were in chapel, at the Maundy Thursday liturgy, shows that in Vito's apprehension, community observance, the eucharistic celebration of the Lord, service in the Congregation's infirmary and the needs of a neighbor, were held in one coadunating mystery. Love is Love is Love. Gertrude was as clear a declarer of that unifying charity as Saint Francesco. One day "she desired to entertain herself in prayer but a work of charity was to be performed," so the Lord said she had a choice, "Tell me, Gertrude, do you intend that I should serve you or that you should serve me?"[86] Vito knew her answer must be his answer.

"You in your turn ought to wash one another's feet." As that Maundy Thursday liturgy was suggesting, there is a Christian reciprocity in all such charity. Vito himself was taken ill and received the kindest attention from a secular priest.

Late on a July night in 1745, returning from Troia, where Alphonsus had sent him begging, on account of their having so little money left for food, Vito got himself as far as the gates of d'Iliceto town, about six miles from the Redemptorist house. He was exhausted. It was dark. Beginning to rain. He applied to a local monastery for a night's lodging. But he looked so much like his old pistol-packing self in his dusty patched jacket that the respectable Benedictines were alarmed and shut their door against him. It was raining much more heavily now. But that was not their worry. Vito, having struggled some way further along the street, was forced from sheer exhaustion to lie down to sleep.[87] His eagerness to do whatever the Fathers wanted had led him to endanger his health often enough before this. Perhaps he thought that his habit of going sockless and shoeless as he worked in the vegetable garden, and of never wearing a hat in winter or summer, had hardened him against all that the local climate might do.[88] He had, certainly, gone through a whole winter without anyone's noticing that he had not been given an allocation of warmer clothes when summer ended.[89] But this was malaria country.[90] So it was not surprising that obediently resuming his journey in the early morning he almost at once collapsed at the gate of the town with the shivers. There, he was found by a secular priest coming from saying the first Mass of the day in the parish church. This good man took him up in his arms and carried him home to his presbytery.[91] Vito was a long time ill. Forty-nine days and nights. Then, being asked by his kind but inexpert carer whether he wanted to go on living or was ready to die, he had Gertrude's answer. "I wish only what God wishes," he replied resignedly, "But if I am given the choice, I should prefer to die."[92] The good priest asked him if, before the Holy Viaticum was administered, he would like to go to confession. Vito was still able to keep alive Gertrude's sense of the Lord and the communicant. "By God's grace," he murmured, "I have no need to confess." No strength left for those violent tears as he received Communion this time. Exhausted in service, he could go, like Gertrude still, to meet the Lord as his commending commanding officer, assuredly, but now, as she said, "face to face, as friend to dear friend."[93] He died in the good man's house, on September 18, 1745.

The Fathers came at once to claim their Brother. The body was carried across the fields to the Redemptorist church, escorted by the parish clergy, the local confraternities, and a large crowd of townsfolk assuring one another that "a saint is dead."[94]

Tannoia recorded that at the d'Iliceto house church, Alphonsus, singing the Requiem Mass, had now and again to pause, breaking into affecting tears for their Brother.[95] "Will tears shed for you through human affection do you any harm?" Gertrude had asked solicitously. "Not at all," Brother Hermann replied, "these tears are to me as the kindnesses of a friend who consoles his friend when he's afflicted; and when I come into perfect happiness, they will go on giving me as much joy as any congratulations or welcoming applause from those I love."[96] He added, as Alphonsus would have expected Vito to add, "I have merited this consolation by my faithfulness in your service."

The final prayer having been said, the crypt stone having been raised, the body having been lifted from the bier, things suddenly went at a faster pace. Everyone was eager to have a relic before the stone was shut down again. Not only the enthusiastically canonizing townsfolk. Monsignore Amato, bishop of Lacedogna, grabbed Vito's skull. He kept it on his prie-dieu for the next twenty years.[97]

In the Congregation, Vito's chief relic was the living memory later Brothers kept of his exemplary integrity. The first Brother had shown them what was entailed in vows of utter hardihood, utter faithfulness, and utter obedience to their King. What it meant to be keeping a brave face for him in all their troubling service, to come through life with him in eucharistic companionship, and, on his account, for love of him, to sustain an order of prayer and work. Whatever the Fathers were requiring of them, they knew now that they were their King's squires. They were to be, every one of them, after Vito, men of Christian honor.

The Brothers especially noted that Vito had nothing about him of the sneak. It became received wisdom among them that a Christian gentleman does not carry tales of another. And does not demean himself, if some tale has been carried about him, by offering a defense. Whether the accusation be true or false. The good Brother will understand simply that his being "a living copy of Jesus Christ" is most perfectly exhibited in his maintaining an honorable silence before his accusers. Whatever the reproof. "He never makes excuses."[98]

Gennaro Rendina

Apostle-like in their conviction that it would not be right for them to neglect the word of God in order to wait at tables, the Fathers were interviewing candidates without offering any precise job description of the Brother in the Congregation. Certainly it was not long before they were taking that account of the Brothers occupying the places of deacons in their apostolic mission to be not much more than a piece of pious fiction. Nevertheless, generous men came in numbers to offer themselves for the work.

Their rules for the reception of Brothers enjoined Rectors to ensure they did not encourage the ambitions of bastards, of introspective grousers, of those who would beg off work on account of some tubercular cough. There was in the first of these regulations a surprising parallel to the barrier erected against bastards at the Naples Law School.[1] Was the design that it should be as bourgeoisly respectable to enroll as a brother in "the College at d'Iliceto" as in the College of Doctors? And was there, at least at first, before the foundations in the Papal States, an unstated but effective barrier against foreigners, as at Alphonsus' old College? Perhaps that was what was meant by the Fathers' requirement that Brothers be "of decent parentage," "*onesti natali.*"

Certainly, the Fathers quickly became rather too choosy among the candidates who knocked at their doors. In 1746, Antonio Lauro, 1723–1763, applying to Rector Rossi at Ciorani was at first judged to be too short. However, a glance at the diminutive Cafaro must render this objection rather weak. Antonio insisted. He had at first been caught between the desire for a pleasing wife, the attractions of pop music, and the virtues of life among the Camaldolese. But having at least put aside thoughts of a wife and started to consider seriously a future among holy men, he had heard a mission given by the Fathers at Lanzara and been so attracted by their tone that he'd exclaimed "These are the ones, there's no other Order for me!"[2]

Perhaps it was on account of his ignoring Antonio's shortness that that year Alphonsus discovered some of the Fathers, Villani among them, plotting to withdraw the Rector Major's authority to grant any dispensation in the matter of the qualifications of novice Brothers. He was, he told Sportelli, determined to fight "these gentlemen." It involved, after all, "a matter of conscience" for him. He must have entire freedom. He'd have the Chapter postponed if any such limit of the Rector Major's powers seemed likely to be discussed, let alone voted.[3]

Besides that quibble about height, Fathers were proposing other barriers. In 1749, Paolo Amato was almost rejected on account of his not having brought bedsheets with him. It had, after all, been insisted in one of Alphonsus' own first jottings of "constitutions" that "those who enter must bring their clothing and twelve sheets."[4] But Paolo was sure he had found his vocation. "I had to be enrolled within the company of Don Alphonsus, this institute then being born in the world, and known even by me for the great reputation it was gathering for holiness." He proved in this opinion too stubborn to be kept away. Told by Carmine Fiocchi, 1721–1776, to come back in a fortnight, he returned punctually to the minute. Told to come back in another fortnight, he did so just as punctually. "After this, I returned about six times." The Fathers decided that he'd do for them at Ciorani. "In the end, I was received on October 23, 1749."

Paolo Amato had been a rough-house brawler. Doubtless, the Fathers intended those forthrightly delays to be a test of the lad's having quieted down enough to be their houseman. But Paolo very well knew the difference of domestic *servus* from Brother. He had the larger service in mind that October day. He had become the *famulus* of Christ. "The Lord took me up and by his infinite mercy, praised ever be the Lord, I shall persevere to the death in the place where he put me."[5]

As the number of places and jobs to do in those places increased, the Fathers were, however, being brought to ask a few questions. About the range of jobs appropriate for Brothers to do. They could never, obviously be appointed Rectors or Preachers, but could they, without derogation of the Fathers' status, be Bursars or Schoolmasters? And about the interchangeability of Brothers. They could not do a Father's job but could they be expected to do one another's jobs? Should the Rector Major or the Rector of a house take into account some quirk of talent of a Brother when assignments were being made? Some individual Brother might, evidently, have an individual skill. Nicola Casoria, 1725–1765, was thought by several Fathers, on account of the boy's coming from a decent family, to be unsuited to physical labor, but he had gotten hold of some knowledge of potions and remedies from his druggist father. Mattia Fazzano, 1735(?)–1795, was dextrous in the dismantling and rebuilding of a faulty clock.[6] Stefano Sperduto, 1725–1805, was quite a good enough carpenter to be esteemed a cabinetmaker.[7] But should the Superior simply establish such a Brother in the infirmary or horological workshop or leave him to finish the vestment press and the altar of Saint Stanislaus in his own time? Might there not be a wisdom in shifting this Brother from job to job, just like the rest of them?

These were not entirely new questions. They had arisen on the arrival in 1734, of Gennaro Rendina, 1708–1789, from Naples. They continued all his time with the Congregation, right up to his death. For Gennaro was a civilizing conversationalist, ready with a curiosity of history to enliven the evening's report of a dull day, and a practical man, as ready to get on with any job in the house.

There was a hint of difficulty at the very start. On Alphonsus' seeking Falcoia's written approval for continuing to talk with Gennaro about entry to the Institute, the bishop was uncharacteristically circumspect:

> I know we have talked about him but I can't remember in what sense. I want some factual information. When it comes, I'll reply. Especially you must give me some more assured notice of his age, talents, virtues, health, birth, etc., and either that you are sure of his vocation or that you suspect the contrary,and what studies he's made.[8]

That question of studies was to prove important in the review of Gennaro's fitness for their needs. Vito had the gifts of a man of business, an estate manager, capable of recognizing when a laborer was overworked or underworking, when an agent was creaming off an excessive amount in his bookkeeping. These were practical skills, well suited to the Brother's proper occupations among them. Gennaro was a quite different sort of man. Everyone was telling them so. He was "a good example," Don Pietro

Strozzi, his parish priest, attested, "to all his neighbors," "a good living man," "frequenting the Sacraments," just the sort to be a fine seminarian.[9] Yet, given the already large number of clergy in their diocese, there could be no question of Gennaro, or the like-situated Filippo Vito, being accepted for the priesthood. In these reformist times, when Tridentine regulations were being more religiously observed than before, no bishop would agree to ordaining a man so obviously in excess of local requirements. It was a further consideration that Francesco and Maddalena Rendina, the boy's parents, could not afford to provide him with a patrimony.

Realizing the likely difficulties, Filippo Vito went away. Gennaro, however, stayed and applied to be a Brother. "He is not displeasing," Falcoia wrote to Alphonsus, May 8, 1734, "If you have need of another Brother, you could well take this one."[10]

Alphonsus had no doubts about receiving Gennaro. The young man had been encouraged to apply not only by Don Pietro Strozzi but also by Don Francesco de Viva, who was himself, all through the summer of 1734, in an indecision about joining the new Institute.[11] Alphonsus had no need to encourage young Gennaro. Only to forward thanks to his self-sacrificing parents for sending them such a fine boy. "Leave word at the house of the Rendina that their Gennaro is content, and that I love him as my own brother. Live Jesus and Mary!"[12]

Meanwhile, Falcoia was making some simple practical arrangements. "For now, he can sleep in the room with the other Brother, but not in the same bed."[13]

Not every question was so quickly answered. There might be no great harm in accepting this Brother of decent family and some education to whom it had been explained that such things would gain him no exemptions from hard work in kitchen and field. But what if this bright young recruit got it into his head that he'd like a bit more learning? Falcoia had been absolutely clear about preventing a Brother from being educated above his station. "Do not put to studying those who are accepted to be lay Brothers, that would be destructive of Community life, stirring up grumbles and all sorts of disorder."[14] His experience in the Pious Workers preserved him from such a category mistake.[15] So the new Institute's rules would make it plain that "a youngster who wishes to become a lay Brother may become a saint in his proper place, but he's not to be put in a priest's place."[16]

"Well, do you want to be a saint?" Alphonsus had asked Gennaro when he first presented himself, "If so, you are welcome."[17] But the difficulty persisted of discerning how to define the Brother's peculiar way of becoming a saint in the midst of the diverse calls upon the Institute. "I rejoice," Falcoia wrote, "that Gennaro is well behaved. I bless him from my heart."[18] But then that education got in the way again. The priests had assured the Scala people that they would set up a town school. Alphonsus had thought of honoring this pledge by employing the literate and numerate Gennaro as a teacher between his kitchen and garden jobs. "My dear son, I'm not at all pleased that a Brother should be mixed up in this business with the school."[19] It would just be a sorry mixture of temptations for him. "He'd be bound to get sick of teaching." The enterprise would collapse. They would all be in bad odor with the townsfolk. Then, there was the matter of Gennaro's status on the street. He could not be called "Reverend," because he was not a cleric and was not going to be. And there was the difficulty of his status in the classroom. Only Don Saverio should be called "Master." Perhaps a Brother might be "Assistant." No, better Gennaro be introduced to the children and their parents as "a student teacher."[20] Best that he should not be in school at all.

Nevertheless, Alphonsus went ahead with the school at Scala. Don Saverio Rossi, 1706–1758, who had only been approved by Falcoia in hope he would become "more mature" one day, was put in place as headmaster. Gennaro was to assist with the teaching of reading and writing and history.[21] A dozen or so families sent their children to class but no one in the town made any move to pay the teacher or the student teacher. This was all the more vexing when there were so many calling for Alphonsus to establish houses in their areas. So, though not for the reasons he had alleged, the schoolroom scheme collapsed as Falcoia had foretold. Alphonsus, March 5, 1736, took both Rossi and Gennaro, who had come to be firm friends, with him to found the Ciorani house.[22] Falcoia, along with the pleasure of knowing that what he had said would happen had happened, had the happiness of reporting good things of their new man, and in redeploying that language which Alphonsus had known would content him. "I have received a letter from P. D. Alphonsus," he wrote to Sportelli, "who tells us that the rose of D. Gennaro is flowering."[23]

Not everyone was so delighted. There were, even then, those who did not at all care for a Brother's so clearly demonstrating his potential. They made this plain to him. In June 1736 Gennaro went to see their Father. "Brother Rendina," Falcoia wrote to Alphonsus, "was much troubled about his vocation. Show him some sign of good will and confidence," and added with a hint of rebuke at Alphonsus' mode of governing the Community, "It displeases me that he should have had to come to me. I don't say more."[24]

But if Gennaro's educated presence among the Brothers was felt to be somehow disruptive, it had to be allowed that Alphonsus could not have contemplated so literary a vocation for himself if Gennaro had not been available as a copyist, proofreader, and general office gofer.[25] Alphonsus, in a rush to prepare a sermon, wrote to Sarnelli, who had requested copies of a bundle of Alphonsus' little writings, "I told Brother Gennaro to copy the Canticles because I really cannot do it myself. But I'll revise them."[26] Gennaro could keep rudimentary accounts, too. "I have already received the twenty carlins," Alphonsus wrote to Margotta in the midst of another shuffle about book prices and Mass intentions and stipends, "and Brother Gennaro's list of the twenty Masses."[27] Still, better, generally, the Fathers thought, to keep him down at the vegetable patch. "It would be good," Francesco Garzillo, 1690–1786, supposed, as he looked at the rows of cabbages, "to get him a spade to dig out those lanky weeds."[28] Mostly, though, Gennaro was told to boil the cabbages.[29]

A Good Cook, As Cooks Go

In the Congregation's kitchens, from the first rough place allotted Vito in the Casa Anastasia at Scala, everything was articulating, shouting, poverty. No Brother would be able to boast the equippedness of his shelves and cupboards. The spoons and forks were of iron, the drinking cups, plates, dishes, of common earthenware.[30] "He heard that Father Carminiello Fiocchi had bought pewter dishes for the d'Iliceto house in place of the earthenware ones; he immediately wrote to him telling him to sell all these new dishes. It was in vain that diverse reasons were alleged for keeping them, and that he was told that since the earthenware dishes broke easily and the house was far from a pottery, they actually cost more."[31]

On these rough plates were served rougher meals. Alphonsus was notorious for his carelessness in the matter of food. And for something more deliberate. "On missions pay attention to the food. What aids us to make our missions give great edification is that we are satisfied with the little that the Rule permits in accordance with what has been our practice up to now. During the time of the mission I absolutely forbid the eating of chicken."[32] This was a matter of principle. "If now we begin to relax in this, we shall in a short time relax in everything." They might have a little cheese. This was not always a delicacy, however. "At the mission of Salerno, they had every day a rancid cheese, and a Father took the liberty of asking the Brother to roast his morsel. Alphonsus immediately reprimanded him, "though he was an old man and a zealous missioner."[33]

On the other hand, those who came to make retreats in a Redemptorist house should not have anything to complain about their meals. No sense distracting them from the good that the retreat was promoting. And returning missioners might have their plates piled higher with the usual community stodge.[34]

Even under this strict oversight, a Brother might distinguish himself in the kitchen. It was noted that Gennaro's personableness was a great help to him and to them all in their dealings with tradespeople. The meat, fish, vegetable, sellers who came to the back door found him much more affable to them than the Fathers. Liked him. Even to lowering their prices a little. Would do things for him. So that when the Fathers had some trouble with a grumpy mailman, and necessary business was being delayed, Sportelli suggested that the agreeable Gennaro would know how to persuade his friend the salt-seller to carry Alphonsus' letters to Falcoia.[35]

Gradually, not only Rossi and Sportelli but Margotta and Garzillo and others among the Fathers, had come to appreciate Gennaro's special talents. He was, time and again, when they came for a chat, an illicit chat, at the kitchen door, proving to have a natural intelligence required for a transference of skills. So his advice was being sought in November 1748 during community discussions about the restoration of the Materdomini buildings. And not only about the design of the kitchen. About hiring and overseeing workmen, selecting building materials, obtaining better discount from local suppliers. Then it was back to doing the dishes.[36]

That Father who acknowledges the talent of a Brother is likely to have a pleasanter time of it in the house. There was an order from Alphonsus that no one was to keep chocolate or tobacco in his room. So the sweet-toothed Sportelli long remembered the cups of hot chocolate Gennaro made for him in the kitchen.[37] These were, however, rare occasions of such cameraderie. Gennaro was increasingly ill at ease in that kitchen. It was evident to him that his talents were not being used to the full. Just as his parents had feared. Was he to be merely perpetual cook?[38] Gennaro complained to Alphonsus. And received the suitably religious response. "When I went to him to complain of my difficulties, my sufferings, he would never fail to reply, 'Ah Brother, so you do not wish to become a saint?' "[39]

Naturally enough, Gennaro became a little bitter at this waste of his gifts by the Fathers and, of course, such being the structure of the world, ways of getting his own back presented themselves. By 1752, he had grown so tyrannical in his kitchen, so mean when serving in the refectory, so insufferably rude to everyone in the Materdomini house, "not only the Community but visitors as well," that Francesco Margotta, the Rector, wrote to Alphonsus, asking how he was to get this Brother to dish out more of that stodge on the Fathers' platters. How, indeed, he was to get him to be ordinarily civil. Alphonsus' immediate response was to repeat his order that everyone should have enough to eat, even if what they ate was not particularly tasteful.[40] Then he turned to providing a list of progressively severer measures to discipline the Brother: the Rector should first issue a private reprimand, then, should this fail to secure submissiveness, as in their deboshed times it might well fail, he should make the reprimand public, with the added warning that the Rector Major was standing ready to dismiss every offender from the Congregation. Forthwith. Alphonsus had only just finished with such a one. He was in no mood to indulge a cook. Gennaro must understand this. "The door is open."[41]

Things should not come to that. Alphonsus knew precisely how to humble an awkward chef. Make him the scullery boy. "I may withdraw this Brother from your house to Ciorani and set him to work under the cook there."[42] Gennaro would be back to the beginning among the dirty dishes. That should make him think again. If he prove stubborn, he'll have to go. Back to those parents. "Tell him this, word for word."

Gennaro's grumbling about the house cannot have been much lessened by his becoming more and more deaf. But he handed the Materdomini bursar and cook job to another, younger, Brother without more than his usual muttering, and turned again to busying himself with the congregation's building program. He could still get on with bricklayers and carpenters, evidently, and architects. They may all of them have been cheered when Gennaro hired a gang of teenage girls to carry the hods of bricks. They were cheaper than the boys. But more distracting. Not to Fathers, of course. But to Students. "Be on your guard," Alphonsus warned Caione on hearing of these dangerous gigglers, "we shall have to remove the young men to another place."[43] Gennaro was safe enough, they decided. He was forty-five, nearly forty-six, years old.

Hiring the girls had been one of the few concessions Gennaro would make to economy during his time on site. He knew that it was no use skimping on materials. But the costs of the building works mounted alarmingly. Draining resources from the kitchen as from every other room in the house. Alphonsus warned them, again. "The Community should not, on account of the improvements being made, suffer privations of food or clothing."[44]

Gennaro had not very long to wait before the chaos came that he knew must come under this entirely new kitchen management—money being so short and all. His poor substitute, Gasparo Corvino, 1722–1785, had not been trained to the work. He had no idea how to organize meals for so many. The house accounts were a shambles. Tradesmen had to represent their bills. They grew tired of delivering their goods on tick. They stopped calling at the back door. And, most galling for those Fathers and Students, whose complaints had precipitated the change, the meals were no better yet. Getting worse if anything. There was a change of Rector at the end of the summer. Giovanni Mazzini, 1704–1792, having found the house not good for his health, was removed within a year. Gasparo Caione, 1722–1809, succeeded him. This luckless man was almost immediately in trouble for allowing the sisters of Bernardo Apice, 1728–1769, to come inquiring after the health of their brother. Rumors about the new Brother's cooking had reached them even at Castellammare.[45] Caione's own stomach could not deal with the amount of oil Brother Gasparo assumed to be the essential ingredient for each and every dish he set before the Fathers. The doctor had to be called.[46]

Since they were all so below par, Caione asked if the unexperienced priest, Francesco Saveno di Leo, 1728–1811, who had proved resilient under the new cooking, might be allowed to help out with the men's confessions at weekends. The request was firmly refused.[47] Francesco Giovenale, 1719–1782, was the next to fall ill. Andrea Strina, 1726–1797, followed him down.[48] Fathers were by now thinking very favorably of those good old days when Gennaro was in the kitchen. But he was busier than ever on the building site.[49] Alphonsus, on being consulted about their household arrangements, suggested that Gerard Majella was strong enough to be bursar.[50] But he could not cook. Angelo Latessa died on October 5, 1754. The Student Pietro Picone, 1733–1754, died on November 9.[51] Don Donato Antonio came all the way from Bovino, determined to bring home his Student son, Francesco Saverio Manfredonia, b. 1735, fled 1755, returned to be dispensed 1756. The boy had written to his parents declaring that he felt "as if there were a hot iron in my intestines." Caione had to let the father talk to his son, but was so alarmed that he bundled Francesco Saverio away by night to stay with Alphonsus at Pagani.[52] Parents were always a coddling nuisance.

After all this, quite understandably, the substituting Gasparo's own health collapsed. He could not stomach the refectory grumblings of Fathers and Students. Even some of the Brothers. Even the refectory Brother, Carmine Santaniello, 1738–1807, who didn't care for the grim looks he got when serving the Fathers the awful soup. So bursar Gerard announced that he'd take over the cooking. But when dinnertime came Carmine was appalled to discover that the kitchen door was still locked. Nothing prepared. He rushed to the chapel where, sure enough, Gerard was still at his prayers. A fine cook he'd turned out to be. They'd all be in deep trouble. Gerard had simply left it to the angels. They had certainly better culinary skills than he. And the angels had most obligingly cooked them quite a meal.[53] But they couldn't rely on angels coming every day. Rector Caione was forced to acknowledge their need of Gennaro. He wrote to ask Alphonsus if reappointing Gennaro were compatible with all their dignities.

Happily, Alphonsus was less reluctant than most to accept this loss of face. "As for the bursar," he wrote to Caione, "Your Reverence is the Rector. Appoint Brother Gennaro for this charge if you think fit."[54] The Rector should be aware that there were other opportunities for him to demonstrate his authority. "You may employ Brother Gasparo where you please."

Gennaro was thereupon called back from his open-air job with bricklayers and architects and girls. For a while Gerard replaced him as site overseer. Then, after the collapse of his health, a Father was appointed to manage the building project. He thought to show them all what a good economist could do. He could save them a lot of money by using less expensive materials when work was restarted on the church dome. Gennaro, seeing what was happening, must have had some gloomy prophecies to make, but he was a beneficiary of this recosting of the project. He was allowed more money to spend on food. So his cooking, if it were not quite up to the angels' standard, was a great improvement on Gasparo's efforts.

Gasparo, not entirely recovered from his kitchen distress, was set to look after one of the older sick Fathers. He could listen to his daily grumblings about Brother Gennaro and the food. It was, Tannoia recorded, "a touching thing" to watch the old priest dragging himself to the church at Materdomini, supported by "one of the lay Brothers."[55] Any Brother would do service as a stick.

Gasparo was transferred, later that summer, to be with Rector Villani at Saint Angelo a Cupolo. His remaining there for the next fifty years was extraordinary. The ordinary thing was for Alphonsus to swap Brothers from house to house as jobs demanded. Like the rest of us, a Brother, once drafted, could usually be brought to do a range of jobs about the house. At the Minister's beck any Brother might be called upon to make a fist at answering the door, tolling the bell for Office, weeding the garden, gathering in the hay, feeding the mule even. Any Brother might hold himself ready to be sent to the Sacristan and then be told to get on dusting the benches, scrubbing the tiles, repainting the vaults. And any Brother might be expected to be capable of collecting the bedtime straw, spreading out the palliasse on the mission house floor, cleaning the latrines. If sometimes a particular expertise were required for a man to quit himself in a job well enough for the flourishment of the Congregation, the contentment of a house, well, "he can be made to learn."[56] Nothing difficult there. In an age of journeymen, apprentices, and master craftsmen, it seemed the ordinary thing for a Brother to learn an older Brother's trade. Or even to be told to retrain in middle life. Sometimes, to the rest of the Fathers' regret, Alphonsus seemed not at all to care what degree of expertness a Brother acquired before setting him to do the job. Who could care whether or no Brother Rafaele Daniele became a tidy barber?[57] Alphonsus always wore his beard "*al vagabondo*."[58] But whether or not the others shared his notions of any Brother's being able to do the cook's duties or take a quick snip at their hair, there were, he would agree, some jobs which made quite particular demands on a Brother. Not everyone, for example, should be given charge of the medicine cupboard.

Alphonsus, from his lengthy experiences as a patient, fancied himself well able to give advice about a range of medical matters from tuberculosis to hernia. When, at Sant' Agata, secretary Felice Verzella brought a starving child to the bishop, Alphonsus at once set about mixing vinegar, spiritous liquors, and a little chocolate, and spooned this cocktail between the clenched jaws of the nervous child.[59] He could not, of course, recognize such a natural talent for medical matters in every member of the Congregation. Fathers were generally useless in the dispensary and infirmary. But Vito had proved capable of mixing a healthful potion or two. It was on his recommendation that Bishop Falcoia had told Cesare Sportelli to apply a balm to Brother Crescenzo's chest.[60] Brother Francesco Saverio Schiavino, 1729–1779, the one-time barber and bloodletter who became bursar at Ciorani could always be consulted in a crisis. Young Nicola Casoria knew a lot about herbal teas. Another young Brother, Pietro Sant Agata, 1736–1794, was even more highly esteemed, having had a little training as a bone cutter.

Not every Brother was by temperament well-fitted to the carer's job. It was not only Sarnelli who was made to feel that his last illness was bothersome for a Brother.[61] Brother Carminiello's spiritual advice proved less than comforting to Gerard, rousing the dying man to protest "why do you speak to me of scruples?"[62] And there was the famous occasion when on Alphonsus' telling his nursing Brother that he was thirsty, he gave him a vase of old flower water to drink.[63] That time he made no complaint. But in his last illness, unable to do anything for himself, having submitted to the kindly attempt to shave him by Brother Rafaele,[64] even he made a piteous moan when the Brothers changed his shirt: "They have taken off my underpants…they have touched my bottom!" The horrors of the Incurabili ward had come crowding into his imagination.

Only on his being assured that it was only his old and trusted Brother Leonardo who was changing his clothes could he be quieted."[65]

As much delicacy and willingness to deal with physical unpleasantness was required when the Brothers had to lay out, clean, and redress the dead for exposition and burial. Sarnelli's body smelt attractively. But this was often a nasty job. Sometimes a little surprising. Preparing the body of Angelo Latessa, "one of our Brothers in cutting his hair inadvertently pierced the skin and the flow of blood from this trifling wound was so great that all his clothes were steeped in it." This was the sort of incident that anyone who was devoted to San Gennaro would appreciate. "We were obliged to tear them up and distribute the pieces among the faithful to gratify their devotion."[66]

Neapolitans did not need a spout of blood to prompt their carrying away such relics. There was a rush of mourners to tear pieces off Sarnelli's habit while he lay in his coffin. Happily, Sarnelli had told the Brothers sent to nurse him that the habit hanging behind the door was far too good to be buried in,[67] so they found some well-patched one.[68]

Sarnelli was recognizing the expertness of the Brother tailors. Redemptorist habits had to be precisely cut. The Rule insisted on the Father's habit reaching just the inch over the shoe. Sometimes a man might come fully trained to the Congregation, Francesco Tartaglione, for instance, Gerard Majella, or "the young tailor," Nicola Casoria,[69] but more often the tailor Brother would find himself training an apprentice who had no experience or natural bent for the work. This was not a matter of any interest to the Fathers. But once trained, the skilled Brother was in demand. That there were not so many who had become expert enough, when there was an obvious need for wielders of scissors and paper patterns, is hinted in Alphonsus' impatient note to Caione in December 1758 "that Brother tailor has not yet come and here we are expecting him."[70]

And As Good Cooks Go, He Went

There was at least as much anxiety in a house while they were waiting for a cook to be assigned. It was supremely ironic that the Rector who had been so urgent about getting him out of the kitchen should be protesting when Gennaro was ordered to Naples at the request of Benedetto

Grazioli. "I have promised that he should go," Alphonsus replied, "and I cannot take back my word."[71] Caione must be content to have some other Brother in his place. He wanted Leonardo Cicchetti from Pagani. He was good at mental arithmetic, useful for dealing with rascally tradespeople. Alphonsus, mentioning Caione's proposal to the Pagani Rector, was thoroughly repulsed. "Brother Leonardo," the Rector had said, "takes care of all temporal affairs of the house, keeps account of Mass stipends, looks after the pantry stores, and everything else." The Rector had been very bold. "It is not possible, I am told, to take him off." Caione could have the seventeen-year-old Domenico Picardi, 1740–1778. He was "young," "discreet," "literate." It was unclear whether he knew how to add and subtract.[72] Caione must make up his mind. It would be Domenico or no one. He must make up his mind at once. "I say 'at once' because Don Benedetto wishes to have Brother Gennaro immediately, and there can be no delaying his departure. This is important."[73] If he does want Dominico in Gennaro's place, Caione must, of course, provide the mule to bring the young Brother and his pack from Pagani. But he would be reimbursed the expenses of sending Gennaro to Naples. Someone would keep accounts. "Take courage," Alphonsus had upbraided the still hesitating Caione, "Brother Gennaro must be sent at once to Atella; then he goes to Naples."[74]

Whether he could add or not, it was very soon clear that Domenico could not bake. The Fathers were soon grumbling again. Reasonably, they complained to Alphonsus who had sent them this unsatisfactory Brother cook. Alphonsus very fast returned their complaint to Rector Caione. "The bread, I'm told, is badly made; it is brown and of a bad quality."[75] Caione must do something. "I beg you, at least have the flour sifted." Alphonsus now conveniently forgot how it had been the withdrawing of Gennaro that begun the disruption of Caione's kitchen. So, since he'd been given Domenico, he would have to surrender some other Brother. What about Paschal? or Matteo? Better Matteo, since as everyone knows, Paschal always manages to overwork at Pagani and make himself ill. "So send Matteo along."[76]

The course of this whole affair seemed a proof to Alphonsus, if any of them had ever needed proof, of the folly of taking a Brother's particular skills into account when arranging assignments to a house. Fancy a Community noticing which Brother was serving them. Fathers should not be troubling themselves with such matters. Certainly the Rector Major should not. Alphonsus appears, as he surveyed the greater and greater numbers of Brothers entering the Congregation, who were naturally possessed of a range of diverse talents, to have grown more and more convinced that they should be conditioned into regarding themselves as indistinguishingly disposable when any position became anywhere vacant. It became, therefore, quite impossible for any Rector to plan for some complementarity of jobs and workers in a house. But, at the same time, since a Rector had always to be reckoning on the absence of several Fathers with their attendant Brothers on the missions, he must come more and more to rely on the permanent residency of other Brothers for the continued running of the house. So these had to be men of all work. Those missioners on their return would expect someone to have washed the bed linen, cleaned out the latrines, paid the tradesmen, chopped the wood, kept the accounts, trimmed the candles, seen to the beggars, arranged the Mass stipends, taken in the mail, kept up chapel prayers for them while they were preaching, gone shopping, and have a meal ready for them on their return. They were proving particularly interested in Brothers' kitchen skills.

In the good old days, Vito, having ruined a batch of baking, had simply eaten the unappetizing bread himself. Domenico was not made of the same stuff. None of them were. Even Alphonsus was now acknowledging the value of a good plain cook. He allotted twenty carlins to Brother Rafaele for all the extra work he done when on loan from Rector Tannoia "This Brother has, as it were, kept me alive, for I have had him here for four days to be my cook, since my hired cook was obliged to go to Cava to assist his dying wife."[77] Alphonsus had absolutely no intention of letting the Brother return to d'Iliceto yet. Though, as ever when there is some difficulty with another Father, Alphonsus manages to make it appear somehow the Brother's fault that he is not doing his proper work in his proper place, "You must excuse him for delaying his return."[78]

Tannoia had, this time, to be properly gracious in the matter of the Brother's extended absence. But the Fathers could not always remain quiet when Alphonsus played musical chairs with Brothers in their houses. Community and Rector at d'Iliceto proved astonishingly restive under orders to send Brother Antonio Maria Oliva to Saint Angelo a

Cupolo, so that he might from there be sent to Scifelli. Rector Tannoia recognized the value of a Brother in the house who, as well as being able and willing to "do the work of three men," tailor, bursar, and odd-jobber, was "always cheerful," "joyfully embracing any burden."[79] So Tannoia screwed his courage to the sticking point and replied to the order with a protestation that "I do not wish to send him." The Rector at Scifelli was quick to complain to the Rector Major at this refusal. Alphonsus could hardly require anyone's prompting to recognize the effects of a demon of disobedience when he met them. Tannoia was threatening the very existence of the Congregation by this disputatiousness. "This discloses to me the principal reason why the Congregation is at present in so trying a condition, namely, that Rectors are the first to fail in obedience." Well, he should see. They all should see. "I have been appointed Director of the Congregation by both the Pope and the King. From this day forward, I intend to change my style. I will be obeyed."[80] The letter announcing this new style of government, which cannot have seemed to any of them to have much new about it, ends with a particular instruction. Tannoia had better obey. "Send without fail the said Brother Antonio."[81]

Others, of course, Alphonsus realizes, must have been aiding and abetting Rector Tannoia in this appalling resistance. Too many folk were interfering in the matter of the Brother's exchange of houses, discussing his usefulness. Inside the house. Consultors probably. And outside. "Beware of allowing any interference on the part of that Bishop who is now with you. Even if he thinks he can use his influence to retain the services of the Brother. You must do everything you can to get him to give up all such notions."[82] There'll certainly be no excusing Tannoia if he starts alleging the wishes of either Consultors or bishop. "Do not answer me that you have failed in your efforts, for if you do not send the Brother, you will have to report to me and will assuredly repent this negligence." There's no mention, amid references to Rector, Consultors, Bishop, of what the Brother might be feeling on being told to pack his bag. But, as usual with him, Alphonsus closes with the personal appeal that no one upset him. "I hope that you will not give me this pain." Tannoia could resist neither threat nor appeal. Antonio was sent to Scifelli to become a saint.

Alphonsus could not, however, be entirely sure that threat and appeal would always work. So he now lets all Rectors know his plain will for the future conduct of these transferals of Brothers from house to house. "I mean to dismiss anyone who refuses to obey, even if he be my own brother." Every man in the Kingdom of Naples would recognize the enormity of an offense that could entail its judge's disregarding the claims of Home and Family. Or even of confraternity. Doubtless their response would be to lodge an appeal. Alphonsus is ready for them. "Let no one think of invoking the aid of the courts, for the King who has appointed me Director, and is very favorable to me, will listen to me rather than to anyone else."[83]

Alphonsus entrusted Brother Antonio and Brother Stefano, who was also posted to Scifelli, with copies of his *Homo Apostolicus*, his *Preparation for Death,* and two copies of *Sermons for Every Sunday,* thus ensuring that the Scifelli Fathers should be equipped for hearing the confessions of those who came to church, for practicing proper asceticism, and for preaching the right sort of sermon.[84] The community was as happy with the bearer as with the gifts. Reporting Brother Antonio's safe arrival, the Rector pronounced them all "enchanted with his affability and his good manners." But Scifelli was never a healthy place. Perhaps Alphonsus had intended that the books should be read by the Brother at the bedsides of the sick. Brother Antonio himself died within two years of being posted there. His epitaph, written at the bottom of his posthumous portrait, exculpates him from any part in his Superior's tendency to resist an order. "A model of obedience and patience, vile in his own eyes, but dear to everyone else, he died joyfully, June 22, 1775, devoutly kissing the crucifix. He was forty-five years old."[85] The portrait shows him to have been a darkly handsome man, with a fine forehead, properly long nose, and neat moustache. A little sad-eyed perhaps, but this is not at all the face of a man who should die of the damp.

Alphonsus' reference to the King and his favor was meant as much for Rectors as for Brothers. In the matter of transfers they were mere equals. Five Rectors found themselves as helpless as the three Brothers involved in an extraordinary round of exchanges at the start of November 1777. By this time, Gennaro was back at Ciorani, feeling himself, at nearly seventy years of age, rather pushed into a corner. He was left to say his prayers, collect a few lemons from the garth trees, and observe the unsafe state of the church cupola. So it was as a pleasing disturbance in his day that he heard that a new Brother was arriving. There was the added interest that, having been told to expect Brother Pompilio at the Brothers' table, it was Brother Matteo who sat down to dinner with him.

The shuffle was begun on account of Alphonsus' hearing that Brother Pompilio was in poor health at Scifelli and, as always in such cases, trusting to a change of air to work a cure, he decided that Pompilio should be moved to Ciorani.[86] The Rector there, poor coughing Bartolomeo Corrado, was told to expect the new tailor.[87] By the same post, Alphonsus informed the Rector at Scifelli, Deodato Criscuoli, 1738–1804, that Brother Matteo would come from Materdomini. Rector Lorenzo Nigro, 1736–1799, was instructed to put him on the donkey for Pagani. He would change animals there. When Brother Matteo arrived at Pagani, however, he was coughing badly and quite clearly in no sort of state to be put on a second donkey to the unhealthy Scifelli house. So Tommaso Mazzini, the Pagani Rector, was told to find him a temporary job and a room. Then, having given the matter a little thought, Alphonsus wrote to Caione, now Rector at Benevento, telling him that Matteo would come to live with him. "The air will do him good, as it is more salubrious than that of Caposele for chest troubles."[88] Caione was also told that Brother Rafaele would be taken from the Benevento house to be the substitute for Pompilio at Scifelli. He, too, would travel by way of Pagani. That way the Rector Major would have a chance to quiz him, as Caione realized he would, about the conduct of Rector and Fathers at Benevento. "I expect to see Brother Rafaele here." The five Rectors were to be uncomplaining while their Communities were thus being reconstructed. "I have nothing more to say."[89]

Four days later, however, Alphonsus did have more to say. Caione at Benevento was now to understand that all is changed. The news from Scifelli is now that Brother Pompilio is recovering. So Brother Rafaele is to remain at Benevento for the unforeseeable future. "Keep him until you receive different orders."[90] Brother Matteo will not, therefore, be arriving at Caione's door. He has already been posted to Ciorani, and received the welcome prepared for Pompilio. But they must none of them think that Alphonsus had put them into permanent place. "I have written to him to remain there for the present, later it will be decided whether he is to go to Scifelli or to some other house."[91] Caione should be alert to the likelihood of those further orders. His Brother may yet be on the move. If Pompilio has a relapse, "it will be better to send Brother Rafaele."

And now that Alphonsus has begun to speak about personnel, it occurs to him that Caione may not have enough missioners in his house to satisfy the demands being made by the cardinal. "If you should need subjects belonging to other houses, just write to me."[92]

All this chopping and changing of Brothers, and the suggestion that there might be further chopping and changing of Fathers, disturbed the Rectors again. Caione found courage enough to protest at the effect these changes would have on the smooth running of the Benevento house. Why had Alphonsus thought of sending Brother Rafaele to Scifelli? Now there was trouble in the community at Materdomini. Brother Matteo had been important for the smooth running of their house. Who was to replace him? Did Ciorani really need him? There was further trouble at Scifelli. Were they to expect Brother Matteo or not? If not, then surely some other Brother tailor? They had to make their plans. It was time they started on the winter smallclothes. Pompilio was beginning to cough again. Alphonsus decided that he could only deal with one awkward Rector at a time. Better keep Benevento quiet. "As for Brother Rafaele, I understand that he is very useful to your house, and since I wish to please your Reverence, I will leave him with you, as you wish."[93] But what to do about the Fathers at Scifelli? They were now suggesting that a little extra cash, perhaps for food and thicker blankets and brighter fires, would help.[94] Then they all, Pompilio and the rest of their coughers, might recover their healths. It was not the air, they told him, but the regimen of poverty which was damaging them. But Alphonsus told Francesc' Antonio de Paola at Frosinone, when he, too, started to grumble, "My purse is empty. I can send nothing."[95] There must, however, be some way to help those sick men at Scifelli. Speaking of sickness, he should not have been advised to keep Matteo at Pagani. It was not the best place for a cougher. "I have been kept in bed several days myself, suffering from a catarrh that threatened to turn out badly." However, "today I am better."[96]

Settling Down Again

If they had needed any argument to persuade Alphonsus of the way such sudden redeployments of good men might lessen their capacity to sustain a first fervor, those Rectors had only to look to the souring of Gennaro's temper over the years. Taking it for granted that his youthful enthusiasm would survive whatever they required of him, the Fathers had never made much effort to discern a settled use for Gennaro's undoubted talents, and when the generous youngster, who had stayed to serve as their Brother when Filippo Vito went back home, became so unaccountably mean with the pasta, they had responded by demoting him to be second cook in another house. It does not seem to have occurred to any of them to inquire into the causes of his increasingly awkward temper. No one seems to have considered that their ordinary assumption that a Brother could live anywhere and do any job, might suggest to the most willing of them, to Gennaro, that he had no especial gift to offer them.

Being ignored is never all bad. So Gennaro must have reckoned in the late summer and fall of 1779. Discussion about that unsafe cupola, about workmen, building materials, suppliers' estimates, was proceeding noisily. There were sharpish expressions of opinion along the corridors, questioning the congruence of any cupola with the Congregation's mission to the poor, the structural reliability of the design, the cost. Everyone had his opinion.[97] Not only the usual men, Villani, Mazzini, Criscuolo, but Stefano Liguori, 1722–1800,[98] Michele Tozzoli, 1749–1820, Francesco di Leo, 1728–1811, and the discontented Fabrizio Cimino, 1733–1818, who left the next year in low dudgeon.[99] Each making his appeal to one or other of the architects that they had together and individually consulted, Pietro Cimafonte, his equally opinionated brother Salvadore, and their more subtle rival, Andrea Para. Each hoping to bring Alphonsus, the amateur architect, onto side.[100] Having a word with Brother Francesco Romito who took Alphonsus' letters at dictation. Or with Brother Leonardo Ciochetti who had become almost Para's official spokesman in the house. But not, it seems, with old Brother Gennaro, though he had been their first site manager at Ciorani. Still, he had some fun on the sidelines.

Things came to a finely dramatic climax when, just as the final stage of construction was reached, one party in the community delated their opposites to the Rector Major. And then descended into a pretty farce. First, in October, Alphonsus replied decisively that "God has made it known to me that the cupola should be taken down."[101] They were, therefore, as a matter of obedience, to attend to the cupola's deconstruction. That was the way, they would show themselves "men who wish to become saints." Gennaro would have recognized this reassertion of their old values in their old language. But then, in the first week of November, another letter came from Alphonsus. Andrea Para had been to see him. "I have decided that the cupola should not be taken down." On this matter, as on all matters, "I am resolved to be obeyed," for in this, as in all matters, he was simply communicating "what God commands."[102]

Gennaro from his corner might observe how Fathers responded to this altered demand for perfecting obedience. They were being treated like Brothers. And not liking it. Alphonsus observed this also. "I see that the Fathers at Ciorani make very little of me and my letters."[103] But, ignoring the Fathers and their shifts to escape the demands of obedience, Gennaro was keeping his mind fixed on becoming the saint Alphonsus had consistently told him he was to be. The Rule laid it down that a working Brother was to be allowed one day of "Retreat" each month, and to be allotted on that day not more than three hours of manual labor, and that labor to be such "as will not be distracting."[104] All Gennaro's days were Retreat days now. Arriving on Alphonsus' doorstep so long ago, he had already the reputation for "the habit of virtue." Falcoia, sending Gennaro off with a mission team, had rightly guessed that he would, just be his ordinary demeanor, "edify" the people.[105] These things are mostly a matter of temperament, but temperament may be cribb'd, cabin'd, and confin'd by experiences of others' failures of sympathy. It is notable that, whatever had happened during Gennaro's over-fifty years in the Congregation, it was still being remarked that he was "constant in his way of life." Gennaro seemed, as he kept steadily going, "as regular as the Ciorani clock."

Gennaro's portrait shows him, aged eighty-one, high-foreheaded, bright-eyed, alert, capable even of a secret smile. He evidently appeared to the painter to have emerged from an angry middle age into a relieved acceptance of the conditions of his vocation. Ready for anything that life may chuck at him. More than ready for death. His habit neatly pressed. His white moustache neatly combed.

Once acquired, the reputation of a curmudgeon is not easily shed. Others in the Congregation may have thought it appropriate that Brother Gennaro should die, January 7, 1789, of a fit of apoplexy. But that local painter has arranged that the naive portrait should present this Brother's devotion to his suffering Redeemer. Gennaro holds his crucifix not as a missioner holds the standard as he goes out to battle for the Lord, but rather tucked, half-hidden, into the fold of his habit, the token of some shared understanding between intimate, experienced friends. He died, the subscription added to this reassuring portrait declares "with a reputation for holiness."[106]

Francesco Tartaglione

Bishop Falcoia wrote in 1742 protesting against a suggestion by the head of the Sarnelli family at Ciorani that Alphonsus should come with a Brother to set up a house of the Congregation in his fiefdom. Falcoia was becoming, as he noted Alphonsus' tendency to think himself in charge, a querulous correspondent. But this time he had a substantial point to make. "I value highly Signor Don Gennaro and his influence, but I cannot agree with his design, on this account: what sort of a figure could you make, alone with your one Brother? How could you present the Congregation of the Most Holy Savior there alone when your own Rule lays down that there should not be a priest by himself in a House?"[1]

It was not only a question of the Rule and the priest by himself. There was also the Brother by himself to be considered. How would things look? This was a time, Falcoia now recognized, for him to point out to Alphonsus an especial awkwardness for Vito. "You should not, if you can avoid it, allow a servant to be humiliated." It is now not just a question of Vito. There's the impression this carelessness of the good of a Brother will make on the others. "They will be badly affected by this treatment of one of them."[2]

The bishop was entirely right in his suggestion that what happened to Vito would be taken by the other Brothers as happening to them. There were ten of them by the time Vito died in 1745. Each of them took his understanding of what it was to be a Brother, his fraternal tone, from what he thought Vito would do and say.

During his thirty-eight years in the Congregation, Francesco Tartaglione became ever more urgent in his efforts to ensure that each new batch of Brothers should be made aware of their tradition. He had himself, as Tannoia noted, "endeavored to follow all the good examples

Brother Vito Curzio had given him at Ciorani."[3] Tannoia had the ordinary notion of what sort of good example a Brother should be taking from a Brother. He firstly approved Francesco's "never neglecting an opportunity of imitating his profound humility."[4] It was only secondly that he allowed that Francesco had found in Vito a model of "exceeding charity."[5]

As the principal account of Vito is the obituary notice in which Alphonsus hoped to fix his image of the paradigm Brother for all later entrants, so the principal account of this Brother is Tannoia's obituary notice, written with at least as keen an interest in the formation of present and future Brothers. It was certainly more important to the obituarist to establish Francesco as an example for them than to check his birth date. "Brother Francesco Tartaglione, that model of humility, was born near Marcianisi, in the diocese of Capua," he says, "on August 7, 1713."[6] Perhaps Francesco, when he made his application to the Congregation had pretended he was two years older than he actually was. Like a youngster too eager to get himself into the army.

At any rate, Tannoia is not much interested in that kind of detail. He had been given some information about Francesco's parents by those at Capua who still remembered the family, but he'd decided, disappointedly, that there was nothing he could use. Ferdinando and Aurelia Tartaglione get scarce a mention. But he does want his readers to know that Francesco was remembered as a model child and a model youngster, "inclined to piety from his very infancy" and "at twelve years of age determining to enter religion." "As he admired the exemplary lives of the lay Brothers of the Society of Jesus, he requested to be admitted among them."

The Jesuit Superiors were disposed to receive Francesco, having assured themselves of his coupling proper piety with a useful household talent. "He was an excellent tailor."[7] Piety and tailoring were not, however, enough. Francesco became ill, so "they sent him away."[8]

It was "because God wished him to enter our Congregation" that he'd become sick among the Jesuits.[9] So, even after he had regained his health, he did not reapply to the Society. He started on the way of life which, unknowingly, would fit him for the Congregation. Restored to health, he "fled laziness," "loved hard work," and "began to frequent the Sacraments."[10] So it was, still within the Providence of God, that Francesco learned that Alphonsus was preaching a mission at nearby Recauata. There, "after listening to the sermon on hell," he resolved to leave the world. There are New Testament models now to be added to those of the Society. Francesco realizes, in his response to Alphonsus' preaching, an imitation of the conversion moments of Saints Matthew, James, John, and Mary Magdalene: he "left his companions," "followed Father Alphonsus," "and cast himself at his feet."

Francesco has done "what all must do if they would join us" and is well on the way to paradigmatic status in this telling of his story. So Tannoia now takes the opportunity to describe the peculiar virtue of the Redemptorist life. Here even Jesuit models must fail. Giovanni Mazzini, the Master of Brothers explained to the urgent Francesco, "My good friend, our table is not like that of the Jesuits, and we have not the comforts which they enjoy: those who are in our Congregation have to suffer much, for we are very poor." But, again proving a proximate exemplar to all later Brothers, Francesco had the only worthy goal in mind. "I am ready to suffer everything in order to save my soul." And he knows the only means to reach that goal.

Tannoia is now into his perfect stride as a shaper of this narrative. He sets Mazzini up, getting the Master of Brothers to suggest that the eager young man go home to think about his vocation. Francesco's horrified response proves he has the true Redemptorist's understanding of these matters. "No, Father, if I return home, I shall not come back again." Francesco makes an exemplary disclosure of the natural alliance of parents and demons. "I know how artful the devil is. I wish to be saved. I can do very well without my parents' consent."[11]

Only after establishing his character as paradigm applicant does Tannoia allow the reader any sense of Francesco's personal quality. Suddenly, a most attractive fellow springs into view. He is "a very handsome young man." He has "the greatest liveliness of manner." And, as suddenly, he is whisked away. "After he entered the House of God," Tannoia says, with a nod of complacent approval, "he soon became very different."[12] The biographer wants his subject to be dull and uninteresting. That's what a Father wants in a Brother. "Mazzini wrote to us," Tannoia recalls, "that Francesco had changed most pleasingly." Now, he was "always humble." Now, he was "subject to everyone." Even the distinguishing talent which had gained Francesco approval among the Jesuits is eclipsed in a praise of that generalized usefulness which was a Brother's best recommendation. "Though our tailor, he was ready for any job." Ready for instance "to carry the builders' materials" to the site of the new wing of the house. The handsome lad was moving among those village girls on site. But he was still "a model in every way." Gennaro, a strict foreman, would certainly not have encouraged any of them to waste time in idle chat. But then again, the lively Francesco bursts through Tannoia's careful study in conventional piety as the biographer is forced to acknowledge the good Brother's enduring "cheerfulness."[13]

We are not surprised, therefore, that on his being first sent to Ciorani, Francesco gained the heart of Father Rossi. It cannot have been, of course, his handsomeness, his liveliness, his cheerfulness that attracted the Rector. These personal traits are not to Tannoia's purpose. He is only wanting to promote a reader's interest in Francesco's uniting "a love of labor" with "a love of meditation," for these are the virtues of every good Martha-and-Mary Brother.[14]

In his first years with the Congregation, Francesco had ample opportunity to observe and, if he would, imitate a nice range of others. He had been one of Villani's companions at Ciorani in 1737.[15] He was left with Sarnelli in July 1742 to run the mission at Sant' Aniello di Barra.[16] He was with Sportelli at Castellammare in April 1743, taking turns to sit with the dying Falcoia.[17] Then, in June 1744, he was with Sarnelli again in his dying days. Francesco was perhaps, by then, too tired to make the best use of this last good example of how to die in the Congregation. There was an awkward moment when Sarnelli, already a skeleton on the bed, "nothing but skin and bones," found the Brother's attentions rather too brusque: "My Brother, for the love of Jesus Christ, have patience, I cannot live long."[18] But on most other occasions there can be no doubting that it was the example of Vito, with whom Francesco was working at Ciorani after the evacuation of Scala in 1738,[19] which influenced most powerfully his sense of what it was to be a Brother in the Congregation.

Francesco's most perfect adoption of Vito's tone as a Christian man of honor is projected in a story that Tannoia retells from Brother Michele Ilardo's store of such improving anecdotes. Francesco figures as Potiphar's steward. There was about him more than a remnant of good looks, clearly. "As his appearance was most attractive a lady conceived a bad attachment towards him." Beekeeper Tannoia gets rather too excited in his bodice-ripping novelettish description of the lady's "impudent embraces" and "immodest entreaties" and of the indignant Brother's only just managing to "tear himself free from her." But the hagiographer recovers well enough to set down Francesco's Christian response. That mission sermon of Alphonsus has its long term effect. "Madam, there is God and there is hell." Then Francesco shifts into a recapitulation of Vito's gentlemanly voice. "The Brothers of our Congregation are not in the habit of committing such crimes." That the country boy from Capua has caught exactly the tone of the gallant Vito is further demonstrated in Francesco's gallant bow at the door and his saying loud enough for the servants to hear, "Madam, I quite understand you, your business shall be carried out." Then, having preserved for the lady that reputation for virtue which she had been so willing to throw away, like young Joseph, he fled.[20]

Getting the Rule Approved and Enjoying a Good Cheese

Like young Joseph, Francesco enjoyed the talents of an administrator.[21] Brothers were now expected to be able to read and write before they presented themselves to the Congregation. At least, ready and eager to be taught. "If there is a Brother who does not know how to read but seems capable of learning, he will have to be taught by one of them."[22] Alphonsus was not consistently impressed, however, with the results of the Brothers' teaching. "I beg you," he wrote in a note to Canon Giuseppe Spatano, 1709–1776, accompanying the *Life* of Sarnelli he'd written for the Congregation of Apostolic Missions, "make what corrections you think best in this manuscript, and especially to correct the spelling mistakes that you may find in it, for I had one of our Brothers copy it, and now the postman is ready to go, and I cannot look it over."[23] But, it may be, the Canon was known to be pernickity about spelling. Sending him the manuscript of *Visits to the Blessed Sacrament,* which had been copied at leisure, Alphonsus made just the same disclaimer on behalf of another Brother copyist.[24]

Brothers were not consistently expected to be able to add and subtract. Alphonsus interested himself enough in the numeracy of the Brothers to write a little book on arithmetic for their instruction.[25] Some were evidently to be bursars as well as secretaries. In a Kingdom where less than one in ten of the population was both literate and numerate, and even the majority of bourgeois citizens would falter at such educational demands, Brothers were expected to welcome this schooling.[26] To take it as part of their general training in service.[27]

There was no doubt at all of Francesco's competence in these arts. As the astute Villani observed. On his being detailed, at the end of October 1748, to obtain official papal approval of the Institute and its Rule, he asked that Francesco should be freed to accompany him to Rome.

After a five-day cart journey and some very frugal meals and rough sleeping, Father and Brother arrived in Rome on November 13, the feast of Saint Stanislaus, and Villani, as the Congregation's Novice Master, insisted they should go at once to see the young saint's room. Everything seemed that day to be arranged for their particular convenience. Leaving the Collegio Romano, they were suddenly aware that the Pope was coming down the street and, kneeling, had his blessing.[28]

Francesco was not likely to be overawed by the city. He had seen Naples. Villani, however, could not resist walking across the Tiber to Saint Peter's so that he might venerate the tomb of the Apostle and gawk at the reliquaries in the basilica's treasury. The next day, he made his early bow to Cardinal Domenico Orsini, 1719–1789, a relative of Alphonsus' old Amatrice client and a near-neighbor of the Villani at Solofra, who promised his good offices. Then Villani began his progress through curial departments, monsignorial withdrawing rooms, cardinalitial antechambers, coming back at the end of his morning's tramp that first day, and each of several days after, with the same complaint, "Words, words, costing them nothing...."[29] He called on the two friendly experts in the Curia that Alphonsus had recommended he consult. Both advised him that the proposed Rule would have to be radically altered before it would have a chance of being accepted. To both he returned the reply, "I have come to Rome not to change the Rule but to ask for its approbation."[30] Neither would waste another minute on such a man after that. Still, he found that Francesco Sanseverino, 1723–1793, "our Ciccio," who had been professed in their Congregation in 1744 but had left on account of ill-health, had recovered enough to take a job in the Curia and was now very ready to proffer expert advice on the ways of officialdom.[31] Another old acquaintance, Giuseppe de Rosa, 1727–1792(?), a subdeacon from Pagani, "an angel—and a Doctor of Theology," gave the pair of them two rent-free rooms in his house.[32] Francsco, who was keeping their money, had to pay only for the bread and cheese he bought for them in the Trastevere market. They could manage on very little, really.

Somewhere along the corridors of power, they encountered the Basilian Abbot, Giuseppe Muscari, 1714–1792, who, to their rather overwhelmed astoundment, professed himself so eager to be in the Congregation that he'd join them "even if," Villani reported to Alphonsus in one of his dutifully regular letters, "he had to put on the habit of a Brother."[33] The Abbot promised to sit down with them and devise a way through the curial maze. And, during a remarkably hardworking Christmastide, the three of them finished a Curia-friendly redrafting of their petition.

Villani trudged from office to drawing room to antechamber all over again. And again. And again. He increased his fasts in hope of bringing yet more saints onto his side in the affair. He venerated more relics. Of course, he became overtired and one day, having paid no heed to Francesco's directions as he set out, got quite lost on his way back from the Vatican and arrived late home in bedraggled need of the Brother's comfort. They were firm friends now. They'd come to value one another among the tricksy monsignori. And their prayers together were answered. The proposed Rule was put on the order-paper for the meeting of the Congregation of the Council fixed for January 25, 1749. Come the day, Villani could not bear the suspense. He sent Francesco to the Vatican to wait in the antechamber.[34]

Early in the afternoon, Francesco returned with the disappointing news that the cardinals had gone to lunch before reaching the Congregation's business. Still, Cardinal Orsini had remarked comfortingly to the Brother, they would certainly consider the matter at their next meeting. In a month's time. Villani had learned a thing or two about the way Roman business was done. Next month there would be Carnival. Then Lent. Then Easter....He would not endure it. He would do something. He would do something fast. "I'll stir up the Secretary," he promised Alphonsus. Poor, good-natured, tired, Cardinal Gioacchino Besozzi, 1684–1755, the Sacred Penitentiary appointed to examine the proposed Rule, had already signed everything put in front of him and, not wanting to be cornered again, hurried off to the country. Now the bestirred Secretary went off to persuade the Cardinal Prefect of the Council, Antonio Gentili, 1708–1780, to peruse the papers after supper.[35] He, in his turn, proved entirely willing to be helpful and gave his approval immediately after breakfast on January 28. This sensible man, too, quit Rome. On getting the news from Francesco of the Rule's being agreed, Villani stopped in the midst of writing one of those letters home to Alphonsus to scrawl "GLORIA PATRI" in large letters at the top of the paper and sent Francesco off to ensure that the good news went with the very next carrier to Naples.[36]

Perhaps it was at the end of this most satisfactory day that Francesco thought to give the exhausted negotiator a treat and bought a rather better piece of cheese. The story goes that on Villani's protesting against this waste of Congregation money, Francesco risked a fib, assuring the scandalized Father that all cheese cost the same at the market. He'd be grinning widely as he made this absurd defense. Doubtless, Villani laughed with him. A cheerful handsome charmer might get away with some such thing now and again.[37] So Villani brought Francesco along to his audience with Pope Benedict XIV at the end of their Roman stay and he took his chance to get the Pope to bless the whole Tartaglione clan.[38] Then the pair of them set off on a little pilgrimage to Loreto.[39]

On their return to Naples at the end of March, Francesco went back to odd-jobbing, while Villani and the other Fathers took order for the October summoning of a General Chapter which would inaugurate the new Congregation.[40] In the midst of their preparations, Abbot Muscari arrived. He had obtained leave from the Superior of the Basilians to try his vocation in the Congregation, and on Villani's grateful recommendation, he had also been given dispensation from anything so tiresomely delaying as a novitiate among the Redemptorists.[41] He had been received into the Congregation immediately in Rome by Cardinal Orsini, appointed Alphonsus' delegate for the purpose. So he arrived among them as a fully fledged Father. And such was his hustle and bustle method that the twenty-four priests assembled at Ciorani for the Chapter accepted this latest arrival as their guiding expert in the arrangement of capitular business. Muscari explained that Canon Law required there be new elections. Accepting his judgment, authoritatively expressed, the office-holders all resigned, Alphonsus included.

It must have been a little curious for Francesco to observe that a Brother who had signed the first vow of perseverance and who had had such a part in the effort to secure pontifical approbation of the new Rule now had no vote, while, in this newcomer's arrangements, even the latest arrival among the Students was enfranchised.

Keeping to his design of providing later Brothers with an example of how a good Brother behaves in the business of an ordinary day, Tannoia makes no mention of this Roman embassage in his *Life* of Francesco. This was too extraordinary an event. But the journey proved significant for Francesco's self-appreciation and, quite without official encouragement, became for all succeeding Brothers an exemplary instance of their sharing to the full in the experience of the Congregation. While the relation between Villani and Francesco might have been, at the beginning of their escapade, undefined enough for those they met on the road to Rome to make that old mistake of supposing them master and servant, by the end of their time together, Father and Brother had become coworkers, reliant on each other and provedly reliable.

From then on, at every crisis of resentment against the Fathers' style, Brothers would make their appeal to the 1749 Rule as a guarantee of Brothers being entitled to the same treatment as Fathers in the Congregation, in matters of food, clothing, working, and praying times, and the valuation of their vocation. That they were unlikely ever to gain their point with the Fathers must have been suggested to the brightest among them by the very different treatment, in the next two years, afforded Students, Reverend Brothers, and one of their own.

Students and Children

Alphonsus was urgent that the Students should know they could always come crying to him. As Ercole had come crying to him. "When it is a matter of consoling one of my brothers and children I leave everything,"[42] They would learn that along with offers to "kiss it better," Alphonsus was ready to administer punishment on the "this hurts me more than it does you" principle. But there was nothing in his dealings with any of these children to suggest that he was happy to see them turn into adults.

The row which erupted in October 1751 had its origins in Alphonsus' inability to cope with his own desire to keep Students as children. Abbot Muscari, arrived from Rome that June, was, at the October Chapter meeting, elected a Consultor General. And on account of his being a learned man, Alphonsus had put him in charge of the studies of the dozen young men at Pagani. But he could not stop worrying about what the youngsters were being taught. Too much history, evidently, too much philosophy, too many languages. Alphonsus could have no real complaint against an education so well balanced, so like his own except that it made no provision for keyboard practice. He had himself been conducting classes in cosmology[43] and arithmetic and grammar. But there was something uncongenial in the tutor's tone. He was throughly aroused on the discovery that the Abbot was not only giving a dangerous emphasis to academic excellence, actually awarding marks for essays, but was suggesting to his students *en passant* that some of the penitential practices that they had all kept up since the good old Scala days, like eating a meal kneeling on the refectory floor, or making a sign of the cross on the floor with one's tongue, were rather "childish."[44] Not fit for grown men. Most horridly destructive of the way Alphonsus ran the Congregation, the Abbot was fostering the notion that any one of them discovering a fault in another should speak quietly to his fellow about this lapse rather than go sneaking to the Rector like a toddler.[45] No matter that the learned Abbot was citing Aquinas to his purpose. That just made Alphonsus even more annoyed. So the Abbot withdrew for a respite from them all and began to think about founding another missionary Institute.

Muscari had, however, been an inspiring Student Master. Attractive enough to draw these children from their Father. "Four of these young men, the best of them, resolved to turn their backs on the institute and follow their new Founder."[46] They would soon be off, Tannoia guessed sarcastically, to the Mogol Empire, or Paraguay, perhaps, or China....[47] Neither he nor Alphonsus, when fretting about all this, cared to recall Alphonsus' own young ambition to be off to foreign parts, a missionary to the Cape of Good Hope, or India, perhaps, or China....[48] On October 13, the four best young Reverend Brothers, Adinolfi, Spera, Cacciatore, and Siviglia, presented themselves to Alphonsus with staves in their hands and mantles over their arms, demanding to be set free of their Redemptorist vows.[49] They were adolescents with fine Christian imaginations supposing themselves old enough to set out just like Jesus' original disciples to preach the Good News. They were asserting themselves, preposterously no doubt but seriously, as men who should be given men's work. They needed to be assigned something to do that connected them with the mission of the Church, to be shown that they were, as they grew up in the Congregation, being taken into confidence by the Father. But Alphonsus thought to deal with these little ones by becoming no higher than a toddler himself, getting down on his knees,[50] and by employing the strategems of a toddler, tears gushing from his eyes, to get his own way.[51] "What harm have I done you?" He summoned the language of bedtime story to make the little ones listen. They were acting out one of Basile's folk tales of ogres and innocent babes walking into the trap. Everything took on a nursery tone. "He seemed like a frantic mother," Paschal Caprioli, 1728–1813, their fascinated classmate, observed.[52]

Alphonsus was reprising the only way he'd been shown by Don Giuseppe for a father to persuade a child. Such falling down, weeping, warning, had continued to be his way of handling a crisis long after the children had grown up.[53] It was exactly his response to Alphonsus' declaring his own decision to lead a life different from that his father had planned for him. To lead a missioner's life. Everyone could see a likeness of Alphonsus to his father. Sometimes this was of practical use. Villani had very recently been assuring Alphonsus that "the frail bargue of the Congregation" required a reliable Captain.[54] But this time it was quite ineffective. "Wait," said Don Giuseppe. "Just take more time to think," said Don Giuseppe. "I love you," said Don Giuseppe, "don't upset me." "Wait" said Alphonsus. "Go on a eight-day Retreat," said Alphonsus. "No Father," wrote Tannoia, "could have done more."[55] But somehow this sort of thing had no effect this time either. All they replied was "We have to go." Just as if they were so many grownup sons. They left. "Poor children," Alphonsus wept. They had been "such angels."[56] He had to write to the whole Congregation about them. "They have abandoned God."[57] Their futures must be terrible. "They will find the exercise of prayer very difficult because in prayer they will be plagued by remorse of conscience for having left God." So they will abandon prayer. "God knows where they will end." Well, they still have a student left, Nicodemo de Angelis, 1730–1792, who is "truly an angel."[58] Alphonsus is recovering very quickly from this disappointment.

And then the prodigals returned. Well, two of the four returned and another of them hung around. Gaetano Spera, 1730–1762, was back with them almost immediately and proceeded without further incident to ordination by Bishop Tommaso Pacelli, 1715–1780, of Bovino in June

1753, and, less than a decade later, to "the death of a saint" at Pagani.[59] Domenico Angelo Siviglia, 1730–1797, delayed his reentry for a few months, but was pleasedly greeted by Alphonsus, making his profession, April 29, 1752, being ordained in December by Bishop Gerardo Volpi, 1692–1768, of Nocera-Pagani, becoming an effective spiritual director of those many contemporaries who suffered from too scrupulous a conscience, and dying in Pagani of a sudden stroke.[60] The dilly-dallying Domenico Cacciatore, 1730–1781(?), was granted readmission to "our family" in 1759, but he could not settle in the house; he remained an auxillary of the Congregation for the rest of his life, coming over from Salerno to celebrate the greater feasts with the community at Materdomini.[61] The most complex of them, Paschal Adinolfi, b. 1728, "my dear companion in the novitiate," "the Benjamin of Muscari," "touched by a demon,"[62] returned with Spera on Friday, October 16, 1751, left again Tuesday, October 20, taking his brother, a priest at the Chinese College, with him, went off to Rome, in quest of Muscari. There the Abbot circulated a long letter of complaint against Alphonsus, which he said had been written by young Paschal.[63] It may have been.

Francesco, watching all their antics, must have been very disheartened to hear Muscari coupled with that demon, for the Abbot had seemed one of the few good guys when Villani and he were dealing with the Curia. Perhaps he could understand how those Students had been charmed by the cheerfully civilized tone of the Abbot's conversation. Perhaps he could sympathize with their hopes of being assigned to some work that would use more of their talents. But, giving a high value to perseverance in service, Francesco cannot have respected these flighty young men. If Alphonsus and the Fathers were now, so soon after denouncing them as "furies from hell," quite willing to have them back, to talk again of "angels," it was not his place, of course, to make an objection. He must just get back to work in the kitchen.

Chucking the Glass

Just what clerical distinction those Fathers made between a scalliwag Student, even a Reverend Brother like a fury from hell, and a lay Brother was made quite plain in a sorry sequence of events involving chronicler Tannoia himself.[64] Francesco was this time deemed to be offering them all a warning example rather than an encouraging model. But such a warning to the Brothers was not at all opposed to Tannoia's purpose when putting his obituary together. He could show that good came out of this shocking affair.

It all happened at the start of May 1752. While Francesco was setting the table at Pagani, someone, it may well have been one of those pesky Reverend Brothers, threw him a cheeky remark and the suddenly exasperated Francesco chucked a drinking glass at him.[65] It is reassuring that there's no suggestion in any of the several versions of this story which went round that the cheeky chap made a complaint against the out-of-line Brother. Rather, Francesco himself, aghast at his resort to violence, and certainly not going to wait to be accused, at once reported his fault to the Rector.[66] His punishment, like everything else about Francesco, must be exemplary. Indeed the Rector and Consultors were of the opinion that Francesco who had taken the vow of perseverance but was not, of course, "in vows," should be immediately dismissed from the Congregation.[67] No matter that he had been working for them, working with them, working well for sixteen years. No matter that it had been his capable support which had sustained Villani in the 1748 negotiations for their nice new Rule.

Happily, "our Father Alphonsus happened to be in the house."[68] He was inclined to be lenient. He allowed that chucking the glass had been "a most serious fault," but noted, too, that Francesco had not planned it. He'd simply responded without thinking. The severer Fathers had right on their side, of course, but there must always be room for some discretionary kindness. "He doesn't deserve sympathy," Alphonsus wrote to Rossi, Francesco's old friend at Ciorani, "but we mean to be indulgent towards him."[69] Francesco was to be given a second chance at the novitiate. It was with him as with the noncommissioned officer who, drummed out of the regiment, knows no other life and re-presents himself to the recruiting sergeant to be signed up as a trooper. "Since he no longer belongs to the Congregation," Alphonsus wrote indulgently, "his position is that of an ordinary postulant." The thirty-seven-year-old was stripped of his Brother's habit and returned to the postulancy at Ciorani under Tannoia's direction, told not to leave the building, forbidden to associate with the Community in the Common Room or the Refectory. "In regard to meals, impose some further mortification on him, I leave it to you."[70] Francesco was, however, as a gracious concession in this penitential regime, to be allowed to go to Communion once a week.

Having got this matter settled, Alphonsus could turn to another. "Send me a little more of that roasted coffee." Then his mind came back to the Brother. Would he be properly grateful? Would he realize who had been his protector? Alphonsus, like the rest of us, liked to be liked. Liked to be thanked. "Tell Brother Francesco that it is to me that he owes this indulgence, because I wish him well; I hardly think that any other superior would have done all this for him."[71] But, just in case the Fathers failed to insist on its being on account of Alphonsus' personal intervention that all this kindness was being shown Francesco, Alphonsus wrote a letter to the Brother. And the Brother wrote back.

Francesco proved properly grateful to Alphonsus. "My dear Father," he wrote from his second novitiate, "I heartily thank you for not having expelled me from the Congregation."[72] His letter, however, is not entirely simple thanks. Francesco can turn a little homily himself as he explains their situation to Alphonsus. God is being good to them both, Father and Brother together. Alphonsus must be happy and grateful to have such an opportunity to be kind to Francesco. "God will reward you for your charity towards me." As for himself, "It seems to me that the Lord must be at a loss what more he can do to make me love Him." They can see together, punisher and punished, the gracious hand of God in their experience. "I feel great sorrow for the fault I committed, but that which appears to be a disgrace in the eyes of men, is really a favor from God." They can see that together, too. Francesco finds the explaining language for his story in the Church's celebration of Adam's sin, "I often repeat 'Happy fault' for," he adds, moving swiftly into the happier language of *imitatio*, "in all it has caused me to suffer, I have simply been made to resemble Jesus Christ." Francesco's meditations have brought him to a precise christocentric meaning for the humiliating stripping he has endured. "He too was despoiled of His own garments."[73]

If, reading this letter, Alphonsus begins to shift uncomfortably at the possibility of being himself likened to Pilate, he has to read on. Francesco is not to be stopped from his Christian account of what has happened to them. "I tell you this frankly."[74] Things have not been as others may have supposed. Alphonsus must know that to a Christian mind the punishment he has imposed is not at all shaming. Francesco has had always before him the image of the abused Jesus. "The first time I went out of the house, I was so absorbed in contemplating Jesus dressed as a madman that I did not even notice that I was wearing secular clothes." It is, most evidently, an honor to be stripped of the habit. Alphonsus should know that Francesco thanks God for all that has happened. It is God's own doing. So he must be off again to tell the Lord that he will endure any penance so long as he is not sent away from the congregation. "I keep cheerful," he assures Alphonsus over his shoulder as he goes off to chapel.

Francesco was yet entirely aware of himself as an exemplar of how things should not be. So he must ask pardon of "the Brothers whom I have scandalized," confident at the same time "that they have not ceased to pray to God for me," keeping him in mind as Brother among Brothers.[75] Perhaps they had been scandalized. Perhaps not.[76] But watching his humiliation, remembering in years to come, Brothers would certainly be aware how largely it appeared to the Fathers that a Brother's self-respect as their *famulus* was tied to his wearing that habit.

Tannoia had no desire to stir up any further talk about the habit. All he wanted was to give an improving twist to this sorry tale. "Brother Francesco bore all with patience, and if his fall had given us scandal, his submission to all the penances enjoined on him gave us far greater cause for edification."[77] So it was, Tannoia records, that having undergone six months novitiate, "to my great satisfaction," Francesco was again clothed in the habit.

He was told to stay awhile at Ciorani under the eye of Tannoia. He was to be assistant to the Brother Infirmarian, measuring out a cordial or two, getting a glass of water from the kitchen, emptying a chamber-pot. There he tended Andrea Zabatti, 1731–1753, another of those Students vomiting blood. Francesco had never been much good with the dying. That had been plain to poor Gennaro Sarnelli in 1744. But Francesco was doing his best. Rather clumsily, perhaps, when he brought Zabatti his thin milk-sops, he attempted to cheer the pious Student by turning the conversation to that happy time with Villani in Rome and their celebratory pilgrimage. "I was so happy to see the house of the most holy Virgin at Loreto," he told Zabatti, "but you, you are going to see the Virgin herself in Paradise."[78] Was there anything more he could do? Yes? He read him Alphonsus' "Prayer for a Good Death."[79]

On Zabatti's dying, Francesco was first sent with a mission team, to shake out mattresses, cook soups, teach a little catechism, but, at the close of the Marianella mission, he was kept at Naples to do an assortment of jobs, including now the delivery of packets at the porters' lodges of the great men involved in Alphonsus' affairs, and sometimes the delivery of word-of-mouth messages to the great men themselves. As Alphonsus became more the author, Francesco became more the secretary, literary agent, and book carrier, scurrying between printing house and bookstore and customs office. And again, the scope of his work changed. His cheerful efficiency as Alphonsus' gofer encouraged other Fathers to employ Francesco. He was soon, Tannoia observes, unmarvelingly, doing innumerable errands for the whole Congregation.

This was a time when the Congregation was engaged in a series of ungainly lawsuits with the squireling neighbors of the houses at Ciorani and d'Iliceto.[80] There was a great deal of to-ing and fro-ing, messengering from office to office through the government center of Naples. Brother Francesco was dealing with civil service committees, ministerial under-Secretaries, lawyers, archivists, prelates. Yet Garzilli remembered that during that whole time, "we never heard a single complaint against him."[81] Landi recognized that Francesco's cheerful handsomeness must have been a help at such interviews, "Everyone learned to recognize him, calling him by name, and he was known throughout Naples for his affable manner and likeableness and readiness to give a genial reply."[82] After the lawsuits had quieted down, Francesco remained a well-known and liked character to the gentlemen of the city. Tannoia was struck that Gennaro Fatigati, Alphonsus' old chum at the Chinese College, should have had the greatest possible affection for the Brother. He could not, however, be content with an explanation which set this popularity down to the natural attraction of a cheery countenance. It was rather, he states assuredly, "the good Brother's humility and recollection" which won the Congregation the good will of the grandees.[83] Indeed, "Councillor Vitale and Secretary of State Brancone both came to esteem Francesco as a saint." A like estimate, surely, would have been made by those Fathers who, arriving unannounced at the Naples house just as Francesco was about to have his late supper, were fed with his bowl of the soup.[84]

Gradually, Francesco had become "the Brother at Naples," "our Brother in Naples," even "our Brother Procurator at Naples," and at last, in

Alphonsus' letters to the Remondini, "the Brother in charge."[85] Under the direction of Father Ferrara, he acquired a range of expertise in the book trade: packing copies of Alphonsus' publications for buyers in the Kingdom, then handling the bills of lading when the Remondini consignments arrived at the Custom House, and at last entrusted with the dispatch of Alphonsus' corrected proofs to Bassano. "I wrote to the Brother in Naples to send you together with the *True Bride of Christ,* two other little works recently composed by me. They are quite small, but very useful."[86] But if they were to be used, the Remondini really must reduce their prices for the Kingdom markets. The priests were impoverished. The nuns had bought *True Bride* long ago. And though he had sent his orders to the Brother about selling books in the city convents, "He tells me that they have been unable to dispose of them." It must certainly have pleased Alphonsus more than the Remondini that "our Brother Procurator" was, however, reporting that the stocks of the reasonably priced *Selva,* which Alphonsus himself had had published in Naples for his impoverished priests, were quite exhausted.[87]

Then, in August 1767, Ferrara died. He, too, was exhausted.[88] He left a huge stock of the *Selva* unsold after an ambitious second printing at Naples, and quite a pile of the Remondini edition of *Theologia Moralis.* And somewhere there must be a store of those books by other Remondini authors which Alphonsus had once promised he would sell in the Kingdom. "I think," Alphonsus wrote hopefully, "I think he put some Father in charge of the volumes he had in his possession." Surely that number could not just disappear? Cupboards would have to be searched. But he himself had, of course, no time for all this. "Father Ferrara's death has cast the whole business into doubt. I have now no one who possesses his ability or who wishes to undertake this task." No Father, anyway. It was a relief to learn that Francesco had the books in a secure warehouse in Naples, but they must now be consigned to some professional bookseller, otherwise "I am afraid they will become the prey of mice and moths."[89] The first prospective buyer proved unsatisfactory. Francesco was sent scouting for another. "My agent informs me that he has spoken to a number of persons concerning the sale but has not been able to complete a bargain with any of them yet." It was very tiresome. Francesco was obviously not so competent. "If I were able to go, I should succeed better."[90]

Still, the Brother, Alphonsus had long ago decided, was able to unpack and pack books, to send a parcel, and to trot off to the post office to collect a packet. He went on using him for these uncomplicated tasks. "I have written to the Brother in Naples to send the book on the Passion and the two accompanying works to Signor Moschini, that he may forward them to you." Francesco could, of course, only be trusted with such business because Alphonsus was keeping a careful watch on him. "The book on the Passion is printed in Naples, and I ordered the Brother to send a copy of it to Signor Moschini, so that he might forward it to you. I suppose the Brother has done so, but I shall write to him again on the subject."[91]

At the Naples Station

It must have surprised Alphonsus that the worldlier Ercole should have greater confidence in Francesco's capacity to deal with a diversity of men. But Ercole had taken his opportunities to make careful note of Francesco. The Brother had lived for a time in an attic of Ercole's newly acquired palazzo on the Via Saint Maria ante Saecula. There, as if Francesco were indeed another Vito, almost one of the Liguori class, Ercole would sometimes invite him down to dine with him, ask his advice, persuade him to transact a difficult piece of business for him.[92] Francesco's manners were evidently good enough not only for him to represent Ercole in negotiations with a tradesman but to be called to supervise the Liguori boys, Pepito and little Alfonsino, when their papa went off to the Marianella estate.[93]

Perhaps it was through superintending the boys that Francesco himself was becoming, as Garzilli recalled, when Tannoia asked for reminiscences of the Brother, "a man of singular patience," "always steady," "always constant in his goodness," "always praying," "according," the dutiful Father was quick to add, "to our Rule."[94] Once the boys had been packed off to the College of the Nunziatella, Ercole brought Francesco down more often. They would discuss a diversity of topics over an evening pipe. When alone in the house, Francesco was, like Vito, "a great reader" after the business of the day was done.[95]

But life was not likely to go calmly for any Brother in that firing line between the Liguori brothers. Any more than for the Brother in the line between Rector Major and a Rector. Irritated that Ercole had done nothing about the water mill, Alphonsus quickly identified the culprit. "It was Brother Francesco, I know, who was at fault, telling you that the Carmignano affair had been settled."[96] Francesco was in hot water again during one of Alphonsus' rare visits to the palazzo. Going to waken Alphonsus in the morning, Ercole found him stretched in a fainting fit on the bed and at once sent for the doctors. On his coming to his senses, Alphonsus discovered he'd been undressed and put to bed. He had a horror of anyone's touching him, at least since his days on the Incurabili wards, and was furious with Francesco for having permitted the outrage.[97] Francesco moved out of the Liguori palazzo and rented a room in another part of town. His time and energies should be entirely at Alphonsus' disposal.

Life, however, went hardly more calmly for him. There was the time when Alphonsus, on his way through Naples to give a mission at Benevento, met Francesco in a city bookstore. "What are you doing here?" "Looking for the new edition of Augustine's sermons that Father Caione has commissioned me to buy." Thoroughly roused, Alphonsus at once rattled off a short sharp letter to Caione, deploring his spending the money that way. The house, Alphonsus was sure, had a set of Augustine already, even if it were not well-printed and the bindings were collapsing. If they had money to spend they would be better buying Rinaldo's *Compendium* of Baronio's *History of the Church.*[98] It would obviously be better, he wrote on reaching Benevento, if Francesco were to return to the ordinary occupations of a Brother. He really should not be browsing in a bookstore. Alphonsus had a handy list of just the jobs for him. Francesco must take the clock back to the maker and swap it for one that chimed the hours and half hours, he must go to the bank to arrange a bill of credit and convey funds for the new plasterwork at Materdomini, and for a change of pace, he should take himself off more often to the Incurabili, sign up as one of their regular volunteers, and, oh, yes, he should go back to the palazzo and stay with Ercole until their ninety-four-year-old mother, then in what must be her last illness, died.[99]

Back again in the tenement, Francesco was, like Vito at Scala, as he must have remarked, himself a house of the Congregation.

Tannoia hardly noticed the time, thirty years in all, that Francesco was left to manage at Naples, no Community support, simply Community duties. An unceasing series of commissions. Keeping a copy of Bianoni's *On the Power of the Church* ready for Abbot Muscari to collect, sending copies of *True Bride* back to Remondini, dispatching fifty ducats to Villani, carrying fifteen ducats to Don Giovanni Oliviero, rearranging the distribution of ten of those Villani ducats to Angelo Maione, getting sometimes in a muddle, but regularly collecting Alphonsus' pension from the College of Doctors, and every now and again succumbing to fever because the air in the hired room was bad for him.[100] "Ah well, *Fiat voluntas tua,*" sighed Alphonsus when told of another of these bouts of illness.[101]

Francesco overworked himself into continuous physical discomfort. "I have learned that Brother Francesco is afflicted with a hernia," Alphonsus wrote in August 1771 to Father Maione who had been posted for a while to Naples. "Have some person of experience in such matters examine him at my expense, in troubles of this kind such persons are preferable to certificate-physicians."[102] He rather fancied himself as such a person. "First of all, reduce the hernia little by little, gently." A soothing ointment often aids this process. "Then a truss should be applied to keep everything back in place." Not a wooden truss. "That, I know from experience, would be useless." One made of cloth which would fit itself to the body would be far better. Getting into his medical stride, Alphonsus shifts from particular care for the Brother into some generalities about trusses. "It is necessary to keep it pretty tight—I do not mean when one is lying down at night, but whenever one is going about or standing." He shifts again into considerations of the Congregation's business. There is a tacit acknowledgment now that Francesco is running things at Naples, and not at all incompetently. Derivingly, there is an acknowledgment that other Brothers may not be incompetent either. One of them might well have to substitute for him if he got too ill for the work. "Should the Brother have to go to Pagani, you must, I beseech you, acquaint yourself with every aspect of his work in Naples, so that you may be able to instruct the replacement Brother."[103] Maione must be particularly careful to identify the cupboards in which Francesco has been keeping the unsold copies of Alphonsus' own books. And "it is of the utmost importance" that Maione continue the little arrangement that Francesco had with the porter at the College of Doctors to give him the nod when new candidates were being aggregated, "so that we may go to the College on the day and claim the fee."[104] It was almost as important that Maione get hold of whatever money was in the Naples cash box. It was quite ordinary for Francesco to be holding as much as one hundred ducats at a time. He does not expect other Brothers to be as reliable. "I did not wish just any Brother to take care of it, we cannot trust everybody." And then, with the money, Maione would have to pay the bills of the printer and the paper dealer and Girolamo Cuomo, their usual bookbinder. Alphonsus had never had to deal directly with the man, but the Brother had told him that he was "very methodical in his business affairs," so that part of these tedious affairs should go well. Alphonsus is evidently to-ing and fro-ing in his opinion about one Brother's being capable of supplying the place of another. "Tell me also what Brother seems to you most fit to take Brother Francesco's position, should he be unable to continue." Happily, this time, Francesco very soon decided that he was well enough to return to his station.

He was not getting more cheerful in his work. Francesco's uneasiness of temper was that of an essentially serious man. Serious about the use of time. Whenever he heard the new clock strike, he said, "Another half an hour of our life has gone." Serious about a lifetime's end. "There is God and there is hell," he had told the lascivious dame. "Every Christian," he was now telling young Brother Michele, "should have death before his eyes, that will secure that he will always be anxious not to become unpleasing to God, and so he will always be in grace."[105]

Michele Ilardo, 1745–1795, was not then ready to appreciate what this tedious old man was telling him of the significance of that vow of perseverance which he had so lately taken. For him, as for most young men taking any vow at any time, the idea of perseverance, of staying, keeping at it, was only notionally connected with the oncoming reality of his own death.

Francesco had been, doubtless, sensitive to this difference between them. But he was right to continue to tell Michele what he had learned from his experience. He wanted to warn the young Brother against the risks to his Christian quiet in the rush of city business which was, rather too evidently, beginning to exert its attraction on this bright youngster. "During the short visits I used to pay him, he never spoke of anything but death." The recollection of their conversations would sustain Michele during his own last years, when he should contemplate with a wry and thankful sympathy what Francesco had been saying of "the shortness of life." Francesco had seemed, at fifty-nine, an old man to him. Michele himself died, worn out by all the jobs his quickness had convinced others he could do, aged fifty.

Living simply in the tenement block, above the room of a widow, an old fear came to Francesco as he sat with her and her three little boys of an evening. The old man, not quite realizing that he was no longer a temptation to ladies, began to worry about his reputation and that of the widow. What were the other tenement dwellers saying? So when he went up to his own room, at the end of an evening's pleasant chat, he was careful to take a couple of the boys with him. They would sleep in his room and thus put a stop to any unpleasant gossip.[106]

So it was, the Monday night of Passion Week, March 21, 1774, declining to stay for supper, for he'd already eaten a little dry toast and salad, Francesco went straight up to bed, taking the two boys with him as usual. During the night they were a little alarmed at hearing the old man utter a short groan and then thoroughly frightened when he fell out of bed, speechless. They called their mother. She woke their neighbors. They went off for the parish priest, who arrived just before Francesco died. Tannoia has no details. But it is evident that Francesco had a death just like Vito's death; taken ill while doing the Congregation's business, out of the house, none of the Fathers with him, just the local parish priest.

It seemed for a while that Francesco would not be given a Community funeral, on account of the trouble and cost of bringing a body from Naples the twenty miles to Pagani. But Don Ercole would not hear of Francesco's being interred in the parish cemetery. He was as aware as the next rich man of the need to scrimp and save, probably more aware, but this was a moment for noble generosity. "He has done so much for me," he declared, "that I will not be ungrateful to him now. I will have him buried among his Brothers."[107] He put Francesco's body on a cart and sent him, with a priest to pray as they went, to Pagani. "The corpse," Tannoia says precisely, "arrived at the first hour of the night, and he was buried the next morning.

"There'll never be a Brother like him," Landi wrote, "No one could do as much as was managed by this blessed Brother."[108] Alphonsus was not so sure. "You have probably learned the misfortune that has befallen me in losing our good Brother Francesco," he wrote to the Remondini,

May 22, 1774, "He used to transact all my business in Naples." However, a substitute had been quickly found.[109] "I have stationed another Brother there now."[110]

Gioacchino Gaudiello

In 1756, leaving Pietro Romano as Rector at Scala with Giulio Marocco and Vito, and Mazzini at Villa degli Schiavi with Cesare Sportelli and Andrea,[1] Alphonsus had taken Saverio Rossi and Gennaro with him to erect the Ciorani house on the income generated by the Sarnelli vineyard.[2] Rossi, the Minister, started to look over architectural drawings. Gennaro gradually slipped into the work of both assistant architect and assistant building site manager. By mid-1738, one lengthy wing had been built, capable of housing the returned missioners, together with some inquiring young men and a few retreatants. Like Saint Alessio, Alphonsus found a neat little room for himself under the stairs. The smallest of the study-bedrooms, it was the most convenient for observing the comings and goings of everyone in the house. After this wing of rooms, Rossi and Gennaro saw to the erection of a chapel which Alphonsus blessed in July that year.[3] Their time and effort and money had been well expended on this building. First the house at Villa degli Schiavi[4] and then the house at Scala had to be closed down and all the Fathers and Brothers to be lodged at Ciorani.

This was not a cheerful time for any of them. But, restoring their sense of being at the start of something significant in the Christian life of the Kingdom, they were joined, on January 20, 1738, by Gioacchino Gaudiello, 1719–1741, the enthusiastic young nephew of Don Angelo Gaudiello, the good parish priest of Ciorani.[5]

Tannoia starts his *Life* of Brother Gioacchino with a florid assertion of his holy childhood: "fed with the milk of piety" when a baby, he'd come early within Redemptorist influence "from his very infancy," when he was brought from Bracigliano, where he had been born in 1719, to live with his father's brother at the presbytery. Seeing his uncle and his two brothers go in and out of the Ciorani house, he had formed a great attachment for the Fathers while he was growing up, "without," as doubtless his Salerno aunts had told Tannoia, "inconveniencing anyone."[6]

It was but according to the order of grace that Gioacchino should in mid-teens fix on becoming a lay Brother in the Congregation. And as according to the order of nature that his uncle, the priest, should think this too humble a position in life for his youngest nephew. But the determined Gioacchino had his answer ready. He'd been talking to Vito among the Ciorani lemon trees. "I mean to become a saint."[7] So his uncle went off to arrange matters with Alphonsus. Gioacchino was eighteen years old at his clothing in the habit. He had now to be shown how to become a saint.

Among those good people who were agreed that the height of human possibility might be fulfilled in a uniting life with Christ, there was an ongoing struggle to describe the way of entering upon that Union. For some, Celeste Crostarosa for an instance, it seemed that such a Union was being offered by Christ to any who would receive Him in Holy Communion. The eucharistic Christ, "substantial, real, divine" has as his sole purpose "the transforming of human beings into God." These human beings have only to accept their share in the suffering life of Christ in order to enjoy his resurrection energy and, even now, that intimacy which is the glorious reality of heaven. "He has made it possible for humanity, united to his life, to participate in those divine perfections which he, united to God, shared in his sacred manhood, and which he has made our common property as his brothers."[8] Vito had come to enjoy such a sense of Union. Though for a time he had been obstructed by the nervous Falcoia.

The bishop was among those who were convinced that such a Union was beyond the ordinary dullness of women and men. They were not fitted to enjoy such a mystery. The most part of Christians should value Communion as a reception of gracious strengths to keep them going along the right way. Taking that way, they would come after death into the Kingdom of His Divine Majesty. "It is necessary," the *Regole Grandi* text has it, "that they have a firm will, resolving never to make peace with their inclinations and appetites, but war and constant battle: this is what the saints did to arrive there, this is what the Saint of saints, their divine Master did." Christ is always the paradigm. Alphonsus, at least for this time, accepts Falcoia's version of his exemplarity. Christians are to be united to their Master, siding with him in this battle, making his virtuous rejection of self and circumstances, putting themselves apart from this mondo." So far as one is detached from creatures, thus far one is united with Christ."[9] Such an account of the possibilities of Christian life, choosing to be at Christ's side, "against the world," his grace then enabling the practice of perfecting virtues towards heavenly reward, was easier to fit with the forms of popular instruction and devotion, the sermon, the schoolroom lesson, the talk to novices, than any exalted declaration of Union now. Falcoia showed how much easier in his correspondence with Vito. To the Christian inquirer's disappointment with his spiritual director.

Falcoia had settled for a review of those exemplary battling saints. Not every saint would do. Not every story of a saint. But saints who did the more obvious sort of good. Practical saints.[10] It was necessary, therefore, that Falcoia should check Vito's litany. Point him towards the most useful saints. A fine range of exhortatory stories about these saints was available to those who directed struggling women and men along the narrow path of virtue towards the Kingdom's rewards. *Lives* of such effective models were written, printed, sold on street-hawkers' trays, in vast numbers.[11] Falcoia would direct this son's reading.

Having been shown these models, "the Father" would have the members of the new Institute apply themselves to the exercise of a distinct, identifiable, imitatable virtue each month. The Fathers were happy to employ this handy system in the shaping of others' saintlike futures. The 1745 *Compendio* of Bovino had put an especial emphasis on this exercise of the monthly virtue: "On this they will make their individual meditations, draw their special resolutions, read matter pertaining to it, hold their spiritual conferences on it."[12] There would be an effective self-training in such a program, when conducted under the supervision of an appointed Director.

At the 1749 Ciorani Chapter, it was ruled that "a virtue and a patron saint are to be assigned for each month" in accord with "our ancient custom." So each member of the Institute would be including the month's saint in his litany along with the general protectors of the Congregation, Saint Teresa of Ávila one of the chief, and those personal guardians appropriate to each one's status and function. Some saints and their virtues would keep more than a month-long place in these devotions. So director Paolo Cafaro wrote in simple terms to Celestino de Robertis, who sometimes fantasized about a Carthusian lifestyle, suggesting that they had always a need to be "Martha and Mary equally" or, rather, "more Martha than Mary."[13] Vito prayed to both saints each day. It would be said of the exemplary Gioacchino that "though he loves Mary, he does not neglect Martha."[14] Much the same praise was given to Gerard. Practicing the virtues of these saints together, a Brother might be readied to take his part in the missioner enterprise now and in the Kingdom later. Fathers might, given their priestly vocation, find their example in "the saint of Saints."[15]

Along with differences of emphasis among those who promoted ideas of divine Union and human Virtue, there were differences, too, in the ways virtue-emphasizing directors described the good life, between those who were suggesting a personal "imitation" of the virtuous Christ and those who proposed that the Christian should set about "following" Christ in purposeful practice of his virtues. Falcoia generally employed the language of "imitating" or, with a cognate meaning, of "conforming" and "reforming" oneself to the pattern of Christ. Alphonsus generally preferred a language of "following." The following was for him in the preaching. Like Paul in his preaching. "Apostolic preaching" represents the perfecting experience of his vocation. But that Falcoia and Alphonsus were neither of them likely to insist on either "imitating" or "following" language is suggested by the various versions they made of rules for the new Institute.[16]

Later Redemptorists have been able to make nice distinctions between "spiritualities" of imitating and following, and have found these distinctions helpful in their elucidations of what it might be for them and others to be "in Christ," but these and other languages seem to have been employed rather indistinguishingly by those Fathers who undertook to be Prefects of Brothers. Their addresses evidently varied. Mazzini, at his funeral sermon, assured them all that Vito was "the ideal of the perfect Brother in a Congregation which has as its purpose to make its members living copies of Jesus Christ." Echoing a different director, Francesco assured Alphonsus that "in all that has happened, I have had an opportunity of imitating Christ."[17] Gioacchino became notorious in the Congregation for his refusing to allow any imperfection to distract him from the Brother's vocation to unifying perfection. But on his first entering

Ciorani, he had been taught a different usage. "I want to become a saint and to follow the vilified Christ."[18] To these three Brothers, and to them all, it seemed that however they expressed their hopes in the Congregation, the Congregation would be replying in terms of "obedience."

Assigned at the start of his novitiate to assist Brother Gennaro in the kitchen, and realizing that he was as unsuited as Vito to a life among pots and pans, it must have seemed to Gioacchino merely self-preservation rather than self-subduing that he should be precise in his obedience to this cook. "Go and wash these endives in the pond," he was told. He at once gathered up the leaves, marched straight out into the garden, and threw the whole lot into the pond. There they floated. As Gioacchino stood on the edge, they floated further and further to the middle of the pond. So, deciding they were now washed, Gioacchino looked about for some way of retrieving the vegetables. He got a fishing rod from the shed. He was found by the cook, who had got tired of waiting for his return with the endives, contentedly catching them, leaf by leaf. "When he was reproved for his silliness, he artlessly replied that he'd been told to do so."[19] Even Gennaro, even in the middle of a busy morning, could not be long angry with him. Still, there was some general feeling that he must not be allowed to get away with such a thing too often. "Father Mazzini told me that it was necessary to be most prudent in giving him directions, for fear of the consequences of his literal obedience."[20]

It had to be admitted, even by a hagiographer who was trying to present Gioacchino as an exemplary Brother, that he was not always so literally obedient. Gioacchino figures as the careless hero in a Tannoia narrative which has a very well-known shape. Alphonsus knew a story like it. About a nun who was hoeing a line of lettuces in the convent garden. She eats one for the sheer pleasure of it, and is soon in the grip of terrible stomach pains; being presented to the local exorcist, her offense is quickly discovered, and the exorcist begins his prayer to rid her of whatever demon she'd let inside her. Now comes the surprising part. At the first drop of the exorcist's holy water, the demon protested loudly, "What harm have I done? I was just sitting on the lettuce and she came and ate me."[21] Tannoia's tale of Gioacchino has a parallel start. This is a story, likely, from the very first days of his novitiate, when the youngster had been sent to work with Gennaro. "One day when he was gathering figs in the garden, he weakly yielded to temptation."[22] "It was a weakness,"

Tannoia says, "either of greed or hunger," with no suggestion of there being much a distinction between the two. But for us, as we listen, Gioacchino is like many another folk-tale hero who unthinkingly puts himself into the power of an unfriendly rose-grower, gold-spinner, or porridge-maker. He eats one. Then another. Then a third. Here the story parts a little from Alphonsus' narrative of the naughty nun. There's no protesting imp. But hagiographer and listener are well aware that "the enemy of mankind" has got him in his grip. There's a further resonance in this storytelling of old Adam under the Tree. Gioacchino is at once assailed by the knowledge that he has committed what was then as now a grievous sin.[23]

He had yet something to learn of what Vito was meaning by self-respect. Gioacchino found it repugnant to admit his fault to the others in the house. But he was still the youngster who had declared his willingness to be like the despised Jesus. He must humble himself at the next community Chapter of Faults. He did so with such manifest sorrow that every one of the Fathers, Tannoia was told, was most deeply touched by his penitence. Thus, to the confusion of the demon, what had been feared as a moment of shame became an occasion of honor. "Our Father Alphonsus thought that this glorious victory over self would be the precursor of the greatest sanctity. So it proved."[24]

What might have resulted at the worst in an intimate, Community-bound, transitory, loss of reputation was vastly exceeded in distastefulness for the new Brother, Tannoia realized, at the twice-weekly public testing that Gioacchino underwent at Ciorani. While his uncle the parish priest, who had been so sensitive to the dignity of the family when his nephew had first proposed becoming "only a Brother," looked on, along with Gioacchino's two respectable elder brothers, one of them a priest himself by now, the Brother had to carry the kneaded dough from the house kitchen to the local bakery to be ovened. "This must have been a cause of real repugnance to him." No gentleman carries a parcel. Or so I was told by a reproving Father at the Birmingham Oratory. Birmingham, England. "But Gioacchino overcame nature."[25] He'd caught something of Vito's tone in telling himself how he should overcome nature. In the fight against every demon, the great hall crucifix and the smaller crucifix at his waist were "my rapier" and "my dagger."[26] Gioacchino had certainly caught Vito's habit of talking to himself. Carrying the dough across the street had been trial by combat. A tourney. "Beat the drum, Brother Gioacchino!" he had exhorted himself, "Win, Brother!"[27]

Gioacchino and the Three Brothers

He would catch more of the first Brother's tone when he was sent to work with Vito and Andrea at Scala. "It may be said that Vito was his Novice Master."[28] Vito had certainly been on the lookout for Gioacchino's joining them for the last six months. He'd added this promising youngster's patron saint to his evening litany in protective expectation of his vocation. Not that a Brother could actually be a Novice Master. But he could show him a thing or two. And not only how to avoid getting into trouble on the corridor or in the kitchen. "It was by his example that Gioacchino was excited to the greatest virtue." Tannoia was thinking of Vito's hardworking life amid cooking pans and garden spades and water buckets. Gioacchino, under this tutelage, became as unremitting as Vito in "all the virtues but especially penitence and mortification." And was approved by all who witnessed his exercise in the appropriate spirituality of a Brother. "He began to imitate the proper virtues of Jesus Christ, that is humility and obedience."[29]

Gioacchino certainly learned from the first Brother's patient, obedient, penitential, acceptance of every shoulder-breaking job. But Gioacchino had also opportunities to discern that Vito was "enlightened" in "the sublimest sort of prayer," most especially in his contemplation of the Lord's Passion.[30]

This was a time of no little disturbance of community life in the Scala house. The Rector, Pietro Romano, who had never given a sign of moving out of his canon's residence down the street, severed his tenuous connection with the Community in April 1738. Giovanni Mazzini, who was sent to replace him, arrived with Andrea Villani on May 16. Within three months, he had informed Alphonsus that there was no pleasing the town corporation. They really could not stay in the house. Falcoia settled the matter for them. They must start packing. On May 27, Mazzini, Villani, and Vito were all back at Ciorani. Francesco and Gennaro were already working on the building site.[31]

These three Brothers, Vito the gun-toting land-manager from an upper-class clan, Francesco the decent skilled workman, Gennaro the schoolmastery encourager, presented a range of brotherly sharings in the life of the cross, none of them quite what the Fathers were expecting. They were enabling each other to become better aware, each moment of their days, of the diverse possibilities of the Brother's vocation to be a saint.

Living in the house with these three men, working with them, praying with them, Gioacchino took the most obvious way of imitating them. He was the quick observer of all their mortifications, and the diligent copier of their penances, of hair-shirtedness, of iron chains cutting into his arms and legs, of whippings to blood, of fastings several times a week, and abstentions from all but the meagerest serving of that ill-seasoned soup which was, "at that time," Tannoia recalled with an old man's sigh for the good old days of austerity, when Redemptorists really were Redemptorists, "quite a luxury with us."[32] This Brother was certainly one of that old school. "He would not even take that soup without adding bitter herbs to the bowl." He often used to eat this mess stretched out on the refectory floor. But Tannoia's modern reader should not suppose this to have been at all remarkable. "All these mortifications were in common use amongst us." And, Tannoia is implying, should be again. Though, of course, now it must be more difficult to keep up the practice of such mortifications since they do not any longer have the example of Alphonsus among them. or his nod of approval.

As in his *Life* of Francesco Tartaglione, Tannoia finds himself having to walk carefully among exemplars. Gioacchino is living with both Vito and Alphonsus. "It would be hard to decide which of them edified this Brother the more." Vito had been making that thin soup for years. For those same years, Alphonsus had been adding those bitter herbs. They had all been becoming saints. "This holy Brother had such a great and sincere desire to become more and more holy, that he turned all the good examples of all the Fathers to account," as Fathers Mazzini and Villani had themselves immodestly remarked to Tannoia, "for the good of his soul."[33]

Gioacchino was kept thinning that soup which, like Tannoia, though with nothing of Tannoia's nostalgia, Rector Villani particularly remembered.[34] They all particularly remembered. It was not, perhaps, served to the ordinandi who were sent by friendly bishops to make their retreats at Ciorani, in numbers large enough to warrant Alphonsus' authorizing

Rossi to draw up plans for a second wing of room. No sense in their losing this income on account of some reputation for being stingy with the deacons' victuals. However, that poor soup must have played a part in the decisions of Father Giulio Marocco in June 1740, and Father Carlo Marjorino, to return to their family parishes, and thus in persuading Alphonsus that the time had come to think again about written Constitutions, or at least about some written promise of the members to stay in the Congregation. Protestations of brotherly affection had not been enough to prevent their going or to bring them back. "Do you believe," Alphonsus wrote to Marocco, "that we shall not receive you with the same love as before? Here you will find more than Brothers."[35] He would, since fraternity was apparently so little valued by these men, have to put their familiarity on a different basis. Each would now have to bind and vow himself to stay "among the Brothers."

On July 21, 1740, on the vigil of the feast of Cesare Sportelli's special protectress, Saint Mary Magdalene, Alphonsus with four of the Fathers, Giovanni Mazzini, Cesare Sportelli, Saverio Rossi, Andrea Villani, and the four Brothers, Vito Curzio, Gennaro Rendina, Francesco Tartaglione, and Gioacchino Gaudiello, made the Vow of Perseverance:

> Eternal, omnipotent, most lovable and my most loving Savior and God, I find myself, through no merits of my own, numbered among the Brothers of this Holy Congregation of the Most Holy Savior for the purpose of serving your divine Son and my Savior Jesus Christ. Trusting therefore in your infinite loving kindness, I am moved by a desire to consecrate myself entirely to your holy love and to bind myself to serve with all my power of imitating the life and virtues of Jesus Christ, which is the only way of pleasing you and is the principal purpose of this holy institute.
>
> After many days of reflection and prayer, prostrate in your divine presence and in the presence of my dear Mother Mary, Saint Michael, Saint Joseph, the holy Apostles, Saint Mary Magdalene, Saint Teresa of Jesus, my Guardian Angel and the Guardian Angel of my Congregation, and finally before the whole court of heaven, I bind myself and vow in the hands of Mgr. Tommaso Falcoia, Bishop of Castellammare and director of this my Congregation to persevere, through divine grace from the merits of the blood of Jesus Christ, until death in this holy Congregation of the Most Holy Savior.

> I intend to make this vow with the understanding and express condition that it can be dispensed only by the actual Major Superior or by the Sovereign Pontiff, and by no one else.
>
> Therefore, my God, my Father, and my only and every Good, I a poor sinner who see myself the most ungrateful and unworthy whom you have among all men, offer you the present vow. And in conformity with it, I intend to give myself entirely to you. And so I pray you, through the tenderness of your mercy, through the merits of the blood of Jesus Christ, and of the Most Holy Mary, and of all the holy advocates and protectors, to accept it and to make me all your own through their merits.
>
> Therefore my Savior, since you have given me the grace to make it, so I pray you to give me the grace to fullfill it for your greater glory and that of my Savior Jesus Christ. With your help then, thus do I resolve and thus do I hope, so that I may bless you and love you with all my heart both in this life and in the next for all eternity. Amen.[36]

Sportelli, who had, on account of his intimacy with the bishop, gradually become accepted as their "corresponding secretary," sent their signed paper to Falcoia, who had drafted the formula for the vow. He added a note suggesting their next step. They should have an Archive, like other Congregations. "All these my Fathers and Brothers made the vow of perseverance in the hands of Your Reverence in the manner you will see from the attached sheet. We ask you to send it back to us with some word of advice, so that we can preserve it."[37] Falcoia replied, "I accept and confirm the offering made to the Lord of your liberty with the vow of perseverance in the Congregation of the Most Holy Savior.[38] He added then his note. They should recognize that they were establishing a tradition, like other Congregations. "This is to be done by everyone who wishes to be admitted into this holy Congregation, after the two-year probation, in perpetuity."

Things were beginning to come to order. Among all the other things, the Fathers were coming to some more settled view of what they were wanting in a Brother. And the Brothers were, the Fathers thought, settling into this view of themselves. In Tannoia's representation of him at least, Gioacchino had no doubt of the character of his vocation. "God has called me to be a servant." And he had no doubt what being a servant entailed. He had served in Gennaro's kitchen. And worse places. "It is not for me to question, whether the command I'm given comes from a Father or a Brother.[39]

Gioacchino's understanding of "servant" had been extended by that vow of perseverance. For "serving" had there been declared to be the Redemptorist way of "imitating" the life and virtues of Jesus Christ, of "conforming" to Christ, and thus of pleasing God. And if that vow had been made on the vigil of Saint Mary, the Brother must know that he is called to be "more Martha." There could be no time off from this demanding vocation. "There are twenty-four hours to my day."[40]

That sort of day, repeated day after week after month, must be wearying. Joined with the austerities and mortifications the Brother practiced, it was likely to leave him open to all sorts of illness. Many of them were, indeed, getting ill. May 16, 1740, Sportelli wrote to tell Falcoia that Brother Saverio, who by his marvelous obedience had put the health of his body in danger, was at last taking a little milk. The doctor had good hope of Father Giovanni's recovery from the fever. Father Andrea was now much better. The young student Crescenzio was also in bed, suffering from asthma. Brother Gioacchino, "our angel," was still very unwell with an obstruction, however with the use of rhubarb he should begin to recover.[41] So he did. And was very fast put back to work in the kitchen.

Tannoia would always present Gioacchino as eager to get back to work. This Brother had "an ardent love of labor," "he always chose the most laborious jobs for his own share of the work," "he was in the habit of saying that love of labor is the true test of the virtue of a Brother."[42] Doing the work, Gioacchino was fulfilling the demands which his spiritual directors had identified for his following of the life and imitation of the virtues of Christ. So, "his humility always caused him to select the most menial offices," and "his charity led him to relieve his Brothers from what was most fatiguing them."[43] Thus he increased in virtue every day. Or nearly every day. It must seem now that the model of a Brother that was being proposed to him must, if accepted, inevitably make a man more than ordinarily tired. Liable, therefore, to bouts of grumpiness.

Somehow, once he had been put in charge of the cooking himself, Gioacchino managed to combine Vito's command of infernal imagery with Gennaro's propensity to irritated grumbling. He had never perhaps made a full recovery from that obstruction. Having filled the corridor with smoke from his stove, he'd turn to explain the facts of life to some inoffensive visitor at the kitchen door, even if he were a proper gentleman. "Well," he'd say in defense of this good Redemptorist smoke, "the world is filled with worse smoke." If they did not take his meaning at once, he barked out the explanatory phrase, "The smoke of hell."[44] It could not surprise him, therefore, that even with this smoke coming out of the stove, all sorts of gentlemen should be trying to step into his kitchen, out of the nasty world. But woe betide such a foolhardy person. Whosoever he might be. There were Constitutions to be as austerely observed as any Order's strict Rule. "Don Andrea Sarnelli, the priest, son of that Baron who was one of our greatest benefactors, was standing in the courtyard with Don Gaudiello, Gioacchino's brother, the priest, when a heavy shower suddenly came down. They both ran into the kitchen for shelter." Gioacchino knew that the Rule forbade any stranger to come into the kitchen. So he pushed them out of doors in double-quick time. The two priests had to run the length of the house and round the corner to the baronial mansion. All in the pelting rain. They could not but appreciate such punctiliousness. It must be, they knew, the result of a grace. There was certainly virtue in it. Already a hint of reward and kingdom. Soaked to the skin, but remarkably cheerful, Don Andrea turned to Don Gaudiello: "Now that's what I call a saint!"[45]

It did not, it seems, occur to either of them at the time, or to Tannoia later, that Gioacchino may just have been having a harmless little fun with the two young priests, in return for their jokes about him and the dough-tray.

Gioacchino's portrait shows a thin-faced youth, holding a mission crucifix and a rosary in his crossed hands, just about to grin, but keeping eyes raised to heaven. In life, Gioacchino, when addressed by a Rector, had learned like Vito to keep his eyes on the ground. Villani told Tannoia that no one in the house knew what color eyes Gioacchino had. It may be he had first learned to mind himself at home. Francesco Tartaglione told Tannoia that he had seen Gioacchino, talking with his mother, keep just the same look to the ground. This would be the safest policy with all of them if, as the local artist's work suggests, Gioacchino were often about to grin. At any rate, this humble stance must have kept him out of all sorts of trouble in the shortish time he was in the Congregation.

It became plain to everyone that Gioacchino, the youngest and newest recruit, was likely to be the first of them to succumb to their shared austerities. He was every day less and less vigorous in body. And in mind. Small draughts gave him a cold. Small faults, hardly faults at all, gave him wracking attacks of the scruples. It was not simply that, as the young new Brother, Gioacchino was enthusiastically careful for every observance of every regulation laid down by Chapter and Rector and Brother-Master—on discovering from some precise Father that he had one more holy picture pasted to his wall than the Rule stipulated, Gioacchino was in a rush to tear it down[46]—but that, as he stayed in the house, he gradually became tormented by a series of imaginary offenses. He saw fault in his reusing a length of pack-thread he'd found on the ground: it was not his property, he'd become a thief, worse he'd ceased to be a man of that poverty to which he had vowed himself. And then there was that scrap of paper he'd found in the trash and picked up to use again. "These are the two great sins," Tannoia remembers indulgently, as if none of the Fathers, Rector, Minister, Prefect of Brothers, had any responsibility to help him out of these delusions, "for which Brother Gioacchino was always accusing himself in the Chapter of Faults."[47] But from time to time, Gioacchino supposed himself guilty in other sinnings. After dinner, he was accustomed to examine himself to discover whether he might not have taken some pleasure in what he he'd been eating. That thin soup had become a luxury. He was worrying about that connection of "serving" with "imitating" which had been established for him at the vow as "the only way of pleasing" God. "My Father," he said to Villani, when he was again confined to bed and a bowl of that soup had been brought up to his room, "can one so dainty as I ever come to be like Jesus?" and "is it possible to become pleasing to God by living thus?"[48]

He had seemed, for some long time before this, not to be living at all daintily. Falcoia, in December 1740, had written to Sportelli expressing some worry about their Brother. Gioacchino was, he suspected, putting himself through too tough an eating regimen. "It is a matter of both quality and quantity."[49] Falcoia had been concerned enough to go into detailed recommendations about sprinkling medicinal saffron over the soup, stuffing the ravioli, having half a glass of good wine, dunking biscuits in a late night cup of hot chocolate. That's what Sportelli, Gioacchino, and all of them should try. Sportelli was already trying the chocolate.

Others were not so stomach-minded. In later days Villani, like most of those who had an oversight of the Brother's prayers and practices, was content for Gioacchino to exhibit the delicacy of his conscience in the matter of meals. He indulged the lad's scruples about that soup. He absolved him of his sinful greediness. In this, the confessor was, after all, simply continuing along the line drawn when the Community had solemnly approved Gioacchino's remorse on eating those figs. It was always difficult in a Congregation founded by so scrupulous a holy man to make much of an objection to such carefulness. Alphonsus often said to others, "Gioacchino gives us many a lesson."[50]

So Gioacchino was left to make himself more dangerously ill. He was a young man, just twenty-one years old, with no history of illness. But none of them seems to have been surprised when his health collapsed totally. A low fever wracked him. He began to spit blood. They all knew what such signs signified. And still the Fathers did not intervene to put a stop to his mortifications. They simply stood back and marveled that these sufferings formed "a new school of perfection" for their Brother, "for while his body wasted away, his virtues only acquired fresh vigor.[51]

While the Fathers remained content to take any mortification as a sign of virtue, they were missing the true significance of Gioacchino's sufferings. They did not inquire what precisely he was making of all their talk of "imitating," "resembling", "conforming." Perhaps, indeed, they could not yet entertain the idea that a Brother was capable of so delicate a life of the Spirit as Gioacchino had come to live.

He had entered the Congregation hoping by this to be made a saint. To be laid open to graces, enabled to practice virtues, fitted for the Kingdom. That was the first motive for all those self-whippings. He was beating the demon out of himself in the pursuit of personal perfection. Like the exorcist beating that nun who had eaten the demon along with the lettuce. But he had come, even through meditating on those exhortations to conformist virtue that he had received from Fathers who thought he could have no larger notion of the imitation of Christ, to understand himself as a servant imitating the Suffering Servant. His motive now in his penitential exercises was to be united with Jesus in his suffering. He was anxious to be, at his self-whippings, with Jesus at the post in the Roman barracks. "O that I could be like Thee, O my Jesus! who wert so cruelly scourged for me." He would not let go this wondrous possibility. "Let me be wounded, my Jesus, that I may be conformed to you."[52]

The Bed of His Cross

The Fathers had grown used to retelling the anecdote about the endive leaves, the fishing rod, and Gennaro coming furious from the kitchen. They could very well suppose that it was simply the continued workings of exact obedience which drove the invalid Brother Gioacchino to stumble towards a steep hill near their house. Mistaking a wave of Villani's hand in that general direction, Gioacchino had set out, they said, in the properly obedient belief that it was up that hill that the Father Rector meant him to take his exercise. They do not seem to have been aware that there was for Gioacchino an image of Calvary in this steep hill and a share in the Way of the Cross in his struggling along the path to its top.[53] And that he had supposed the Rector to be opening this Way for him. Clumsy, unimaginative, insensitive, these Fathers were, disappointingly, much like the rest of us. They missed the signals that he was giving them all the time he was in sick bay, signals of something more vital to him than the ordinary practice of obedience.

At the very last, one of the Fathers, Mazzini most likely, a mite more sensitive to what was happening among them, did begin to catch something of Gioacchino's appropriation of crucifixion, of his conformity with Christ stretched on the cross. And to publish something of the Christ-likeness of this Brother. "Once when he was asked how he passed the day all alone, stretched out on a bed of suffering, he pointed to his crucifix, and said "I look in my mirror where I see what I ought to become."[54]

This was a language of a great tradition. It was also a contemporary language. The Fathers, hearing him talk of this mirroring, should have made their meditation on what Falcoia had been meaning by his accommodation of a verse from Wisdom so that Christ should say to the Redemptorist, in one of those drafts of Rule VI of the *Regole Grandi*: "I am the mirror without spot" in whom "those whose eyes are clear and limpid" may look for ever.[55] They had used such language themselves. "This is the mirror," they had said of the Cross, in the Bovino *Compendio*, "in which the disciples of Christ must see themselves."[56] Yet, somehow, the Fathers missed that reciprocity of the Christian mirrored in the mirroring Christ which was being presented to them in Gioacchino's sickroom. They saw only the physical likeness. The young man's body on the bed had just the look of the body on the wall. They took comfort from this outward appearance. "His appearance itself gave us all consolation."[57]

Everything which Rectors and Prefects had been telling Gioacchino of "example," "imitating," "following," everything which he had been putting into penitential practice, was now being transmuted within a mystery of identification with the crucified Christ in whom the Father is well pleased. This young Brother, on the cross of his bed, could cry out in his joyful pain, "God is my Father, I go to Him as His Son."[58]

They could all see that Gioacchino was finally realizing the demand for service made in the very first Rule of their *Regole Grandi:* "You must do this, no matter what fatigue and sweat it may cost you, even death itself."[59] They could see, too, that he had responded to the call made upon every subject of the Institute, in Constitution I, "to be like him in his dying after they have been like him in his living."[60] But hardly one of them could appreciate such a realization as Gioacchino was presenting of Rule XII: "Whoever wishes to become one with my spirit and my heart and not only like me in external appearances, let him love the divine will as I have loved it, and let him equally, always, love the Cross as I have loved it and do love it."[61]

On the hill of Calvary at the last, with Mary "my own Mamma" standing by him, Gioacchino experiences for a while Jesus' own pain of abandonment, "the pain of aridity," but then the pressures of Jesus' own loving are yet more unbearable, only the evangelist's image of the piercing of Jesus' side will fit him: "Get a knife and open up my breast."[62]

It is a wonder that some well-meaning Father did not take him literally. Bleed him at least. But Mazzini gets his meaning. He knows, as this Brother stays looking into that crucifix-mirror, that he must speak the simplest truth. And that his usual language of "imitating," "following," is inadequate here. The two parts of his attempt to express this experience declare a shift in his sympathetic understanding. "You are beginning to resemble Him," he stutters, and then, in a language of present tense identity, "Your bed is your Cross."[63]

Mazzini is being forced by the intensity of the experience into a stranger language yet, stranger, at least to him, as he brings "bed" and "Cross" together. Falcoia had allowed a little space for this language in the texts which were put together in the *Regole Grandi*. The Redemptorist should respond to the Lord's presentment of his Cross as an offer of the most intimate union with him. "In that nuptial chamber I have desired to greet all my wedded souls in union with me."[64] They are to be "my spouses on the Cross." The nervous Falcoia had been rather startled by his own words. He sees to it that the *Regole Grandi* shall scurry back into the more comfortable convention of the day-to-day imitation. "You, if you want to be imitators of me," the Redemptorists are told, "must deny yourselves always," so "always crucified on the Cross, you will be like me."[65] But then Falcoia, as Celeste Crostarosa's sister remarked, was essentially a timid man. Celeste herself had heard the Lord's loving praise of those who "embrace the Cross and lie on it as on a wedding bed." She had written a nicely balanced verse of the Cross as bed and rack:

> On this bed of pain
> And sorrows
> Your are stretching Yourself
> My sweet Lord.[66]

So, in the description of the Institute that Alphonsus put together, with some suggestions of content and phrasing from Villani and Sportelli, for Archbishop Giuseppe Nicolai of Conza in 1747, they were all three ready to recognize the Cross as the moment at which the Lord was "carried away by desire," "embracing that dear wood with tenderness," "stretched out on it," and had come into "the desired wedding with his Church," and Redemptorists must know experiencingly, "with his beloved souls."[67]

It is within this wonder and within this language for wonder that Mazzini makes his sudden affirmation to the dying Gioacchino, "Your bed is your Cross."

There is more. There is life after the wedding of the Cross. Alphonsus, repeating that *Corona* of psalms each day, had been trying so manfully to make his way into the splendor of that prayer "that he may enable us to share in his resurrection by grace." So Gioacchino is sustained from crucifixion into resurrection. He can put down the rapier and the dagger, and come, like the risen Christ in those holy pictures pasted on his wall, holding the lance with its fluttering pennant, from dying to life. "I carry the standard," he cries.[68]

They could all say "Win, Brother!" now, and mean "Win for us!" Gioacchino's death made them all feel more of a Congregation. He was the first to become the saint that each, at his first coming, had heard Alphonsus say he could be. They liked to talk of him. In their own terms. "The Fathers never wearied of calling to mind his virtues." Falcoia thought they exaggerated. "If the other Brothers were to come upon such high-flown praises, they would be scandalized at them, for they would remember the shortcomings they must have observed in him."[69] But he was assured by the Fathers that none of the Brothers remembered seeing Gioacchino commit the least fault. He had always been good. From first day until last. Yet, though Alphonsus, proving himself more sensitive than his companions, observed in his obituary inscription that it was "not on the wood of the Cross but in desiring the Cross that he embraced the Crucified,"[70] they went on for the most part talking of the "obedience," "humility," "modesty," and "purity" of his following, rather than of Gioacchino's mysterious final oneness with Christ.

It is perfectly in accord with the Fathers' presumption that Tannoia, having collected the materials for his *Life* of this Brother, should construct a narrative which leads to the climactic assertion of appropriate virtue. "His last moments were consecrated to the obedience which he had practiced so faithfully during his life." He refers to the incident of the chicken vermicelli soup. This is a cleverly retrogressive strategy. The reader is back with the business of the daintiness of appetite, the anxiety about possible sinning, the Father who brings consoling absolution. This time a fly has fallen into the soup. Gioacchino wonders if he has permission to consume the fly. Happily, Villani is on hand to bless fly and soup. So Gioacchino in one saintly gulp drinks them down.[71] Tannoia can conclude his *Life* of the Brother with an incident that combines mortification with obedience.

Gerard Majella

Gerard, a schoolmaster reported, had been "always cheerful" in class, as an apprentice he had chosen a wrong moment to laugh at the foreman of the tailor's shop, later as the domestic servant of an irascible bishop, he had managed to "keep a good smile on him."[1] He maintained this reputation for merriment through his years in the Congregation: questioned about a rumor that he had been taking a dip in the sea, "Gerard replied with a laugh..."; hearing the music of a village flute-player, "he began to leap and dance"; sitting with the archbishop's secretary, "he laughed a lot at his jokes..."; on someone's beginning to play an air from a modern opera on the recreation room harpsichord, Gerard seized an astonished Father "and danced round the room with him."[2] He was even caught grinning towards the Lord in the Tabernacle as he passed through the chapel.[3] Recording Gerard's salute to Alphonsus as they passed on the corridor, "My Father, you have the face of an angel," Gaspare Caione, Gerard's first biographer, had to add quickly, "and he wasn't being funny."[4]

Gerard wanted others to be jollier. "Stay cheerful," he commands Maria di Gesu when she is not reelected Prioress at Ripacandida.[5] Letting Maria Celeste dello Spirito Santo know that he has at last located a copy of the songbook she had been asking for all year, he tells her to "Sing in your cell," that way, he declares, she'll become a great saint.[6] His immediate response to Caione's anxious inquiry about his health is to say "You really must cheer up, my dear Father."[7] He set about jollying laymen, too. Bartolomeo Melchione had been a bright spark about town when a bachelor, but after a year of marriage, "he had become dull and heavy." Gerard cooked him a meal and then spent the evening singing songs with him.[8] Melchione kept up a chorus all the way home to his wife. His friends thought it a miracle. And it must be supposed that his wife forgave Gerard for keeping Melchione out so late. A nice smile turneth away anger.

There were, inevitably, occasions when this easygoingness made life more difficult for another Brother. Tannoia tells a story of Francesco Tartaglione, who had to cook the community supper, sending Gerard to the Naples fish market, and of Gerard's meeting a poor man on the way and handing over all the housekeeping money in exchange for his tray of tinder boxes. Being questioned by the waiting Brother on his return, "Where's our fish?" the cheerful Gerard settled down to tell Francesco how he'd met the man with the tray, how the poor man was hungry, and how he had bought all his stock, and how he was sure "they'll come in handy some day."[9] "This answer" Tannoia records drily, "annoyed Brother Francesco not a little."

Gerard's smiling had gone along with such sudden alms-giving even in his apprentice days. Wondering what he should do with his life, since tailoring did not really interest him, the adolescent Gerard had gone to consult his Capuchin uncle, Eustachio Gabella, at the Santomenna friary: "On seeing how miserably Gerard was dressed, he bought him a greatcoat; but when Gerard, coming out of the friary, met a poor man wrapped in rags, he took compassion on him, and immediately took off the coat and gave it to him." Tannoia records that "his uncle was not best pleased."[10] Gerard took his reproof in good part and went on grinning.

The ex-apprentice, unsatisfactory nephew, had a try at being an assistant schoolmaster. But his grins betrayed him. Taking him to be quite mad, the boys bound him with ropes and hauled him up and down the street. That schoolmaster reported Gerard to be "always suffering" as well as "always cheerful." But he seemed strangely content to accept the role of village idiot.

There is a tradition of Jesus as madman, as mad in his love for humanity. Reading back from such incidents, therefore, Tannoia takes Gerard's escapades as evidences of an *imitatio* of Jesus as the madman. "What affected him most as he contemplated the Passion, was to see the way our Blessed Lord was reviled as a fool; he therefore resolved to simulate madness so that he could share in His humiliation."[11] Tannoia constructs a narrative in which the village boys are acting like the Roman soldiers who tormented the Lord and Gerard is responding with joy at recognizing his likeness to the derided Christ: "This is little enough to endure for the love of Jesus Christ who made Himself of no reputation for my sake."[12]

Assuredly, the school assistant might have picked up a phrase or two of this "madman" tradition, but it is likelier, more in character, to suppose that Gerard was, in these episodes, simply making an adolescent experiment in self-discovery. "He resolved to simulate madness."[13] Like young Hamlet, he put on "an antic disposition."

Gerard had always been an enthusiastic actor. He had as a little boy, so his sisters Birgitte and Anna Elizabetta giggled to recall, played at "altars," taking, of course, the priest's starring role, "imitating the ceremonies," lots of bowings, genuflections, and breast-beatings, lots of small statues of saints and candle ends and tablecloth copes. His Godfather, Alessandro del Piccolo, the goldsmith of Muro, added that Gerard would go back and forth in front of the figurines, imitating the priest's swings of the thurible. No one at the time seems to have thought this altar-making as at all odd. It was just what imaginative little boys did, between playing cops and brigands.

Gerard had placed a statute of the Archangel Michael at the center of the "Blessed Spirits" venerated at his altar. He presumed that this courteous spirit would make some appropriate response to his low bow. And Piccolo recalled a nice reciprocity in their relation. Seeing the congregation get up for Communion, the boy, quite naturally, attached himself to the end of the line. When the priest refused to allow Gerard to receive Communion until he had been properly instructed, Gerard was sure that those to whom a good boy prays will come to help him. So it proved. He came down to breakfast one morning to announce that the wondrous archangel had flown to him in the night and brought him Communion just as he'd wanted. That should teach the parish priest a thing or two. "This," says the surely back-to-front Tannoia, "was the origin of the great devotion which this holy Brother entertained all his life for Saint Michael."[14]

There's another reference forward in Gerard's own telling of another childhood anecdote. One day, coming back from a wander round town, he'd brought home a very fine loaf. On his mother's demanding where he had got this bread, Gerard replied easily that a little boy had given it to him. There the matter had been left. But later, when he was a Brother, reminiscing with his sister, he said he now knew, what he hadn't realized as a boy, that the child who had given him the bread was Jesus. "Fancy, I thought he was just one of the village boys!" Birgitte laughed aloud at this fine notion. "Her brother was giving himself some very pious airs now that he was wearing the habit. "You'd better come back to Muro and see if you can find that boy again!" Gerard, paying no heed at all to the sorts of distinction others might make between childhood imaginings and wondrous vision and every day experience in the house chapel, replied equally cheerfully, "Oh, I can find him everywhere."[15]

He had more stories yet of his pious boyhood. At Caposele, when the community was sitting round the fire in the recreation room, Brother Gerard told them how he would often stay all night in the unlit church, and how one dawn as he came out of the side door he had been met by a terrible ferocious dog ready to tear him into bloody pieces. A demon straight out of hell it was, for sure. Gerard had a great repertory of these deliciously frightening tales. He told them well. With the true anecdotalist's delight. So the community, of course, shivered and encouraged him to frighten them again. There had been another time, he told them, when a great carving had been hurled down at him as he prayed, a huge wooden figure. He'd barely escaped with his life. Tannoia, trying hard to maintain his character as a reliable historian remarks: "I do not know whether this should be viewed as an accident or not."[16] Less scientific Fathers, on a winter's night, were of a mind to believe that a bad spirit had been aiming at Gerard. And Gerard had to agree with them.

Play-acting As "Real Life"

Even the lad who has been chased by a demon and survived, even the lad who can hold a room of adults fascinated with his story of the demon, must earn a living. So, being a pious lad with an unspoilt notion of the clergy, Gerard answered an advertisement for the general dogsbody job at the house of Claudio Albini, 1679–1744, who had been appointed Bishop of Lacedognia in 1736. He soon discovered why it was that no servant stayed with the bishop for long. "He was absolutely unpleasable," as Don Pelosi, the agent of the Orsini cardinal of Gravina observed. But, Archdeacon Cantore added, "Gerard was quite the hero, never complaining of his ill-treatment." He was, Caione says again, "always cheerful."[17]

The death of the irascible Albini left Gerard again at a loose end. And having, perhaps, on his visits to uncle Eustachio, enjoyed some talk with Saint Francis and Saint Anthony, whose statues were allowed to be most life-like by all who stood before the Santomenna altar, Gerard wondered if he might fit in the friary community. But the Capuchins declined to receive him. Not after that business with their overcoat. Then, in August 1748, the famed Redemptorist missioner, Don Francesco Antonio Garzilli, 1690–1786, came to preach at Muro, appealing for money for the building of a house at Caposele. Brother Onofrio Ricca, 1727–1792, came with him, to shake out his bedding, cook his supper, and count the collection. Gerard cornered Onofrio, pestering him with questions about the Redemptorists and, delighted with what he was told, soon declared "I will live with you." Onofrio was not impressed. This tailor's apprentice was far too thin for them. "The Congregation is not for you. Among us, hardship is the norm, sleeping on straw, rising to a rigorous day...." And, "with a happy face," Gerard answered, "That's just what I've been looking for."[18] Garzilli was, however, as dismissive as Onofrio. So Gerard, the resilient adolescent, determined to go off as a hermit. He told his new plan to his friend Felice Farenga and the pair of them set off for the woods.

Gerard made a rule for their lives in the hermitage, with a fine catalogue of austerities and mortifications. He said later, it was another of his recreation-room anecdotes, that they had determined to eat nothing but roots and grasses but after three days their teeth went quite green.[19] So they went back to their mothers' cooking. And to some earlier play-actings. Not quite so usual among altar boys. Gerard had seen pictures of the Lord at the flagellation post. "His sisters have told me, that from the time he was nine years old, he used to discipline himself several times a day, especially after Holy Communion, with knotted cords, which he had tied together."[20] But the teenager had grown dissatisfied with this *imitatio*. He needed someone else to play the Roman soldier. "Felice Farenga, who was Gerard's great pal, affirms that he several times tied him to a post at his insistence, and then scourged his bare shoulders with a wet and knotted rope." Gerard was always ready for more floggings. "If his friend wanted to stop he pleaded with him to continue, until at length his back became one wound, blood gushing forth all over the place."[21] This, too, on their mothers' discovering what was going on, was forbidden them.

Gerard found the opportunity for a more approveable acting at the performance of the Muro Passion Play on Good Friday. Nothing elaborate. A reading of the Gospel narrative illustrated by a sequence of tableaux. Gerard, deemed the best actor among the lads, perhaps simply the best actor among those lads the cathedral priest thought respectable enough, was chosen to play Jesus. That priest had a fine sense of the dramatic, as fine as Gerard's own. He staged a stupendous climax. At the Gospel announcement of Jesus' death, the high double doors of the cathedral were thrown open and there was the crucified Lord dying on the huge Cross. Relatives of amateur actors are not likely to be their severest critics. But so convincing was Gerard's performance as the bloody, naked, Jesus that when she saw the soldier thrust his lance, and the body shudder, Gerard's mother fainted clean away. "He often used to repeat this story for our amusement in the recreation room."[22] However unfeeling it might be to make such sport of his poor mother, this was too good an anecdote to pass up.

That Passion Play at Muro was performed on Good Friday, April 4, 1749; on Low Sunday the missioners arrived in town. They were led this time by the even more famous Paolo Cafaro, a very small priest with a huge head, so fiery a preacher that he was nicknamed by his fellow missioners, "the Anger of God." The Sunday evening service ended with Cafaro's dramatic exhibition of self-lashing. Just the sort of stuff to fascinate a theatrical boy like Gerard. He stuck like a burr to Cafaro, refusing to be put off by his appearance or by his gruff answers. Gerard's sisters went off to tell their mother.[23] She was as adamant as Don Paolo that her son should give up all thought of running away to be a missioner. Gerard was not the only barnstormer in the family. His mother cast herself as Mary, the sword-pierced Mother of Sorrows: "My son, I conjure you not to cause me this pain by the sword which pierced my heart when I saw you transfixed on the cross."[24] Suiting the action to the words, she struck a splendidly dramatic pose. Tannoia recalled that the Brother made an anecdote out of this, too, gestures and all. It was better than his grimace when he pretended to show them his green teeth. Continuing her part in a melodrama, the day of the missioners' departure, Gerard's mother locked him in his room. But he had seen how romantic heroes in touring company plays effected their getaways. He made his sheets into a rope, tied this to the bed, and slid down. "With one bound he was free." The missioners were already on the road to Rionero, but Gerard caught up with them and repeated his plea to be accepted as one of their company. "You haven't strength to be our Brother," Cafaro insisted, "just go home." But Gerard grinned again. Put on the charm. He knew exactly what the romantic hero would say. "Put me to the test." He was ready to prove his worth. So Cafaro sent him on to d'Iliceto, "rather for the sake of getting rid of him than for a wish to receive him."[25]

Gerard never lost his enthusiasm for performing in a Passion. Going down, as a novice at d'Iliceto, to the cave in which Blessed Felice of Cosaro had practiced his severest penances, he organized new representations of the flogging of Jesus. He could find young men in the nearby township who, like Farenga, were willing to take part in these performances. "His ardent desires were seconded by a man whom he had converted and in whom he placed great confidence, and by a youth of Lacedogna named Andrea Longarello, who was anxious to become a lay Brother; while Gerard acted the part of the victim they served as the executioners." This first assistant was Francesco Teta, another one-time tailor much given to depression, whom Gerard had accosted on the road to Sant' Agata and brought home to Father Fiocchi.[26] Andrea remained Gerard's friend and admirer for life. If the Muro priest directing the Passion Play had very well understood the powers of signs and symbols, it had been the intense realism of Gerard's acting which had affected his mother. And the whole crowd in the church square. It was with just such a realism that he directed his play of the Passion in the hermit's cave. "He caused them to tie his hands together and fasten them to a beam, after which he made them strike his shoulders with knotted ropes until blood poured forth in all directions and his body was a mass of wounds."[27]

Gerard had by this time collected more props. "After the flogging, he placed a crown of sharp thorns on his head and persuaded them to beat them into his head with a hammer." Then one of the large commemorative crosses placed against the church wall at the close of a mission was brought into play. Reading the Baroque devotions of *L'Anno doloroso*, 1690, by Antonio da Olivadi, Gerard had been discovering all sort of new details of the Passion and Death of Jesus. "He had read that the hands and feet of Jesus did not reach the augur holes which had been made for the nails, so the executioners had to draw them to the holes by main force." Gerard determined to share this suffering also. "He had his limbs stretched on the cross until his bones were dislocated." But this limb-stretching was the end of such plays. "The Anger of God" had been provoked. "Brother Gerard went on with these tortures for a great part of the time he was at d'Iliceto and only left them off in obedience to the order of Father Cafaro."[28]

There is a tradition that Cafaro, or some other Father on the Rionera mission, had sent home a message that the community was to expect "a useless Brother." It was not unknown for a Father to use that language about a Brother, any Brother. Or, indeed, about a Father. In a very bad moment, Alphonsus described the great de Paola as "a useless subject."[29] However, it was not another but Gerard himself who made this judgment, on his deathbed, "I am a useless subject for the Congregation."[30] Observing him about the house, Cafaro had in fact been very ready to allow that the thin lad was proving a good Brother. He was passing that test he had asked to take. Cafaro's estimate was quite different from that of the maniacally self-important Don Matteo Criscuoli, b. 1718, professed 1747, dismissed 1755, who was left in charge when Cafaro went off to preach a mission. In this man's eyes, Gerard could do no right. He was always down on him. Imposing severe penances. Forcing him to eat on his knees. Denying him Communion. Many times requiring Gerard to trace forty or fifty or sixty crosses with his tongue on the floor until his tongue bled so profusely that the pavement was stained red. The other Brothers were appalled. So was a young Student in the house, Francesco Maria Tannoia, but he was also, he said later, filled with wonder at Gerard's constancy in these trials. It was as early as this, he remembered, that "we began to say "Brother Gerard is a great saint."[31]

Getting a Story Straight

The Congregation's memory of this saint shows that no one of them knew quite how to place Gerard. They were unable to get their memories into agreed shape. There's no settled tradition of the stories they wanted to tell of Gerard's hearing the unuttered commands of a Rector, of his leading a troupe of Students on pilgrimage, of his leading a company of village louts into the church, of his encountering a gang of laborers at a swollen river's bank, of his being accused of gross misconduct with a girl.[32] There are at least two versions of all these and more stories. Gerard had been unpigeonholeable since birth, or at least since two different dates of his baptism were reported by the parish priest of Muro.[33]

In one pair of stories, Gerard set out to ride from Melfi to Lacedogna, late at night, and in the dark lost his way in the wood of Olfante. Rains fell. Thick fog surrounded him. There was real danger of his horse's missing his footing and both of them being flung to their deaths down a ravine. Then a footpad comes out of the dark. "Behold, my hour is come," he snarls above the noise of wind and rain, "You are in my power." He laughs horribly. Devilishly. But Gerard can handle him. "I command you in the name of the most adorable Trinity to take my horse's bridle and lead me safely to Lacedogna." The brigand bent his head submissively, took the bridle, and led him right to the door of Don Constantino Capucci. This good man, being roused from his bed, for it was now ten o'clock at night, was very surprised to find Gerard tapping at his door. Thus far the story as Capucci repeated Gerard's tale to Tannoia. But, though a good story, it is not quite good enough.

Constructing a context for his revised version, Tannoia would have it that Gerard sat down to a late supper with Capucci and explained how he came to be at his door so late. He can now reorder the narrative as the Redemptorists, Don Carmine Fiocchi, 1721–1776, the gossipy Rector of d'Iliceto, for instance, or Don Francesco Giovenale, 1719–1782, liked to tell it. Gerard recounts his horrid experience of rain and dark and ravine. "Then a man," he says, but at once corrects himself, "or rather a demon," came out of the dark. "Behold the hour and the man," he shouts, "Now I am your master. Hope for nothing. You have disobeyed your Superiors and God will not forgive you." The demon now seems not only to be "in human form" but in the precise form of a Redemptorist Rector as he points to disobedience as the way a subject slips into the power of a demon. Gerard says nicely, "I was a little surprised by what he said." He knows full well that he is not a disobedient subject. The demon, therefore, is lying. He can have no power over Gerard. "Fiend that thou art, I command thee in the name of the most holy Trinity to take the bridle of my horse and to lead me straight to Lacedogna without doing me any hurt." And so, in enforced obedience to the obedient Brother, the demon did. This is now a story entirely fit for Redemptorists to hear and retell. After all, as Tannoia says, "the faithful servant was not like a light hidden under a bushel, but God placed him on a candlestick that men might see his works, and that souls might thus be led to glorify their heavenly Father."[34]

Tannoia, poor honest beekeeper, was always plodding after the sprightly Gerard. He well discerned that this Brother could not be kept within the bounds of what Fathers thought appropriate. Gerard, he knew, was almost, at times, indistinguishable from a Reverend Brother. There was that little pile of books in the tailor's shop, for instance. Scholarly books. Cafaro was accustomed to give little elementary talks to the Brothers on the mysteries of Christian faith. He found that Gerard was following up what he had been hearing with real excitement. "When Gerard was in our house, during that rest hour which the Rule allots to each subject, he ordinarily used the time not for sleep but for reading."[35] He became as lively a theologian as any of the Students. More than most of them. More than most of the parochial clergy around. They acknowledged this willingly. All over the area. Whenever Gerard went with the missioners. At Naples, learned gentlemen came to hear him expound the doctrines of the Church, most especially the doctrine of the most holy Trinity.[36] The Canons of Corato got him to speak to them of "the mysteries of God."[37] Bishop Muojo of Muro, when Gerard went back to his hometown, was much impressed by "the precision of his disquisitions on theological topics."[38] So were bishops Basta of Melfi[39] and Amato of Lacedogna.[40] Don Giuseppe de Lucia remembered how, on his entering a conversation with Gerard, he expounded the doctrine of the Incarnation as perfectly as Saint Augustine or Saint Thomas could have done."[41] Some, of course, were not so pleased that a lay Brother should be received as a theologian. Not that it did them much good to complain. Celestino de Robertis thought it great fun to spread the story of the Naples priest who entered into controversy with their uneducated Brother about the Most Holy Trinity.[42] The opinionated cleric had to make a hasty retreat. Paolo Cafaro's resigned comment must have come to mind again: "Wherever Gerard goes everything is turned topsy-turvy."[43]

As Tannoia, the ex-novice Master recognized, the wonder of Gerard was not that he had learned so much. Given a sabbatical year, Tannoia might himself have learned as much. No, the wonder was rather his being so splendid a teacher. Don Donato Antonio Spicci, one of Gerard's hometown Muro priests, coming one day into the tailor's shop at d'Iliceto, saw a copy of the *Life* of Maria Crocifissa Tomasi, 1645–1699, on the table, open at her account of the inward loneliness of Christ on the cross and of the reciprocating loneliness of the Christian.[44] The priest's face showed the superior surprise he felt at a Brother's reading so sophisticated a book. So, since Don Donato Antonio was ready enough to take up the book and flip through the pages, Gerard asked for his comments on the passage. Not much impressed by the priest's pious waffle, Gerard allowed himself another little laugh, "You a theologian! And you don't get the sense!" So he put him to a seemingly simpler test, requiring the priest to comment on the first verse of the fourth Gospel, "*In principio erat Verbum....*" Finding that he now kept total silence, Gerard could not stop himself going a step further with his teasing, "Come on, it is not in French or Hebrew, so anyone should be able to understand it." He told him to study the passage for a while and then tell him what he thought. So the priest sat down to read again what he read each morning at the end of his Mass. But after reading, and rereading, and considering, he had nothing to say. "You've read it?" asked Gerard looking up from his sewing, "Yes," said Don Donato Antonio, by this time having given up all sacerdotal swagger. "Well, let's hear what you think it means." The house physician, Doctor Nicola Santorelli, had stopped by the workroom and, seeing how the priest reddened in his confusion, could not prevent himself laughing aloud at his discomfiture. This made him redden more brightly. "Now then, Donato, don't blush so," said Gerard with a grin, putting them on equal Christian name informality, "Come here." Then, making the sign of the Cross on his forehead, he told him to give exegesis another try. And the priest began to interpret so confidently and well "that it seemed his words had come from Paradise," so, thoroughly pleased, he trotted off to tell Caione how very well he now understood Saint John's meaning.[45] Even Doctor Santorelli began to feel that he could do a little theological reading too. "His words," he owned, "rendered the most abstruse doctrines intelligible and those which seemed the most obscure became clear and plain as he talked."[46]

It was a puzzle to most of these educated persons, priests and laymen, as Doctor Santorelli said, how such things could possibly be understood by "a poor lay Brother." It is a puzzle, now, that none of them seem to have noticed how natively intelligent Gerard was. Even his exercise of a skilled worker's intelligence had to be set down to some miraculous power. Don Donato Antonio, coming back to the tailor's shop, discovered Gerard, having put aside his book, pouring over a paper pattern intent on cutting the cloth so that he would get, as the Rector had ordered, two habits out of it. "Anyone could see," Donato Antonio said later, "that it just couldn't be done." There wasn't enough cloth in the bolt. But Gerard, pausing only to remark that a man must do what obedience says he must do, turned the paper pattern about, took out his scissors, and cut. When he'd done, there were the two habits ready to be sewn. But everyone else in the shop was simply convinced that there was more cloth in the pieces on the shop floor than in the original bolt. It was all a great mystery.[47]

They were, these priests and doctors, able to deal much more easily with Gerard's quickness in discovering what was going on in another's heart.

"He laid open the deepest wounds of their souls to some, and set before others the duties of their station, and their infidelities in the performance of them."[48] It may seem more remarkable now that, so far from these strangers' resenting such invasions of their minds and hearts, "the fame of the spiritual endowments with which God had favored Gerard, and the sway he exercised over the hearts of men, caused him to be sought after on all sides."[49] They sought him at Melfi, where he quietly exposed a hypocrite mystic, at Cedogna where he stopped a townsman in the street to talk about his secret vice, and at Naples where a shopkeeper came back from chatting with the Brother at the door to tell his other customer that Gerard had spoken of something which he had supposed known "only to God and me."[50]

His contemporaries were as ready to credit Gerard with as fine a knowledge of their physical condition as of their hearts' secrets. There was this Alessandro, a middle-aged widower, who had recently married again. He brought his new wife to Caposele. There they met Gerard and fell to explaining their hopes for a child. "Your wife should be happy and of good heart," said the grinning Brother, always the encourager, "After all you've suffered, she is forty days pregnant," and, he added to complete their joy, "It will be a boy." All came true. Just exactly as Gerard prophesied. Alessandro, of course, was already calling the child in the womb by this kind Brother's name. And every time he called "Gerard, Gerard," he could feel the baby kick in response.[51] So the bachelor Gerard slipped into a reputation for knowing about pregnant mothers. And their unborn children. And their anxious husbands.

Gerard's gracious fame could not but be spreading.[52] "The populace followed him."[53] So did others. On Doctor Giuseppe Salvadore of Liveto's coming to visit with Abbot Prosper d'Aquila from Sant' Andrea, Gerard, to avoid any boring pious talk, turned the attention of these grandees towards the Abbot's servant. He asked the young peasant to play him something on the harpsichord. The villager said he knew nothing of music. He wished to be excused. "The Abbot and the doctor meanwhile amused themselves at his embarrassment." But Gerard again asked the lad to play for him. And so, perhaps he had been practicing in secret on the Abbot's expensive instrument, he sat down at the keyboard and played for them. Gerard could evidently establish an immediate sympathy with such a young man. The two poor men's sons were allies in an escapade. Abbot and doctor were left to think whatever they might.[54] There's a similar camaraderie revealed in the story of Gerard's meeting another youngster carrying a vast cord of wood, far too heavy for him, and Gerard's heaving up one end and bearing the burden with him all the way to d'Iliceto.[55] That camaraderie was felt in the house, too. The Student, Domenico Blasucci, was commonly to be found at the door of the tailor's shop, knowing that when Gerard arrived they would be swapping a few cheery words. Domenico was a fellow Muro townsman, but there was more than local patriotism bringing the two young men together. There was real affection. So Domenico often thought of a reason for passing that way through the house. Like the time he found a needle in his cupboard and recognized at once that poverty demand he return it to the house tailor that very minute.[56]

Perhaps such easy friendliness with a fellow youngster is not so remarkable. But as evidently, Gerard was capable of working his way into friendship with a late-middle-aged Canon. Camillo Bozio of Atella was brought to admit, after a moment of professional outrage that a Brother should be talking theology in his sacristy, that this Brother was not only a competent commentator on Scripture, but a fine companion on a lengthy walk. There was a cheerful piety about his talk. Quite unlike the stuff he had to endure at meetings of the diocesan Chapter. He long remembered the time he and his new friend came upon a country church and how, going in, Gerard had sat himself down at the organ to play an impromptu hymn:

O happy flowers, night and day
Near my Jesus you can stay

Bozio remembered, too, the fun they'd had when he tried to join in.[57] He just couldn't keep up with the jaunty rhythms Gerard was giving the hymn tune. He hadn't Gerard's warmth for such devotions. "My voice was too cold."

Bozio turned out to be a likable Canon. But Gerard was managing to make friends even with the "Anger of God." He discerned the essential fineness of the man. Cafaro was a courteous Christian, unable to sit quiet when he noticed, as he too often had to notice, an incivility in the house. He let Alphonsus know that the d'Iliceto Bursar, Father Lorenzo d'Antonio, 1711–1769, was "too down on the Brothers." He let Brother Gabriele Puzzo, 1722–1750, know that he should not be putting himself "above the others," and exemplified his egalitarian appreciation of the Redemptorist vocation in signing himself to this lay Brother as to each Father, "Your Servant and Brother."[58] On Falcoia's death, Alphonsus had chosen Cafaro to be his spiritual director. Gerard had made the same choice.

There came to be such a sympathy of heart and mind between them that when Rector Cafaro died at Materdomini, in the summer of 1753, Gerard remarked assuredly in the recreation room, "Don Paolo is a great saint. He enjoys the sight of God in heaven." Cafaro had been the ideal Redemptorist. He had been the true imitator of Paul in all things. "And his throne of glory is not far from Saint Paul's, on account of the thorn in the flesh from which he suffered." Apostle and Redemptorist would be talking of their recoveries together. Like patients released from hospital. Tannoia's gossipy interest is hooked by this reference to some secret thorn. And Alphonsus was intrigued that Gerard knew so much. The Rector Major had supposed himself the only one of them privy to Cafaro's special pain.[59]

Perhaps the true wonder was how little interest any of the others in the community had taken in their Rector. Not thinking it their business to ask what made him so angry in the pulpit. It may be that Gerard, in his ordinary companionableness, recognized another sufferer. For he was at various times himself the victim of terrible bouts of depression. There is a famous instance of such a time in September 1751. Gerard, trudging down the d'Iliceto corridor, was overheard muttering, "I can bear it no longer." These were, the Brother who overheard him insisted, Gerard's very words. "His heart was so dried up in him that he felt almost driven to despair." His friend Domenico was coming the other way down the corridor. Seeing the usually cheerful Gerard in such depression, Domenico, quite heedless of the Rule, stops to talk, "Brother Gerard, what's up?" And he, with a bitter sigh says again quite aloud for anyone to hear, "I cannot bear it any more." Domenico knew just what Gerard needed. The Student gave the Brother a hug, making, as the nervous chroniclers aver, the sign of the Cross on his breast. So Gerard was freed from his dumps. He returned to a wanted cheerfulness. And to those accustomed occupations of a Brother.[60]

Taking Risks, Getting Accused

Gerard made a note to remind himself of what that little demonstration of brotherly sympathy had meant to him and what it might mean to another. He wouldn't every time risk an impetuous hug, but he'd do his friendliest best for anyone in the house suffering a like distress, "anyone who is where it has pleased the divine will to place them and they cannot bear it any longer."[61] He'd put them in his prayers. He'd give them a grin when they passed in the corridor.

As Gerard was popularly esteemed to have powers for the quieting of an uneasy spirit, so he was celebrated as the carrier of others' physical burdens. That incident with the cord of wood is an instance. There's another story of his getting a gang of log rollers to swing into action with him, manage the unmanageable tree trunk together, and raise the roof beam high.[62] Another of his meeting a poor old woman on the steep path up to Sant' Agata. She had a load of washing on her head. Though he was by now gentleman enough to go red with shame, he took the bundle and carried the washing right through town into the public square. There are many Christian exemplars for such a carrying of another's burden on a steep hill path, from Simon of Cyrene onwards. But, in relating this story, Tannoia properly recalled stories of the gentleman Vito and the Amalfi porters. "In this, he imitated Brother Curzio, with whose manner of life he was well acquainted."[63] Gerard, as he stooped to lift the laundry basket, like Gioacchino when he carried the tray of loaves, was accepting a further demand of that code of brotherly honor which Vito had established among them.

In the more popular forms of knightly romance, that old woman would have revealed herself as a powerful fairy able to translate the questing hero on the instant to the palace of his lady. But those who followed Vito could expect no such shortcuts. And men of his honor would have to be very careful in dealing with any lady. Gaudiello's experience with the infatuated Neapolitan dame should be a warning to them all. Yet the smiling Gerard was a little careless of appearances in such matters. He was always easy in his relations with women. They could see that this Brother was not a power-seeker. Simply a sharer of what he had been given. They could speak as equals, even when they were asking for direction. He was "continually writing letters to troubled souls" and "giving marvelous support" to the weary, showing himself to be in command of "a unique teaching in the school of prayer."[64] Especially did Gerard delight in the Teresian nuns of Ripacandida and their young Prioress, Mary of Jesus. "When they conversed together on spiritual topics," Tannoia says, "they were as two burning flames mutually enkindling each other."[65] For a time not a week passed without his writing to the nuns and their writing to him. So inflamed were they that on one of his visits when they were contemplating the wondrous love of Christ for them, Gerard had to take such a grip on the grill between them to moderate his transport of desire that it bent within his grasp, "as if it had been melted wax."[66] It was shortly after this, in 1752, that the worried bishop of Melfi stopped all Gerard's communications with these nuns, both visits and correspondence. Gerard wrote all smiles to the bishop, reassuring him that they were all entirely ready to do whatever he wanted of them. "Your Most Reverence must be cheerful."[67] He seems not have been sensible of the danger at which the bishop had been hinting.

It sometimes appears that it was more than ordinarily difficult for Gerard to appreciate any danger of the kind. He was not ignorant of the nastier aspects of small-town gossip. The Muro population had included a few calumniators. He certainly knew that he should not go about alone. Once, at Oliveto, Gerard was told that Don Fiore would not be traveling with him on account of some sickness. Gerard sent him the message that he must recover at once. And he worked the necessary miracle to get him well enough to travel.[68] But Gerard could not be forever taking such precautions. Not when there was good to be done. Doctor Gaetano Federico of Castelgrande recalled that Gerard, being woken at two in the night by Sibyl Sebastiano, agreed to say a prayer with her daughter, Caterina Mucciaccio, who was writhing in the Doctor's doorway. On a sudden the demon molesting her cried out in defeat. "Grr, the wretch wins!" The Brother, thus encouraged, took off the cord around his waist and strung it about the girl, all the time whispering to her.[69] At least he had the sense that time to tell the Doctor not to leave them alone. Another time at Codogna, when he was staying with Don Constantino Capucci and his family, he did not take even that elementary precaution. Donna Emmanuella in the kitchen was not at all happy that Gerard should be talking with their two daughters and the young maid in the room above. "Saints have always trembled when they were in dangerous situations, but this man is conversing with my daughters and my maid without any fear or restraint whatever." On Gerard's coming down into the kitchen with his usual grin, Donna Emmanuella didn't care for his smiling and asked him just what he found so funny. "I have to thank you," Gerard replied, "for having remembered my weakness, I wish all mothers were as thoughtful." It was awkward for her to talk of such things with him. She had no liking for the embarrassing turn this conversation was taking. "Do you not remember," Gerard asked, "what you were saying to yourself only a minute ago?"[70] He knew this mother had been muttering sense.

But even if he remembered Donna Emmanuella's scolding, Gerard was not able to preserve himself from an even riskier entanglement with another Lacedogna family, friends, or at least acquaintances, of Don Constantino and his wife. The magistrate Candido Caggiano had three daughters and a son. The boy being already a subdeacon and two of his sisters, Saveria and Veronica, being nuns, it seemed to the youngest Nerea, a girl of twenty years, that she should enter a convent, too. This provided a financial problem for her parents. Three dowers in so short a time would threaten even a comfortably off family. So Gerard, as he had so often done for girls in such circumstances, collected the necessary two hundred ducats from his richer patrons.[71] But three weeks after she had been received at Foggia, it was apparent to Mother Celeste Crostorosa that Nerea did not have a vocation for their convent and she was sent home. No girl at that time could easily face her townsfolk as "a failed nun." And three weeks was quite long enough to give her such a reputation. Nerea was full of resentment against Gerard who was so clearly responsible for getting her into this mess. She felt outraged. She flung accusations about.

It is not entirely clear what Nerea alleged. It may be that she told the parish priest, Don Benigno Bonaventura, that Gerard had molested her. It was certainly he who forwarded the accusation to Alphonsus. But it is likelier that she told her family with sensible self-preserving care against parental fury, that Gerard had been playing around with another girl. There's a version of this nasty little tale which suggests that Nerea accused him of sinning with the fourteen-year-old Nicoletta Capucci, one of those girls with whom Gerard had been laughing in the upper room while her mother prepared supper. Perhaps Nerea had wanted to be sharing that seductive laughter. Perhaps she even believed there might be something to her accusation. After all, Donna Emmanuella had been made nervous by Gerard's behavior in the house. There was another report that Nerea had allowed herself to be seduced by her confessor, and that, on her becoming pregnant, this priest had been the first to suggest that they put the blame on Gerard.[72]

Celeste, knowing nothing of what was going on, celebrated Holy Week 1754 with unperturbed devotion. Gerard was there, too. He gave her a crucifix with a striking quotation from the liturgy they had sung together that week. "O wood more wondrous than every other wood, being found worthy to carry the Son of God."[73] But he said nothing of what the ex-postulant was doing. They were not to meet again.

Nerea was making an accusation to which every missioner, wandering from village to village, house to house, sleeping in strange beds, eating at strange tables, felt himself exposed. This accusation had been made against Alphonsus himself at Villa dei Schiavi in 1737. And by the local clergy. They resented the missioners getting money from their parishioners for Mass stipends. "They went so far as to say that the missioners intrigued with a woman whom they identified, alleging that she was received into the missioners' house by night; and this wretched creature lent herself to the accusation, defaming Alphonsus even more than the others."[74] Going to the local Baron for protection of his name, Alphonsus had been met with unlooked for reproaches. "What have we here, one of those filthy hermits?" But he had been vindicated very fast. And had written into the 1747 Constitutions that none of the Fathers should go parish visiting unless accompanied by a Brother or some local priest.[75] The Fathers had not supposed perhaps that a Brother could have any reputation to lose. Or that anyone would bother to accuse a Brother.

Now, it seemed to everyone who had been greeted by Gerard's easy smile when they passed in those draughty corridors of d'Iliceto that the charge had some credibility. Gerard was a really attractive young man. They had been recognizing this when they were sending him out to charm money from the local gentry and their ladies. "Women wanted to give him their earrings and men would have him take their best waistcoat buttons."[76] But he was, it had to be admitted, very high spirited. Too high spirited for his own good, perhaps. Dancing in the recreation room, indeed. Very likely the girls did find him sexy.

When Villani arrived at d'Iliceto, sent by Alphonsus to investigate, no one in the community was prepared to say that such a thing as Nerea alleged was downright impossible.

Gerard was, therefore, sent, already in disgrace, judged quite capable of getting into such a scrape, to be sentenced by Alphonsus at Pagani. This was, likely, the first time they'd met. And, "since men of eminent sanctity have fallen under similar circumstances,"[77] since he himself was always quick to discern an occasion of sexual sin, since the d'Iliceto community had not given a character reference for their Brother, Alphonsus felt inclined to believe the accusation. He set the enormity of it before Gerard. Later, it seemed to Alphonsus that he had arranged this interview with Gerard so that the accused could provide a full explanation, a self-defense. At the time, it must have felt to Gerard that Alphonsus was simply following the line marked out by the d'Iliceto Fathers. So Gerard said nothing against his accusers. It was, he knew from Antonio Torres, impossible to remember the calumnies and the blasphemies thrown against Jesus and then to seek to vindicate one's character.[78] The significance of the carved Crucifix he gave to Celeste was plain to Gerard. "For your sake the Savior died on a Cross, saturated with opprobrium."

Alphonsus had customarily talked and written of "the theater of the Passion" and now, in this most intense of all the dramas in which Gerard was representing Jesus, Alphonsus assigned himself the part of Pilate. Not having the evidence to warrant dismissing Gerard but feeling that he must fulfill the expectations of all who were watching them, inside and outside the Congregation, Alphonsus acted in quick defense of the Congregation and its reputation. He could not think of Gerard's reputation at such a time. Later, he might have come to think that it was only by the justification of an innocent member of the Congregation that there could be any effective justification of the Congregation. But for now, Alphonsus forbade Gerard's receiving Holy Communion. He was not to have any communication with anyone outside the Congregation. He was to take himself off to Ciorani.

Gerard, secure in his innocence, secure in the just God's working his purpose out, knew that in this silent *imitatio* of the unjustly accused Christ he was behaving just as Vito would have the Brother behave. A man of honor does not defend himself against vulgar abuse.

It was saddeningly evident to Gerard that Alphonsus had put himself into a most awkward position. As the bishop of Melfi had discovered during the affair of the Ripacandida nuns, Gerard's consciousness of his own innocence allowed him to think only of the peace of mind of his superior. He felt he should be comforting the Rector Major ahead of the dark time. Alphonsus seems obscurely to have felt some mysterious reversal in their situation. He did not know what to do with this Brother who said nothing for himself but who, meeting him in the corridor declared, as if he were determined to sustain Alphonsus' sense of his own integrity against the shock that must come, "Father, you have the face of an angel."[79] And Gerard's smiling ways were having their effect again. Guilt does not look so. If Alphonsus were not sometimes disturbed by Gerard's serene care for him, others in the Ciorani community were becoming very restless about their part in this affair. Most especially about the ban on his receiving Communion. They wanted it over. One of them suggested that at least Gerard could serve his Mass. "Don't tempt me," said Gerard, "I should snatch the Host out of your hands." Caione remembered an incident on the stairway. One of the Fathers suggested going to the Rector Major and asking that the ban on Communion be lifted. Gerard hesitated a moment before saying, "No. No." Then giving a hard blow with his hand to the balustrade to steady himself. "We must continue under the pressure of the will of my dear God."[80]

Meanwhile, not having obtained a confession from the Brother, nor any evidence of his guilt or innocence, Alphonsus was getting very frustrated. Don Saverio Rossi, the Rector of Ciorani, was now required to make more regular reports on this Brother's behavior. Tannoia himself remembered being set by Alphonsus to be an unofficial spy, "watch him as narrowly as possible."[81] But it was not by such snooping that the truth was discovered. It is, in fact, not at all clear how the truth was discovered. It may be that the seductive priest himself wrote a letter to Alphonsus. Caione says that the man was now on his deathbed, and that his confessor required that he disclose his part in the affair. Or maybe it was Nerea who wrote. Perhaps she could not bear the weight of her own conscience. Or maybe it was her confessor who imposed this recantation. Or again, she may have at last told her family the truth. Her appalled parents, the magistrate and his wife, may have written to Alphonsus. Or their son, the subdeacon.[82] There was, Tannoia knew, more than one letter to the correspondence. He did not want to linger on these. He was anxious to get his *Life* of Gerard back on course. But there was still that second interview with Alphonsus to be mentioned.

Making a Claim to the Rule

Alphonsus felt now, as any good Superior, any good man, would feel, very uncomfortable with himself and his government of his subjects. By this time he had listened to Margotta's account of Gerard's goodness. And to the satisfactory reports of Rossi and Tannoia that they had nothing to report. There was no more doubt about this Brother's obedience than about his chastity. Alphonsus must clear things up. This time, he felt it better not to order Gerard to travel to him. Roles were, to his mind, already somewhat reversed. He came across from Pagani to Ciorani. But that was condescension enough. He would see the Brother across a desk. And Gerard, seeing his difficulties, was anxious to help him. He was certainly not going to explain how well Alphonsus had played Pilate in their scene together. But he was hoping to make his sense of a good Redemptorist Brother absolutely clear to the Rector Major. So, to Alphonsus' urgent question "Why did you not defend yourself?" Gerard answered, as only Alphonsus could have told Tannoia (unless some Father were at the keyhole), "How could I, since the Rule commands us not to make excuses, but to bear every mortification in silence."[83]

This scene has been a favorite with Redemptorist illustrators. Paintings of Gerard pointing to an open copy of the Rule on Alphonsus' desk are on every house wall. Its significance has not, however, always been thoroughly appreciated. Developing a sentence from the old *Regole Grandi,* it had been suggested in Rule VIII of the 1744 Bovino text that the Fathers, "these beloved disciples of the Divine Majesty," might, in their search for meekness of heart, "attempt the humblest and most menial tasks in the community" and the example had been given of "sometimes working in the garden." In this same Rule VIII, it is ordered that these same disciples who are to do occasional gardening as a mortifying exercise shall never "excuse or defend themselves" to a Superior, "even if accused or calumniated falsely."[84] This Rule is itself developed further in the Eighth Constitution of the Conza text, the first official Rule of the Congregation, in force from 1747 until the promulgation of the Pontifical Rule in 1749. "They shall try as much as is in them, not to excuse or defend themselves," even though they be calumniated. In this, they will be imitating the Saint of saints. "The Lord never defended himself or excused himself, no matter how greatly calumniated or accused, except in those things which concerned the glory of His heavenly Father." Again in their seeking after humility, it is recommended that they sometimes work in the garden, even wash dishes, wait at table. Seeking after humility is to be an hieratic activity. Decently graded. "The Superior, to edify his subjects, may serve at table on Friday."[85] As plainly, Chapter I of Part II of the 1749 Pontifical Rule, organizing the relations of Fathers in a house, declares "they shall not excuse themselves or defend themselves" when rebuked by a Rector.[86] Silence under accusation, like gardening and waiting at table, is being presented as an extraordinary perfecting discipline in the spiritual lives of Fathers. Neither this Rule, which lies open in those paintings, nor any of the earlier texts is making reference to the conduct of Brothers.

The Pontifical Rule had been obtained by a Father and Brother praying together, working together, suffering together in Rome. That much had been gracefully recognized by Villani when he brought Francesco with him to take leave of Pope Benedict. As the first to know themselves to be members of the new Congregation of the Most Holy Redeemer, Father and Brother had gone on a grateful pilgrimage to Loreto together. But the Fathers had not, as they read, translated the Rule into the language of shared vocation. Nor, of course, had the Brothers. There is a shock for all of them in that pictured scene of Alphonsus and Gerard with the Rule open between them. They had taken Brothers' endurance of blames for granted, as they had taken their garden and refectory and latrine services. Brothers were naturally treated as those at the base of every hieratic organization were treated. As rightless domestic servants were treated. Gerard is asserting the startling new notion that the Rule applies to Brothers as to Fathers. He has exercised his right to perfecting silence precisely as a Redemptorist living within the Rule. Like a Father.

Alphonsus was, of course, intelligent enough to catch at Gerard's meaning. At the development Gerard was proposing for his self-understanding within the Congregation. There was in this claim much to unsettle Alphonsus. Much that he would instinctively resist, at least when the same claim to live under the Rule like Fathers was made by other Brothers.

Meanwhile, Gerard, in energetic harmony with the Rector Major, is repeating his version of Alphonsus' own exhortatory sequence: "How necessary it is to become a saint," "I have been given this opportunity to become a saint," "What, then, must I do to become a saint?" Answering that question, he recognizes that he is not being asked to do very much individually. They are all called to be saints together in the Congregation. "I have what I need to be a saint because others are paying the price."[87]

The Rector Major may have found Gerard, after their second interview, an awkward reminder of a moment when the Congregation had proved to be a less than transparent figure of the Communion of Saints. So Francesco Margotta had quite easily persuaded Alphonsus that Gerard should go back with him to the Naples station for a while. Be out of the Rector Major's sight for a bit.[88] It was during this next stay in the city that Gerard's sense of their all being Redemptorists together in one mission community, Brothers with Fathers becoming saints within the protective Rule, working with the citizens for the realization of the Kingdom of God, achieved its largest expression.

Long ago, taking a gaggle of Students on an expedition, Gerard had slipped into a Father's mode, talking of "my family."[89] Rather like Alphonsus himself. No one of those youngsters had thought this odd. At least no one of them is recorded as thinking his paternal use, expressing a paternal care, as odd. Now, he was dressing as well as talking and generally behaving in the ways that Fathers dressed, talked, generally behaved in the city. The Congregation's reputation was generally enhanced by his playing the Father's part. "My Father," the poor madmen at the asylum would say after one of the Brother's catechetical instructions, "we wish you would stay with us and never leave us again; you must not go away, no one tells us such beautiful things as you do."[90] Gerard's pastoral care was exercised for several priests of the city, too. "Monsignore Amato himself, the flower of bishops in that time, was never weary of listening to him."[91] He was announcing the Gospel of repentance and forgiveness. In ways that Tannoia recognized as almost priestly. There was "an innumerable multitude of people who might almost be called his penitents."[92] Gerard was chatting pastorally at the doors of librarians, printers, and "other tradespeople of our acquaintance."[93] Naples, like Melfi, becomes a "theater" in which Gerard made his appearance.[94] He'd take any chance for a spot of comic acting. On one famous occasion he opened the door to find a servant of the Duchess of Maddaloni there with a message that his mistress wished to meet the famous Brother. Gerard knew how some crotchety, nose-out-of-joint Father might reply. He did his imitation. "I cannot make out why such a fuss is made over this Brother. He's half a simpleton. They are strangely deceived about him in Naples, I see. Tell this to Her Grace, if you please."

Gerard could never give up joking. Or acting. But he had learned to be more careful in one important concern. Coming out of Santo Spirito church, he was stopped by a lady who said winningly, "Brother Gerard, I hope that you will do me the favor of coming to my house: I have a son who is ill and suffering greatly." Even the sick lad's pain did not confuse Gerard's clearer sense of the old danger. "Madam, what use could my visit be? However, I promise to recommend him to our Blessed Lady." This was not the only occasion during this stay in Naples when Gerard's attractiveness was recognized by a lady. But Tannoia simply notes that "he used always to make similar answers at such times."[95]

Whether or not these events happened in quite the way Tannoia describes, Francesco Margotta thought that far too many stories were going the round of Naples. Gerard was living a life altogether too exciting for a young man. Part of the difficulty was that, in his kindly haste to get Gerard away from the scene of that punishment time, Margotta had not stopped to think what work Gerard would be doing in Naples. There was no set job for him. He was simply going about doing good. And making friends. Among these, Alphonsus' favorite Naples Jesuit, Don Francesco Pepe, who gave Gerard coadjutor authority to distribute several thousand plenary indulgences to whomsoever he deemed would perform the required pious acts in a proper spirit. This was perhaps Pepe's kind return for Gerard's sending a couple of poor girls to try their vocations as lay Sisters in the city convent that Pepe had founded.[96] Alphonsus would have been entirely approving of such a hustling of girls into religious life. Out of the danger of marriage. Even after the Nerea incident. He was not pleased, however, that Margotta was teaching Gerard to beg for his midday meal with the other starving folk at the door of the San Girolamo monastery.[97] And neither Margotta nor Alphonsus cared for the reputation that Gerard was, quite deservedly, acquiring as a wonder-worker on the city streets. He was prompting madmen at the hospital, grocers at their shop doors, prostitutes at the ally corner, and passersby, however too much in a hurry to buy a tinderbox, to pause for a moment and consider whether they might not be living in a communion where miracles could happen. It was, evidently, still true that "wherever Gerard goes everything is turned upside down." So Margotta wrote to Alphonsus suggesting that he recall Gerard to Materdomini.

Alphonsus took up the suggestion. No sense letting a Brother get a reputation in what was the Fathers' line of work. He remembered that there was some fuss at Materdomini about the cooking, another case of a Brother's looking indispensable.

> Since Brother Gerard is back again, let him be Bursar, especially since, as I recall, Brother Gennaro is deaf, and, moreover, has been put to working on the building site.[98]

At Materdomini, a Father died, a Student died,[99] most of the community had a bout of sickness. Gerard himself became ill. But not from the cooking. Or the bad air of the place. Or from some personal weakness. He was discovering the price he should be paying for the good of another.

The Price of Another's Good

"God had afflicted Father Margotta for some months with such an interior desolation and aridity that he was in a most pitiable state."[100] No pilgrimage Margotta made to the various Neapolitan shrines relieved his depression. Gerard had warned him as much. But the poor man would persist. The conventional remedies were failing the conventional man. Margotta was the more distraught. Gerard could not leave him to his suffering. One day, Doctor Santorelli found Gerard at his bursar's table obviously engaged with a business which both pleased and saddened him. "I am writing to Father Margotta to tell him that his trial is over, and to congratulate him." Soon a letter arrived from Naples to tell the community that Margotta's sufferings had ceased. Gerard was paying the price for Margotta's recovery. "He lost his wonted cheerfulness on the day he sent his letter to Naples, he became quite pale and cast down." Caione, struck by this unaccountable alteration, ordered Gerard to declare the cause. "I could not bear to see Father Margotta suffer any longer, so I prayed to God to let me suffer in his stead."

Gerard recovered from that sympathetic illness. But he had the firm notion that the recurrent bouts of sickness from which he was emerging weaker each time would lead to his death. In January 1755, he told Brother Gennaro that he was certain he would die soon, and die alone.[101] Early in March, he asked Doctor Santorelli, "Do you realize that I am to die this year of consumption?"[102] He recalled those indulgences that he had been given by Father Pepe, and wrote off to Celeste Crostarosa, on March 8, assuring her that she and all her nuns and all those who followed them into the Foggia convent should enjoy these indulgences in perpetuity. The Jesuit had taken some care to hand over just those indulgences that would give Gerard most satisfaction to distribute. He had them for the Feast of the Blessed Trinity, and for all Feasts of Christ, all Feasts of Mamma Mary, Feasts of Saints Michael the Archangel, Gioacchino and Anne, Joseph, Elizabeth and John the Baptist.[103] They must be careful to keep his authorizing letter safe, in perpetuity. It strikes him that he is in such a case that he should now be making a holy bargain with them: "I set it down that whoever is Prioress of the convent when I die shall see to it that all the Sisters apply, for the next eight days, what indulgences they can for my soul, and I in return agree to pray to the Lord God for them."[104]

Between bouts of sickness, he was still at work. Still using his charms on possible benefactors for the Congregation. Still assisting missioners. In the spring and early summer of 1755, the last year of his life, Gerard went the round of villages in the valley of Sele: San Andrea di Conza, Serino, Calitri, Senerchia, Oliveto Citra, Contursi, Auletta, Vietri di Potenza, San Gregorio, Buccino.[105] It was while he was collecting money at San Gregorio in July that he began to vomit blood at night. Hearing this from the archpriest Salvadore at Oliveto Citra, the Rector wrote to inquire their Brother's own sense of his condition. Gerard wrote home at the start of August, "If you wish me to return, I will do so at once, on the other hand, if you wish me to go on with the collection, I will do so; just send me an order and all will be well."[106] Caione decided that he should stay at the archpriest's house until he was ready to continue begging. But, by the end of August, it was evident to Gerard that he was not regaining strength, rather his fever was coming more often, and with increasing force. He must return home. At Materdomini, he fell into dysentery, violent perspiration, delirium, frequently passing into total unconsciousness, and spitting more than a pint of blood each day.

Filippo Gallela, a young apprentice joiner, another of those country lads with whom Gerard so readily established a grinful easiness, walked the twenty or more miles of mountains from Muro to Materdomini, thinking only to be in the house with him. That would be happiness enough. But Gerard had his visitor called up to the infirmary, assuring him with a smile that he would delay his death a few days. There was a short period of remission, during which, by a curious reversal of expectation, on September 14, it was the holy Prioress who died at Foggia. Gerard, on being told, at once confirmed that Celeste was "now enjoying the beatific vision."[107] He knew her well enough, he knew the goodness of God well enough, to be able to say that. Then Gerard's health fast deteriorated. The younger Brothers in the house, Andrea D'Anticona, 1733–1822, Saverio D'Auria,1734(?)–1802, and the novice Brother Carmine Santaniello, 1737(?)–1807, who had just joined the Congregation, took turns with the elder Stefano Sperduto, 1725–1805, in a twenty-four-hour watch.

In the evening of October 15, Brother Stefano sat by him and, seeing him so obviously near death, asked quietly, "We have always loved one another; will you remember me when you enter into the presence of

God?" One Brother to another, Gerard replied, "How could I ever forget you?"[108] Later, he said he was thirsty. Brother Stefano went out to fetch a cup of water. The kitchen was, as usual, locked at night, so it took some time to get the key, the cup, the water. By the time he returned, Gerard was facing the wall, unconscious. He was dying alone. Like Vito, and, as Maria Crocifissa had taught him, like Christ.

After the news was known, Caione reported to Alphonsus, "a multitude of people," "a great gathering of folk," crowded to the church, manifesting "a universal esteem," "a universal sorrow," as they snatched for relics.[109] "The people," Tannoia remembered, not unsympathetically, "began to cut off his hair and tear pieces from his cassock."[110] They wanted to hang onto him. So did the Fathers. Don Francesco Buonamano, 1706–1777, the Rector, was so enthusiastic for dipping napkins in the dead Brother's blood that he had a vein opened in Gerard's arm not once but twice, immediately after his death and then again while the bier was standing in the church. Andrea Strina, 1726–1797, held the basin to catch the gush of blood. But the Fathers found themselves being thrust aside. "It was necessary to post guards to protect the body."[111] There could however be no resisting the people. Gerard was already their saint.

The Fathers made another effort to secure Gerard for themselves. On the discovery that the local painter was out of town, they had two death masks made. On the man's hurried return to retrieve his share of the memento market, Caione had a posthumous likeness taken as the body lay on the bier. Don Benedetto Grazioli of Atella paid for a large number of death-cards to be printed from this portrait. The Fathers sent one of the masks to Alphonsus. Don Benedetto forwarded a couple of the cards.[112]

In a further effort to keep Gerard as their own, to retain their control of their Brother's posthumous celebrity, Redemptorists began to put their memories of Gerard down on paper. Giovenale's jottings were posted to Alphonsus towards the end of 1755. Mauro Buono Murante, 1735–1761, the fifteen-year-old for whom Alphonsus had in 1752, on a moment's extraordinary enthusiasm, founded a one-pupil school at Ciorani, was also required to set down what he recalled of missioner Gerard's visits to his hometown.[113] "Do not forget," Alphonsus wrote, "to bring me the accounts you will have been able to collect about the Brother Gerard."[114] By then Caione had composed a decent little obituary essay, demonstrating his talent for ordering bits of evidence, so Alphonsus sent him Giovenale's *memoire* with a fussing set of instructions on how he should combine the different pieces of evidence that the Fathers would send him. "I send you herewith the notes taken by Father Giovenale on the life of Brother Gerard. Preserve and take a copy of them as well as you can, as I have asked you to do. See also about the time that you devote to this matter. It would be well for you to spend about a quarter of an hour every day on the work, and thus you will gradually get the work done. I send you also your own manuscript. It will serve to remind you of a great many things."[115]

Caione worked to a model. After introductory stories of the strange adventures of the child, of his untaught wisdom by which he put to shame theologically expert scholars, of his leaving his mother to follow his divine vocation, he shapes his central narrative after the Lukan pattern of Jesus' setting his face towards Jerusalem, the Mount of Olives, and beyond. Caione sets Gerard on a journey through Senarchia, Auletta, Vietri di Potenza, San Gregorio, until he comes to Oliveto. On his way, like Jesus, he works a range of miracles, multiplying loaves, raising an epileptic child, casting out demons, subduing winds and waves, confronting the women and men he meets with their hidden sins.[116]

Gerard's journey, on this telling, is most like Jesus' journey at its close. Tannoia may have been making conventional use of the spiritual directors' language when he wrote that, in the service of irascible Bishop Albini, Gerard "did not drag his cross but carried it joyfully."[117] But Caione had recognized that Gerard had himself made his dying a crucifixion. "Uniting his sufferings with those of his Redeemer."[118] Keenly sensitive to what was happening in this dying, he preserved every fragment of the Brother's conversation which hinted at compassionate identification with Jesus. "I write to you from the Cross," Gerard had assured Maria of Jesus, "suffering my agony." "I am hidden in the sacred wounds of Jesus," Gerard had told Gerardo Gisone, 1720–1765, "and his wounds are in me."[119] Along with this inward psychological reciprocity, there were sickroom circumstances which seemed to be furthering his desire for identity with the Crucified. "They have all abandoned me."[120] This was not said regretfully. Gerard was content to be abandoned as Jesus had been abandoned. He was content to be sharing each experience. It was quite happily that he confided to Gisone, "I suffer continually all the pains, all the sorrows that Jesus Christ suffered during his Passion."[121] Others were ready to recognize this identity. It had been clear to Brother Carminiello that at his cry, "My God, my God, where are You?" Gerard endured a desolation which was just the desolation of the dying Jesus. Carminiello had thereupon responded like the good thief on Calvary. "Remember me when you enter the presence of God." Brother Saverio, too, understood Gerard's asking for water as an echo of Jesus' cry, "I thirst."[122]

There may seem something "staged" in the ways that Gerard's carers and Gerard himself attended to such likenings. It was always difficult for others, difficult for Gerard himself, to tell the difference between his play-acting and his truth. Probably there was not much difference. The pains of those dramatic whippings, arm-stretchings, were real enough. And it seemed to those with him in the infirmary that, more truly than at the moment of the Muro Passion play which had so disturbed his mother, Gerard was "thrust through by the lance," truly fulfilling the pattern of Jesus' death.[123] If there ever were much value in a distinction of "following" from "imitating" Christ, Caione thought it quite irrelevant to his presentation of the mystery of Gerard's death.

It is striking that Caione, who had had an opportunity to know Gerard well during the last months of his life, should think it right to put his life story into that Gospel shape. That he should authorize a wholly Christic version of Gerard's dying. And record without any demur, Gerard's identifying self-awareness: "I have figured out that this bed is the will of God for me: I am nailed to this bed as he himself was nailed."[124] It is as striking, and touching, that Caione should close his narrative of this imitation of Christ with a personal prayer expressing just Gerard's sense of Father and Brother living together within a Rule towards the companionable Kingdom:

> My dearest Brother, pray God, whom you love most ardently, for me, a poor sinner. Make my heart burn with love of Christ God, so that I may be in your company.[125]

"*Gloria Patri...*"

While Caione, more sensitive in this at least than Giuseppe Landi, 1725–1797, certainly more sensitive than Tannoia, who was also obediently setting down his recollections of Gerard, could well recognize the likeness of the suffering Christ in this Brother, Gerard himself had been a yet more imaginative contemplator of the mystery of the Cross and our sharing in this mystery. He had appreciated the Trinitarian value of his sufferings.

Of a sudden, sometimes, others were made privy to Gerard's expertness in theology. "One day when I was at Naples," Celestino de Robertis chucklingly recalled, a priest began asking Brother Gerard all his old seminary questions about "the difficult mysteries," such as "the generation of the Word," "His co-eternity with the Father," "the Procession of the Holy Spirit from the Father and the Son." De Robertis was proudly astonished to hear his Brother deal with each *quaestio.* "He expressed himself with ease and clarity on matters which the best theologians treat with caution."[126] Gerard had been meditating intelligently on what he had learned in his unsystematic reading, especially what he had gathered of Augustinian and Thomist comment on the fourth Gospel. He had been placing what he had further understood through these meditations within that Trinitarian tradition of a Christian's relation to Christ which is most vitally expressed in the writings of Saint Teresa of Ávila, 1515–1582, and, his personal find, Maria Crocifissa Tomasi.

Alphonsus, in his meditations, had so identified with Jesus, the heir, that it became difficult for him to contemplate the crucifixion as anything but a manifestation of the inexorable outward demand of the Father's justice. Gerard, unencumbered by any anxieties concerned with fatherhood and authority, was free to appreciate the Cross as a presentation of loving. Of loving within the Trinity. Of love overflowing. The Father's love sustains the Son in his awful expression of their love for us.

He could hear, too, with the Evangelist, that at the climactic instant love at the Cross, Jesus handed over the divine Spirit to the Christian. "The grace of the Holy Spirit," he could write to Gaetano Santorelli during the terrible Eastertide of 1754, is "always within the spirit."[127] Sharing the Spirit, the Christian will be alive with Jesus to do the will of the Father.

Gerard's language, as he makes his grand effort to articulate his sense of the divine will within his living, becomes so intense that only one of the transcribers of his Rule of Life was prepared to copy out his climactic apostrophe:

> To do what God wills it is necessary only that I should will, yes I, I, I, should will only God, and it is by God's will that I will God, that I will only what God wills.[128]

That "I, I, I" proclaims that nothing of himself is lost, nothing of his will, in willing only what God wills. Those repeated affirmations are of a self who is finding himself, and finding himself free to will, as he wills what God wills.[129]

What God wills is total loving. "The Holy Spirit will enable you," Gerard told a lay companion, "to know how much more you should suffer for the love of him who suffered so much for our love."[130] Love is sustaining. Total love is totally sustaining. So it is that when, under the loving will of the Father, that compassionate suffering with his Son seems too great to bear, "the grace and consolation of our Holy Spirit," will keep us loving.[131] At this apprehension of "our Holy Spirit" Gerard no longer felt like a madman in his loving.[132] No longer felt that he could not endure life in the house a moment longer. He could make sense of himself. He could endure. For, through "our Holy Spirit," he could see how it was that Jesus should endure each loving demand of the Father. Gerard could see the Father upholding his crucified Son in his arms under the loving hover of the Spirit. He could appreciate the Cross as the showing forth of the love of the Triune Godhead:

> Whenever I see the Cross, I am determined to make this little devotion of always saying a *Gloria Patri.*[133]

As it is with the Crucified, it is with Gerard. He is experiencing that love. He had come through reading, meditating, waiting, into an appreciation of Christians' enjoying together the inwardest life of the Trinity. "You cannot imagine," he told Isabella Salvadore, in his very last letter, "how much I love you in God."[134] In the wonder of Trinitarian life, Gerard is at last discerning the way, both self-aware and aware of the girl's feelings, to speak of love. There is not going to be anything so juvenilely romantic as the grill's melting between them; this love,"I must repeat," and there is a quickening of pace as Gerard attempts to prevent any repetition of the Nerea misunderstanding, "is a love divinized in God." That, he tells the archpriest's niece, must be their shared truth.

She and he and all those blessed spirits who have stood by him since his altar-playing days and all of us may be of good heart, joining in that grand shout, "Blessed be our Most Holy Trinity."[135]

Brothers As Rebels

After his death, no one was much interested in remembering Gerard as a sensitive expounder of the doctrine of the Trinity. Or in his academic renewal of the languages of "imitating" and "following." "From my Chair of the Cross," Maria Crocifissa Tomasi had heard the professorial Jesus say, "I will teach you things mysterious and divine."[136] So Gerard, writing to Maria di Gesu, had explained, "He is my teacher. I am his student. It is right that I should learn from him and follow in his footsteps."[137] None of them, probably, wanted to remember him as a professor. However, having in his lifetime had no thought of the distinction of the Reverend Brother theological student from the Brother studying theology, Gerard became after death a teacher in the Congregation. If not as Professor of Dogmatics, then, as interpreter of the Rule as the announcement of a Redemptorist following.

At Pagani, Brother Antonio Lauro, recognized by later Redemptorists to have been attempting an "emulation" of Gerard, was quick to appreciate the significance for them all of Gerard's affirmation of equality within the Rule and to find his own expression for this equality in the precise demands of religious obedience. As he stated them plainly even to Alphonsus himself. The exhausted Rector Major had collapsed into bed on return to Pagani after conducting a six-week Naples-wide mission for the demanding Archbishop Sersale. He had been committed to the infirmarian's charge. He felt like death. Their sensible doctor prescribed complete rest and a strengthening diet. Brother Antonio was detailed to be his temporary *famulus*. He saw a nice opportunity for insisting on their equality, Father and Brother, within their Rule. "Having to have supper in bed, and not eating much more than a slice of local bread, when the doctor had ordered him to eat more," this Brother said to him, "Father, what Your Paternity tells others to do, you must do yourself, setting an example." He raised the plate towards him. "I'm in the wrong," Alphonsus admitted. He began to eat.[138] Rector Major and Brother were both better aware, after Gerard's endurance, of the meaning of their having willed themselves, freely willed, to the shared life of Christ's obedience.

They were, Alphonsus and Antonio both, capable of recognizing the divine imperative for obedience, unto death, even death on a cross. But it was difficult for Alphonsus, recalling only the domestic demands that his father had made of him and his brothers, as difficult for Alphonsus as for Antonio or any of the Brothers, to give more than a notional assent to Gerard's presentation of the Father as loving sustainer of their obedient lives. Gerard's sense of the Rule as opening upon the obedient son's relation to his loving Father was put aside as they retold the exemplary history of Gerard's own heroic obedience under calumny and heard how he died.

Antonio Lauro was not alone in interpreting Gerard's meaning. Others, Fathers and Brothers, were recognizing the importance of getting a general acceptance for their version of this Brother. The story of Gerard was, as ever with stories about him, being told in two versions. He was being reconstructed by some as the paradigm of Brotherly virtues, especially the virtue of obedience, and he was being deconstructed by others into a hero Brother offering resistance to authoritarian governance in the name of the Rule. Nothing of such a deconstruction need be written plainly. Hinted merely in conversation. Signaled at the raising of an eyebrow. Alphonsus read the signs.

In the very same January 1756 letter that he was telling Gaspare Caione to start work on a hagiography of Gerard, he was warning him to "keep a watchful eye" for signs of ambition in the lay Brothers of the Materdomini house. Most disturbing things were happening. In the house where Gerard's unfortunate business had begun. Other Brothers, far less subtle than Gerard, were making their own claims. "At d'Iliceto there has been a semi-revolution." Caione should know the extent of their scandalous behavior. And write accordingly.

The Brothers had been claiming that they should have precedence in the house over the Student Novices, that they should have time for prayer in common with the Fathers immediately after the midday meal not at the end of their tiring day, that they should, like Fathers and Students, be allowed a siesta before starting their afternoon work in the kitchen or the field, and that they should not have always to do the dishes but should, like Carmelite and Franciscan Brothers, have time off from these chores. Alphonsus was astounded. "This is a fine state of affairs, truly!"

Caione must reestablish the true Redemptorist tradition: "Let us be careful to avoid customs that may afterwards give rise to disputes." Every Father must be put on the alert to stop the rise of such house customs. "Read my letter to Father Apice," "read it to the Fathers of the house."

Two days later, Alphonsus was writing to Tannoia, then Rector at d'Iliceto, which was beginning to figure in his imaginings as a center of revolutionary talk about "the Brotherhood of Man" and, more dangerous yet, "the Rights of Man." They all knew where that kind of talk leads. "The Father" had warned them all, years before, of the horrors that would follow any appeal of the Brothers to "a Right."[139] Alphonsus was still angrily nervous at the thought of the d'Iliceto Brothers' tendency to murmur against his government. No Bourbon or Hapsburg would endure such impertinence. This was a matter of fealty. Of keeping faith.[140] He said he would deal with the ringleader himself. He wrote to Tannoia. "I cannot pardon that novice Brother: send him away. At once."[141]

If the Rector were worried about the Brother's reaction, "he may do some mischief," "he may take some other Brothers along with him," Alphonsus has his device ready. Equivocation would come in handy here. The naughty man might be left to think that he had been taken back into the ordinary life of the Congregation. "Tell him to take a letter to Lacedogna or somewhere at a distance, which will inform the recipient that the bearer is no longer a member of the Congregation and should, therefore, be dismissed." Alphonsus seems to be remembering what some theater-going Spaniard had told him of Claudius, Hamlet, and the sudden end of those unsuspecting letter bearers, Rosencrantz and Guildenstern. After this the lieutenant-rebel may be punished. "Take the habit from Brother Giacomo until further orders; he should eat his meals outside the refectory, and receive Communion only on Sundays."[142] Once the ringleaders have been put down, Tannoia should be able to pick off the other rebels at his leisure. "Call the lay Brothers to you, one at a time, and tell them that I am angry with them, etc." Then he is to let the Brothers see the letter Alphonsus has written to them. He is to put an end to all this talk of Carmelites and Franciscans, insist simply on their Redemptorist customs, and see to it that unruly Brothers understand that they are called to be "men of all works." There are to be no more murmurings about "this is not our job." To prevent further rebellions, Tannoia has then to adopt Alphonsus' own favorite strategem. He should engage a helpful sneak. Brother Cesare Apostolico, 1746(?)–after 1781, would do. "Tell him privately from me that he should watch to see who murmurs and complains and report the matter to you." Then, of course, the name must be forwarded to the spymaster. "You should tell me who it is."

There's nothing in his correspondence with Tannoia to suggest that Alphonsus thought it worth his while making inquiry about the immediate causes of the rumpus. He seems, for instance, to think that he is turning to a quite distinct matter when he tells Tannoia that he is very well aware of the miserable state of the d'Iliceto finances:

> I do not know how you can subsist without grain, without oil, without linen, and without money. I send you ten ducats. But will this be sufficient?[143]

Alphonsus' attention was already engaged by a need for him to write around to quash rebel elements in other houses. He was convinced that the cause of all these troubles lay in the unsuitable characters of the present Brothers. He would therefore have to look more carefully than before at those who put themselves forward. Caione was told to issue a further declaration to his Brothers that they should not now hope to be admitted to profession until after a probation of ten years.[144] This new regulation would take effect immediately. "As for those that have already received the habit and are to be professed, you must inform me of the least fault they commit, so that I may defer their profession. Perhaps."

Girolamo Ferrara, now Minister at d'Iliceto, and therefore having charge of the Brothers, is also to let them know of this new arrangement. "Tell the novice Brothers who have or who have not yet received the habit (and tell each one separately each time, so as to prevent their plotting together) that I have no intention of admitting any to profession except after a very long trial of their virtue."[145]

Since, he now realizes, any one of them may be impertinent enough to ask the reason for his profession's being delayed, it will be necessary to have an answer ready. Alphonsus will have to keep files on them all. "For this purpose take care to collect information, put it down on paper, and send it to me, specifying the particular defects of the lay Brothers in your house so that I may use your report as a legitimate pretext when they ask me to admit them to profession."[146] It will be a great advantage to keep these men waiting. They'll be more eager to please meanwhile.

"It has been remarked that these good Brothers after profession begin to relax their fervor. They become very imperfect."

Mid January 1756, in the midst of his efforts to secure the cooperation of Rectors and Fathers in his dealings with the rebels, Alphonsus composed a letter to the Brothers at d'Iliceto, in which the particular difficulties he'd been encountering during the last few weeks were confronted and together dispatched. He began, as ever, autobiographically, with the effect their rebellion had had on him, "God knows what great pain it caused me to hear of your faults," continued with a condemnation of pride when "it should be your duty to acquire the virtue of humility which is the proper virtue of a Brother," and reached to a preliminary assertion of pardon and punishment now and forever:

> Well, speaking in general, I pardon you all; but I beg you not to force me to chastise you again, for such chastisement may and will draw after it eternal punishment: if you oblige me to expel you from the Congregation, I do not know what will become of you. I should tremble for your eternal salvation.[147]

They have come very near expulsion and the consequent likelihood of damnation, and are not free of the threat yet. Alphonsus would have them know that he is arguing from strength:

> Do not think to intimidate me by saying that you wish to leave. Every day I am forced to refuse admission to men who wish to enter the Congregation; however, even if no newcomers were to arrive, Brothers might be obtained from other houses, wherever they happen to be numerous. Hence I beg you not to talk any more about leaving, for that alone would induce me to dismiss you from the Congregation.

So they have no alternative to submitting the future conduct of their lives to the reasonable demands that the Congregation is making on them.

> Now that the winter is here, you will make your common exercises of the day at evening, for then you have time, as you do not have to study like the Chorists. Moreover, as the days are short, the siesta is not necessary, the night's sleep is enough for you. That is the practice in the other houses.

Alphonsus next takes up the comparison that these Brothers have been suggesting with the ways other communities treat Brothers. He quickly turns the comparison against them. Using it to reassert his threat of expulsion.

> The Carmelites and Franciscans are members of Orders, making solemn vows; you belong to a Congregation in which the Rector Major can dismiss subjects, whenever he sees fit.

So they had better get back to work. No more talk of Carmelites or Franciscans. Alphonsus starts a different comparison:

> The duties of Chorists are to preach, to hear confessions, and to study.

That's plain. But there can be no such listing of the duties of Brothers:

> The duty of the Brother is to serve, to do whatever is commanded.

Alphonsus is thinking of the Brother not as the *servus*, the slave, but as the *famulus* who, in gratitude for the Chorists' protection, accepts that he may be commanded to anything. This *famulus* is not yet come into that Christian relation which lasts into eternity. Not yet the *frater*. The Brother must know that he is one of those crowding dependants who can be sent away from the homestead. Kept from bliss. For them now, Alphonsus' proleptic judgment as Rector Major is a foretaste of the eternal Judgment of God. "I bless all those Brothers who have a good intention" and "I curse all those who have bad intentions." These ungrateful men will not be coming out of their *famulus* status. "My curse will be accompanied by the curse of Jesus Christ."[148]

He was still thinking of these difficult Brothers when he was composing his notes for some Epiphany meditations. Starting forbiddingly from Jeremiah 2:20, "These are the ones who say, 'I will not serve.'" Alphonsus asks his meditator, "What say you, my brother, have you too been one of these?" and goes on to describe, in the language of Deuteronomy 28:47, what his brother's grousing will get him, what his life will be like when sent away, "Because you did not serve the Lord thy God with joy and gladness of heart, thou shalt serve thine enemy in hunger and thirst and nakedness and in want."[149] This is the *servus*. The Brother who rebels is slipping into being such a *servus,* losing his true character as the *famulus* called to eternal life as freedman of God. The Brother, then, should tremble, as Alphonsus trembled, for his salvation. The Lord is at least as disappointed as Alphonsus with such a Brother.

By this time, the novice Brother, Bartolomeo, not wanting to be thrown out, was writing to Alphonsus, complaining that Tannoia had misrepresented him. "It's not fair." "It's not my fault." Alphonsus, on the specious excuse of having to keep to the approved lines of communication, managed to dodge a straight answer but left the impression that he would intervene to temper the well-known severity of the Rector. Accordingly, Tannoia is now told to rescind the order of expulsion which Alphonsus himself had decreed. And, since this is all a muddle, Tannoia had better find a way also to reintegrate the true culprit, Andrea Lungariello, 1722–1805.[150] Or rather, as Alphonsus continues to distance himself from his first swift sentence, he tells the student Pietro Paolo Blasucci, brother of Domenico, to write to Tannoia on his behalf, putting straight whatever needs to be put straight. Tannoia must have squirmed to discover, as he read this letter, that he had been cast in the role of muddler.

Young Blasucci, sensitive to the awkwardness of his conveying the Rector Major's displeasure with a Rector's management of a house, was careful to maintain a distancing formality:

> I write on behalf of our Father.
>
> It is a question of how to deal with Brother Bartolomeo. He is not guilty of that which the Father had supposed from Your Reverence's letter. The guilt belongs rather to Brother Andrea, that is, the guilt of insolence and of false rumor-mongering. The Father, believing that Brother Bartolomeo had been lax in performing his duties, had given his order for the dismissal of that Brother, but it was really Brother Andrea who had been lax. Now he wishes that they should both be reinstated in the habit and their bad conduct ended by the imposition of some other mortification.
>
> More, he wishes Your Reverence to tell this Bartolomeo and all the other novice Brothers that the Father has determined not to allow any Brother to make the vows now and that for some time to come he will not think of any of them being allowed to make the vows until God has inspired him to allow them.
>
> That mistake, to which I have alluded, was caused by your confused letter.
>
> As regards Brother Andrea, he wishes that he be given a large

and lengthy penance for his faults. The same goes for Brother Giacomo.

The Father has written another letter before this saying the same thing about Brother Bartolomeo, *et al.* You have perhaps already got this from the Brother who brings this letter.

No more.[151]

But it seemed to Tannoia that there was a lot more to be said. He had been placed in a wretched position. Just by doing his duty. He had written to Alphonsus about these Brothers. Alphonsus, misunderstanding what he had written about two of them, had instructed Tannoia to get rid of Bartolomeo. So, of course, the dutiful Tannoia had, unprotestingly, told Bartolomeo that he was to start packing. But Bartolomeo had protested.[152] Now Tannoia was being told to withdraw the expulsion order. The Brother would naturally attribute his change of fortune to his protesting over the Rector's head to the Rector Major. He would be an ever-present reminder to everyone in the house that Tannoia had been overruled by the kinder Alphonsus. He'd feel secure enough to resist the Rector in future. So would other Brothers. Tannoia wrote again to Alphonsus. He sent the bothersome Brother Giacomo to bear his letter to Pagani.

Alphonsus had no wish to have this business reopened. He had managed things very nicely. "I have spoken kindly to Brother Giacomo and he has confessed his guilt." If he had, "through some mistake," dismissed Bartolomeo, he had put the mistake right. There was no more to be done. They must all settle down again. Anyway, no Brother should feel secure after this. "Let us see how he behaves himself; if he behave badly, he can be dismissed. Then he'll be sorry. I shall not be sorry. I shall feel sorry for my sins, but not for an act of justice."[153]

The bad examples of Andrea, Giacomo, Bartolomeo, and the rest of them at d'Iliceto were, such was the communications network of the Brothers, swiftly followed by revolters first at Ciorani and then at Pagani. They were visited with exemplary punishments. On January 15, 1756, Brother Carlo Califano, 1724–1781, and Brother Giuseppe Trobetta, 1726–1780, at Ciorani were sentenced to be imprisoned in the house attics, "*carcerati.*"[154] Brother Domenico Picardi, 1740–1778, the sixteen-year-old jackanapes, was similarly immured at Pagani. So was Brother Crescenzio, who muttered something about "rights." "All the others who have been murmuring have been given their penances."[155] Tannoia, recovered from that moment of disgruntlement, makes no mention in his *Life* of his own murmuring. "As their discontent had been public, Alphonsus wished that their punishment should also be public."[156] The Rector Major deprived the Pagani Two of the habit, sentenced them additionally to kneel while eating in the outer refectory, to go without fruit, and forbade their receiving Holy Communion oftener than once a week. Some men, however, are incorrigible. On January 20, Crescenzio, who had been in the Congregation since May 1742, had to be dismissed on account of his refusing to stay pent up in his prison. He'd wandered down the corridor as if he were a free man.[157] Rector Tannoia and Minister Ferrara should now know just what they were to do with Andrea, Giacomo, Bartolomeo, and the rest. "I leave it all to Your Reverence."[158]

Alphonsus went off to Naples in the first days of February 1756, and preached a set of evening sermons for his clergy.[159] But his mind was not yet entirely clear of that episode with the Brothers. He was still thinking of things he should have said to them. So, one day during this sermon series, "having compassion on the servants of the cardinal," he assembled them in the palace hall, "even the very lowest of them," and instructed them on the duties of their condition. "It was," Tannoia wrote later, "as a salutary stream which flowed and penetrated to the depths of their hearts." The scullery maids and boot boys and footmen and major domo and all decided to behave better and attend more carefully to their duties. "The cardinal shed tears of joy."[160]

It was on the close of this mission that Alphonsus had collapsed into bed at Pagani. This was the moment for Antonio Lauro's admonition of an equality in obedience.

Alphonsus had been quite quickly quieted. Others were not as sensitive to the resonances for their own lives of Gerard's tremendous appreciation of Christ's obedience. Tannoia understood that if peace were to be restored in the d'Iliceto house, the Brothers needed to hear something from Gerard's exemplary history. Most happily, he found precisely what he wanted among the anecdotes he was collecting for his *Life* of their model Brother.

Tannoia retells the tale of Gerard's being knocked down by a rough estate guard of Duke Giovanni Guevara of Bovino.[161] The Redemptorist Brother was on his way to Foggia, just across the fields from their own d'Iliceto house, and was taking his usual short cut across the Duke's land. The estate guard made his sudden appearance on the bridle path. "As soon as he saw Gerard, he rushed upon him and struck him so violently with the butt of his musket that it caused the servant of God to fall." But that was not enough for this ruffian. He repeatedly jabbed the barrel end of his gun into poor Gerard's stomach and chest. "I have long been wanting to revenge myself on a monk," said he. Taking the bully to be God's instrument to reprehend whatever unknown faults he had committed against the Rule, Gerard cried out, "Strike brother, for you have cause," and fell to the ground. Thereupon the guard was covered in confusion. "O, what have I done? I have killed a saint!" Lifting Gerard back on his beast, he brought the half-dead Brother to d'Iliceto. This very house. Getting home, the injured Gerard did not sneak on his attacker, rather, he asked that the guard should be given a meal. Rather a better meal, it was to be hoped, than these they'd all been having lately. So far, the story had done Alphonsus' work. The Brother has been a humble hero. He has been properly self-scrutinizing about offenses against obedience. He has been patient in suffering. Gerard has so far been showing how one of those religious, those Carmelites, for instance, for whom he has naturally enough been mistaken, should behave. Tannoia means next to turn the story to the Brothers' advantage.

Now, returning to his station on the Duke's path, the brute should learn what it meant to meet a Brother of that other Order with whom they'd been comparing themselves. The guard had taken his musket and stopped another traveler. "This one managed to jump down from his horse and, while begging for mercy in the name of Saint Anthony and in the name of Saint Francis, he adroitly slipped below him and seized the musket from him. He then inflicted so many blows on his body that he left him in his turn, half dead." Then, finding that he had a nasty bruise himself from this encounter, the friar went off to the Duke in his country house, complaining. He was very quick to tell tales. So the Duke gave him some money for his pains. But really that Brother had no business making his complaint to this landlord. As Alphonsus was always telling them, there is rather a Divinity that shapes our ends. There was worse to come for the attacker. "Divine Justice did not allow the cruel guard to go unpunished." Very soon after, he was killed. By a musket shot.

This tale is perfectly told. Having set up, in the first episode, a contrast between the sort of religious that the ruffian had encountered before and the good Redemptorist Brother, Tannoia has gone on to set up an even more effective contrast between the Redemptorist and those Franciscans the Brothers were always wanting to allege in their murmurings. Tannoia does not have to be so impolite as to identify the second traveler's Order. His invoking Saint Anthony and Saint Francis gave him away. The Brothers at d'Iliceto will all note the pleasing difference between Gerard, on his way to becoming a saint in their Congregation, accepting hardship as his ordinary way of serving God, and the self-defensive, self-preserving, Franciscan. Certainly they should all see that there was no cause at all for any of them to be wanting to be a Brother of that kind.

Francesc' Antonio Romito

Other Brothers, who had kept their heads below the parapet while these exchanges were taking place, could not long remain undisturbed. It is significant for what it says of the strengths of their fellowship that that very Brother whom Alphonsus had selected to sneak on his brothers was now thinking himself unsuited to life under Alphonsus' regime. "Brother Cesare Apostolico writes to me that he is disquieted and on the point of losing his vocation."[1] Alphonsus was not pleased. "That this trouble should also come up!" He did not intend to let Cesare go. This time, he assured Tannoia, he had acted impeccably. Done nothing to diminish the Rector's authority. Just stiffened the Brother. "I have answered him firmly and kindly. Told him he should stay." Tannoia was to take especial care of this useful reporter. Even to grant this Brother that siesta so recently refused the rest. "Try if possible to calm him by kind treatment. Allow him more sleep if he wish it."

Tannoia discovered, on calling Cesare to see him, that this Brother was no stranger to fits of depression. He recalled for Tannoia the time when, very much down, he had encountered Domenico Blasucci in the corridor and how that kind Student had given him a hug and cheered him up. What had worked for Gerard had worked for Cesare.[2] Tannoia did not, it seems, offer to give him a hug in his office. He knew that Alphonsus was not keen on such cheering methods.

The whole business was near to becoming too much for Alphonsus. "O my God! These Brothers!"[3] He told himself not to expect success in any further dealings with them. They would always prove unbiddable. They were certainly being unbiddable at Pagani. Once he'd gotten rid of those two malcontents, things should have settled back to normal quiet. But there was an air of resentment in the kitchen. A grumbling in the cabbage patch. Even some surliness on the corridor. The old lag had found out another like himself. "In regard to the two Brothers, Saverio and Domenico, if they do not do what they should, they will be dismissed without fail."[4] None of them could be trusted to persevere in good ways. Saverio had been the Brother that the dying Gerard had called to chase away a demon from his sickroom.[5] So what had gone wrong? But then, happily, none of them was quite beyond recall. Or so, for a while, Alphonsus persuaded himself. He supposed he might turn the revolting Domenico into another of his spies. A few encouraging words should do the trick. But in this Alphonsus was mistaken.[6]

Brothers were, rather more often, tempted to sneak off for a swig from the refectory decanter or the cooking-wine bottle in the kitchen. This was the ordinary temptation for a servant in a gentleman's establishment. Some Fathers thought it hardly worth noting in a Brother. Francesco Fiore, 1715–1787, who was with Gerard at Castelgrande in 1753 and again at Oliveto, had been allowed to decline into an inoffensive old soak, taking his own time to die in the Congregation.[7] Nicola Piccialli, 1762–after 1807, was perhaps happier in his Rector. Michele Tozzoli, 1749–1820, wrote to Rector Tannoia from Materdomini for support for his request to Vicar Villani that this Brother be posted to the d'Iliceto house. The people of Caposele were making comments. It was not good for their Students and Novices to see him like this. They'd never be able to correct him at Materdomini. "He thinks everyone here is his enemy." At d'Iliceto, Nicola would be unknown. Maybe, he could make a new start. And perhaps, in the new community, he would not find so many reasons for drinking. "Consider that he is old not to say near death. It cannot be good for him to be in this state."[8]

At least Brother Nicola had, for even this brief late moment, got the attention of three Rectors. Unlike that anonymous man, "from one of the best families" of Melfi who, in 1744, "left home and relatives to become a serving Brother," about whom Tannoia had nothing more to relate.[9] Unlike, too, Giuseppe Sereno, at whose death in 1789, aged sixty-five, Kuntz admitted, "Of this Brother we know nothing."[10] Almost nothing is known of another head-down Brother, Francesc' Antonio Romito, for the first twenty years of his time in the Congregation.

Francesc' Antonio arrived the same year as that Melfi aristocrat, 1744, when he was just twenty-two years old, after trying out the career of a salesman, first in his father's shop in Tribunali area of the city and then in Bartolomeo d'Auria's bookshop in the Giudeca, the Jewish Quarter of Naples. He was sent almost at once to assist Francesco Tartaglione in taking care of the ailing Sarnelli who, it was obvious to everyone, must soon be dead. But Sarnelli was an unconscionable time a-dying. Or so it seemed to Francesco. He wanted to get back to his jobs. Francesc' Antonio was better prepared to sit by the bed. "Don't let me stop saying the rosary," Sarnelli had insisted in weakening accents, "I want to die saying the rosary." On June 30, 1744, they had reached the third sorrowful mystery when Francesc' Antonio saw that Sarnelli had begun his death agony. "Bless us now," he said, urgently, and the near-dead man held up his hand to give the two Brothers his last benediction. Francesco then began to teach Francesc' Antonio how to clean and lay out the corpse.[11]

The two Brothers sat alongside the bier, waiting until his old friends from the Apostolic Mission came, "on account of the ties of brotherhood," to take Sarnelli's body to San Maria dell'Aiuto.[12] After this quiet funeral, it was back to d'Iliceto and the ordinary anonymity of a Brother for Francesc' Antonio. He was there for the last week of Vito's life. Made his vows on June 20, 1745. And was taken by Alphonsus, along with a troupe of fourteen Fathers and Brother Teodosio Flumeri, 1727–1798, to Troia and then on to Foggia in the last week of November 1745, for a thirty-six day mission.[13] Young Francesc' Antonio was, by a few weeks, the senior of the two Brothers and had, therefore, the sudden responsibility for all their beds, meals, and laundry. He was kept busy. So he missed hearing the Advent sermon which was so graciously received by the Madonna of the Seven Veils.[14] But Francesc' Antonio did get the story at supper that evening: "We heard from the Fathers and all the people that during the sermon that evening, a ray of light coming from the face of the most holy Mary had lit up the countenance of the Servant of God, who was rapt in ecstasy."

Francesc' Antonio, when he arrived at Materdomini Caposele the next year, must have been already well-aware that a Brother could not regard any house of the Congregation as his home, or even his base, and that he could not regard any job as his usual employment. He was not a tailor or a clock repairer, just an odd-job man for the Rector. Or messenger boy, between Rector and Rector. Cesare Sportelli writing, December 22, 1747, to Villani at Ciorani about arrangements for various missions, convinced that they had taken on rather too many assignments, and that more than one poor Father in the house was overworking, mentioned in passing that he had sent Brother Francesc' Antonio to tell Alphonsus just how things were with them. It was simply another evidence of how very busy they all were that he had, yesterday, finished his letter to the Rector Major so late in the afternoon that he had missed the mail coach. He had had to send Brother Francesc' Antonio off on foot.[15]

For the next twenty years, Francesc' Antonio found himself doing different jobs in different houses. He worked well and won moderate approval as a decent man, reliable and pious. If he had died in 1761, very little would have been said of him in the Congregation's obituary that wouldn't have been conventionally said of each of them. But, in 1762, Alphonsus chose him as his house-Brother at Sant' Agata.

Francesc' Antonio, along with Brother Leonardo Cicchetti and the new bishop's Secretary, Don Felice Verzella, a youngish priest of the Nusco diocese who had met Alphonsus while on a clergy retreat at Pagani, was sent a little ahead of the bishop to get things ready.

Brother Leonardo was known to be a careful preserver of his energies. There was a story going around the Brothers of Leonardo's being sent with Gerard to work in the fields and proving, though a sturdy lad, to have little liking for farm labor. "Here, let me do it," had been the thinner Gerard's cheerful suggestion as Leonardo hesitated at the stooks.[16] He was known, too, to be the reteller of grisly off-putting stories about the early days at Scala. He'd like to gossip about how it was that the first Fathers lived in a rundown house, fed only on thin soup very badly cooked, not much in the way of salt to give it flavor, and dry bread to go with it.[17] Leonardo evidently gave some thought to food. On top of all this, the early Redemptorists had, he said, eaten on their knees with heavy stones hung from their necks, and had come out of the refectory only to go into their rooms to discipline themselves at the remorseful thought of their pleasure-filled lives. So it was not surprising, Leonardo would say, "that he who would help the most abandoned was himself abandoned by his companions."[18] All but one had left Alphonsus. But Leonardo's version of the Congregation's history hints at how carefully revisionist the Fathers had been when telling him the story. Somehow Leonardo had been given the impression that Don Giovanni Mazzini was this single faithful follower. There was, in the tradition the novice Brother had received from the Prefect of novices, no mention of Vito.

Francesc' Antonio as he listened to Leonardo's kitchen tales would not have objected to this version of events. Like Leonardo, when it came to his turn to testify to the Auditors, Francesc' Antonio showed that he had been told of the parts played by several priests in the founding of the Congregation, and by a couple of bishops, but nothing of Vito in the Casa Anastasia.[19] Maybe Vito himself was too modest, in those few conversations he and the new Brother had at d'Iliceto before his going to his death, to mention even his regular bell-ringings.

Vito was not the only Brother edited out of the instruction in the Congregation's history. Brother Teodosio Flumeri, 1727–1798, who came now and then to help the other two at Sant' Agata, could actually recall for the Process Auditors that day at Ciorani in 1749 when Villani's letter arrived from Rome announcing that the Papal Brief approving the Congregation had at last been issued and how "our Servant of God jumped in the air for joy" at the news.[20] But he had no recollection of Francesco Tartaglione's being sent with Villani.

The Master of the Bishop's Household

Forgetful of his distinguished predecessors, each of these Brothers was yet very careful of Alphonsus' reputation. Each knew what was expected of him at the Process. So Leonardo had a good story about the straw mattress to prove that Alphonsus was as severe with himself after becoming bishop as he was before. The day Alphonsus made his solemn entry upon his diocese, he'd been a little shocked to see all the presents that had been sent him, especially the cakes and puddings that the local nuns had been cooking for their new bishop. Leonardo had had the rather disspiriting job of carrying most of them back to the Mothers Superior.[21] But there had been even greater episcopal disgruntlement that night, when Alphonsus went off to the room that the Canons had prepared for him. He had been affronted by the immense curtained and betassled bed. However, a night's sleep in that grand four-poster would, Alphonsus correctly surmised, be a most acceptable climax to Ercole's day in the palace, while the. bishop could sleep on his usual mattress. Alphonsus had sent instructions ahead to the Brothers for his straw palliasse, "*il mio pagliaccio*," to be stuffed and laid on the floor. But Leonardo had allowed the Canons to overrule his orders. Such disobedience would normally have merited a severe penance, however the overall cheeriness of the day permitted Alphonsus' contenting himself with one of those little puns which he never grew out of attempting, as a reproof to the foolish fellow. Well, my clown, "*il mio Pagliaccio,*" I ordered you to carry it here, where is it?" Such unusual leniency provoked an unusual response. Leonardo made a brave effort to stand his ground. "Monsignore, I haven't had the time to get the straw this evening, but," he added as Alphonsus' face became less cheery by the second, "tomorrow…." The bishop pulled a pile of clothes together on the floor and slept there for his first night in his diocese.[22]

Francesc' Antonio as chief cook and bottle washer found he was too often getting into trouble on account of Leonardo's easy ways about the house. He could not be everywhere at once. There were so many entrances for trouble to come upon them unannounced. And Leonardo seemed always ready to welcome trouble. There was the time, quite soon after they had all arrived at Sant' Agata, when the fishmonger, thinking it proper to make a present to his bishop, had brought a sturgeon to the back door. Leonardo had, quite unthinkingly, accepted the man's trade sample. He had handed it to the cook, who started thinking of the different ways in which he might stuff the fish. Then, of course, Alphonsus appeared in the kitchen doorway. Nothing miraculous. He'd smelled the fish. It was no good Leonardo's now protesting "But it is a very small sturgeon." There was a sudden explosion all over them. "In this house we eat shad." The rejected fish had to be returned to the surprised fishmonger.[23] It was, Francesc' Antonio had to admit, a great relief when the junior Brother was recalled and he was left to manage things by himself.

Though he may have been introduced to kitchen boys and ostlers and visiting bishops as "master of the house," Francesc' Antonio had still to do all the ordinary serving jobs. Cooking their meal on the cook's day off, fish generally, holding his tongue when Alphonsus ruined a perfectly good piece of shad with a dollop of bitter herbs, washing his bloodstained small clothes, persuading him once in a while to let him shake out the straw in his palliasse, counting the forks when the Vicar General, Giovanni Nicola Rubino, 1725–1807(?), became obsessively suspicious of a house-boy, sharpening quills for Secretary Verzella, and handing out small alms to the local beggars at the palace gateway. He even learned, after some most embarrassing failures, how to strap the packs securely on the mule's back so that Alphonsus should sit safe, side-saddle atop his luggage, as they went along the zigzag mountain paths. Most difficult of all, even after his experience with the dying Sarnelli, Francesc' Antonio accustomed himself to reciting the rosary with the bishop at his intolerably slow pace.

Not everything went smoothly. After that night among the rags, in the middle of his first Sunday sermon at Sant' Agata, one of Alphonsus' two remaining teeth began to give him pain. After Mass, he summoned Francesc' Antonio to give it a pull. To Alphonsus' astonishment, for he'd come very fast to think Francesc' Antonio capable of anything, the Brother professed himself quite unable to extract teeth. The Brother's fastidious modesty delivered the bishop into the hands of a man not much more skilled. His Canons had recommended that Alphonsus summon the celebrated Matteo Moretto from Naples, but he had demanded, "Have we no barber in this diocese?" They all knew of a barber in San Maria de Vico, but he could not be sent for that day on account of his always being drunk by noon. However, next morning early the barber presented himself at the door. He sat Alphonsus down on the floor and, standing over him from behind, tugged the rotten tooth out with his pliers. Alphonsus now had only one tooth left, and this proved quite useless for any chewing. When the inaugural city mission was at an end, therefore, the barber was summoned a second time. This tooth being sounder than the other, and it may be the time of day being nearer noon, the barber, again standing behind the bishop, took three attempts before getting the tooth out. Alphonsus, who had sat all the while clutching his crucifix, just managed to say ruefully, "Many thanks, Master Nicodemo, I'll not be giving you any more custom."[24] He still thought that Brother Francesc' Antonio had rather shirked his duty in this matter of the tooth. As he told him.

Francesc' Antonio knew just what his job description should include. Teeth, no. Habits, yes. Alphonsus' everyday black habit was a sad case. Too patched for any further mending. He really ought to have a new one. Since it was obvious that Alphonsus would never sanction the expense, the master-proud Brother bought a length of cloth out of the household petty cash and stayed up all night to cut and sew a new habit for him. In the morning, going as usual to dress the bishop, Francesc' Antonio adroitly substituted the new one. He hoped that Alphonsus would think he had only sewn new sleeves into the old habit. So he did. For one moment. But then he exploded. "Am I the master here or you? This is a new habit." Francesc' Antonio stood his ground. He knew he was right. "You could not go on wearing that old thing, it wasn't decent." Alphonsus was not be so easily put off. "Bring it back here at once." But now Francesc' Antonio played his trump card. "If you won't wear this, you will just have to wear nothing at all. I've given that old one away to a passing beggar." Alphonsus knew when he was beaten. "You're always getting your own way," he growled.[25] Francesc' Antonio was indeed finding his way of getting Alphonsus to behave, insisting that he take his medicine, wear his galoshes, eat up his soup. Put on his new habit. His experience of managing the bishop would prove immensely helpful to everyone at Pagani at the close of the Rector Major's life, when the Fathers were finding him too difficult to control.

Alphonsus accustomed himself to Francesc' Antonio's little deceptions. He recognized well enough that they were done out of kindness. But to the very end he could not resist showing that he could see through them. There was that time when Francesc' Antonio had been keeping notice of Francesco Tartaglione's death from the old man, thinking how much he cared for him, and Alphonsus, who discerned what was happening, had at last to say, "Now you know very well that Brother Francesco has gone to another life, don't you?" Francesc' Antonio, in some confusion, had to admit his deception. The kitchen boy, Aniello, coming in on this touching scene, supposed Alphonsus had had some prior knowledge of Francesco's dying.[26] But then, as Alphonsus himself observed, "these people often take me for a prophet."[27]

Francesc' Antonio was Aniello Vertucci's immediate boss. Not always an easy job. Young Aniello was a continual trial. Especially when he grew into a cheeky teenager. There was the time, for instance, when, as the Carnival procession went past the palace, Aniello stood at the kitchen door with another lad, Giuseppe Sevastano, and they got to nudging each other as a well-dressed, beautiful, woman walked by. "The devil tempted me to commit a sin with her," Aniello said at the beatification process in 1788, thinking to put a pious front on the whole incident, "but I told myself it was impossible, because she seemed such a decent woman." It had not been his fault. He'd told his mate that this was a virtuous maiden. But Sevastano was sure she would be an easy conquest.

He'd gone straight up to her and told her what Aniello had been thinking. Things had gotten out of his control. She had invited them both to her lodgings that night, giving them precise directions. Aniello, his bluff properly called, had protested to his friend that he dare not leave the palace at night. The bishop was sure to hear him lift the latch. Or Brother Francesc' Antonio would hear, and that would be almost as bad. "Say no more," said Sevastano, I'll get her to come here tomorrow night, secretly enough." She came. Sevastano let her in, and told her how to reach Aniello's room which was on the ground floor, not far from the door. "But just as I was beginning to play a pleasant game with the girl, there was a terrible rattle of chains, a stamping noise, and a furious blast of wind, as if it would bring down every house in the district." It quieted down. They began their game again. And the racket started up again. Recognizing that there must be some connection between his game, "that old man" upstairs, and the horrid noises, Aniello came to his senses and let the girl out of the door. Three days later, on being summoned by the bishop, Aniello was bending to kiss his hand as usual when Alphonsus drew back. "Aniello, Aniello, on Wednesday night you were going to offend God, and the Devil was preparing to carry you off to Hell, but 'that old man' prayed for you. Take heed, another time God will not pardon you." Starting at this awkward reminder of the Shrove Tuesday Carnival and the Ash Wednesday escapade, Aniello took a quick glance at the bishop. It seemed sensible to deny the whole thing. But Alphonsus asked him, "Did you not hear the chains rattle?" He had just begun his usual penitential regime for Lent. "At this, dumbfounded and blushing and ashamed, I went back to the kitchen and began to cry."[28] Francesc' Antonio, who had his own ways of knowing what was happening in the house, was standing ready with a whole stack of new work to take his mind off his tears.

Aniello had not been so confused, however, that he did not have another go. There was a poor girl from Airola who came to Arienzo each week to receive alms from the Brother, along with those others who came crowding each Saturday, many of them relatives of men held in the town gaol. One day as the girl from Airola started for home, having tied the coins in her scarf, the weather turned, it began to rain. Aniello called her back. She could get dry in his room. He had a little fire. By now the busy Brother was bustling at the other end of the house. But Aniello had not calculated the detective skills of the bishop. Especially when there was some sexual naughtiness going on. He was stretching out his hand to shut the door, when he heard Alphonsus' voice in the room above. "Alas," Aniello said to himself, "that old man is at his prayers again, what am I going to do, what was I hoping to do?" Leaving the girl by the fireside, he went straight upstairs to knock at Alphonsus' door. The bishop turned to greet him and, appreciating the pretty comedy of the boy's confusion, could not but forgive him at once: "Aniello, you are a real scoundrel." Alphonsus' forgiving grin had its saving effect. "From that moment on, I was free from all bad thoughts," Aniello assured the Auditors.[29]

Aniello's reformation must have made the day-to-day running of the household a little less taxing for Francesc' Antonio. But it was never an easy business for the shopkeeper's son to balance the bishop's budget. Parish priests hardly ever paid their contributions for the episcopal table on time. They might forward a fraction with the promise of the rest later, after the tithes had come in from the harvesters, if the harvests were not ruined by the rains. So Francesc' Antonio had to keep a complex set of running entries in his record books. Receipts from the book business in Naples were, perhaps, even more complicated. And Alphonsus took it for granted that Francesc' Antonio should do the bulk of the calculations for him. So did the rest of them. It was straight to Francesc' Antonio that Michele Ilardo had written on his first day as supply agent in Naples.[30] So Francesc' Antonio had very fast to get acquainted with book-printing, book-selling, book-pirating. He learned to keep separate files on the different editions printed at Naples, Venice, Liege, Cologne, "and other places in Germany."[31] All very interesting, no doubt. But tiring.

Interested or not, tired or not, whenever a beggar came to the door, the bishop always assumed that Francesc' Antonio would find some money somewhere in the house. It was Francesc' Antonio's vocation to hand out alms, deacon-like. Francesc' Antonio could plan for regulars, like the girl who caught Aniello's eye, but he could only so far reduce the kitchen allowance to find the funds for these strays, otherwise the cook would be marching upstairs to disturb Alphonsus at his book-writing. And then he was suddenly to find funds for a woman at the gate so that her children should not have to sleep all together in one bed. They both knew the risk of incest in such conditions.

There were too many sudden extra calls for his energies. Alphonsus had not been convinced by his protestations during the tooth-drawing episode. He had it in mind that Francesc' Antonio should fulfill his vocation as a paramedic. At the end of a day, for example, when Francesc' Antonio had had to look after two important guests, making up beds for bishops Niccolo Borgia, 1700–1779, of Cava dei Tirreni and Angelo Antonio Pallante, 1703–1765, of San Severo, shopping for a better than ordinary bottle of wine, planning their meals over the next days, persuading the cook, fixing times for their Masses, and settling the stabling of their horses with the ostler, the tired Brother found himself called to turn nurse again. The bishops' coachman, having driven to Sant' Agata through the rain, had got wet through. He fell into pneumonia immediately upon descending from the box. Francesc' Antonio put him to bed between blankets, but whatever Alphonsus' estimate of the Brother's nursing skills, whatever his renown as an infirmarian in the Congregation, the poor coachman became so much worse that the Vicar General, who had not the Redemptorists' confidence, administered the last Rites. The fellow's son was hurriedly called from Naples. He, too, was given a bed and board. Then, with the Brother s nursing, the coachman did start to get better. Well, Alphonsus had kept popping into the sick room with all sorts of advice concerning the effectivest remedies. Father and son were able to leave the palace together after a month as Alphonsus' guests.[32]

"He Is Prudent. You May Depend on It."

Along with his duties as housekeeper, accountant, nurse, Francesc' Antonio was required to function as an under-Secretary if Verzella were indisposed. He thus got to know most of what was happening in the diocese. He knew about the stipulations of a legacy to the Pious Workers requiring them to preach at San Maria a Vico.[33] About the row provoked by the parish priest at San Felice when the chaplain of the Duke of Maddaloni was inducted to the chapel-of-ease at Taverna di Cancello.[34] And the other great row with the archpriest of Frasso who was not content that the bishop should be founding a chapel at Crisci for the poor people of the hills.[35] And the lengthy negotiations between bishop and the Collegiate Chapter at Arienzo which followed the archpriest's objection. And Alphonsus' finally determining to ordain a squad of local men who could be sent at his order to say Mass anywhere in the diocese whether parish priest, archpriest, or Canon, were pleased or not.[36]

Francesc' Antonio's discretion being proven by his keeping silent about the tantrums of those senior clergy encouraged Alphonsus to employ him when he was conducting Congregation business which he did not think Verzella should see. "I cannot write myself," he wrote to Villani during another of his bouts of illness, "but in secret matters I employ Francesc' Antonio, whom I trust."[37]

This secretarying was for Francesc' Antonio a quite congenial occupation. He was good at it. He knew he was good at it. In time, he was regularly composing letters for Alphonsus to sign.[38] Alphonsus, content with this arrangement which saved him so much energy, assumed that the Fathers would be entirely happy to accept this Brother's having so privileged a position in the Congregation.

They were not, not all of them at any rate, comfortable at Francesc' Antonio's entry upon this new position. There was perhaps no harm to be discerned in Alphonsus' using a Brother as secretary when writing to the Chinese College about Ripa when there was a question of beatifying his old friend.[39] But there was an awkwardness in Francesc' Antonio's being the secretary to whom Alphonsus dictated letters to the Father Vicar. There was something more than awkwardness, something a little infra dig, in Francesco's writing those letters to six separate Fathers in one day which conveyed the Rector Major's orders to return to proper observance.[40] That Alphonsus himself felt something of this is shown by his writing separately to Mattia Corrado, who had gone to live with his parents:

> This order has been sent to all; it was written in the same terms and in the same form by Brother Francesc' Antonio. But as I entertain great esteem for you personally, I have taken it upon myself to address a special letter to you, different from the letter sent to the others.[41]

Those others were tempted to excuse themselves from their irritating orders by asking rhetorically, how were they to be sure that Francesc' Antonio had truly transmitted Alphonsus' will in the matter. The Brother cannot have endeared himself to such grumblers when, to preempt that sort of complaining, he added to his letters an affidavit that he had put down only what Alphonsus wanted.[42]

However congenial, this secretarial work, added to that of the bursar's office, proved very demanding. Francesc' Antonio was sometimes unable to keep going. There were days when he had to climb straight back into bed of a morning, and Alphonsus had to find, to his expressed irritation, someone else to write his letters to the Fathers.

Francesc' Antonio was not only a competent adder-up of the household accounts and a trustworthy letter-scribe. He was also a great reader. At least a great reader in the range of Alphonsus' works, very ready to have a chat with the 1806 Auditors about the *Novena for Christmas,* the treatise *Against Atheists and Deists,* the more difficult, "but still very beautiful," tract against Febronius, and "that little book of *Visits to the Blessed Sacrament.*"[43] He had become, too, during his time as under-Secretary, acquainted with the author's and publisher's view of a book as well as a reader's. He chatted as easily with Alphonsus and Vicar General Rubino about editions of the *Visits* lately produced in Hungarian, about the difficulty of persuading the Remondini to publish a Collected Edition of Alphonsus' ascetical works and about the wonderful stories of the *Glories of Mary,* "that golden book."[44] It was a climactic moment of Francesc' Antonio's peculiar service in Alphonsus' household when, alongside Secretary Verzella and Archdeacon Ottaviano Raione, he was drafted to assist in the sorting, correction, and amplification of the preliminary research notes of Geronimo Ferrara, 1715–1767, for Alphonsus' 1769 book on *Celebrating Mass.* Nothing of this sort was in the *curriculum vitae* of any other Brother. Alessio Pollio had, notoriously, not noticed when he was serving Garzilli's Mass that the poor old Father had omitted the Consecration.[45]

Though he had before thought of Brothers as interchangeable, Alphonsus out of the house, off the mission roster, while he was bishop, recognized Francesc' Antonio as his personal link with the Congregation. They meditated together morning and evening, recited the Office together during the day, said the rosary together, with Alphonsus often getting his Mysteries into a muddle, ate together, talked together without much sense of those distinctions between Father and Brother which had seemed so important when he was directing the day to night business of the Congregation at close quarter.[46] Francesc' Antonio had "long conversations" with Alphonsus. Alphonsus had "long conversations" with Francesc' Antonio.[47] Intimate conversations in which the bishop entertained the Brother with anecdotes of when he was a boy, a young man in the Law Courts, a missioner on Procida. Felice Verzella remarked, without any animosity, so Francesc' Antonio must have been always polite in his dealings with the Secretary, that Alphonsus treated the Brother as he treated himself.[48]

Francesc' Antonio, years and years later, delighted to recall these intimate times, bringing back for a delicate moment Alphonsus' "inimitable sweetness of heart" and, such had been their easiness in each other's company, his "cheerful grin," "*ilarita di volto*," as the bishop retold another anecdote to amuse his Brother. Francesc' Antonio had entered into such a sympathy with Alphonsus that he could recall, too, without any fuss, Alphonsus' efforts, however he was by nature "impetuous" and "peevish," to moderate his temperament.[49] They'd come to calmness together. And more than calmness. Prompted by something that Francesc' Antonio read aloud from Scripture, for the *Life* of a saint, from a favorite book of devotion, while he had been eating his meal, Alphonsus would afterward explain what the passage had meant to him. They were, sometimes, both of them together, "elevated in mind," "transported with joy," as Alphonsus spoke of God's love.[50]

There were, as well as these intimate, happy, times, other times in which Francesc' Antonio felt what the rest of the household felt. No one could live at close quarters with Alphonsus for any length of time without finding himself in a temper at having to share in an obsessively enforced deprivation. Vicar General Rubino said at the beatification process that he could find nothing positive to say about the bishop.[51] Secretary Verzella left in 1773, unable to bear the regimen of the palace any longer.[52] Father Angelo Maione, seconded by Villani to be Alphonsus' assistant, asked to be recalled within the year.[53] Francesc' Antonio did not have, nor did he expect to have, such a recourse, but it must have seemed sometimes to Francesc' Antonio very jealous-making that Alessio Pollio, the man servant, left every night to go home to his wife and children. Like many bachelors, he may have supposed that married life was all apple pie and welcoming slippers. And of an evening, once Alessio had left, the Brother found that he had become so necessary, gradually, to Alphonsus that he was rarely left to sit down in the kitchen to eat his supper. Getting up from the table to do at once what Alphonsus required, he became "a martyr to his indigestion."

The day came when the poor Brother, so irritated at being on call the whole long day, could not stop himself shouting his complaints about the house, knowing full well that Alphonsus must hear him.[54]

That was a noticeable tantrum, recorded because so singular. Generally he was more understanding of the old man's querulousness. Grateful that Alphonsus was so usually understanding of his own irritabilities. They knew they had to get on together.[55] When, at Pagani after Alphonsus' death, the old Brother talked to the youngsters of these old days, Francesc' Antonio was keen that they should recognize a reciprocity in their life. Just as he had a hand in the writing of the book on the correct celebration of the Mass, so Alphonsus had, literally, a hand in washing the supper plates. "I have seen thousands and thousands of times with my own eyes," he would say with affectionate exaggeration, "our Rector Major wash pots and work in the kitchen along with a Brother after a meal," not hesitating to take up, as a nervous novice Brother with them at the sink had noted too, the very greasiest pots. The poor youngster had wanted, Francesc' Antonio knew, to grab the dirtiest dishes for himself to wash so that Alphonsus' hands should not be so soiled. "Am I perhaps better than you?" demanded the old man. There was no answering him, of course.[56] Francesc' Antonio could only turn away to smile. Within that imperious tone, he could hear, even if the nervous youngster could not, Alphonsus' eagerness to be their Brother.

Alessio Pollio

Arriving at Sant' Agata after his consecration in Rome, Alphonsus had very soon decided that the servants of Monsignore Flaminio Danza, 1691–1762 his predecessor, were unsatisfactory. "I have sent Domenico Antonio away," he wrote to Ercole, "and the coachman will follow him."[1] Within another five days, a third servant was discharged. And last of all the cook. But he went willingly, already distressed by the plainness of the fare he was now ordered to prepare. Brother Francesc' Antonio was left to cope singlehandedly. But Alphonsus had formed a plan for the restaffing of his palace. He had it in mind to recruit a cobbler who, a month or so earlier, had been brought by Don Urbano Cimino to receive his blessing, while the newly nominated Alphonsus was spending a little time with his proud brother.

It was likely that, considering Alphonsus was about to be bishop of the diocese, that the cobbler had mentioned that he'd spent his childhood at Sant' Agata. Perhaps, among all those who came to call upon him when he was in Naples, this man had remained in Alphonsus' mind on account of his being christened Alessio after that saint in whose opera Alphonsus had made such a showing. Such adolescent triumphs quite commonly stick in an amateur's memory. So Alphonsus made him an offer.

Cobbling seems not to have been a very rewarding trade. Neapolitans were not much worried by a few holes in their soles. Brother Leonardo was certainly not alone in going for walks through town improperly shod. Or perhaps Alessio Pollio was not a great cobbler. Or a great business man. At any rate, "I was called to his service," he remembered for the Auditors at the 1806 beatification process, "and I answered with greatest pleasure."[2]

Life in Alphonsus' household was as properly regulated as in the communities of the Congregation. Alessio and the new cook and the odd-jobbing laborers were expected to go to Mass each morning and to Communion on all principal feasts, at least once each two weeks. There was to be no evening visit to the local wine-bar, no game of ball in the courtyard, and if they played cards on the premises they were not to place even the smallest wager on the game. And certainly there were to be no romantic episodes.[3] The replacement cook, though he was making a quite decent attempt at the sort of dull dishes Alphonsus required, found that his dallying with a local girl brought the order not for simple dismissal but exile beyond the frontier of the diocese. He, quite wrongly supposing that he was a free man and could live where he liked, took lodgings in town and went on with his dallying. But the bishop set the police on him. Only by bribing their sergeant when they came to apprehend him did this dallyer escape prison. Alphonsus relished the intelligence that the episode had ended with the criminous cook's being out of pocket.

He was delighted, too, with his being able to appoint next a man who knew even less about cooking food. The exquisite Giovanni Nicola Rubino, who had come over from Conza to be Alphonsus' Vicar General, had to be content with even poorer meals after this new man's appointment. He and Secretary Felice Verzella hated this cook. The previous man's sexual adventures had not much concerned them. But it was clear to the twenty-four year-old Alessio after this, if it had not been clear before, that he had better simply find a nice girl with a little money and settle down.[4]

Alessio found Fortunata Leone, the widow's daughter, and married her during one of Alphonsus' trips to Naples, October 13, 1766. They found a small house in Arienzo, the city to which Alphonsus had retired on account of his suffering so many chills and fevers at Sant' Agata. Not that the air was entirely healthful at Arienzo. Within a year of taking up residence there, Alphonsus had begun to hope that he might use his continuing ill-health as an excuse for resigning the bishopric. He actually wrote out a letter of resignation to Pope Clement XIII, but then deciding to wait awhile yet, put the paper in the box under the bed where he kept his whip and other most private things. Alessio, making his usual rounds of the house, came "quite casually" across the letter in the box and, as casually doubtless, read it through. He thought himself entirely warranted in intervening in his master's affairs and took away the letter.

It may be that he had divined that Alphonsus was in two minds about this resigning, and would not be unpleased to have some further excuse for not posting it to Rome. "The Servant of God, not finding it, said nothing."[5]

The Sicilian Grumble. And Others.

Alessio would have heard, just as casually that October 1766, that back in the Congregation others were saying a great deal. About the length of that habit which Francesc' Antonio wore in and out of the house.

This was a long-running noise. Not insignificant. They were, Alphonsus, priests down the road at the Collegiate church, Brothers, all of a mind with Polonius. The apparel oft proclaims the man. In the very first weeks of his episcopate, Alphonsus had been several times shocked to see quite a number of the local clergy, Canons at the cathedral even, not wearing the long cassock, some of them not even while they were celebrating Mass. He had at once determined that they should dress more seemly. He had issued a circular letter to all the clergy of his diocese. That was in July 1762. So it, was "with no little grief" that he had to remind them of this dress code in June 1764. "Ecclesiastics have taken the liberty of wearing civilian clothes." In July 1767, to his "great sorrow," he was again having to insist on their putting on "the long buttoned cassock." He was forced again, in 1770, to rebuke them all, even those Canons again, about "clothes of fashionable colors." Meanwhile, Vicar Villani was having, again, to rebuke Brothers who, having served their first six months' probation in civilian clothes, were getting themselves fitted for habits that were longer than they should be.[6] Alphonsus must have thought he was living in a mad world. Priests were wanting to look like laymen. Lay Brothers were wanting to look like priests.

This time, Brothers were behaving badly not only at d'Iliceto and Ciorani and Pagani. From Sicily, Pietro Paolo Blasucci, reporting to Villani on the state of the Agrigento house, had a sorry tale to tell the Father Vicar:

> Brother Pasquale, Brother Nunzio, and Cosmas have for the past year been unhappy with the Rector. Nunzio and Cosmas especially. On account of their having to shorten their habit by a palm. First they complained about the Chapter decision. Then about their being

> brow-beaten by Rector Apice, who made Cosmas cut another strip off the habit which he had had made to measure at Ciorani. Nunzio had also had one made, by a tailor at Agrigento, which he had trimmed, unknown to the Brother, quite stealthily. The Rector attaches so much importance to this business of the length that he goes cane in hand to measure their habits, not only the new ones but also those the Brothers have been wearing in other houses. This excess of care for mathematical exactitude in reducing the habit to the regulation mid-leg length is disturbing the Brothers, especially because they're laughed at in the streets of Agrigento. I have tried to quiet and comfort them, but they are going about their work with a very bad grace. They do what they're told but not cheerfully. Of the four, only Brother Vincenzo stays cheerful and in good spirits.

Things came to such a pass in the house that Blasucci thought that they would settle down only if urgent prayers were said for the lot of them:

> So, as far as I can see before God, the relations of Fathers and Brothers here must simply be entrusted to the grace of God.[7]

Having written this private letter to Villani on October 10, letting him know the actual disposition of the community, Blasucci evidently felt that he need not mention anything about the habits in the official report which as Vicar Ordinary he forwarded to the Father Vicar two days later.[8] But this did contain one unitive suggestion. About clothing. Observing that, "unless they are legitimately excused," the Brothers wore the white linen cotta when serving the Fathers' Masses, Blasucci recommended that "the same decency of wearing the cotta" be adopted by the Fathers when they took a turn to serve.[9]

Alessio wore the cotta as a matter of course when serving the bishop's Mass. That was the start of their day together, though earlier Alessio had lit the kitchen fire and earlier still Alphonsus had been saying his morning prayers. So they continued for the thirteen years of Alphonsus' episcopate. Alessio was Alphonsus' general factotum, cutting his hair, mending his slippers, during winter fetching coals for the fire bucket in the bishop's study, during summer bringing him a glass of cold water last thing at night, all year carrying little messages about the town.[10] It was his especial pleasure to drive the bishop's four-wheel carriage on excursions to investigate what progress had been made in building the church at San Maria a Vico which Alphonsus had planned to serve the hillside folk.[11] Rather more wearisome to Alessio was the time spent escorting Alphonsus from palace to cathedral to make his daily visit to the Blessed Sacrament. He remarked at the Process that these visits lasted so long that he used to leave the bishop at his prayers, do his household chores, and then return to collect him.[12] And, just as he thought Brother Francesc' Antonio was out doing the shopping, and he might have a little rest, there would be a lady at the door and Alessio would have to stand behind the bishop's chair for the whole visit because Alphonsus would never be left alone with a female, not with one of his own family, not even, Alessio found later, when he had brought his two-year-old daughter to work with him one morning, with the smallest girl. "Alessio, don't bring her again, it disturbs me."[13] But perhaps it was the toddler's noise that had disrupted Alphonsus' concentration. The proud father had not thought of that.

The factotum did not, it appears, begrudge being kept from his wife and two daughters on those evenings when he was required to stay and recite the rosary with Francesc' Antonio and Alphonsus. There was a companionship in their kneeling together. But Fortunata may justifiably have grumbled. Alessio could not warn his wife what time he would be home, on account of his never knowing if five decades would suffice for Alphonsus' evening devotions. The old man simply continued from mystery to mystery until he felt it was time for him to make his end-of-the-day examination of conscience, to recite the Litany of Loreto, and say a few more prayers before eating. Sometimes in the middle of these devotions, he rang his little hand bell to warn the cook to start reheating supper. Only on his at last rising from his knees could Alessio think of going home.

Alessio very fast made it his business to know all about the running costs of the house. He'd looked over Francesc' Antonio's account books, quite casually. Noted the bishop's correspondence in and out of the house. So he was able to tell the Auditors at the Process that Alphonsus had, in addition to his income from the bishopric funds, what Alessio called, echoing Alphonsus, "his own money," and the pension from the College of Doctors, and another from the Congregation of Knights of the magistry of Portanova and, not so regularly, amounts from his brother

Don Ercole.[14] Revealing a peasant's interest in the ways of rich men, he was also able to tell the Auditors that he had often seen Alphonsus use the backs of envelopes.[15] Not that his bishop had been mean. Alessio had kept an eye on the outgoings, too. He had noted that five carlini were regularly given to poor persons at the door whether known to the bishop or not.[16] Brother Francesc' Antonio had charge of that. And Alessio had made the immediate calculation of a connection between such giving and their all eating nothing much but rough bread and a soup as thin as that in any Redemptorist refectory.[17]

The memory of those awful meals lingered. And alms-giving was not the only cause of their being such meager fare. Alphonsus was, it seemed, quite unable to insist on regular payments of the "table money" which parish priests should have been forwarding to the palace bursar. He was equally reluctant to press for the rents from his tenant farmers. Alessio knew for a fact that old "Tollo" Judavaja of Durazzano owed rents amounting to a really substantial sum.[18] And, if he were unwilling to press the clergy for their payments, he was far too ready to send money to any priest he heard was ill. There was that minor Canon of the cathedral, for example, who was really no more than a silly fool, but Alphonsus would insist that Francesc' Antonio....[19] There were, too, Alessio was convinced, some more handings-out of moneys that never got into the ledgers.

Alessio himself, however, was sometimes ready to prompt Alphonsus into making a handout when he liked the petitioner. It was surely at Alessio's suggestion that a falsely accused woman, who lived in one of the bishop's tied cottages, on being summoned to defend herself, declared not only that she was not "that sort of person," but that she had Saint Joseph as her patron; the saint was, as Alphonsus knew, Alessio's own patron. There would seem to be a little conspiracy here between his clients. "Well," said the smiling bishop, "St. Joseph has heard your prayer and told me not to turn you out of the cottage." Her saint next emboldened the woman to suggest that the bishop might reduce her rent. And Alphonsus agreed.[20] But Monsignore Onofrio Rossi, 1717–1784, his successor, as Alessio had been interested enough to find out, raised the rent back, higher than it had been. Perhaps she had not kept up her prayers to Saint Joseph.

Alessio liked to emphasize Alphonsus' own devotion to his patron.

"He used to preach in honor of Saint Joseph on the Wednesdays preceding his feast. And at the Novena."[21] Though not always, he had to admit, to his taste. There was the notorious time when Alphonsus, despite not having prepared a sermon, decided that he would preach for the triduum of Saint Joseph at Montevergine. Alessio offered a few pointers. The sermon should be an encouragement for the saint's fellow workers to some general jollity in the town square, "come to the celebration." But Alphonsus knew better. Saint Joseph would only be satisfied if the congregation "leave off sinning" and it was about their sinning that he would preach. "No longer offend God" was the text and whole matter of the sermon that feast day.[22]

Though he never recovered from the shock of Alphonsus' disregard of the usual courtesies on his holy patron's feast, for it could never seem quite right that Alphonsus should that great day preach his ordinary sermon about human sin and God's merciful forgiveness, Alessio did come to appreciate a consistency in his master's way of living. That soup in the private dining room, those self-whippings in the attic, those secret alms-givings, were of a piece with the very raggedness of his cassock.

Visiting Fathers told him that Alphonsus had always gone about in patched clothes, even in Naples itself. So it was no wonder that he dressed so poorly in Sant' Agata. Alessio knew that all the thirteen years Alphonsus was the bishop, taking part in the great ceremonies of the diocese, he never had a decent cape and was always wearing a hole in his slippers.[23]

Those Fathers told him, also, that the Rector Major had always occupied just that sort of bare room he was occupying at Arienzo, two or three benches piled with books, a small table, and a mattress on a low hurdle bed frame. Alessio and Francesc' Antonio took surreptitious turns at pushing the straw back into Alphonsus' palliasse but neither ever felt he had made a bearable bed for the bishop. At least, at Arienzo, Alphonsus had had a few paper pictures pasted on the wall and a small altar set up for when he was too ill to go across to the Collegiate Church for Mass. It seemed to Alessio in 1796, that the life he and Francesc' Antonio shared with Alphonsus "shone with poverty."[24] But even after all that time, Alessio had not come to terms with the behavior of that cook.

It was apparent to everyone in the house that the new cook was unable to prepare a decent meal. However much the Vicar General and the rest of them complained, they could not persuade the bishop to dismiss him. So the meat went on being ruined. Variously, from meal to meal. Oversalted. Insipid. Underdone. Burnt. Still the bishop did nothing. The awful meat-marrer stayed in the house right up to the day Alphonsus himself left.[25] Not a day after. The diocesan Administrator fired him that very morning. Alessio's favorite horror story of this cook was not precisely about the standard of his cooking. It was rather about his not knowing a servant's place. Once when Monsignore Antonio Puoti, 1716–1792, archbishop of Amalfi, who'd been born in Arienzo, was coming for the consecration of the newly completed cathedral, Alessio had highest hopes of their all having a fine luncheon. He just happened to be around when Alphonsus called the cook to give him his orders for the meal. The cook had always had his own explanation for the poor quality of their meals. He had never been allowed to show off his true skill. Not with the ingredients Brother Francesc' Antonio was buying. But alas, Alphonsus had called him to ensure that there would be nothing like a banquet for the visiting notables. Just their usual lunch. The cook protested. "But Monsignore, that's a meal to give a scullery boy." Aniello might have had something to say about that. So might Alessio. Alphonsus returned a mild reply. "Well, say what you wish," and then, rather less mildly, even perhaps a little threateningly, he went on to make a reference to the Brothers, "there are other men who are more biddable." The cook did not suppose Alphonsus was about to replace him by a Brother. And, indeed, Alphonsus was perhaps simply stating the facts and hoping the cook would be likewise obedient. But he rather had the boldness to continue. "Well, of course, Most Illustrious sir, you can give them your soup if you wish." He turned on his heel and, at the beatification process, Alessio was still shocked to recall, "muttering all the while," made for his kitchen. Alphonsus said nothing to all this. Turning in expectation of an awesome frown, Alessio was surprised to find him laughing at the absurdity of the situation. "Now, look how he does take on."[26] Still, it was rather reckless of Felice Verzella to encourage the cook to prepare something more exotic than Alphonsus had intended. They got away with it while the guests were in the palace, but afterwards Alessio happened to hear Alphonsus say to Verzella, "The table of a bishop is not the table of a King."[27] This was, in his repertory of rebuke, a rather strong thing for Alphonsus to say to the Secretary. It seemed to Alessio, however, quite an exaggerated response to the extra dish that the cook had placed on their table. It had not been at all the dish for a King. It had not, indeed, been very well cooked.

Alphonsus must have himself told the story which would confirm Alessio's views both of Alphonsus' patched cassock and of the general unpleasantness of cooks. Alphonsus had come to the garden back door of bishop Filippo Gentile, 1692–1771, of Telese, who was then residing, as he much preferred, in Cerreto, the more charming township. He had been met by the bishop's cook. The ignorant man took this shabbily dressed traveler for some no-good vagrant, and observing grandly that his master was then far too busy to grant him an audience, sat Alphonsus down on a bench by the wall. Told him to wait. After a while, Alphonsus asked again for an audience with the bishop, to which the impertinent fellow replied, "Wait, I'm busy," and then again, "Monsignore is not at leisure." After another while, he went casually to let his master know that this pestering tramp was in the hall. On hearing Alphonsus' name the bishop rushed down to embrace him, took him up to his study with every mark of reverence and affection. The cook hovered nervously about. Alphonsus must be telling his master of his ill reception. "But it was not like that," Alessio boasted, "because the venerable servant of God had kept quiet. Never said a word."[28]

Well, as Alessio had at once to admit as he chatted with the Auditors, it wasn't only cooks who mistook Alphonsus' patched habit. There was that Abbot presiding at First Vespers of the Assumption at the Regina Caeli convent who, looking round the congregation and, noticing Alphonsus in his patched habit, risked saying, "That's the sort of thing which brings shame on us all." Alessio warms to telling this story. It so redounds to his master's credit. And, therefore, to the credit of his master's servant. "The church was full of ladies and cavaliers; the prince of Montemiletto had seen him but not being acquainted with him, asked me if that really were Monsignore Liguori, and on my assuring him that it was, he at once presented himself with a respectful kiss of the hand and then went on to introduce the duke of Andria who also kissed his hand and asked his blessing, then a whole troupe of gentlemen and cavaliers came up. The Abbot was much confused by all these courtesies."[29] Better yet, Alessio had another story of when Alphonsus was summoned to the King's court in Naples, and of two Cavaliers of the Order of San

Gennaro who wondered who "that old man" standing in the ante-chamber could be, and who, on learning from Alessio that it was the bishop of Sant' Agata at once sent to offer him their seats. "No, no," said Alphonsus confusedly, "I could not inconvenience a cavalier." He began to hurry down the stairs.[30]

"All Shall Live in the Same Manner"

Alphonsus might seem to the casual observer not at all the man to appreciate others' concerns with clothes. Alessio knew better. He'd divined the meaning of his master's patched apparel. Went on thinking it their secret. Kept quiet. Very soon after this, however, when others were becoming grumbly about what they looked like in their habits, Alphonsus was to demonstrate that he, like every Neapolitan, quite understood the signifying power of clothes.

Their wearing the habit distinguished the Brothers of the Congregation from gentlemen's servants in the street and marketplace. And their wearing the calf-length habit ensured that they were distinguished everywhere from the Fathers. But in the sacristy, their habit's shortness might lead a visitor to confuse the Brother with one of those disreputable "*diaconi selvaggi*," bossy tonsured sacristans who swept the church floor, rang the bells, trimmed the candle wicks, and sometimes taught catechism to the parish urchins. These were, from their knee-length overalls and their love of clerical scandal, popularly known as "half-habit clergy." No decent man would want to be mistaken for one of these.[31]

In the early summer of 1773, the Brothers somehow got together long enough to compose a lengthy letter to Alphonsus.[32] This was their grand remonstrance. Complaining of many slights and disrespects but chiefly of their low status in the Congregation's being so openly signified by their being no longer allowed to wear the same clothes as the Fathers and Students. First the zimarra overcoat had been taken from them. Now they were being put back into a habit of ten or eleven inches shorter than that of the Fathers. Such outward signs signified. The Brothers did not look like respected members of the community. They did not feel respected. Was this really what the Rule meant by the affirmation that "all shall live in the same manner"? Surely decent old men wanting to stay modest, to say nothing of decent young men, should not have to wear so leg-revealing a costume, when it was thought proper that Students be covered to the shoe?

Alphonsus professed himself astonished at their grumbling. They were merely being told to observe "the custom in our Institute from the beginning."[33] They should know that the zimarra had been worn by Brothers for a year at most. Bishop Falcoia had put an end to this abuse of clerical garb. "To this I alone can testify, since there is no other Father left from that time."[34]

Falcoia had, in 1733, been keen on the Fathers' wearing, along with a dark red habit, a pair of blue stockings.[35] Alphonsus had absolutely refused to get into such an outfit. He had, he said, in the good set terms of a man who knows he is a gentleman, no intention of looking like some fool actor.[36] So Falcoia had to content himself with ruling that "in the matter of Clothing: all the Fathers, Students and Novices who are not Brothers should wear the same clothing." The same zimarra. The same cassock. The same small clothes, cotton in summer, wool in winter. But, in regulating what was appropriate "for the Brothers," he had allowed himself to be in class-distinguishing mode: "It is forbidden for them to wear the zimarra and the habit ought to be shorter."[37]

Falcoia had not, however, been able to stop Redemptorists talking about clothes. There was a history of discussion about their habit. By 1747 and the Conza text, all Redemptorists were being admonished to be "well content with some poverty in dress," accepting that they were to have a habit "made of ordinary wool" and "the same for all seasons."[38] Nothing distinguishing is said in that text about the Brothers' habit. But at the General Congregation assembling on October 17 that year, the Fathers having first laid it down, in Edict IV, that a youngster could not be received as a Brother before his eighteenth birthday, they went on to make edicts about how the received youngster should dress among them. For the first twelve months in the community, he should wear his own secular clothing, at the end of that year the Rector Major might allow him to be clothed in a habit of appropriate length.[39] "The habit of the Fathers," they had decided, should "overlap the shoe buckle by a finger's length, although when new-made there should be a two-finger gap all round "because they always stretch."[40] However, in the language we still employ in measuring the height of a horse, the Fathers decreed that the Brothers' habit "ought to be a hand more off the ground."

Last time there had been a "murmuring" among the Brothers, they had talked of Carmelites and Franciscans. This time it is Alphonsus who introduces the counter-example of those Brothers at the Chinese College. These also wear the short habit.

> It is not at all true that this usage is against modesty; on the contrary, it is conformable to the humility that should be shown by those who are not priests.[41]

Alphonsus has managed another of his useful word-plays here. The Brothers had been talking of a physical modesty and the moral danger their exposed calves might pose for others. Alphonsus has shifted into talk of psychological modesty and the moral danger to which the Brothers themselves were exposed. They were becoming proud again.

But all this talk of the relation of habit length and calves and modesty was, whether Alphonsus was willing to recognize it or not, a distraction from what the Brothers were trying to tell him.

They found it difficult to express their obscure sense that while they were commonly now doing clerical work, teaching catechism, adding up accounts, they were being kept within conventions established for Brothers who had at first been employed mainly in cooking meals and cleaning latrines. They saw the insistence on the short habit as a sign that the Fathers were not acknowledging their development as sharers in the active vocation of the Congregation. And were not taking into account what outsiders, seeing their habits, were judging their work to be.

The motives of some Brothers may well have been rather mixed. So may those of Fathers who did not want them to look like Fathers. But there was, of course, no real likelihood of either Fathers or Brothers being given much encouragement to discuss these matters. Alphonsus takes all responsibility, all authority, to himself

> It is not the Fathers that have always recommended the wearing of the short habit by the Brothers, but I myself, in order that they may be kept in humility, that they may be distinguished from the Fathers, and that the people may not call them "Your Reverence" as they do the priests.[42]

He seized upon the example of that Brother who had worn a habit not quite as short as that of the other Brothers. "He wished people to think that he was one of the Fathers."[43] Alphonsus was asserting this same connection of long robe and priestly character when he insisted, at Sant' Agata, on that "long cassock" for the clergy.[44] Longer or shorter, they had all of them, always, recognized that the habit signified. On Andrea's being let go in 1738, Falcoia was fast to assure Alphonsus, "I have made him leave the habit behind."[45] That Brother was no longer "one of us." Contrastedly, Pietrangelo Picone, 1733–1754, dying of tuberculosis at Materdomini, wrote to his old novice Master, Tannoia, "O what a fine thing it is to see me wearing my Redemptorist habit!"[46] But now, for Fathers and Brothers, length mattered.

Tannoia himself, as sensitive as any to the possibilities for disputatiousness at the Brothers' table, was hoping to get away with describing Gerard's clothing when he came in vision to cure the lady at Benevento simply as "the habit of our Congregation."[47] But the Brothers, having listened to this grand story, came questioning him about what length the heavenly Gerard's habit was. So Tannoia told them another story of another vision of Gerard in which the holy Brother, having no truck with all quarrel-stirring clothes, came "this time most richly clothed, resplendent in glory."[48] Anything for a quieter life.

This was a nervous time for them all. Certainly for Tannoia, never the calmest of persons, who suspected that someone in his community was spreading an unpleasant rumor, a calumny, against him. He was sure that Villani believed it.[49] After all, he'd believed that calumny against Brother Gerard. Tannoia had lost all joy in being a Rector. He simply wanted to get on with his bees and his writing. To be free of all responsibilities in the house at such a disturbing time.[50] Or at least to be on easier terms with Brothers and Fathers. But, thoroughly irritated that something might be happening without his knowing, and not being fully apprized of whatever rumor was going around, Alphonsus wrote to Tannoia and to all Rectors reminding them to appoint a special Zelator to inform him just what the Brothers were doing wrong outside the house when they were away on mission.[51] There had been some disturbing gossip. Well, he would know how to deal with them. So, dreading another unpleasantness in the kitchen or the garden shed or anywhere, Tannoia told a story which should give the Brothers their own reason for not hankering to look like a Father in a longer habit. He told a story of Francesco Tartaglione.

One day, as Francesco was returning to Naples from an errand to Castellammare, he was met at a narrow place in the road by a gang of young ne'er-do-wells who stopped his poor hired beast going any further. Mistaking him in his habit for a priest, the youths began to mock him. "O if that poor mother who put her son into the priesthood could see him now, riding an ass!" They took up stones from the roadside and started chucking them at him. That habit had got him into a real mess. It was only on account of Francesco's being such a fine Brother that he wasn't killed for being a silly priest. For Francesco had flung himself down on his knees in front of the louts and urged them on. "Strike, my friends! Strike a sinner!" And they, no longer of course mistaking him for a priest, were thoroughly ashamed of themselves. "Alas," they said, "we have struck a saint!" Less perfect Brothers, hearing the Rector tell that story, would be less eager to make a claim to the longer habit.[52]

Alphonsus, not having to concern himself with the day to day running of a house, generally took a shorter way than Tannoia when a dispute arose in the Congregation. He did so in 1773. He gave the Brothers, at a stroke, all they had ever asked:

> I wish you well as I do all the Fathers, for we are all brothers.

He is giving them his brotherly salute on account of their all belonging together in this new company of brothers:

> You have left your families to give yourselves entirely to God and to become saints.

Then, with as quick a stroke, he takes it all back again:

> But if any one is proud, I will not acknowledge him as my brother, for the proud are hated by God.[53]

Proud talk of that sort about the habit would lose them, at the heavenly tribunal, the loving care of the Lady. They must listen to her counsel. "I hope that the Blessed Virgin will put this notion out of your heads." She may yet help them to become saints. "That's what I hope."[54]

But if the Blessed Virgin should put that thought out of their heads, Alphonsus should be suggesting some other, encouraging, thought about their arriving as persevering Brothers at that heavenly tribunal. He had not, however, got clear enough for himself yet the Pauline distinction, so particularly impressively analyzed in Estius' *Commentary,* of the *servus* from the *famulus* who is, within the Christian community, on the way to being the *frater,* a brother among the saints. He could not yet, therefore, offer an explanation of the habit of the *famulus* on the way which should affirm in some immediately intelligible manner how this differed from the apron and clogs of the *servus,* who was simply the futureless slave.

The Brothers, considering among themselves what it might mean for them to become saints could not well see the connection of saintliness and the short habit. They had enough stories to tell among themselves of Gerard's being thought to be one of those full-length priests. And of his being content to be thought so:

> He met a poor countryman by the way who complained to him of the manner in which the mice destroyed all his crops, and as he took him for a priest, the man asked him to curse the mice for him. Gerard, having some sympathy for the poor man, made the sign of the Cross over the field, after which it was instantly covered with the bodies of dead or dying mice.[55]

They had that less ambiguous story of Gerard's being received by the patients in the asylum courtyard as a priest who, singularly, was able to understand them and talk to them in their own way of the Lord:

> "My Father, you are so good to us, we want you to stay with us and never go away. No. You must never go away. No one else says such beautiful things as you do."[56]

And another story of the Naples shopkeeper returning from a chat with Gerard at his store front to say plainly to his Redemptorist companion,

> That Father is a great saint.[57]

Tannoia knew these stories. He was prepared to tell them to the Brothers of his house, knowing their effect. He was acknowledging that Gerard at least was a Brother accepted every where by every one in the city as doing the work of a Father:

> Innumerable multitudes of people, whom one might almost call his penitents, surrounded him even late into the night, that they might listen to his edifying conversation.[58]

Late into those nights, Gerard had been doing the work not of any Father but of their Father Alphonsus himself. Gerard had been conducting his own Evening Chapels.

There was an irony, which would not go unnoticed by the Brothers, in the lengthy-habited Gerard's being presented as an exemplar to them by the very Fathers who were insisting that they wear the short habit. Telling them that their complainings were all pride. Going on telling them so. Kuntz very much lamented that "the letter of our blessed Father had no lasting effect" on account of the Brothers' harboring objections "in the pride of their thoughts."[59] But for now, Alphonsus was himself not going to argue the matter any longer. They had better just all settle down to fulfill his hopes for them.

Not every matter could be so smartly put aside. The air of Arienzo proved as little healthful to Alessio as to Alphonsus. He well remembered that when he was kept at home in bed, Alphonsus had called and left some money with Fortunata.[60] The widow Leone's family having steadfastly neglected to pay the sixty-four ducats of her dowry, and the two girls always needing food and clothes, Alessio always needed money.[61] Fortunata had begun to take in washing. She laundered the palace linens and sent them on each week to Antonio Biscardi in hopes that he would be able to darn them again. But the bishop's small clothes and the Pollio family finances were as threadbare as the other. Alphonsus had to bring money round to the house more than once. He made a will leaving Alessio fifty-six ducats and eighty-seven grains in a bill of credit he had drawn on the bank of San Maria del Popolo, "to be paid immediately on my death," declaring this generous sum to be simply "in recompense for the good service he has given me."[62] Such care secures devotion.

Alessio's view of Alphonsus is perhaps best instanced by his taking a vial when Alphonsus was being bled for a fever and preserving some of the blood.[63] He was treating Alphonsus as all good Neapolitans treat their saints; crowding to the liquefaction of the blood of Saint Stephen in the monastery of San Gaudioso, of the blood of San Pantaleone at Ravello, and of course, the blood of San Gennaro at both the cathedral in Naples and the execution rock at Pozzuoli, "celebrated," as Alphonsus himself cheerfully supposed, "in the whole Christian world."[64] Alessio had taken his vial of Alphonsus' blood in the expectation of its working miracles for the sick and, at the Process, Don Carlo Desiderio confirmed that the blood was still working them.

When, in July 1775, Alphonsus did at last retire from the bishopric, he asked Alessio to go back with him to Pagani, and Alessio felt himself in honor bound to keep an eye on his old master. Perhaps he had no real choice. The Vicar General, who had put himself at a distance from Alphonsus, had no good opinion of any of the bishop's domestics. Alphonsus' familiar use of Alessio as his letter-bearer in his dealings with archdeacons, rural deans, parish priests, cannot have endeared him to those who misliked the contents of the letters they were receiving. So Alessio would have no realistic hope of getting another job in the town or the neighboring villages. If he were to earn anything to support his wife and daughters, he would have to leave Sant' Agata and Arienzo behind him. He had, it seems, no desire to return to cobbling. He felt comfortable in his life as Alphonsus' servant. Alphonsus felt comfortable with him. So it was arranged that he should go along with the old man and that Fortunata should stay with the children at Arienzo.

Perhaps, these things happen, Fortunata and Alessio had discovered that they were happier if they were not too often in one another's company. Lack of money, the onset of ill-health, worries about the children's futures may bring wife and husband closer. Or they may not. Alessio was probably quick to blame Fortunata's family for all their troubles. She cannot have been pleased when he worked so late so many nights. Things did not improve for them. Fortunata's health was affected. She became bedridden. Their money problems became the more acute. Her slow illness both required their buying medicines and prevented her from taking in the laundry work. She died, it seems during the autumn of 1779 while Alphonsus was making a last effort to get the d'Ambrosio family to do something for her and Alessio.[65] Alphonsus wrote very soon after to Mother Maria Angelica recommending that he receive one of Alessio's daughters as a postulant among the Redemptoristines at Sant'

Agata. He allowed that there was no possibility of her bringing much money to the convent:

> I recommend her to your charity and, if you can be a little lenient in the matter of dowry, I shall be most happy, for Alessio is embarrassed enough in consequence of the expenses he has to incur.[66]

Perhaps, despite the d'Ambrosio efforts, Fortunata's relations never paid up. But Alphonsus was already hurrying forward to the day when Alessio would be accompanying his daughter to the convent door. And now he espied a drawback to the whole arrangement. He added a plaintive postscript to the Prioress:

> Please send Alessio back immediately, for I need him.[67]

He gave forty ducats to assist the marriage of Alessio's other daughter to "a decent young man" of Sant' Agata, and it was settled that Alessio would himself stay with Alphonsus.

Alphonsus had had the prescience, so very long ago, to insist that the Rector Major should have the scope to dispense a candidate from any novitiate. He had, indeed, been especially furious when Villani allowed a General Chapter to start talking of legislating on this very matter:

> I hear that you have brought to the consideration of others the question about the novitiate of the Brothers. Your Reverence, it seems to me could have, I say, told me secretly your idea on this point without undertaking to have the Chapter decide that the Rector Major cannot grant a dispensation when there is a question of the novitiate. This is equivalent to overthrowing absolutely the powers of the Rector Major and to destroy the principle traced out by our Father of *government by a single head* like the government of the Church.[68]

So Alessio stayed as a Brother.

Out of the Bishopric, Into the *Regolamento*

Returning to Pagani, Alphonsus should have been much quieter in himself than he had been at Sant' Agata and Arienzo. He had, it would appear, developed, before being appointed to Sant' Agata, a psychological distaste for being made a bishop which, as Frederick Jones observed, "verged on the obsessive."[69] His father had thought promotion to a fine see would go some way to recovering his career.[70] His brother had been willing even to lend him money to pay the expenses entailed in such a promotion.[71] But Alphonsus had "never settled down to enjoy his episcopate," he talked even of his "natural repugnance" for "this difficult and wearisome position of bishop."[72] He was referring to a terror he had of those pastoral responsibilities upon whose discharge he would be required to give an account on Judgment Day. The bishopric came, indeed, to seem to him itself, Frederick Jones says, already "a punishment for his sins."[73] But there was also the more natural repugnance at being at a distance from his brothers. "He believed he was being banished from the Congregation."[74] So, in November 1774, while he told Vicar Villani, "I want to return to die in the Congregation," he was at least as greatly looking forward to living among them again. "When I have once returned to one of our houses, I may be useful to the subjects, particularly the young men."[75] He had not considered the effect of this announcement on those who had been running things in his absence, Villani at Pagani, Pietro Paolo Blasucci on Sicily, de Paola in the Papal States. Villani was stunned. Alphonsus had to write again. "You do not say a word on the matter," "I am astonished that you say nothing on the subject," "Write to me."[76] But the Vicar kept his head.[77] He gave no sign of resigning when Alphonsus returned to Pagani. Alphonsus hardly noticed this vexing detail.

Alphonsus had come back with his old familiar assertion. "I do nothing but pray for you," he told Fathers and Brothers, "whom I hold dearer than all my relatives."[78] He had taken his old authoritative command of affairs. "At the start of the mission year, I thought I should give you some counsel," and such needful and durable counsel that "this letter is to be kept and read every year in October before the Fathers set out on the missions."[79] Reviewing what Villani, Blasucci, de Paola, and the rest of them had been doing while he'd been away, he saw at once the necessity of getting things back to what they should be, had been, always. "I do not wish to violate a rule established by our Father, Mgr. Falcoia."[80] He is, after all as he had had to tell the Brothers in 1773, "the sole survivor" from those Falcoian times. "To this only I can testify." As in 1773, again, he turned to setting up an informer network. "Tell me what Father Blasucci is doing."[81] He would need regular reports from all of them. "Before anything else, write to me. Often."[82] "Write to me every week."[83] "Write to me by every post."[84] The Fathers proved not at all keen on making these regular reports. "You have not written to me for some time." "I have been expecting an answer from you for two or three weeks." "Today I finally received a letter from you."[85] They slipped from under him. "Using one pretext or another, they've not heeded my order."[86] Slipped away. "A long time ago, I issued a general prohibition for all subjects of our houses, against their leaving the Nocera house without having asked my permission: I wish to know when subjects leave so that I can give them the necessary advice."[87] They didn't want his advice. "The Fathers at Ciorani make very little of me and my letters." They told him as much. "You are suggesting that it would be better for me not to write so many letters."[88] But he had to communicate to his brothers those "lights that God gives me." They didn't want to know about those peculiar lights. They wanted to get on with the day-to-day running of the houses as best they could, by the ordinary lights God was giving them.

It is not so surprising, therefore, that he should for a while draw back somewhat from all he had said about families and the dangers for any Redemptorist who retained an interest in his sisters and his cousins and his aunts, and should turn expectantly to his brother, Ercole and his brother's family, for some comforting attention. Not that he'd ask for any sympathy. He'd just tell them what they were to do. From Pagani, he wrote, as *de facto* head of the family, to regulate the education of Ercole's sons, Giuseppe and Alfonsino. "You may come and talk it over with me and the Fathers."[89] Perhaps their sitting down all together to fix the futures of the boys, Alphonsus at the head of the table, would encourage his brother and his brothers to renew the proper, shared, recognition of Brother Alphonsus.

His brother, however, thought him merely interfering. His brothers were going to some lengths to avoid his attentions. That famous "*Regolamento* crisis" was in significant part brought about by senior Fathers who were hoping to achieve a constitutional acknowledgment of their competence to deal with the ordinary problems of the Congregation in a modern way.

In the old days, Paolo Cafaro had resolved entirely to depend "on the

Rector Major and the local Rector."[90] But the manners of those old days seemed to some distinguished Redemptorists no longer appropriate to the complexities of Congregation government. In 1774 already, Pietro Paolo Blasucci was speculating how the Consultors' position might be strengthened against those of Rectors and Rector Major. An opportunity for some strengthening of the sort came when, in January 1776, civil service discussion of the appropriate official attitude to the Congregation reached the Giunta degli Abusi. These were the gentlemen who had so nicely solved all problems arriving at the suppressing of the Jesuits and the redistribution of their General's powers in the Kingdom. During the next year it became clearer to Alphonsus that it was time to make some accommodation with the Ministers. With his usual enjoyment of a shared secret, he insisted that the two Consultors charged with the business, Angelo Maione, 1733–1787, and Fabrizio Cimino, 1733–1818, should take their oaths not to divulge anything of the negotiations until all was settled. They were unsuccessful in preventing leaks. Disturbing leaks, some Fathers thought. But they did manage to keep one secret. They kept it from Alphonsus. About his yielding something of his centralizing, centralized, authority. They had been, even those who sympathized with their general modernizing project agreed, a little devious. But Alphonsus had known there would be some changes to endure at the negotiations' end. He had told them to keep quiet. And he had, in order to facilitate Maione's day-to-day conduct of the Congregation's effort to obtain the desirable royal recognition, given him a sheaf of blank sheets with his signature at the bottom of each.[91] Maione could, therefore, well hope to get a reconstructed Rule sealed and, since it was already signed, in place before Alphonsus, whose chief aim of a royal recognition of the Congregation had been achieved, could start some awkward fuss about the detail. "The substance of the Rule remains intact," Villani had written soothingly after his 1748 concessions to Curia prejudices.[92] In 1780, Consultor Maione was saying something the same.

The government decree confirming the agreed *Regolamento* was read to Alphonsus at Pagani on March 9, 1780. He saw at once what was happening. Whatever else he'd had in mind when he authorized Maione and Cimino to treat with the government ministers, it was not that he should be sidelined. He roused himself. "I've seen the new *Regolamento*, the work of Father Maione; it is entirely contrary to my views."[93] The Father was being displaced by some unruly younger sons. The Company was being taken over by the management. But surely all decent men could see that this modern *Regolamento* could not be better than the *Regole Grandi* which had been "scrutinized by Mgr. Falcoia who was a holy man"?[94] Or the Pontifical Rule granted by Benedict XIV, by which he had been invested with singular and total government in the Congregation "for life"?[95] "This Father, in order to give authority to the Consultors, has sought to despoil the Rector Major of all his powers."[96] Maione's reconstruction had run well with the ideas of the regalist Ministers. Redemptorist Fathers and their Rector Major should be less like those offensive Jesuits and their General. Maione had seen to it that there should be no more talk of Fathers' being, "in my usual phrase" as Alphonsus said, "cut to pieces" by the Rector Major.[97] In this, if only in this, he had the support of de Paola. And the silent by-standing of Villani.[98]

That shift of power towards Consultors could not, however, please everyone. "The young Fathers here," Alphonsus wrote from Pagani, "are creating a commotion."[99] Old Fathers, feeling out of things in distant d'Iliceto, were making their own commotion. "It is all a great mess," as the panicky Tannoia was foolish enough to inform the Roman Curia, precipitating their interest.[100] The beekeeper, used to queens in the hives, popes in the Church, was put into a dangerous tizzy by the thought that Alphonsus would no longer be the enlightened despot in the Congregation. He shared, evidently, something of the Ministers' assessment of the Congregation's likeness to the Society of Jesus. For this once quite unhistoricist, forgetful of "the brothers of this Congregation" being defined in the Pontifical Rule as a company of secular priests. Tannoia thought it must be destructive of the Congregation's identity and mission effectiveness that, under this *Regolamento*, they soon would all be "nothing better than a Confraternity," a band of do-gooding associates. He was particularly upset that their religious vows were to be converted to mere civil oaths. They'd be civil servants.[101] The Roman authorities were led to think this a main point.

Alphonsus was not at all fussed about proposals to restructure such external forms of their lives together. An oath would bind them as well as a vow.[102] That was not a main point. That was not it at all. "The essential thing is that the internal government of the Congregation remain the same." Nor, all remaking of governmental customs being removed from discussion, could he see as cause for worry about the persisting identity of their Congregation. They should all take comfort that they had upwards of one hundred young Reverend Brothers studying dogma who "if they presented themselves at the Sorbonne or at Louvain would make a good showing":[103] the future was surely safe with them. But it was a little disturbing, on both governmental and recruitment grounds, that Francesco de Paola, always an intelligently energetic man, was supposing this to be the moment when he might start liberating the houses in the Papal States from all those squabbling Neapolitan Fathers.

Alphonsus and those Neapolitan Fathers felt themselves driven between the Scylla of the royal determination to bring the Congregation within civil jurisdiction and the Charybdis of the Roman refusal to sanction a lessening of the ecclesiastical remit. Neither would budge. "Maione wishes to obtain a new decree by which whoever refuses to accept the *Regolamento* shall be expelled."[104] Complementarily, by September 1780, the curial investigators were deciding to shut down the Redemptorist enterprise in the Kingdom. Alphonsus wrote to Pope Pius VI, Braschi, 1717–1799, outlining the history since "the day that some priests and I formed an Association to preach missions to the country people of the Kingdom" until their present negotiations with the difficult Ministers of their King and declaring that by accepting the royal decree "I have saved the work of the missions from shipwreck." He was returning to the high seas language of Don Giuseppe's bedtime yarns.[105] His letter was not received with any sympathy at the Curia. The Naples Fathers were already regarded there as "no longer members of the Congregation," no longer enjoying "the privileges and favors" granted to their predecessors in the reign of Pope Benedict. Alphonsus was at a loss what to do. It was no longer a question of the Rector Major's powers. "It is not this that affects me." They were all, now, being prevented from making an effective response to those needs of the poor which had first prompted those secular priests to come together. "The blow that really hurts is the withdrawal of the faculties for the missioners, without these we can render only feeble service to souls."[106] It was very soon known to everyone in the Kingdom that the Fathers in the Naples houses were operating without papal authorization. By the spring of 1781 there was not one Student remaining in the Dogma class. Or any other class.

"When a man is on the point of drowning," Alphonsus wrote to Pietro Paolo Blasucci, "he makes a grab for whatever's within reach."[107] So would Blasucci come to Pagani? He could take charge. As Alphonsus' man. By-passing those awkward Consultors. Blasucci, correctly, surmised that if they all kept quiet on Sicily neither Naples nor Rome would have will and energy to move against them. The Agrigento Fathers should keep themselves to themselves. Like, but not entirely like, the Roman Fathers. "The *Regolamento* is directed to the secular priests living by royal permission in the four houses of the Kingdom of Naples."[108] Sicily is a separate Kingdom. So, it is left for all to make the inference, Agrigento is a separate house in a separate Kingdom. Some Agrigento Fathers were rocking Blasucci's boat. But he could deal with them. There was a one in the morning meeting of the Rector's allies in Brother Vincenzo's room.[109] Perhaps it does not signify that Brothers Pasquale and Cosmas were not of that conspiratorial company. Brother Nunzio Bergantino had died in 1779.

Alphonsus felt himself very much alone. "I will write neither report nor letter, for I see that all I do turns against me."[110] He felt as much ignored in the Pagani house as in the wider Church. "Such a slight to my authority now prevents my companions from showing me any respect."[111] He complained even to de Paola about the lot of them. "I will request Fathers Corrado and Pavone to call upon me tomorrow; but I fear that they will not respond to my appeal; I see that they do not listen to me any more."[112]

Every man needs someone to listen. Alphonsus turned to Francesc' Antonio and Alessio. He told them all about those ungrateful Fathers. About that scheming Consultor. These confidences, had the delicious tone of shared secrets. They were becoming friends.

Francesc' Antonio and Alessio never forgot these beginnings of true intimacy with Alphonsus. Nearly ten years later, when Maione was dead and Cimino was bishop of Oria, the two Brothers recalled together for the notary, Don Domenico Cavalli, how, so trusting was Alphonsus, the untrustworthy Maione had been able to put words on those presigned blank sheets that did not at all express Alphonsus' mind. The poor deceived old man had been sure that "in the end it would turn out that he had been honest in fulling his commission," but it proved not so.[113] Maione's treachery had been a very great shock. The Brothers had, of course, frowned and tutted appropriately as Alphonsus poured out his self-justifying complaints. They were his sympathetic listeners.

The Brother As Father

Alphonsus looked about him for a few others who should listen to him. It was not easy. "The weakness of my head prevents my being able to say clearly what I mean, and I cannot pronounce my words properly."[114] However, he could just about dictate a letter to Francesc' Antonio.[115] And get Alessio to hand it to the mailman. If the Fathers wouldn't do as he wanted, his youngest brother would. That resignation of primogeniture rights had always been for him a legal fiction. "Don Ercole will do as I tell him." This plan to have Giuseppe married to the daughter of State Counselor Nicolo Vespoli, prince of Cimitile, must be scrapped.[116] The next generation of Liguori would have to do like their father. Alphonsus' nephews must spend their 1780 Easter vacation at Pagani. "I expect you here to give you my last blessing and my last commands."[117]

The boys proved as wary as their father of obeying a summons from the old man. Alphonsus would have to bless them at a distance and content himself with putting these commands in writing.

In April 1780, Alphonsus is in the middle of the *Regolamento* crisis. He is writing to the boys in the same week as he is writing to Diodato Criscuoli, 1738–1804, at Ciorani summoning him to a meeting of delegates from all the houses. The Congregation seems in danger of slipping out of his fatherly grip.[118] It is, perhaps, a relief to him, for a moment, to be able to assert paternal rights in the clan.

In the long letter to the boys that he now writes, the longest he wrote to any member of his family ever, Alphonsus is exploring what it means to him to be a father, the father at the head of the clan, certainly, but also the Father of the men in the Congregation. He begins with a reverence towards the Father from whom all fatherhood comes. Giuseppe and his brother are to love their heavenly Father "with a tender and filial affection." Then, derivedly, they are to love Alphonsus as their father. "Love God, my dear children—I call you 'my dear children' because I love you with all the tenderness of a father." Perhaps, after that long time, he can recognize "filial affection" responding to "the tenderness of a father" in his difficult relations with the Captain. Assuredly, it is as the Captain's son that he proceeds to give the boys his counsels. He is chief of the Liguori, affirming the dignity of their ancestry and their good position in present society. "You belong to an honorable family" and "You are at a College directed by masters who join to an illustrious birth their great and admirable virtue." They must remain nobly obedient to their well-born ushers. "I am confident that you will do so, to please God, your father, and myself." Still it was good that he had had the foresight, in that letter Ercole had carried to the College on their first day, to instruct these gentlemanly schoolmen that they should report anything they noted about the boys' conduct straight to him. Their reports were on his desk as he wrote. "I have learned with pain that you neglect your studies: O my children! if only you knew what you are doing!" They have no appreciation of how painful their bunking off is to him. "Study and afford me the consolation of hearing before my death that you profit from my advice."

This is a letter for them to place alongside those of the antique Roman authors they were set to construe in class. "Read this long letter attentively, ask for an explanation of the passages that you do not comprehend, impress it deeply on your memory." He was not going to allow the boys to fall into forgetfulness of his fatherhood as, it seemed to him, so many of his brothers in the Congregation were forgetting him. He would, whatever happened, be their father.

Perhaps he foresaw something of what was going to occur. Perhaps not. "Ercole will give me trouble this year," he remarked to Giambattista di Costanzo. "This was all he said."[119] Ercole died, September 8, 1780. Quite unexpectedly, in his physicians' opinion. He had appointed Prince Nicolo Vespoli together with the family attorney, Pietro Antonio Gavotti, to be guardians of the three children if he were to die before they came of age. So now, a little surprised that he had not been named guardian, which would surely have been the natural thing; Alphonsus dictated a letter to Gavotti.[120] Taking on the management of the boys' futures, Alphonsus thanks his deputy:

> If the death of my brother, Don Ercole, whom God may have in his glory, has brought me no slight grief and distress, it has also filled my mind, as soon as I heard the news, with a thousand painful thoughts about the care of my nephews which I thought I should take upon myself, left as they are without any father or mother. But having heard only today that your most Illustrious Lordship was

> chosen by my brother as guardian of these children, my grief is moderated and my mind relieved from all these anxious thoughts which oppress it, because I think them in good hands, and am certain that with your help and devotedness, not only will they profit by your wise counsel, but their temporal affairs will be excellently managed.
>
> I thank God continually and at the same time express my most devoted gratitude to your most Illustrious Lordship for having been willing to undertake this new burden, which will ever be for me an additional obligation to all that I owe you.

Ercole's death had, however distressingly, opened a clear way for Alphonsus' directing the boys' futures. Gavotti was to realize that Alphonsus would be overlooking his shoulder. He could not have missed the carefulness of Alphonsus' postscripting suggestion that he continue to employ the family agent, Gaetano Celano, so that they should all be kept informed of any depositions of property the guardians might think good to make. Nor the threat complementary to Alphonsus' promise:

> If you look after these boys, God will look after you.

Alphonsus himself was already looking after Ercole's eighteen-year-old daughter, Teresina.[121] "To a nunnery, go; and quickly too. Farewell."

Reorganizing the Family

Teresa may have been secured as a True Bride of Christ, but the boys escaped the rule of their father's fatherly brother. Alfonsino, having in 1783 made his formal "*cessio*" and "*renunciato*" of all ambition to be a priest, first took an apartment in the Via San Maria ante saecula, in the family's old neighborhood, and then moved to Sorrento so that he might be at convenient visiting distance for his niece Carmela. The surviving twin became Don Giuseppe de' Liguori, prince of Pollica and Celso, received by everyone as the acknowledgeable head of the house. He grew up. He married, in 1784, the princess Maria Guzmana Sambiase, a relative, at a little distance, of the great Minister Montealegre who had been created Duke of Salas. The couple rented a very decent house in the piazza Fiorentini and became well-known revelers in fashionable Naples society.[122]

There had probably been nothing unwelcome to the Fathers in Alphonsus' invitation to take an interest in Ercole's sons. They all of them felt something of that intense Neapolitan interest in their own and others' family connections. They were certainly not at all averse to thinking and talking of their own Congregation as one large family,[123] even of "this least of Congregations" as "this small family of the Most Holy Redeemer," and of house communities as smaller families. Coming home from a round of visitations, Vicar Villani asked the Rectors still to keep him in their family prayers "*una cum familia tua.*" [124] This became their customary use in the Congregation. So Federico Kuntz writes of Gerard as "that most splendid member of our family" and of Alessio's being received into "the Pagani family."[125] There was a structuring value to this language. Encouragement to good community practice. Under the Father Rector, the house family would pray together, stay together, obey together. At d'Iliceto, within the "*Ilicetana familia*,"[126] Tannoia returned time and again in little community talks to reminding them all that "where there is no family there can be no observance."[127]

In their talk of themselves as "family," Fathers Rector were usually expressing an understanding of Fathers' relations with one another as brothers. They were not saying anything about Alphonsus' relative status. They certainly were not, at the time Alphonsus returned from Sant' Agata, ready to accept him as an active *pater familias,* controlling their lives. Alphonsus, however, knew no other way of being a father. His dealings with his family presented them with a warning enough of that. But these Fathers were not nephews to be told what to learn by rote. They were not to be constrained like some young niece. And it is apparent that Alphonsus did not appreciate what had been happening while he was out of the way at Arienzo. He was reduced to blustering incomprehension; how could they resist his will? "When you know that I have said a thing," "When I have written it in a letter bearing my seal."[128] They were not to be brought back to anything like that sticklike obedience which Alphonsus thought religious.[129] The King's Ministers had been right to think there was something "Jesuitical" about him.

Alphonsus had to accommodate himself to the changed conditions within the Congregation. It seemed to many of the Fathers that it must be less painful for him, and for them, if he would just bow out gracefully. Alphonsus was not the man to retire. Under the Pontifical Rule he had been elected for life. But now there was the *Regolamento.* On the Fathers suddenly turning their Pagani consultation, in May 1780, into an electoral Chapter, Alphonsus was shown that it was now by their vote that he could continue as Rector Major, and then only with Corrado, the man who "does not listen to me," as an effective Vicar General. This was the occasion for his recognizing Corrado as "Most Revd. Father and Brother."

Others were showing an even freer spirit. In July 1780, Blasucci wrote to the energetic Francesco de Paola, alarmed at the "choleric" and "impetuous" proceedings of his cousin. He should slow down a bit. As "your brother," Blasucci urged de Paola not to be ambitiously divisive; he and the other Fathers, "your company," should just wait for what Providence would arrange "after the death of Mgr. Liguori."[130] They were unwilling to wait. In September, the Fathers in the houses of the Papal States, having satisfied themselves that they would be free to do better work if separated from their Naples brethren, finally withdrew from Alphonsus' jurisdiction. De Paola was appointed their President. This was the occasion for Alphonsus' ceasing to sign himself "Brother Alphonsus" in their correspondence.

He was still, rather too obviously again, trying to be the "very devoted and affectionate uncle" as he sent his Christmas wish to the young Giuseppe recommending that he now "profit by the time God sends" lest "your neglect be a cause of regret in the future."[131] Then it was back to Congregational affairs.

"The Pope is angry with us." "The King has forbidden us to write to the Pope." "The Blessed Virgin will be the one to set afloat our poor damaged little boat."[132] And so she did. In the time God sent. The good reputation of the missioner Fathers with local bishops persisted. On some happy turns of events, including the death of the Cappellano Maggiore, Mgr. Testa, in April 1782, various of the bishops got up enough courage to write to Rome complaining of a policy that deprived their people of so much good. "If morality and the fear of God prevail among the people of my diocese," wrote Nicola Amato, bishop of Lacedonia, "all is due, Most Holy Father, to these laborers and the untiring zeal of Monsignore Liguori."[133] In Rome, it was also noted that President de Paola, "carried away by his fervent nature," as Cardinal Francesco Banditi, 1706–1796, observed, had managed to provoke an unseemly rebellion in those houses he had been presenting as models of Redemptorist observance. A rebellion, moreover, claiming that there was a falling off in observance of the pontifical Rule.

At Sant' Angelo a Cupolo in the Duchy of Benevento, founded 1755, Scifelli, founded 1773, Frosinone, founded 1776, Benevento itself, founded 1777, Spello in the diocese of Foligno, founded only in 1781, and, the very recentest of the President's foundations, Gubbio, Brothers had subscribed to a petition to Pius VI:

> Most blessed Father,
> The Brothers of the Congregation of the Most Holy Redeemer in the Pontifical States with humble heart before the throne of Your Holiness, humbly point to the introduction of some new abuses in their Congregation which are not actually stated but are practiced in the Congregation.

These Brothers were pointing to some not very new "abuses" being perpetrated by their Rectors; they complained about Brothers' not eating at the common refectory table with Fathers, and, again, about a Brother's shorter habit and his not being provided with a zimarra "against the winter chill." "This is not a matter of the Fathers being charitable to the Brothers."[134] They had the remembrance of Francesco Tartaglione's being in Rome with Villani. Of Brother and Father sharing cheese. Of their going together to get the blessing of the Pope. "It is clearly stated in the Rule that all shall live the same way." But the Alphonsian assertion has been made again by their President:

> All these things have been laid before our Superiors but nothing has been done. The Fathers take no notice. They say that the Rule is not for us, the Brothers. We therefore pray Your Holiness to make known how things really are.

Then they can all get back to being the Christian family Pope Benedict wanted:

> Humbly we pray that we may live according to the Rule that we have professed with no such abuses.

"This proud petition" as the scandalized Kuntz termed it, was given extraordinary short attention by the Prefect of the Congregation, Cardinal Xavier de Zelda, 1756–1801, who simply returned it to the President's Procurator, Isodoro Leggio, 1737–1797, recommending that "the Superiors deal with it according to their Rule."[135]

Hearing some good of Alphonsus and being irritated by de Paola's Brothers and their petition, the cardinals were in a more favorable mood when it came to considering those episcopal petitions. On April 4, 1783, they restored the missioners' faculties.

Within the week of receiving this liberating intelligence, the Fathers were told that the Royal Chamber had decided the Sarnelli lawsuit in their favor. The Fathers could think of reopening for novices. They could be a *familia* again. With "little children." With *famuli*. But first, they must take thought for themselves.

Their missioner faculties having been restored, the discussion of the Rector Major's authority had moved back to the top of their agenda. The reconstructive notions of the disgraced Maoine could now be reexamined. If they were to move forward as a family in the new conditions, it had become clearer to most of them that Alphonsus must be persuaded to step to the side. They must proceed to a new election. They met for this purpose at Ciorani in the summer of 1783. Alphonsus stayed back at Pagani. Out of the way. Upstairs. On August 16, they voted for Villani to be "co-adjutor with right of succession" to the Rector Major of the Naples houses. The Fathers were now and henceforward to be led by one of themselves who had no claim to primogeniture, no claim to be their father by his own right.

The *Famulus* in the New *Familia*

Within such a family, the Fathers were *confratelli*, brothers with a sense of familiar equality, or, in the current fashion among English-speakers, "confreres." These sharing brothers, looking about for a language in which they might next talk of serving Brothers, were attracted by that vichian analysis of the primitive family structure which had seemed to Alphonsus himself to offer a likely start for reflections upon the Brothers' status. But because he had never yet found spare enough time and energy to articulate the Pauline ideas underlying his practice as Brother Alphonsus among Brothers, the Fathers were still thinking in ways that had characterized their bourgeois acquaintance. They were thinking in terms of the masters in the world and their servants. It was not entirely laziness that had led them to take up Alphonsus' language of *famulus* without exploring his Pauline reunderstanding of Vico's sociology. But assuredly the Fathers did not, generally, look very long or very intently at the status and function of Brothers in the community houses. Paolo Cafaro was almost alone in his concern for their peculiar Christian character. Mostly they took little account of the Christian difference of the *famulus* from the *servus* or of the vocation of the *famulus* working among them to be that *frater* whose "Christian fraternity," as Estius said, "lasts into eternity." To these modern users of the language, the serving Brother seemed perfectly well figured by that vichian *famulus* whom they, vichian heroes at the head of the *familia,* were graciously prepared to feed, lodge, and protect as long as the *famulus* identified himself with the interests of the *familia* and worked hard at the work they assigned him.

It could not seem a difficulty to any Father putting these general notions into practice on the corridor and in the garden that, on this thinned-down understanding of *famulus,* Brother Agostino Salvadore, 1719–1789,[136] at d'Iliceto was not definedly distinguishable from Michel' Angielo, the unpaid *servus* to whom they were giving meals and out-house lodging in exchange for a variety of manual labor. Michel' Angielo had been their unpaid workman, odd-job man, since that day in 1745 when Alphonsus and a couple of Fathers, coming out of the house, had been met by "a friendly man of good physique" who said he needed a place to sleep and was ready to work. Alphonsus had liked the look of him and at once accepted him "to serve our house." Everyday thenceforwards Michel' Angielo rose at dawn, went three or four times back and forth between kitchen and spring to fetch water, sawed the day's billets of wood, cleaned out the grate, swept the yard, weeded the vegetable patch, and was in so many ways "the ass of the house." This laborer was not to be identified with a layman of the world. "With these exercises of Martha, Michel' Angielo did not omit those of Mary Magdalene," for his life was "a continuous martyrdom"; he was thrashing himself with whips, sleeping on the church paving-stones, wearing himself out in prayer before the blessed Sacrament. Thus he died. After carrying the morning's logs. And was accorded a community requiem.[137] Just like Brother Agostino.

Even if few of the Brothers would have wished to distance themselves from so excellent a man, most would have been hoping to be distinguished from other, paid, servants. From Gaetano's *lacche,* Giuseppe di Nino, who was paid twelve ducats a month, from Dominico Iannela, whom Alphonsus had felt obliged to take over "*in famulatu*" from Bishop Danza,[138] or that rascal Aniello Vertucci, an eye always on the girls, whom the Fathers described in the Process documents as "*famulus* of the Servant of God," exactly as they described Alessio.[139]

Very aware that Alessio had not endured any novitiate, his domestic service to the bishop at Sant' Agata somehow substituting, the Fathers did not bother to remark just how he had come from *servus* to *famulus* on the way to *frater.* This was not the time to confuse the Auditors with Pauline exegesis. Alessio is often simply "his *famulus,*" "his *famulus* for twenty-five years."[140] Francesc' Antonio hinted at a nicer understanding of what had happened as he and Alessio and Alphonsus had prayed together. It was, he thought, necessary to distinguish. To acknowledge the process. He, therefore, referred to Alessio as "once his servant, now our Brother."[141] But it was significant for all the Brothers that the Fathers had, without much thought, quite indeliberately for the most part, slipped into regarding Alessio the man-servant as the good example of what was required in a Brother.[142] Their view of Alessio informed their expectations of other Brothers. In the Kingdom. And beyond the Alps. In the present. And in the past. Vito is described by Kuntz, without any delaying explanation of how he is using the term, as "*famulus* of the Father."[143] By this time, as they listened to some Fathers telling the story, Brothers might think themselves happy not to be lumped with Giuseppe Savastano, that irresponsible "*garzone du cucina,*" scullery boy, who had encouraged Aniello in his naughtiness.[144]

There was every encouragement in their language of *famulus* for the Fathers to slip into such an estimate of the Brother as the inconsiderable scullion. Alphonsus himself had, in his *Theologia Moralis,* considered it a real question whether the *famulus* could, precisely because he was so much the agent of the heroic head of the *familia,* the servant of his master, be held personally responsible for his actions. For his holding down a horse for his master's pleasure, for example, or his bringing a girl to his bedroom, or his holding the ladder while his master climbed to her bedroom, or his obediently serving his master meat on a day of abstinence. Alphonsus had made his contribution to this debate among contemporary moralists. He had settled for himself that *famuli,* like *coloni,* those serfs whose lease gave them no secure hold on the land they were farming, like women, minors, men of no fixed abode, none of them being "a person" within the legal definition, could not be sworn as witnesses in a Naples court.[145]

But just as the Fathers were placing their Brothers as dependent *famuli* of the family, men without responsibility in the family's determinations for their future, Alphonsus, the displaced hero upon whom those *famuli* had been said by Vico to rely, put from the center of his Brothers' lives, at a distance from his brother's sons, was coming to rely more and more on the goodness of the Brothers in the Pagani house.[146] He did need Alessio. He needed Francesc' Antonio, too.

He began to be better aware of the fineness of the familial service these Brothers had given him at Sant' Agata and Arienzo. His "familiars" had been, he was now realizing, for some long time, truly, his "little family."[147] He was doing some revision of the past himself. He now understood Vito to have been "his whole family."[148] Out of his loneliness, he looked for future possibilities of such family love, too, in the service of Brothers he was meeting for the first time, Giuseppe di Napoli, 1737–1806, and his eager crew. But his old familiar friends were still his most caring Brothers. He could ask anything of them.

There came a time when Alphonsus was calling out for Alessio at any and every hour of the day and night.[149] Francesc' Antonio was as persistently summoned by panicky shouts of the Rector Major. The two of them were set to stand at all times between Alphonsus and the community. Alphonsus was their responsibility. He would create a fuss. Demand what he should do to be saved. Require immediate advice from a Spiritual Director. One of the pair would leave the room in the pretense of going to consult Villani or Mazzini or whosesoever words Alphonsus was likely to respect, wait in the corridor for a credible time, then go back with plain orders for Alphonsus to obey. He would, for a while, be calmed. For he was always ready to recognize his share in that obedience to which these two Brothers were making their assured, companionable appeal. It was a great day for everybody in the Pagani house when Alessio took it upon himself to deal with Alphonsus' awkward insistence that, as a matter of humility, he should be eating with the rest in the refectory, not have his meals carried up to his room. "Monsignore," he had said firmly, "Your Most Illustrious Reverence wishes to go down to the refectory with the community: when you get there you eat very little, because you are not well, but Your Most Illustrious Reverence's shakiness makes you take a long time to eat that little, and the whole community is inconvenienced by having to wait for you; things really cannot go on like this."[150] Alphonsus listened. Did as he was told.

Alessio had understood, like Antonio Lauro, like Francesc' Antonio, the practical implementation of that delicate lesson Alphonsus had learned from Gerard about their shared, uncomplaining, obedient life.

He was beginning to understand from Alphonsus' developing Christian friendship, though Alphonsus was by now past the time when he could articulate this understanding of his life with Brothers, that the three of them were *famuli* of their heroic Redeemer, the head of the Christian *familia,* ever present in the house. They were, the three of them, *famuli* being brought well on the way to enjoying the happiness of eternity, coming at the eucharistic celebration to be *fratres.* Whether those who were calling him upstairs and downstairs appreciated it or not, this was the meaning of his being called "Brother."

The three of them sat together in Alphonsus' little room and Francesc' Antonio read aloud their day's meditation from Alphonsus' own *Visits to the Blessed Sacrament.* Fathers in the house were always mightily relieved when this reading began. Alphonsus was safe at prayer for an hour or more after that. For Alessio, spending his day plumping the palliasse, emptying the slops, wheeling Alphonsus in his chair up and down the corridor, fetching meals on a tray, putting his arms round the old man as he tottered to make the Stations of the Cross along the corridor wall, washing him, undressing him for an early night, these prayerful readings were his opportunity to get some finer appreciation of the meaning of his vocation. Domestic chores were located in eucharistic devotion during Alessio's personal novitiate.

That they should all together be pressing forward from the Cross to the Eucharist was Alphonsus' persistent theme in parish devotions, mission sermons, theological writing. He was ever eager for Christians to recognize that "Jesus would not be separated from us by his death, so he instituted this Sacrament of love in order to be with us to the end of the world."[151] This was the mainspring of Alphonsus' mature understanding of himself within the Christian mystery of redemption. It raised him out of himself. Alessio has, of course wonders to tell his avid hearers of this raising experience. The wonder of that time in the Benedictine chapel at Medugno when Alphonsus was celebrating Mass and Alessio, serving him, had seen him raised more than a hand's breadth into the air. Or, more wondrous still, that time at Arienzo, when he was serving Alphonsus' Mass in the little house chapel, the bishop was then raised at least three hands above the predella.[152] But for himself, he was more often recalling those unspectacular times at Pagani when, immediately on their returning from those carriage drives, taken each afternoon "under doctor's orders," Alphonsus and he would sit side by side, making "those meditations for *Visits to the Blessed Sacrament* which he had published" and which Alessio himself learned almost by heart as he sat with Alphonsus. At these times, Alessio was coming to appreciate how the humility of the Servant is expressed in his being "self-reducingly" among us, "at one time as an infant in a stable, at another as a poor man in a workshop, then as a criminal on a gibbet, and now as bread on an altar."[153] These quiet readings, these meditations alongside Alphonsus, raised for Alessio the possibility of a eucharistic significance to his own service. Gave rewarding value, after Alphonsus' death, to Alessio's own promise to persevere "until death in the Congregation."

Alphonsus had a favorite story. He tells it in those *Visits*.[154] At several other places in his writings.[155] A story expressive of all that he was hoping they might realize together as he listened to the reading with this Brother:

> Tender indeed was the devotion of Saint Wenceslaus, duke of Bohemia, to the Most Holy Sacrament. This holy ruler was so enamored of Jesus there present, that he not only gathered the wheat and grapes, and made the hosts with his own hands, and then gave them to be used in the Holy Sacrifice, but he used, even during the winter, to go at night to visit the church in which the Blessed Sacrament was kept. These visits enkindled in his beautiful soul such flames of divine love, that their ardor imparted itself even to his body and took from the snow on which he walked its wonted cold; for it is related that the servant who accompanied him in these nightly excursions, having to walk through the snow, suffered much

> from the cold, and the holy ruler, on perceiving this, being moved to compassion, and commanded him to follow him, and only to step in his foot marks; he did so, and never afterwards felt the cold.[156]

There is in this story, as Alphonsus tells it, an image of the desirable world in which snow and bitter weather, grapes and ground grain, wine cellar and bakery, come together in environmental harmony, and, along with them, appreciating meanings, duke and attendant have their proper human places in an eucharistic order. This is a story Alessio knew well and understood. He could know, at its repetition, that he was now, to Alphonsus' mind, as Vito had always known he was, Alphonsus' squire, "accompanying the holy man," "*accompagnando il santo,*" persevering with him to the fulfillment of their Grail story.

Persevering to Good Deaths

Going along together could not be easy for any of them. Their shortcomings being so painfully uncovered, their mistakes being so remedied, their offenses being so punished, their work being so demanding, their soup being so thin, it must be something of a surprise that any young men stayed long enough to make the vow of perseverance of the professed Brother. There were, of course, plenty of men who, arriving with the intent of making a life of service as Brothers, concluded that this could not be the future for them. Angelillo, the youngster from Amalfi, who seemed to Falcoia rather too excitable in his first enthusiasm, was the first to leave, on August 8, 1735.[1] Girolamo Ciammo followed him out soon after.[2] This acknowledgment of a big mistake was not always easy for a good man to make. Romualdo di Cristoforo, one of the Brothers admitted in 1741, took more than forty years to consider what he should be doing, and withdrew only in 1785, though he was nearly sent away in 1771, after a bust-up with Brother Bartolomeo, who also left.[3]

They all had need of some encouraging images of putting-up and carrying-on leading to a worthwhile end. Alphonsus insisted that each man who had lived well and come to a good death in the Congregation should be memorialized in a way that would encourage other men to live such a life to such a death. He wrote three such accounts himself, presenting Gennaro Sarnelli, Paolo Cafaro, and Vito Curzio as paradigms of living to death in the *familia*.[4] Generally, in-house chroniclers saw to it that the good Redemptorist's death within the Congregation was better recorded than most events of his life, certainly than anything in the man's experience before he began to live within the Congregation. Most personally, Alphonsus had assured them that it would be precisely in that good dying that each one's experience would make best sense to the man himself. "My Brothers, when death comes, the light of the candle will disclose to us the graces that the Lord has bestowed upon us, in keeping us in the beautiful vocation that he has given us."[5]

"Hold for certain," he told the novice Brothers in 1762, "that whoever dies in the Congregation will not only be saved but will be saved as a saint," hence "I pray to God to send you death rather than permit you to lose your vocation."[6] So, fortified by images of the deaths of Vito in the priest's house and of Francesco in that tenement, each as encouraging as Gaudiello's flag-waving, along with the good deaths of so many persevering men, living Brothers were to "look here upon this picture and on this," as Alphonsus almost says, pointing Hamlet-like to "the presentment of two brothers." They should all reflect upon "the unhappiness of so many still alive who live, or rather drag out a wearisome existence, outside the Congregation."[7] And all through the eighteenth century there was some Brother or other to whom he might point as an exemplary backslider. "You know," he'd said in 1758 already, "the case of that Brother who, having gone away without permission several months ago, continues to live at enmity with God."[8] The Brothers might notice, too, the sad but exemplary case of Carlo Califano, 1724–1781, who had gone in some huff with them all, only to plead on his deathbed six months later, to be readmitted to the Congregation.[9] Such men's misfortune should, he observed, "make us determined to suffer everything rather than the loss of vocation."[10]

Along with retelling these modern instances of alternative endings to a Brother's history, Alphonsus had always been ready with some wise sayings to encourage a Brother in the vocation they shared, to talk with him of how they might, Rector Major and Brother, persevere together to death. Alphonsus went to some great lengths to get them to recognize what they were doing together and the point of it all. "I had a great grouse," Leonardo Cicchetti remembered, "against a certain one of our priests, and the Servant of God called me from Ciorani to meet him at d'Iliceto." The interview went well. "Well now," Alphonsus had said, "You are truly called to be a servant. So am I." Leonardo took it that Alphonsus was telling him, as plainly as the Rector Major may tell a Brother," that there were Fathers who made life difficult for him. Something in Alphonsus' tone suggested that they were in the same boat. But Alphonsus was signaling their shares in more than an irritation with a Father or two. There was a reciprocity in their serving together. "I serve you. You serve me. We serve one another." And Alphonsus was making an affirmation of willed value in their joint perseverance in service. "We intend it all for the service of God."[11] This is what their vow meant. Persevering, they would become saints. They would be *fratres* in a confraternity lasting into eternity.

Alphonsus sent him into the field to think about their lives of service. After a while, he followed him out and they looked at the great rough countryside together. The chill winds howled horribly about them, as they always howl at d'Iliceto. For a man to make himself heard, he must fling his voice against the noise. "Leonardo, these hills seem to you full of demons, because you have given up our usual little prayer. O love," Alphonsus shouted, "O God, I love you!" Leonardo was stymied. "I said nothing in reply, but keeping in mind what he had said to me, I, only out of obedience, made this prayer." Nothing changed. He reported again, as dolefully, to the Rector Major. Then Alphonsus, who knew what it was to be discouraged, told Leonardo how he himself got out of such doldrums. Leonardo, at the beatification process remembered the scene vividly. The Servant of God said to me, "You are too cold!" but he was not commiserating with the Brother after his second venture onto the chill field. He was pointing to a likeness of d'Iliceto weather and the Brother's heart. "You are too cold!" he repeated, "Off with you now to your confessor!" What worked for the Rector Major worked for the Brother. "This I did, and by the grace of the Lord was quieted."[12]

Ciorani seems more than once to have been a lonely, disspiriting, house for a Brother. And, as often, such a house for the Rector Major. And he let more than one Brother know it. And realize their shared service. Brother Apostolico Cesare recalled Alphonsus' remarking to him there, "God knows how much I have to put up with, and just as I have to put up with things and carry on, so must you."[13]

Brothers were having to carry on in the Papal States, too. The Fathers meeting for a Chapter at Scifelli in October 1785 under Francesco de Paola's presidency had had two years to rethink the meaning of the Rule to which the Brothers had appealed in their petition to the Pope. These Fathers had already obtained a papal rescript, on August 5, 1785, sanctioning a separate table for Brothers in the refectory and, further, a separate place in chapel and common room and hall "for any common act."

They now had it in mind to settle a financial claim which had lately proved bothersome, by defining the Brother as unpaid *servus:*

> At the reception of Brothers in future, it shall be stipulated in the official file that if he leave the Congregation, he will have no claim for wages or other recompense.[14]

In deciding whether he leave or persevere, a Brother must now, humanly, take into account the raw economic reality that he would leave penniless. There might be in this an effective counter against any sudden determination to depart after the Fathers' further decreeing that the wearing of the zimarra in winter or the white collar at any season was forbidden to all lay serving Brothers. This was "our custom."[15]

Alphonsus carried on until the early summer of 1787. His Brothers had then to endure the troublesomeness of his dying. The Fathers were properly edified when they brought Communion to the sick man and heard as they came into his room his affecting cries, "Give me the body of Jesus Christ" and "Come, Jesus Christ."[16] But they were spared the terrible scenes when Alphonsus had to have his undershirt and small clothes changed. Francesc' Antonio spoke delicately of Alphonsus' "not being able to pass urine" and of their having to place a poultice "on his lower parts," and of the poor old man's "virginal modesty" when they wanted to clean him, "pulling his shirt down to cover himself," all the time repeating "Don't, don't touch me." Alessio, in less restrained terms spoke of Alphonsus' piteous cries when he and Leonardo Cicchetti lifted the sheet and began to draw up his undershirt, and of their having to hold him down as he struggled, while they put the ointment on his loins, and of his crescending scream filling their ears, "Let go of me! Let go of me!"[17] This must have been a terrible moment for Alphonsus' loyal friend. And not at all easy for him to recall a decade later for the Auditors. Alessio had, too, his memories of dysentery, fever, "gangrene in his guts," convulsions, but he would have those Auditors fix their minds on Alphonsus' saying simply, "Tell me something of God."[18]

The members of the Apostolic Mission let him know that they were praying with their senior brother.[19] His nephew, Don Giuseppe, came to receive his blessing.[20] They showed him a picture of "a servant of God, our lay Brother, who had died many years before with the widest fame of being a saint," but looking at Gerard's portrait, Alphonsus only said, "He is not the one to give me freedom."[21] He did not want to be the latest subject of Gerard's healing power, to be kept alive by some delaying miracle. He was eager to be the freed *famulus* of God in the Kingdom. "I have," he told Francesc' Antonio on July 16, still employing their language of shared work, "just one more job to do." He had to die.[22]

Alessio's devotion to Saint Joseph, which had been put a little out of countenance in that incident of the Montevergine sermon, now reasserted itself. The saint was, after all, the patron of happy deaths. He put a picture of his patron into Alphonsus' hands. Alphonsus held it for a while, turned to the Brother, and asked him, teasingly for the last time, "Is this Saint Joseph?" "Indeed it is," Alessio replied, and, also for the last time, took charge of his Master, "You must recommend yourself to his care."[23] Alphonsus' response was too indistinct for any of them to hear, but he continued looking at the holy picture.

Near his ending, Francesc' Antonio relieved Brother Giuseppe Sereno, 1724–1789, in the corner chair, and sat along with Alessio.[24] The two Brothers were for a while alone with Alphonsus. "He had received the Holy Viaticum," Alessio reported, "I restored him a little with a drip of water down his throat, and after that the Servant of God seemed more at ease, so I with Brother Francesc' Antonio said to him, 'Monsignore, we have served you for so many years, now that you are going to join Jesus Christ in Paradise, bless and pray to Jesus Christ for us.'" Alessio could not forget the moment of kind respect. "He replied, 'Yes, Signore,' and raised his hand to form the sign of the Cross with the words of benediction." For that short moment the three of them were simply brothers, gentlemen, servants of God, together. Then the rest came back, crowding round the deathbed.

At the funeral, Alessio and Francesc' Antonio were, properly, stationed on either side the bier. Some things had not changed from old times with Alphonsus, when his coach stopped on the country road and mothers crowded round with babies in arms, or when the door bell rang at Pagani and they had to go down and bring some infant up for his blessing and downstairs again, for they were still kept busy lifting up small children to touch the holy man.[26] Immediately after the funeral they were, according to his precise instructions, handed the cash sums that Alphonsus had bequeathed them.[27] He had experience himself, in dealings with his brother Ercole after their father's death, of how very inconvenient it might be to wait for a legacy. Alessio and Francesc' Antonio with these bags of coin would be welcomed at any house to which they were assigned after their master's death.

"So Many Petty Troubles and Unhappinesses"

No amount in the bag could make their lives easy in a house. Neither he nor they had thought it could. There were still dishes to be done. Beds to be restuffed. Latrines to be dug. Still Students to be endured. Fathers to be pleased. Fathers Minister to be obeyed. "Remember that you are living in a community of which every member must bear his share of suffering."[28] They would simply be hoping to hold onto their vocation, praying as he had taught them when they recited the *Te Deum* together at Arienzo: "We ask, therefore, that you will sustain your *famuli.*"[29]

"Let each one of you every day while visiting the Blessed Sacrament," Alphonsus had urged them, "ask in a special manner for perseverance in your vocation."[30] Each was to make that response which Alessio had heard read aloud from that little book of *Visits,* "Yes, my sovereign Lord, I now sacrifice to Thee my whole soul, my entire self, my whole will, and my complete life." Their vow of perseverance had just that significance for these Brothers. Each was, as he made that vow, promising "to give myself entirely to you," "to serve you with my whole self," "to serve you with all my powers," "to persevere through divine grace from the merits of Jesus Christ."[31] To be the saint that their sovereign Lord called them to be.

Francesc' Antonio and Alessio, both of them, lived into the reuniting of the seventeen houses of Naples, Rome, and Agrigento Redemptorists, together with those in the Warsaw community, at the March 1793 General Chapter. Andrea Villani had been Alphonsus' successor as Rector Major from August 1787 until his death in April 1792. Francesco de Paola, now very eager for reunification, was ready to resign, and was gratefully named "ex-General." Pietro Paolo Blasucci, the Chapter Secretary, was elected Rector Major at the third ballot, March 12, with precisely the two-thirds of votes needed. After these satisfactory resolutions to so many problems, the capitulars took a moment to declare:

> The habit of the Brothers shall be four fingers shorter than that of Fathers, measured from the shoe buckle, and any overcoat shall be of the same length so that they may be quicker about their manual service.[32]

They were attempting in this Constitution to give some practical coherence to all that had been said during the previous sixty years about the status, work, and clothing of the Brothers. Their habit was now declared, most reasonably, surely, to be shorter to suit the manual labor that men of their status were to do in the houses. Their relating the length of habit to the kind of work rather than to the status of the Brother was likely designed to avoid raising those wearying debates about the Brothers' vocation. Just let them get on with the job for now, sensibly dressed. Certainly, this was not the time for any capitular to ask Alphonsus' grand question: "Do you wish to be a saint?"

The Brothers answered, nonetheless. Francesc' Antonio was one of the seven symbolically representative Brothers at the Chapter who made, on April 15, a renewal of their vows of poverty, chastity, and obedience, and their oath of perseverance.[33]

Francesc' Antonio and Alessio, both of them, persevered. This was perhaps no easier for Francesc' Antonio than for Alessio, but it seems so now. His portrait shows Francesc' Antonio as a comfortably plump old person, wearing the authorized round wool hat against the cold, sitting at a desk, books piled high about him, three volumes of Tannoia's *Life* of Alphonsus among them, pen at hand and a sheet of paper, suggesting that he has been taking dictation or even been making a few notes of his own. He was coming, in these last years, to a quieter contemplation of that scourged Lord who had disturbed the cabin'd imagination of Captain Liguori. "As he sat before the little statue of the *Ecce Homo* in his room, because he could no longer kneel, he was so often seen to be in tears." And to those who recommended themselves to his prayers, he would simply reply, "I am a sinner, but the Most Holy *Ecce Homo* will take care of all."[34] Thus he became a center of stillness in the Pagani house.

"Great was the amiability and sweetness of his temper, and when any Father was distraught, afflicted, he would go to this Brother and be comforted and calmed."[35] He had, they all knew, been a great comforter and calmer of Alphonsus himself. Their Father had always been so effective at "urging the sorry and the timorous to have confidence in their merciful God," and so often ineffective in convincing himself of his own sharing in God's mercy. The Brother had many times to remind Alphonsus, as he told Auditor Andrea Gardellini and Secretary Jacobe de Carpineo, that it had been only by continuously applying to that divine mercy that he had been able to found the Congregation and follow his vocation, keeping it going through such trying times. He must, the Brother had told him, go on hoping. Always. So they would say Alphonsus' favorite prayer together, "My Jesus, You are my hope," and stay a little while in quiet.

"The Novice Masters and Prefects of Students, when any of their charges were troubled about their vocation used to send them to this Brother for reassurance and comforting and thus they did not lose their vocations."[36] There's no record of what Francesc' Antonio said to comfort the younger men. Perhaps he simply repeated what he'd said to comfort Alphonsus, "Go on hoping." Perhaps he told them, as he told the Auditors at the Process, "Read that golden book *On the Necessity of Prayer*." Perhaps, more simply still, like most sensible old men when asked about life by young men, Francesc' Antonio told them that he did not think that there would be any better life for them anywhere else either. They should everywhere be hoping to die. That's what he was hoping. "I desire death," he repeated, "for, after so many petty troubles and unhappinesses, I shall be united with my Jesus."[37]

On Francesc' Antonio's dying that desirable death, November 4, 1807, at Pagani, Rector Felice Spizoco, 1764–1811, wrote to Rector Francesco Saverio Menechini, 1769–1840, at d'Iliceto about the long illness of "this man of decent family," "this good son of the Congregation," "this great servant of God."[38] These young Rectors, along with many of their Redemptorist contemporaries, were supposing that, after Francesc' Antonio's requiem, things could never be the same. But they were not yet out of touching distance with their beginnings. There was still Alessio.

"Forth They Went, Forth They Went Together"

On Alphonsus' death, Alessio had found himself in as awkward a position as at the bishop's retirement from Sant' Agata. Only this time there was no one offering a way forward. Those among the Fathers who had for some time resented this Brother's influence with Alphonsus could now suggest that he be put, this late, through a novitiate program. They were likely supported in this design by those who felt it a difficulty when they would present Alessio as their paradigm of "the Brother as servant" that he had not undergone the usual trial period. It would seem that Alessio was sent, whether for a formal novitiate or not, is unclear now, perhaps it was unclear then, to the Tropea house, founded only in 1790, to learn how to do the jobs he had been doing for a quarter of a century. Just the sort of novitiate some would have wanted for him. But after a while it was realized by those now running the Congregation that they needed him.

He was to be a star witness at the beatification process hearings which they had begun to organize in 1788. Alessio had never been taught to read and write, but with Don Salvadore Tramontano acting as secretary, writing down what he said, his *famulus* for twenty-five years was expected to give useful testimony to the sanctity of their Founder.[39] But however well he thought of Alphonsus, it could not be assumed after their treating him none too well recently that Alessio would do quite what the Fathers wanted. They could not but be a little nervous that this *famulus* was to have a day in court. They need not have worried. Alessio had a better understanding of his place than they.[40]

Questions about the legal status of the *famuli* occurred in the jurists' discussion of Canon as well as Civil Law. Alphonsus had, in *Theologia Moralis,* been content to exempt members of a bishop's household, living at his expense, at his table, "*commensales*," *famuli* in a feudal *familia*, from the general rule that a *famulus* could not be considered an ordainable person. Such a man's title to ordination rested precisely, Alphonsus opined, on his status as *famulus* in an ecclesiastical *familia.* The scope of the hero bishop's protection included, exceptionally, power to confer ecclesiastical title on a nonperson.[41] So it might seem to fit nicely with a definition of the Brother as such a *famulus* that Alphonsus, at the end of his time at Sant' Agata, should have used his authority to secure that the *famulus* Alessio be received as a Brother of the Congregation. But if it seemed to some that Alphonsus were then exercising a bishop-like privilege to entitle his *famulus,* even to dispensing him from the novitiate, it seemed to Alessio, who had been *famulatus* in the episcopal household, that he had been released by Alphonsus into the proleptic freedom of the *frater* serving into the *familia* of God. This was, after all, what was always happening in the Church. It was what had happened to Onesimus.

Understanding himself as already that Christian freedman, Alessio could not be intimidated by the solemnities of the beatification process. He was not a vichian *famulus* whose status prevented his giving testimony in a civil court, but the Pauline *famulus* responding to the call to be *frater*:

> I am a lay Brother in the house of Saint Michael the Archangel, belonging to the secular priests of the Congregation of the Most Holy Redeemer, founded by that Servant of God Don Alphonsus Maria de Liguori, one-time Bishop of Sant' Agata dei Goti.[42]

It had, of course, been carefully explained to Alessio what was required from his testimony about Alphonsus' deathbed. Diplomatically, he recalled that "he blessed the Fathers of the whole Congregation, those in the kingdom and those in the Pontifical States, "as well as the King, his Princes, his Generals, his Ministers, his Judges," but he wasn't going to let the Fathers take all the credit for this embracing benediction: "he blessed them all at my suggestion."[43]

The Fathers were politically interested in evidence of their Founder's making such due acknowledgments of hierarchic propriety. Secular priests had to have a wary eye to the civil authority. Most especially these secular priests after that *Regolamento* fuss. Ferdinand I must be encouraged in his present favorable mood. They had the other eye fixed on the maintenance of decent order in the house. However relieved they were by Alessio's following the official line, they were still telling the Process reporters to record their Brothers as "associates," "companions," they have told them to set down Alessio as his "servant," "*famulus*."[44] Alessio does not care. Alessio knows that he has something worth their all hearing precisely on account of "the long service I gave the venerable servant of God."[45] They might then be able to recognize for themselves the significances of their own services in the Congregation.

Christ is still the paradigm. "Look at him as a servant in the poor cottage at Nazareth," Alphonsus had told them all, "sweeping the house, fetching water from the well, opening and closing the shop."[46] Then they could look at those who accepted this paradigm. They could look at Alessio's patron saint. "Saint Alessio, although he was the son of a Roman gentleman, chose to live the life of a servant in his father's house."[47] Now Alessio was telling them to look at Alphonsus: "*Dei famulum Alphonsum*," "living the life of a poor man," "hard working," "renouncing riches and honors," as Alessio told the Auditors, "swapping decent clothes for a habit."[48] He had already told Tannoia his fine story of Alphonsus' readiness to serve the servant:

> When he went from Arpaja to Airola, he could not procure enough beasts for all his followers; not wishing to inconvenience anyone, he set out on foot, accompanied only by his servant Alessio. It was during the heat of the month of August, but he had pity on the poor young man, who was bathed in sweat: "My son," said he, "it is far too hot for a waistcoat, take it off and give it to me to carry." The servant hesitated, but Alphonsus was so persuasive that he did at last consent to hand over the waistcoat.[49]

"Forth they went together." *Famuli* following, both of them, in the footsteps of Christ.

It would have been rather awkward for the Fathers, after Alessio had given such helpful and impressive testimony "*Venerabili Dei Famulo*"[50] to send him back to the sticks at Tropea. Most happily, the young Don Giuseppe de Liguori, who had done some quiet business with Alessio when procuring that newer carriage and those sturdier horses for the afternoon drives at Pagani, was content that this Brother should occupy one of those upper floor rooms which his uncle had kept for his use in old days.[51] So Alessio was assigned to the Naples station. Alessio practiced what he had been told by Alphonsus, imitating his patron saint in quiet service. He practiced what he himself had told those Auditors, imitating the lifestyle of Alphonsus. He was recognizable still, to those grandees at whose doors he presented the Congregation's messages, as "the servant of Monsignore Liguori."[52] Kuntz, who was in this properly sensitive, observed with especial pleasure that Alessio in Naples made his way to those many churches where the Forty Hours devotion to the Blessed Sacrament was being celebrated as in the time when young Alphonsus was meditating his Christian future.[53] In Alphonsus' places, Alessio was sustaining the Congregation's response to that eucharistic grace which enabled all their loving, persevering, service. He worked hard and late. "It would be little did I die for thee, wear myself out for thee, who didst die for me, and dost sacrifice thy entire self for me every day on the altar."[54]

Alessio wore himself out in Naples. On his growing too infirm to be the Congregation's city messenger boy, Pietro Paolo Blasucci, who was now Superior General of the reunited Congregation, sent the quite recently ordained Francesco Alfano, 1785–1864, to bring Alessio home to Pagani in January 1810. His last day did not come as quickly as they all expected. Not until January 23, 1813.

The community had noted that after death, Alphonsus became "red faced with a sort of cheerful smile."[55] They had none of them noticed his looking like that before. But Alessio had. That ruddiness had suggested a familiar name for the old man. Almost too familiar. Not to be used to his face. Nor when that rascal Aniello was in earshot. A name in use when he and Rafaele and Leonardo and Francesc' Antonio grinned together below stairs. So now, on his own deathbed, Alessio was remembering that ruddy smile: he sat up and called to his brother Alphonsus, just at the moment of becoming the *frater* with him in eternity, "*Mio Cirasiello*,"[56] he called, "My Cherry, My Monsignore, Beautiful Cherry, help me."

Notes

Brother Alphonsus

1. *Vid. egr.* Alphonsus to Pietro Paolo Petrelli, 1726–1771, January 5, 1752, to Gasparo Caione, August 31, 1754, to the Fathers and Brothers, September 24, 1758, and August 27, 1765, to Tannoia, August 12, 1773, to Francesco Antonio de Paola, January 25, March 12 and 24, 1774, to Andrea Villani, April 8 and June 6, 1774, *et al. pl. Lettere di S. Alphonso Maria de' Liguori,* Rome, 3 vols., 1887, English trans. *Letters of St. Alphonsus de Liguori,* ed. Eugene Grimm, 5 vols., New York, 1891. He was "Brother Alphonsus Maria the broken down," *Fratello Alphonso Maria Cionco,* in a sad letter, April 30, 1771; Tannoia, A. M., *Della Vita ed Instituto del Ven. S. di Dio Alphonsus Ma. Liguori,* Naples, 1798, Lib. III, cap. xlix, p 258, hereinafter all references are to the Italian reprint, Materdomini, 1982, of the 1798–1802 edition, since the English trans., *Life of S. Alphonso Maria de Liguori,* anon. Cong. Orat., in *Saints and Servants of God* series supervised by F. Faber, 5 vols., 1848f, does not correspond to the original in chapter division or, quite often, in text.
2. Tannoia, *Vita,* II, xxxvi, pp 231 and 234; II, xl, pp 251 and 252; III, xlviii, pp 249 and 251; III, liv, p 277, for letters of July 27, 1751, July 17 and 18, 1758, August 13, 1760, and *Vita,* III, 1, p 264, for letter of October 1, 1772, and III, liv, p 277, for letter of July 29, 1774. Alphonsus almost always uses *Fratello* for blood brother and Brother in the Congregation; Giuseppe Orlandi reassuringly affirms that "fratello, frate, frabutto, etc." are all synonymous, *Il Regno di Napoli nel Settecento,* Spicilegium Historicum CssR (hereinafter S.H.) XLIV, 1996, p 155.
3. Alphonsus to Margotta, December 7, 1747.
4. Alphonsus to Muscari, October 16, 1751; he was also signing himself "Yours very respectfully" in a letter to Archbishop Antonio Puoti, 1716–1795, February 12, 1763.
5. Letters to de Paola, October 18 and November 10 and 13, 1780, November 25, 1780, January 10 and 29, 1781.
6. *Vita,* IV, xxvi, pp 135f; Bishop Alphonsus was not so regularly willing to recognize even a friendly bishop as his Brother, *vid.* letters to Antonio Puoti of Amalfi, February 12, 1763, to Domenico Cavalcanti of Trani, February 9, 1764, and to Nicola Borgia of Aversa, June 10, 1775. For the ordinary monsignorial

usage, contrast the several letters of Bishop Andrea Lucchesi Palli, 1696–1768, to Alphonsus, signing himself "Your most affectionate and obliged servant," *egr.* December 2, 1761, and then, July 21, 1762, immediately after Alphonsus had been elected bishop of Sant' Agata, "Your most devoted and obliged servant and brother," *Lettere dalla Sicilia a S. Alphonso,* ed. Salvatore Giammusso, Rome, 1991, pp 68 and 100.

7. Alphonsus to Tannoia, November 17 and December 31, 1755, January 13, 20, and 21, March 6, May 2, 11, and 25, June 3 and 24, 1756, *et al. pl.*
8. Alphonsus to Villani and others, April 26, 1775; *cf.* letter to Superior of Missions, 1755(?).
9. Alphonsus to Mauro Murante, 1735–1761(?), January 7, 1756, December 14, 1759, to Giovanni Battista Gargano, 1737–1770(?), December 13, 1758, and to Students at Ciorani, 1761.
10. August 16, 1779, January 28, 1762; *cf.* letters to Luigi Capuano, 1739–after 1781, July 22, August 3, 4, and 7, 1755, and Angelo Maione, 1733–1787, April 9, 1758.
11. Alphonsus to Novices at d'Iliceto, August 1758.
12. Alphonsus to Michele Ilardo, November 14, 1774.
13. Letters of January 13, 1756 and August 1773(?).
14. Lay Brothers in Franciscan, Dominican, and other Orders were known as "*Fratres barbati.*"
15. *Vid.* Maria Celeste Crostarosa, *Autobiografia,* ed. Majorano, S., and Simeoni, A., Materdomini, 1998, *Libro secondo, cap.* 3, p 207, and Swanston, Hamish F. G., *Singing a New Song,* Liguori, 1997, pp 77ff. She had first been convinced of Alphonsus' vocation to address the needs of the people of the Kingdom on October 4, 1730. "The coincidence of this revelation and the feast of S. Francis of Assisi is not accidental," Rey-Mermet, Th., *Il Fondatore* in Chiovaro, F., ed., *Storia della Cong. del SS. Redentore,* 1993, vol. I/1, *Le Origini,* p 151, for a quick suggestion that Franciscan influences in several elements of Celeste's proposal require some studying. References to this ongoing narrative hereinafter as *Storia;* English trans. *History.*
16. Tannoia, *Vita del Servo di Dio Fr. Gerardo Majella,* (hereinafter Tannoia, *Gerardo*), 1811, 7th ed., Naples, 1838, *cap.* III, p 14, English trans. *Lives of Companions of St. Alphonso Liguori,* anon. Cong. Orat., London, 1849, (hereinafter *Companions*), pp 246f.
17. Dumortier, F., *Le Pere Antoine-Marie Tannoia et Quelgues Scolastiques,* 1902, p 179, for Blasucci's notions of becoming a Friar.
18. Tannoia, *Historico-critical memoir of Bl. Benevento of Gubbio;* Benevento died 1231 at Corneto and was buried at d'Iliceto. Tannoia's little book, 160 pp, was published by Alphonsus' Naples printers, the Paci brothers, in 1780.
19. Gregorio, Oreste, "Saint Alphonsus, da laico, fu 'congregato mariano' e 'terziario francescano'?" S.H., XIII, 1975, pp 469–475.

20. For the difficulties encountered by Brother Elias in managing Franciscan Fathers, *vid.* Lempp, E., *Elie de Cortone,* Paris, 1901, *passim.* Brothers were commonly Provincials and Guardians in charge of house communities right up to the time of Bernard von Offida, d. 1694. For Alphonsus' careless beard, *vid. Vita,* II, xliii, p 276, "*con una barbaccia da romito,*" *et al. pl.*
21. But he did, daily, recite the *Corona B. Mariae Virginis* which he thought, like most of his contemporaries, was composed by Saint Bonaventura; *vid.* also Tannoia's note of Alphonsus' admiration for the Franciscans and their many saints, Gregorio, O., S.H., IX, "*Sentimenti,*" No. 75, p 457.
22. Letters of August 30 and November 7, 1762, to Rural Deans.
23. Letter of March 16, 1766; blessing them, "We remain your most devoted servant." The clergy of the diocese were never "Brothers," see Pastoral Letters he wrote July 30, 1762, February 20 and November 28, 1763, February 28, 1764, *et al.*
24. *Vid. egrr.*, letters to Alphonsus from Paolo Cafaro, October 20, 1748, February 11, 1749, November 15, 1752, *Epistolae Ven. Servi Dei Pauli Cafaro, CSSR,* Rome, 1934, pp 22, 28, and 62; from Francesco Garzillo, May 1, 1749, ibid., pp 31f; from Pietro Paolo Blasucci, November 25, 1767, and April 12, 1772, *Lettere dalla Sicilia,* pp 155–158, 201–204. It must have been only by a singular mistake that Cesare Sportelli signed himself "Servant and Brother" in a letter to Alphonsus, July 15, 1739, *Epistolae Ven. Servi Dei Caesaris Sportelli, CSSR,* Rome, 1937, pp 38f.
25. Alphonsus to Villani, July 7, 1774, and to Corrado, February 16, 1781, ed. Gregorio, O., *Manoscritti Inediti di S. Alphonso,* S. H., VI, 1958, pp 337–343. The awkwardnesses of a Vicar General's life are exposed in these letters by the Rector Major's still signing himself everyone's Brother. He would on occasion stretch to avow himself the Brother of a relative in religion, for example in a letter, July 20, 1777, to Antonia de' Liguori in the San Marcellino convent; *ibid.*, pp 331ff, letter at p 339, *vid.* also, Tannoia, *Vita,* IV, xv, p 70; Villani to Rectors CSsR, October 10, 1762; *Documenta Miscellanea ad Regulam et Spiritum Cong. nostrae illustrandum,* Rome, 1904, pp 158f.
26. Alphonsus to Caione, September 21, 1754. *Cf.* the decorums of Falcoia's letters to "the Very Revd. Father Don Cesare Sportelli," February 7, 1736, and, once he had become "the Revd Brother Don Cesare" at Villa de' Schiavi, July 13 and August 10, 1736, Gregorio, O., ed., *Mons. Tommaso Falcoia: Lettere a S. Alphonso ecc.,* (hereinafter Falcoia, *Lettere*), Rome, 1963, pp. 296, 311–312, and 313–314. However, in an *obiter dictum* of Alphonsus, collected by Tannoia when preparing his hagiography, but not used in the final draft, there seems to be a gradual slippage from "Brother" as restricted to lay Brothers to "Brother" as inclusive of every Redemptorist: "The Brothers are to live the perfect life, each doing well in his own office, the cook, the porter, the students, the Fathers, all living in modesty, humility, obedience, recollection." S.H., IX, 1961, pp 439–475, No. 1, p. 447.

27. The great Bellarmine had given theological shape to ways in which the roles of a prince as "servant" and "father" could be exercised in charity; *De officio principis christiani*, Rome, 1619. This was the general theory adopted with incomprehending enthusiasm by Carlo III, Bourbon. *Cf.* Morandi, C., *La politica dell' assolutismo,* Pavia, 1930, and Valsecchi, F., *L'assolutismo illuminato,* 2 vols., Bologna, 1931–1934. For Alphonsus' effort to make something good from kingly examples, *vid. Fidelity of Vassals,* 1777, especially chapter 3, 2.5 on Saint Louis of France.
28. Vangheluwe, A., *De dominio filiorum familias, Collationes Brugenses,* 43, 1947, pp 258–264, and Benzerath, M., *Das Bild des Bruders in der Geschichte* in Wiederkehr, *Die Situation des Bruderberufs heute,* Munich, 1967, pp 53–72.
29. *A mio arbitrio* twice, Alphonsus' personal notebook, Redemptorist Generalate Archive, SAM, VI, 10, 66. *Cf.* for affirmations of obedience to Falcoia, *ibid.* 63 and 64.
30. Note written by Alphonsus in margin of letter from Falcoia, August 24, 1732, Falcoia, *Lettere,* No. 34; *cf.* Alphonsus to "My dear Father," July 24, 1740, and references to "our Father," Alphonsus to Giulio Marocco, July 12, 1740, to Cesare Sportelli, October 26, 1742. *Vid.* Sportelli to the Superior of the Nuns at Scala, June 23, 1744, *Epistolae,* No. 77. Falcoia responded in letters signed "Your dear Father" to Alphonsus, January 23 and January 30 and May 8, 1734.
31. Sportelli to Falcoia, May 16 and September 25, 1740, and January 20, 1742. He was his "most humble, most obsequious, and most devoted S. and Son," September 23, 1737, *Epistolae,* pp 47f, 51f, 61, and 26f. For Falcoia, *vid.* Gregorio, O., *Mons. T. Falcoia, 1663–1743,* Rome, 1955.
32. Alphonsus to Brothers, August 1773.
33. Sportelli to Alphonsus, December 21, 1747, *Epistolae,* No. 167.
34. Sportelli to Villani, December 22, 1747, *Epistolae,* No. 168.
35. Sportelli to Alphonsus, August 6, 1744, February 22, 1745, June 21, 24, and 27, 1745, August 11, 1747, *Epistolae,* pp 97f, 103f, 105f, 107, 109f, 153f.
36. Sportelli to Mazzini, January 29, 1746, *Epistolae,* pp 121f.
37. Sportelli to Cafaro, December 15, 1747, February 22, 1749, *Epistolae,* pp 170ff, 205f; reciprocally the polite Cafaro signed himself the "most humble servant and subject" of Sportelli when writing to the Minister at Ciorani, August 10, 1742, *Epistolae,* p 13. Cafaro himself recognized a danger in "my fiery soul" during his dealings with Brother Francesco Tartaglione and Brother Leonardo Cicchetti, 1724–1808, *vid.* letter to Alphonsus, January 16, 1753, *Epistolae,* p 63. Alphonsus wrote a short *Life* of Cafaro, 1766.
38. Sportelli to Marocco, June 7, 1737, *Epistolae,* pp 24ff. Angelo Verdesca, 1732—after 1767, went a further step of informality, signing his letter to Tannoia, October 27, 1761, "Your servant and affectionate brother Angelo"; *Lettere dalla Sicilia,* p 65. Alphonsus himself closed a letter to Margotta, 1751, since he was endeavoring to get him out of the dumps, with the good wishes of his "most affectionate Brother Alphonsus."

39. Tannoia, *Gerardo,* p 108; *Companions,* p 378.
40. *Vid.* the particular friendliness of Domenico Blasucci and Gerard Majella, Tannoia, *Notizie sullo R. Fr. D. Blasucci,* p 14; *Companions,* p 212.
41. Tannoia, *Gerardo,* pp 67, 73, 94 *et al. pl.; Companions,* pp 319, 329, 358.
42. Alphonsus to Remondini, November 2, 1769.
43. For a good general discussion, *vid.* Gutierrez, P., *La paternite spirituelle selon S. Paul,* Paris 1968, and Sagne, J.-C., *Le pretre comme figure paternelle et fraternelle,* VSS No. 91, November 1969, pp 491–524.
44. *Cf.* the concerns of Alphonsus and Caione about the color and length of the Brothers' habit, Tannoia, *Vita,* II, lxii, p 365. For the extreme measurings adopted by some Rectors in this matter of the Brothers' shins, *vid.* Pietro Paolo Blasucci to Villani, October 10, 1766, *Lettere dalla Sicilia,* p 146.
45. Alphonsus to Caione, July 15, 1757. Domenico Caputo left the Congregation in 1764, a year after the death of his father, the Brother. He attempted to return but was denied, Alphonsus to Villani, March 15 and 21, 1766; Kuntz, Federico, *Annales CSSR,* VII, pp 62f.
46. Alphonsus to Caione, January 11, 1756: "At d'Iliceto there has been a semi-revolution."
47. Alphonsus to the semi-revolutionary Brothers at d'Iliceto, January 13, 1756; he might have added that, practically, passive voting rights had been removed from Conventuals in 1720 and from Capuchins in 1740.
48. For Alphonsus' reading Rousseau, *vid.* his *Reflections on the Truth,* I.2 and 32, III.44, 46, and 50; *Truth of Faith,* I.vi, 2.23 and VI, x; Swanston, H. F. G., *Celebrating Eternity Now,* 1995, pp 7, 77, 186, and 200f.
49. Alphonsus to Brothers at d'Iliceto, January 13, 1756.
50. *Ibid.*
51. *Vid.* Mazzini's testimony, *Proc. Nuceriae Paganorum,* 1794, *Summarium* 24, de Pretioso S. D. Obito, III, p 287, and Francesc' Antonio Romito at the Caracciolo *Relatio,* 1806, *de Obito,* XXVIII, p 738.
52. *Positio super Introductione Causae,* Rome, 1796, Summ. 8, XIV, *art. Proc.* fol. 1134f, and *Ex Proc. S. Agathae Gothorum, Summ.* 9, XIV, art Proc. fol, 1136f, 1141, and 1145.
53. Alphonsus to Caione, January 16, 1756, to Tannoia, January 20, 1756. Frederick M. Jones says, *Alphonsus de Liguori,* Dublin, 1992, p 264, that the booksellers of Naples, "*questi benedetti libraii,*" were "the only ones who could drive him to the verge of imprecations." Alphonsus was, however, similarly driven when considering the litigation begun by a provoking cleric, "*quel benedetto prete di Calvanico,*" Alphonsus to Caione, November 22, 1758.

Part 1: The Blood Brother

1. Basile, Giambattista, *Lo cunto de li cunti,* ed. Rak, M., Cernuscos, N., 1986; *trattenemiento ottava de la gionata seconna, tratt. terzo de la giorn. quarta,* and *tratt. quarta de giorn. quinta.*

2. Swanston, H. F. G., *Singing a New Song,* Liguori, 1997, pp 89ff.
3. Swanston, H. F. G., *Celebrating Eternity Now,* pp 97–106.
4. Tannoia, *Vita,* I, vi, p 22, and, for the entanglements of the Amatrice lawsuit, Swanston, *Celebrating Eternity Now,* 97ff.
5. Alphonsus to Pietro Gavotti, November 18, 1780; Tannoia, *Vita,* IV, xv, p 74. For an analysis of the *cicisbeo* in Neapolitan society at this time, Vidal, M., *La Familia en la Vida y en el pensamiento de Alphonsus de Liguori,* Madrid, n.d., pp 189–203. The *cicisbeo* conventions operated strongly in favor of Nelson and Emma Hamilton at the end of the century when the British fleet was in the Bay.
6. Matteo Migliore, November 29, 1763, *cf.* to Giulio Marocco, April 27, 1763, to the Duke of Maddaloni, December 18, 1763, and to Federico Belluoci, July 25, 1764.
7. Tannoia, *Vita,* III, lix, p 312.
8. *Ibid.,* lx, p 317; Alphonsus to Nicola Pisanti, September 30, 1766.
9. Tannoia, *Vita,* III, lx, p 317.
10. *Ibid.,* p 315 and letter to Tramontano, September 1769(?).
11. Tannoia, *Vita,* III, lx, p 318.
12. *Theologia Moralis, Lib.* III, *tract.* II, "On the Second Commandment," *Cap.* ii, "On Oaths," *dub.* iv; Gaude, 162.
13. Tannoia, *Vita,* III, lx, pp 319–320.
14. *Theologia Moralis,* Lib. IV, *tract.* IV, "On the Sacrament of Penance," cap. I, "The Essence of the Sacrament," *dub.* iii, art. 1; Gaude, 470.
15. Tannoia, *Gerardo,* xxxiii; English trans. *Companions,* ed. Faber, G. W., London, 1849.
16. What Alphonsus says, *Theologia Moralis,* III, IV, i, *dub.* iv, Gaude, 394ff, about the foetus' not being from the first moment a human being represents a pastoral effort for the forgiveness of these panicky young people. At least the poor girl who had aborted a fetus, at some back-street horror, would not be held to have committed murder. Alphonsus was glad, when considering such abortions early in pregnancy, that he had Aristotle and Aquinas with him, and that the same opinion was then shaping the practice of the Sacred Penitentiary in Rome.
17. Tannoia, *Vita,* II, xlvi, p 289; *vid.* Tellería, R., "*Reformatio conservatorii in civitate Gaeta a S. Alphonso suscepta,*" S.H., VIII, 1960, pp 131–137, and "*Iterum de Reformatione conservatoni Caietae,*" S.H., IX, 1961, pp 243–252. *Vid.* also Tannoia, *Vita del Can. D. Giuseppe La Monaca,* Naples, 1787, a biography of the founder of the orphanage at Corato, for continuing Redemptorist interest in such institutions. A similar large hospice for abandoned children was managed by the Confraternity of the Body of Christ based at the cathedral in Catanzano, De Girolamo, A., *Catanzaro e la Riforma Tridentina,* Regio Calabria, 1975, pp 194–195 and 202–205, and Black, C., *Italian Confraternities in the Sixteenth Century,* Cambridge, 1989, p 196. Don Giuseppe bequeathed sixty-

six ducats to the Conservatorio Visita Poveri, the home for such abandoned street children near the arsenal, which was a favorite recipient of support from naval officers, Celano, C., *Delle notizie della citta di Napoli,* Naples 1758, Giornata IV, p 138, and Tellería, R., *Documenta Tria circa Res Familiares D Iosephi de Liguoro et eius Filii, S. Alphonsi,* S.H., V, 1957, pp 237–276, No. 6, p 270.

18. *Avvertimenti ai Predicatori,* 1778, *Instructions for Preachers,* I.l and 3; *cf.* Novena for Christmas, disc. X, "On the birth of Jesus": "Mary invites all, nobles and peasants, rich and poor, saints and sinners, to come into the grotto of Bethlehem"; *Opere ascetiche,* IV, 1939, p 126.
19. *Istruzione al popolo,* 1767, *Instructions for the People,* 4, "the Fourth Commandment," 2.
20. *Ibid.* 1, The story is derived from Louis Abelly, 1603–1691, *Les Verites principales de la foi,* Paris, 1675, p 28. *Cf.* Alphonsus to Giovanni Battista di Costanzo, 1743–1801, January 17, 1782, who had just accepted a teaching post with an unsettled set of Students: "When you begin to teach theology, do not depart from Abelly. Mgr. Giulio Torno thought very highly of this author."
21. Alphonsus to the Fathers and Brothers, June 20, 1767.
22. Kuntz, *Annales,* III, 1749, pp 420f.
23. *Ibid.*
24. Don Giuseppe had enlisted in 1685 as an *aventurero* on "La Capitana"; he was promoted ensign in July 1692, and having married Donna Anna Caterina Cavalieri in May 1695 was successively temporary Captain of the "Padrona," 1707, Commander of the "Daun," 1708, Commander of the refitted "Padrona," 1709, and Captain Commander back on the flag-galley "La Capitana" from 1716 until his enforced retirement as "*Tenente Coronnello*" on the withdrawal of the Hapsburgs in 1734; Tellería, R., "*Duo nova documenta super familia de Liguoro,*" S.H., VII, 1959, pp 205–259. The statuettes are preserved at the Ciorani house.
25. *Simple Exposition of the Passion,* XII.2.
26. Alphonsus' baptismal certificate is printed and illustrated from the parish register of San Maria dei Vergini, *Lib.* xl, *bapt.* f. 127, in Tellería, R., *San Alphonsus Maria de Liguorio,* 2 vols., Madrid, 1950, vol. I, p 8.
27. Jones, F., *op. cit.,* p 9.
28. Alphonsus was taught the elements of cosmology and astronomy by Carminiello Rocca, Italian and Latin grammars and literatures by Domenico Buonaccia, and the theory and practice of keyboard by the great Gaetano Greco, c. 1657–1728, at the Conservatorio dei Poveri di Gesu; *vid.* Tellería, R., "*Sac. D. Dominicus Buonaccia, S. Alfonsi pueruli primis in letteris humanis magister,*" S.H., XII, p 964, pp 205–208.
29. Jones, F., *op. cit.,* p 13.
30. All his life, Alphonsus remained an enthusiastic keyboard player, even on his monthly "retreat" days at Pagani, but he was characteristically reluctant to

approve his enthusiasm: "I must have been mad to lose so much time; but I had to do what my father wanted"; Tannoia, *Vita,* I, iii, p 9.

31. He went on placing favorite verses from the *Aeneid* into his very last writings, *egr. Truth of Faith,* II, iv, ll.
32. George Frederic Handel, 1685–1759, directed the performances of the first version of his *Aci, Galatea, e Polifemo,* for the Alvito wedding, 1708.
33. Giambattista Vico, *Scienza Nuova,* 1725, cap. IX.93. It is probable that Alphonsus was registered by Vico as an incoming student at the Law School in September 1708 and heard the great man's inaugural lecture for the academic year, *De nostri temporis studiorum ratione; Opere,* ed. Battistini, A., Milan, 1990, vol. 1, p 104. For Vico's consideration of justice, *vid. ibid.,* pp 188f. For a suggestion of Alphonsus' acquaintance with the ideas of Vico, the greatest of European intellectuals so far, *vid.* Swanston, H. F. G., "The Voice of the Poor in the Writings of S. Alphonso," S.H., XLV, 1997, pp 526–535.
34. For Alphonsus at the Metastasian opera and the Neapolitan vernacular opera, *ibid.,* pp 535ff.
35. Tannoia, *Vita,* I, vi, p 22; Swanston, H. F. G., *Celebrating Eternity Now,* pp 97–105.
36. Tannoia, *Gerardo, Cap.* vi and *Vita,* II, lviii, p 347.
37. Alphonsus to Francesco Saverio Rossi, 1706–1758, ordering Grassi's expulsion, October 18, 1754.
38. *Brevi notizie della vita del R. P. Paolo Cafaro* in *Via della Salute,* 1766, English trans. Grimm, Miscellany, 1890, p 240.
39. Alphonsus to Caione, October 2, 1754.
40. Tannoia, *Vita,* II, xlii, pp 264–265.
41. Alphonsus to Fathers and Brothers, August 8, 1754, opening section.
42. Alphonsus to Nicolo Pentamelli, November 28, 1761.
43. Tellería, R., "*De Maria Anna (Anna Maria) ac de Maria Luisa (Barbara) de Liguori, sororibus S. Alfonsi, in monasteno S. Hieronymi monialibus,* S.H., IV, 1958, pp 7–24, "*Maria Theresia de Liguori, Herculis de Liguori filia atque ex eodem nepos S. Alfonsi, in monasterio SS Marcellini et Festi sanctimoniales,*" S.H., V, 1957, pp 44–56, and "*Rev. D. Caietanus de Liguori, S. Alfonsi frater, eiusgue nepos Alfonsinus beneficio ecclesiastico muniuntur a duce Gravina Orsini,*" S.H., XIII, 1964, pp 325–357; Vidal, Marciano, *La Familia, passim.*
44. *Analecta CSSR,* xxi, fasc. 5 and 6, December 1959: "*S Alfonsus adolescens Oratorio Philippensi S. Ioseph adscriptus,*" pp 307ff.
45. Tellería, R., S.H., XIII, *art. cit.,* p 327.
46. The Cassinese monastery, founded 845 or 847, had been thoroughly renovated by Benvenuto Tortorelli and Bartolomeo Chiarini in 1571, the Choir of the new church being given a splendid marble atrium. This was destroyed in the earthquake of June 5, 1688. The rebuilt church of 1700 was itself ruined in the 1731 earthquakes. Antonio lived just long enough to admire the restoration of the twenty great cloister frescoes of the life of Saint Benedict by Anto-

nio di Giovanni Solari, 1495–1524, and the new-style decoration in the high-ceilinged refectory. In the Archivio di Stato collection, which is housed in the spacious San Severino buildings, there are eighty-eight bundles of papers treating of monastic affairs in Dom Antonio Benedetto's time. *Arch. dei Monasterii Soppresi Invent. Somm. Pte.* II, No. 6140, busta 28, f. 49. *Vid.* Mazzoleni, J., *L'Archivio del monastero benedettino dei SS Severino e Sossio,* Naples, 1984, and *Per la storia sociale e religiosa del Mezzogiorno d'Italia,* ed. Galasso, G. and Russo, C., 2 vols., Naples, 1980 and 1982.

47. Jones, F., *op. cit.,* p 24.
48. Alphonsus to Maria Saveria Foglia, Prioress of Regina Coeli at Airola, midsummer, 1764.
49. Tannoia, *Vita,* I, i, p 3.
50. *Ibid.*, I, viii, pp 28ff; Abbot di Miro, professed at San Severino in 1672, was a man of delightful culture, with an easy command of Greek and Latin literature, who had studied in Naples, Venice, and at last in Rome with the celebrated Dom Celestino Pezzancher. He was well-liked by both Pope Innocent XII and HRE Karl VI, and on returning to San Severino as Abbot in 1719, had been elected Abbot President of the Cassinese Congregation the next year. He was, even in the midst of these responsibilities, able to find time to compose several odes, eclogues, and epigrams, and a poem in praise of the theology of the benedictine cardinal Joseph Saens d'Aguirre. He died in 1723 almost immediately after Alphonsus' visit. *Vid.* Francois, J., ed., *Bibliotheque generale des ecrivains d. l'Ordre de Saint Benoit,* Bouillon, 1777–1778, anastatic reproduction, Louvain, 1961, vol. II, p 264a, and Armellini, *Biblioteca Monte Cassino,* vol. II, p 27.
51. Vincenzo di Miro, after a career among the diplomats at Vienna, had been employed as Counsellor of San Chiara and Regent del Collaterale by both Philip II of Spain and HRE Karl VI.
52. Tannoia, *Vita,* I, viii, p 29.
53. *Ibid.* I, i, p 3.
54. *Ibid., cf. Hamlet,* IV.7.178. *Vera Sposa di Gesu Cristo,* 1760–1761, XXIV.6; *Op. asc.,* II, p 417, English trans. Grimm, *True Spouse,* p 717.
55. Tannoia, *Vita,* I, viii, p 29; Di Maio was the Chief of the Rota, the panel of judges at the disposal of the Regent di Miro. De Ruggiero, F., *Tela giudiziaria della Vicaria,* Naples, 1758, and Peschia, C., *Storia della Vicaria,* 2 vols., Naples, 1777.
56. *Selva di materie predicabili,* 1760, Pte. I, cap. x; English trans. Grimm, *Dignity and Duties of the Priest,* p 190.
57. *Vera Sposa,* xxiv.3; *True Spouse,* p 715.
58. *Vera Sposa,* xxiv.6; *True Spouse,* p 717.
59. Tannoia, *Vita,* I, vii, p 24.
60. *Miscellany,* p 208.
61. Tannoia, *Vita,* I, iii, pp 9f, suggests an early passion for card games with a set of

youthful cronies at the apartment of Don Carlo Cito. Don Giuseppe was not pleased to see his son frittering away time, and perhaps even a little money, on such things. He put a stop to these late-night sessions. It does not appear to be quite the case, therefore, that it was always Donna Caterina who "kept me out of mischief," *ibid.*, I, ii, p 7.

62. Sarnelli, P., *Nuova guida di Napoli,* Naples, 1781, p 21, cited by Tellería, R., S.H., IV, 1956, *art. cit.*, p 9, note 8.
63. Tellería, R., S.H., IV, 1956, *art. cit.*, Appendix I.
64. Alphonsus to Villani, July 13, 1766 and to Michele N., July 8, 1766. Barbara's godmother, the princess Reitano, was almost the last surviving member of one of the grandest of Sicilian families, *vid.* Bernardo Gonzaga, *Memorie delle Famiglie Nobili delle Province Meridionali d'Italia,* Naples, 1878, vol. V, pp 151ff. On his wife's dying in 1728, Prince Francesco de Liguoro married Beatrice Capece, who proved "truly more loving than if she had been her own daughter" to Donna Antonia de Liguoro, 1707–1782(?). *Cf.* Tellería, R., "*Testamentum, Codicilli et Capellania Codicillaris Exc. mi D. Francisci de Liguoro,*" S.H., V., 1958, pp 264–308, Document II, Codicil, p 302. Tellería, pp 267ff, suggests that Antonia had, like her sister Teresa, been considered by their fathers as a possible wife for Alphonsus. *Vid.* also Gregorio, O., *Manoscritti Inediti,* S.H., VI, 1958, pp 330–352, p 339 for Alphonsus to Antonia, July 2, 1777, and Tannoia, *Vita,* IV, xv, p 73.
65. For Don Giuseppe and the *Monte dei Poveri Vergognosi, vid.* Tellería, R., S.H., IV, *art. cit.* p 19.
66. Alphonsus to Ercole, February 1746.
67. They quite often attempted to retrieve what a previous head of the clan had bequeathed outside the family. The ferocity of duchess Isabella Mastrillo, 1673–1761, in her efforts to grab back such moneys led to the closure of the Marigliano convent of the serafian custom and the removal of the Crostarosa sisters to Scala in 1724; *vid.* Swanston, Hamish F. G., *Singing a New Song,* 1997. Similar feelings for family property prompted Gennaro Maria Sarnelli's relatives to make a try, first, for the repossession of his books, Alphonsus to Canon Giuseppe Sparano, July 17, 1744, and then for the vineyard that their brother Andrea had given to the Congregation. Their suit took its slow way through the courts, 1759–1783; Alphonsus' letters, December 7 and 18, 1774, February 4, March 20 and 25, May 8 and 21, 1775, January 23 and November 4, 1776.
68. It is unclear whether San Girolamo was among those many convents which, after Alphonsus' ordination in December 1726 had him to preach in their chapels, *vid.* Tannoia, *Vita,* I, xi, p 35, and II, xxxvi, p 236; and again unclear whether he stopped awhile in the convent parlor in 1767, when he had come to Naples about the d'Iliceto and Ciorani lawsuits, though Alphonsus had by then a reputation and, receiving so many convent invitations, "he could hardly fix on which to answer first," ibid., III, xl, p 203. But there were "few convents in Naples in which there were no nuns under his direction," *ibid.*, I, xii, p 43.

69. *Vera Sposa,* X.1.5; *True Spouse,* p 284.
70. *Ibid.* II.19.7; *True Spouse,* p 54.
71. Tannoia, *Vita,* III, xlvii, p 245.
72. For S. Gaetano, *vid.*, Chiminelli, P., *San Gaetano Thiene, cuore della Riforma Cattolica,* Vicenza, 1948.
73. Tellería, R., "*Per D. Caietanus de Liguoro S. i Alfonsi frater, eiusque nepos Alfonsinus beneficio ecclesiastico muniumtur a Duce Gravina Orsini,*" S.H., XIII, 1965, pp 325–357.
74. Tannoia, *Vita, Pref.*, vii and I, ii, pp 4f.
75. Tellería, R., S.H., XIII, *art. cit.*, p 326 and Trendari, A., *Emilo Cavalieri dei Pii Operai,* ed. Vizzari, D., Naples, 1969.
76. Most years, the squadron was in dock at Baia for winter refurbishment and Captains were expected to supervise the work of the arsenal teams; Don Giuseppe usually took shore leaves during the summer and early autumn. These things had been reorganized by the Real Junta del Arsenal appointed under the 1715 Reglamento Cesareo de la Marina.
77. Tellería, R., S.H., XII, *art. cit.*, p 330.
78. Tellería, R., S.H.,XIII, *art. cit.*, p 326, note 5, and Archiv. Cong. Orat., "Girolamini" 32, *Libro de' defunti* for a notice of Casimiro Sicola.
79. Tellería, R., *San Alphonsus,* vol. 1, pp 103f; Sparano, G., *Memoriae Istoriche,* 2 vols., Naples, 1768, II, pp 310 and 337, and Mazzochus, A., *De sanct. Neap. Eccl. Episc. cultu,* Naples, 1753, p 5.
80. Tellería, R., S.H., XIII, *art. cit.*, p 332.
81. Tannoia, *Vita,* I, ix, p 31. Domenico Invitti was successively Canon of Naples, 1688, titular bishop of Gratianopolis in Mauritania, 1724, titular metropolitan of Sardis in Lydia, 1725.
82. Ripa, Matteo, *Storia della Fondazione della Congregazione e del Collegio de' Cinesi,* 3 vols., Naples, 1832, vol. 1, p 12.
83. Alphonsus long contemplated a career as a foreign missionary, *vid.* Jones, F., *op. cit.*, pp 90ff, Gregorio, O., *Tommaso Falcoia,* p 125, and Alphonsus to "Chinese Collegers," May 22, 1777, with his letters to Students, July 18 and mid August 1758.
84. Tellería, R., S.H., VI, 1958, pp 265–308, and "*Duo Nova Documenta Super Familia de Liguoro,* S.H., VII, 1959, p 232, note 10.
85. Tannoia, *Vita,* I, vi, pp 20f, *cf.* discussion of marriage-brokering, Gregorio, O., *S. Alphonso, Contributi bio-bibliografici,* Brescia, 1940, p 58. Alphonsus, to please the nuns of her Carmelite convent, wrote a gushing account of the *Vita e morte della S. di D., Sr. Teresa N. de Liguori,* 1761. For the enclosure of Antonia Clara in 1707, *vid.* Archiv. di Stato, Monas. Soppr. S. Marcellino, V.2.867, *Libro delle ufficiali,* 1709–1785.
86. Both daughters had been boarders of the Holy Sacrament convent (which followed the custom of Saint Maria Maddalena de Pazzi), Antonia from 1717, Teresa from 1720. Antonia was professed at S. Marcellino in 1724 or 1725, *vid.*

Gregorio, O., *Contributi,* p 38, note 55. The text of the bequest is printed by Tellería, S.H., VI, *art. cit.*, pp 304ff. Codicil 8 asks that the Prince's second wife shall look after the needs of "*mia amatissima figlia*" Antonia.

87. Tellería, R., S.H., XIII, *art. cit.*, refers to "chapel" and "chaplaincy" but in truth there was only a small altar on the wall squeezed between the main door and the first proper chapel on the Epistle side of the church.
88. Alphonsus' approval of Ferrara's scheme for the exchange of copies of his *Theologia Moralis* for Mass stipends, and his careful inspection of the articles of foundation of the Benevento chaplaincy, suggest a sound interest in financial arrangements of a complex kind. Alphonsus to Villani, October 1, 1756, and to Caione, November 22, 1758.
89. Gaetano was granted title to the chaplaincy "*Per mentre che il medesimo vivera.*"
90. Gaetano to Alphonsus, Archiv. Gen. CSSR, XXIX, 25, printed in Tellería, S.H., XIII, *art. cit.*, p 334.
91. Tellería, R., "*Super domibus Palatiatis Familiae S. Alfonsi,*" S.H., XIII, pp 113 and 335.
92. Tannoia, *Vita,* III, xix, p 94. Alphonsus to Ercole, November 28 and December 13, 1763.
93. Matteo Gennaro Testa, 1708–1782, was granted a doctorate in theology by the College of Doctors, January 17, 1761, consecrated metropolitan of Reggio di Calabria by the Cardinal Henry, Duke of York, April 12, 1761, and promoted to Carthage, December 22, 1766, though never, of course, residing anywhere but Naples all these whiles. He was made Cappellano Maggiore with responsibility for the relations of State and Church by Tanucci.
94. Tannoia, *Vita,* III, xix, p 94.
95. *Ibid.*, p 95.
96. *Ibid.*
97. *Ibid.*, p 200. Alphonsus had enough sense of the fitness of things to object to riding in a coach which bore not his own but his brother's coat-of-arms.
98. *Ibid.*, xlvii, p 248.
99. *Ibid.*
100. Tellería, R., S.H., XIII, *art. cit.*, p 333, note 24.
101. Don Gaetano's act of renunciation to Cardinal Domenico Orsini, 1778, and the authorization by Filippo Orsini, on behalf of his father the cardinal, in Archiv. di Stato, and the installation documents on Alphonsus' being granted the benefice in Archiv. di Curia, Naples. Tellería, R., S.H., XIII, *art. cit.*, pp 351–353.
102. Alphonsus to Ercole, December 4, 1770.
103. Alphonsus' withdrawal described by Tellería, *art. cit.*, S.H., XIII, p 353.
104. Tellería could discover no trace of Gaetano's tomb; *ibid.*, p 345.
105. Gaetano bequeathed everything to his "universal and particular heir, his Excellency Signor Don Giuseppe di Liguori," instructing him to allot fifty ducats to Carluccio Scarola his manservant and a month's salary of twelve ducats to

his odd-jobs-about-the-house-man, Giuseppe di Nino. He was also careful to stipulate that his universal heir should, on his death, transfer twenty ducats to the burial confraternity of "the Seventy-Two Priests" so that they should say Masses for the repose of uncle Gaetano's soul at the rate of two carlini a Mass.

106. At *Theologia Moralis,* Lib. III, *tract.* V, "On the Seventh Commandment," *cap.* iv, *dub.* v, Gaude, 946, Alphonsus made it plain that a man had no obligation to leave anything to his brothers and sisters, unless they were in extreme poverty, and then no more than they absolutely required.
107. Alphonsus to Villani, October 8, 1774: "I have without hesitation told Father Giovanni (Lauria) that he is not obliged to return home, and that neither the temporal nor the spiritual wants of his family oblige him to do so."
108. Alphonsus to Tannoia, July 4, 1756. He was always in a worry about money and its management within the law. In a quite typical twelve months, March 24, 1774, to March 25, 1775, Alphonsus' correspondence shows his dealing with some urgent financial crisis almost every week. Then the whole round begins again. The very next letter, to Angelo Maione, March 29, 1775, is concerned with the cost of a coach ride, and the next after, April 2, 1775, with the difficulty of getting a Redemptorist's family to acquiesce in a dower settlement.
109. "*...quo melius honori suo consultum sit*" as the Pope says. Tellería, R., S.H., IV, 1956, *art. cit.,* pp 10ff for the Brief, October 1, 1707.
110. Don Giuseppe agreed to draw his draft on the Banco di Popolo, September 20, 1707.
111. The act of provisional acceptance by the Abbess and Vicar is printed by Tellería, R., *art. cit.,* pp 12–13.
112. In the certificate of reception, November 20, 1717, Tellería, R., *art. cit.,* p 13, Anna Maria is said to have replied, on being questioned formally about her vocation by Don Pietro de Duce, the Vicar for Religious, "I have come into the presence of Your Illustrious Reverence, to say that, of my free and unprompted will, I wish to be the Bride of O. L. Jesus Christ, becoming a nun in the Convent of San Girolamo of this city and to put on the habit of a novice Choir nun, to have my hair cut off, and to take my part in all the fit customs of the novitiate, and as a novice to observe obedience, poverty, and chastity, and the Rule of Saint Francis." All this she swore, "no one making me do so by force or violence," fully in command of herself, "being 15 years old."
113. Arrangements for the dower were signed by Annella, December 1, 1718; Tellería, R., *art. cit.,* S.H., IV, 1956, pp 14–15. The dower sum was considerably less than that arranged for Maria Luisa (Barbara) on account of the customary reduction when a second blood sister entered the convent community.
114. *Vid.* the agreed statement between Abbess de Costanzo and Francesco Maria di Costanzo, February 13, 1715, concerning the shortfall in payment of 3,000 ducats capital sum and 135 annual income at 4 1/2 percent, and the 500 ducats promised by the Monte de Poveri lenders according to arrangements al-

ready in place, December 31, 1711. Tellería, R., S.H., IV, *art. cit.*, pp 19f. The Monte de Poveri had paid Barbara's school fees, fifty ducats a year, since September 1709, *ibid.* pp 17f.

115. Tannoia, *Vita,* III, xxiv, p 123: the two Nola brothers had to be persuaded by bishop Alphonsus to pay the school fees arrears to the Redemptoristine nuns at Sant' Agata so that their sister might be debtless at profession as a member of the community.

116. Tellería, R., "*D. Iosephus de Liguoro, S. Alfonsi Peter adit haereditatem Patris sui D. Dominici de Liguoro mortui ab intestato an. 1728,*" S.H., IX, 1961, pp 83ff. Don Giuseppe's nephews, Vincenzo and Filippo del Migliore, had recourse to lawyers to get their share of property left by their grandfather to their mother, Don Giuseppe's sister, Donna Geronima. Uncle Giuseppe paid up, or at least instructed his heir, Ercole, to pay over fifteen ducats each to these nephews and their sister, "soon after my death." It was another five years before the Prioress of San Maria Visita Poveri received her legacy of sixty ducats under this same will. Tellería, R., S.H., V, *art. cit.*, pp 236–275.

117. Caterina Carrato was not the only employee at the convent. For an aristocratic nun to require a maid, "some lay sister or some other," was not so very unusual. Such women were not always employed to relieve a Choir nun of the heavier manual work or to take care of her in illness. Brianna Carafa, Alphonsus' persistent correspondent in the San Marcellino convent, supposed that such a cell companion would keep the ghosts of dead nuns at bay. Alphonsus thought this nonsense; letter of May 1, 1769. Brianna took an old nun into her cell so that she might look after her until she died. This was much more to Alphonsus' liking; letter of July 17, 1768. Caterina Carrato was herself exhausted by the demands of caring for Annella and was, in 1769, replaced, with Barbara's consent, by the robuster Margarita Faldarino. Tellería, R., S.H., V, *art. cit.*,p 16.

118. Tellería, R., S.H., IV, *art. cit.*, p 9, citing Archiv. Curiae, Nap., *Sectio Monalium,* S. Girolamo.

119. Santagata, S., *Vita di Giambattista Cacciottoli,* Naples, 1751, p 210.

120. The nuns, though vowed to "the Rule of Saint Francis," were conscious of their standing in society requiring their being given retreats by such fashionable Jesuits as Gennaro d'Ancona, Saverio Sant' Agata, and Matteo Stinja; Archiv. di Stato, Napoli, *Monasteri soppressi,* vol. 2511.

121. *Instructions for the People,* I.4, II.2.

122. Tannoia, *Vita,* III, xl, p 204.

123. *Vera Sposa,* XVIII.2.l; *True Spouse,* pp 41ff.

124. *Ibid.* II.4. Alphonsus is citing Giovanni Battista Scaramelli, *Direttorio ascetico,* tract. 2, *ad* 11, 2.438, Venice, vol. I, p 419. He may well have had in mind the sad history of the young niece of the Ven. Serafina di Dio, 1621–1699, who threw herself down a convent well, *vid.* Serafina, *Trattato sulla conformita alla volunta di Dio* in *Capritana Positio Super Virtutibus,* Rome, 1865, pp 244–248, and Squillante, N., and Pagani, T., *Vita della Ven. Madre Serafina di Dio,* Naples,

1723 and Venice, 1743. The best recent study of this splendid woman is Possanzini, S., *La Venerable Madre Serafina,* Fisciano, 1992. Alphonsus once suggested that Don Giuseppe was driving Ercole to the same desperate dive; letter of end of October, 1737.

125. *Vera Sposa,* II.4.2; *True Spouse,* pp 44f.
126. Tannoia, *Vita,* III, xl, p 204.
127. It was a blessing to them all that Donna Anna Caterina, who had become nunnish in her careful daily recitation of the Little Hours of the Office, was for the last few days of her life relieved from the horrors of her scruples; Tannoia, *Vita,* II, xlii, p 264.
128. Gaetano's anxiety for such a large number of Masses to be said for the repose of his inoffensive little soul suggests that he was, like his mamma, burdened by horrid doubts as to whether he had served God well enough; his contemporaries had no doubt that he had been a decent Treasurer of that chapel where there is now a bust of his brother.
129. *Vera Sposa,* X.1; *True Spouse,* p 284.
130. *Vera Sposa,* I.2; *True Spouse,* pp 21f.
131. Alphonsus' remarks are, designedly, elaborations of a short sharp sentence at 1 Corinthians 7:28.
132. Grimm, distressed at this generalization, translated this last phrase as "the generality of married persons," but Alphonsus had put a deliberate emphasis on "all married women," "tutte…dico tutte." *Vid.* for a discussion of this startling verdict, Raponi, S., "*La chiamata universale alla santita*" in *La Recezione del Pensiero Alfonsiano Nella Chiesa,* ed. Weiss, O., Rome, 1998, S.H., XLV, 1997, pp 169–204, especially pp 178–184. Alphonsus is employing the language of the *Salve Regina,* "*gementes et flentes,*" but there is no heaven at the end for the married woman: she passes from "one inferno in this life" to "another in the next," *Vera Sposa,* I.2.
133. That picture of the married woman would likely fit Donna Anna Caterina's experience. She may have sighed a little to "Fonso," regretting for a tired moment that she had not been left with her sisters at the Pontecorvo convent. There, Teresa had, only twenty years old, died of tuberculosis and gone to heaven, while Cecilia had lived an exemplary quiet life and died a holy abbess. Anna Caterina had been given, a dimmish young woman, to Don Giuseppe, the gallant trireme officer who wanted some bright talk at the supper table and a couple of jolly outings before he had to go back on board the stinking ship. It is not too surprising, given his mother's history, that Tannoia should be able to list many examples he knew of nice girls who were, by Alphonsus' preaching, turned from pledged fiancees into nuns, "hundreds of them"; Tannoia, *Vita,* I, xv, p 54, II, xxxiii, p 220, and xxvi, p 236.
134. Vito Curzio's brother, the Canon, was among his dependents. It is not recorded whether Vito was ever a member of the hunting party.
135. Tannoia, *Vita,* I, vi, p 20.

136. Ippolita married (1) Don Nicolo Tramanto, Baron of Santa Croce, in 1691, and on his death, (2) Hyacinto del Balzo, in 1717. She was alive enough in 1728 to contest Don Giuseppe's pretensions to an exclusive inheritance of their father's property. Jones, F., *op. cit.*, p 11, says that Teresa married the Duke of Praesenzano, "a widower much older than herself," but he does not identify a previous wife of Don Domenico. He also states, p 12, that there were "no children of the marriage." Tellería, R., S.H., IX, *art. cit.*, p 91, identifies Donna Geronima del Balzo as their daughter.
137. King Carlo had made outdoor sports, hunting chiefly, all the rage. The great Minister, Bernardo Tanucci, 1698–1783, used to complain that he had, when commanded to the royal hunt, to miss his daily Mass. Cala-Ulloa, P., *Di Bernardo Tanucci e dei suoi tempi,* Naples, 1875; vid. also, Alphonsus to de Paola, February 18, 1781.
138. Tannoia, *Vita,* I, i, p 3.
139. Jones, F., *op. cit.*, p 501, note 8.
140. *Vera Sposa,* X.1.6; *True Spouse,* pp 284f.
141. Alphonsus to Maria Antonia de Liguori, May 9, 1776, to Giuseppe de Liguori, June 3, 1781, and to Tommaso Falcoia, July 24, 1740.
142. Alphonsus to Ercole, February 1746, May 24, 1761, March 21, 1762.
143. Alphonsus to Ercole, November 12, 1762, December 13, 1763, March 21, 1762, February 22, 1746, May 24, 1761.
144. Alphonsus to Ercole, May 24, 1761 with a reference to "Brother Francesco."
145. Alphonsus to Ercole, February 1746.
146. Alphonsus to Don Giuseppe, mid October 1737.
147. Ercole married Donna Rachele de Liguoro, January 22, 1732. Two of her sons by a previous marriage were the first to greet Alphonsus on his coming down the road from Rome to Naples, June 21, 1762. Tannoia, *Vita,* III, vi, p 22.
148. Alphonsus to Ercole, mid February 1746.
149. Alphonsus to Ercole, February 22, 1746.
150. Alphonsus' will, March 5, 1746, drawn at d'Iliceto, witnessed by two Foggia lawyers, Carlo Ricciardi and Giuseppe Bonasissa, who each of them had in his family a youngster who would join the Congregation, Sebastiano Ricciardi, 1731–1762, and Paschal Bonasissa, 1733–1791.
151. Alphonsus to Ercole, November 23, 1755.
152. Alphonsus to Ercole, May 24, 1761. He is appalled at the annuity interest's lying idle in the bank: "I cannot bear the idea of these maturities accumulating."
152. Alphonsus to Ercole, March 21, 1762. On March 9, within a month of the death of Bishop Danza, one of the Nuncio's staff arrived at Pagani to inform Alphonsus of his nomination to Sant' Agata dei Goti. On his declining the honor, a second messenger came, March 19, from the Nuncio, Giuseppe Maria Locatelli, communicating the express order of Pope Clement XIII, della Torre Rezzonico, 1693–1769, to which Alphonsus submitted.

153. Alphonsus to Ercole, March 21, 1762.
154. Neither Gaetano nor Ercole attended Alphonsus' consecration by Cardinal Ferdinando Maria Rossi, 1696–1775, in the Minerva, June 20, 1762. Tannoia, *Vita,* III, v, p 20, and Tellería, R., *San Alphonso,* vol. II, pp 34f.
155. Tannoia, *Vita,* III, vii, p 29.
156. Alphonsus to Ercole, mid August 1762; *cf.* Alphonsus to Ferdinando IV, 1751–1825, King of the Two Sicilies, end of July 1767.
157. Donna Rachele had had at least two, and perhaps five, children by her previous marriage, but wanting his own proper heir, Ercole was thinking of remarriage within a week of her death. Alphonsus was at least as fast in considering the matter.
158. Alphonsus to Ercole, November 5, 1762.
159. Alphonsus to Ercole, November 12, 1762.
160. Alphonsus to Ercole, December 12, 1762.
161. Tannoia, *Vita,* III, lxvi, p 353.
162. *Ibid.*, xix, p 93.
163. Alphonsus to Ercole, November 22, 1783.
164. Alphonsus to Ercole, March 11, 1764.
165. Tannoia, *Vita,* III, xxvi, p 130.
166. *Ibid.*, xxx, p 152. Nor even, when by some curious chance both brothers were staying at one time with the Prince della Riccia at Airola, though in different wings of the Palazzo, for Alphonsus to allow Ercole and his wife to have a little music in the evening. Somehow, for this one time, he persuaded himself that a harpsichord was "not suitable" for a bishop's residence. *Ibid.*, xv, p 74.
167. Tannoia, *ibid.*, xlvii, p 244.
168. *Ibid.*, p 245.
169. *Ibid.*, xl, p 202 and xlvii, p 244. Tellería, R., *San Alfonso,* vol II, p 153, insists that Gaetano baptized the elder twin, Carlo Maria, thus securing the boy's primogeniture rights; only after this did the parish priest of Marianella, Don Giambattista Giodice, baptize the secondborn twin, Giuseppe Maria. In this version of the history, Don Antonio Fusco stood proxy for Alphonsus, the boys' godfather. Tannoia, *Vita,* III, xlvii, p 245, says that Alphonsus confirmed both boys: if so, he must have done the ceremony more than usually early in their lives, Alphonsus himself was not confirmed until he was twenty-five years old, September 21, 1722.
170. Berthe, Augustin, *Saint Alfonse de Liguori,* 2 ed. Paris, 1900, vol. II, pp 185f; English trans. Castle, H., Dublin, 1905, vol. II, p 175. Whatever bad memories older Redemptorists have of refectory readings and however startling to others the Franco-centricity of the writing, these Berthe volumes remain the good stand-by *Life* of Alphonsus.
171. Antonia de Liguori figures first in Alphonsus' correspondence when, May 1776, she sends him some of the "queen's biscuits" for which the convent had some local fame. Their "Spanish bread" was, doubtless, also tasty.

172. Alphonsus to Brianna Carafa, November 12, 1768.
173. Tannoia, *Vita,* III, xlvii, p 245.
174. Alphonsus to Ercole, December 4, 1770; Tannoia, *Vita,* III, xlvii, p 245.
175. Domenico Pedicino, a priest from Vitulano, had been Alphonsus' choice as the boys' tutor. Tannoia, *Vita,* III, xlvii, p 245. Later, Ercole himself selected a pair of Naples lawyers to govern the boys' education. One of these, Pietro Gavotti was named in Ercole's will as a guardian for his sons in the event of his dying before they were "of age."
176. Tannoia, *Vita,* III, xlvii, p 246. Alphonsus to Ercole, December 15, 1771.
177. Tannoia, *Vita,* III, xlvii, p 247. The "College of Nobles" had both lay Governors and lay teachers under a Principal who was, usually, a serving army Colonel. There was a time-tabled period each day for the study of "the military arts." The boys generally went on to careers as army officers or as functionaries in the royal palace. This might well have suited both Ercole's boys, but Alphonsus was in 1771 already intending Alfonsino to make a commitment to the priestly life. *Cf.* Gregorio, O., "*Alfonsino de Liguoro chierico beneficiato,*" S.H., XX, 1972, pp 24–44.
178. Tannoia, *Vita,* III, xlvii, p 246. It may or may not be an evidence against Alphonsus' assessment of the Cadet College that, during a mission-like exercise there, Alessandro di Meo, 1726–1786, excited such compunction among the young soldiers that many wished to change their choice of futures and become religious "and several of them," di Meo reported cheerfully to Villani, "are anxious to join us." Things turned out differently. Marchal Francesco Pignatelli spoke to Alphonsus about appointing di Meo to the College staff. Avoiding this honor, di Meo had had to preach the Lenten Exercises at the College in February 1786, and then a Triduum for those whose duties had prevented their attending the Exercises. These exertions brought on the first of his heart attacks. He died on March 21, 1786.
179. *Cf.* Gregorio, O., S.H., XX, *art. cit.*, p 29, note 13 for a reference to this dominie in Tanucci's letter to Carlo III, March 5, 1776.
180. *Glorie di Maria, Pte.* I, *cap.* vi.l, *esempio;* Grimm excised this fine story from his English trans.
181. Tannoia, *Vita,* III, xlvii, p 246.
182. *Ibid.*, p 247.
183. *Ibid.*
184. Even the Bambino in the Crib reminded Alphonsus of the infant Hercules, Novena of Christmas, IX.iii, p 133.
185. Conza text, First Rule: Faith, Constitution. *Cf. Regole Grandi* I, English trans. Hoegerl, Carl, *Founding Texts of Redemptorists: Early Rules and Allied Documents,* Rome, 1986, (hereinafter *Founding Texts),* pp 180f and 113.
186. Alphonsus to Novices at d'Iliceto, August 1758; *cf.* to Fathers and Brothers, September 30, 1770, February 26, 1771, and June 27, 1773. For Alphonsus' response to Ercole's boys, *vid.* Tannoia, *Vita,* IV, xxxii, p 169. He was as quick

as any modern amateur analyst to recognize what might be ambiguous in this response, *cf.* Jones, F., *op. cit.*, p 482, and Tannoia, *Vita*, IV, xxx, p 155.

187. "*La tenerezza*" is noted by Tannoia, *Vita*, II, lxii, p 360 and IV, xxxii, p 169.
188. *Vid.* Falcoia to Alphonsus, April 29, 1735, Gregorio, O., ed. *Lettere*, No. 116; Jones, *op. cit.*, p 147 says that Falcoia warned Alphonsus against "*le sue tenerezze*" on another occasion but does not provide a reference.
189. Alphonsus to Canon Giacomo Fontana, January 28, 1751, to Tannoia, mid summer 1754, and June 24, 1756, to a Redemptorist priest, June 3, 1757, to Caione, July 15, 1757. Did Alphonsus remember the pleasure he'd taken in card games?
190. *Vid.* Alphonsus to his nephews, April 4, 1780, and June 3, 1781, to Teresina, July 30, 1781, and May 25, 1782, to Brianna Carafa, September 20, 1781, to Tannoia, April 29, 1758, and to Caione, November 22, 1758. *Cf.* Tannoia, *Vita*, II, xlix, p 353 and IV, xxv, p 185.
191. In at least this respect, Alphonsus' *Breve notizie* of Cafaro are autobiography. He also praises Cafaro's sneaking to the President of his Junior Seminary on those who had broken the rules. Alphonsus remained all his life convinced that such "fraternal denunciations made to a father" would assist the accused child to make due reformation; *Theologia Moralis*, Lib. IV, *cap.* III, *dub.* v, Gaude, 235.
192. *Vid. egrr.* Falcoia to Alphonsus, January 3, 1733, and January 24, 1734; *Lettere* Nos. 47 and 77. Tannoia was fond of the phrase, too, *vid. Vita*, I, xii, p 43, II, xi, p 124, *et al. pl.*
193. *Considerazioni ed affetti sopra la Passione*, 1761, XII; *Quindici Meditazioni*, 1766, VIII; English trans. *Reflections and Affections on the Passion*, pp 112f, *Meditations for the Last Fifteen Days of Lent*, p 442.
194. *Meditations for Last Fifteen Days of Lent*, VII.iii, p 444.
195. *Simple Exposition of the Passion*, Introduction; *Meditations on the Passion*, Wednesday. For this theater image, *vid.* also *Preparation for Death*, xxv.2 and xxvii.1, and *Selva*, Pt. II, Instruction 1.
196. Alphonsus to Luigi Capuano, August 7, 1755.
197. *Glorie di Maria*, Pte. I.l, para. iv; *Glories of Mary*, pp 71ff.
198. Isaiah 9:6, cited at *Glorie di Maria*, I, para. ii; *Glories of Mary*, p 47.
199. *Imitation of Christ*, Book IV, chapter XIX.
200. *Ibid.*
201. Genesis 45:8 and Judges 17:10.
202. *Iliad* XXIV, lines 475–691.
203. *Lear* II.4.153. For Alphonsus' knowledge of Shakespeare, *vid.* Swanston, Hamish F. G., *Celebrating Eternity Now*, p 236, note 120.
204. *Glorie di Maria*, Pte. I, 1.2; *Glories of Mary*, p 47.
205. Gertrude of Helfta, *Revelationes*, ed. by monks of Solesmes, Paris 1877, *Legatus divinae pietatis, cap.* LVI; English trans. *Revelations*, ed. M. Francis Clare, London, 1870, p 258.

206. Falcoia to Sportelli, February 15, 1738, *Lettere,* No. 172.
207. Vincent Contenson, O. P., *Theologia mentis et cordis, Lib.* X, *dissertatio* iv, *cap.* 1, *Speculatio,* 1, *Quartus excessus,* Rome, 1769, Vol. III, p 170. *Glorie di Maria,* V, para. 1; *Glories of Mary,* p 155.
208. *Regole Grandi,* II; *Founding Texts,* p 117. This hard saying was deliberately revised in the Conza text to "your heavenly Father, who is better by far than any father."
209. *Regole Grandi,* Rule 2, Hope, and Rule 1, Faith; *Founding Texts,* pp 117 and 112.
210. *Breve Istruzione degli Esercizi di Missione,* 1760; English trans., *Exercises of the Missions,* VII, p 238.
211. *Ibid.*, II, p 365, IV, pp 114, 185, and 226.
212. Letter of bishop of Molfetta, cited by Jones, *op. cit.*, p 193.
213. SAM IX.III.l, published in *Analecta CSSR* 5, 1926, pp 171–180 and 230–242; *Founding Texts,* pp 75–94.
214. *Compendio,* AGR, SAM IX.III.4; transcribed in Gregorio, O., and Sampers, A., *Documenti intorno alla regola,* Bibl. Hist. CSSR., 4, Rome, 1969, pp 293–317, *Founding Texts,* pp 156–174 with 2 Corinthians citation, p 169.
215. Conza text; *Documenti,* pp 282ff; *Founding Texts,* pp 179ff, where the 1 Corinthians quotation is said to be from the similar 4:16.
216. Pontifical Rule, AGR I A 93, *Documenti,* pp 413–435; *Founding Texts,* pp 297ff, III.2 with note 76.
217. Guilielmi Estii, *In omnes Pauli Epistolas item in Catholicas Commentarii,* Douai, 1614–1616. I have used the editions of Sausen, F., VI tomes, Paris, 1843, and Holzammer, J., 3 vols. Mainz, 1859. Alphonsus is said by Jones, *op. cit.*, p 47, to have had an opportunity to refer to Giulo Torno's own *Annotations on the Commentaries of Estius,* Naples, 1720. I have not had sight of this, but it would evidently be good to do so.
218. Estius, *loc. cit.*, "*parens erat in Christo,*" "*decet autem . . . filios patrem.*"
219. Estius commenting at Philippians 2:22 considers Latin Mss and Ambrosian conjectural emendations before offering his own exegesis: "*velut filius cum patre, serviverit ac totum se contulerit ad Evangelii negotium promovendum.*"
220. Estius at 1 Thessalonians 2:11, "*nunc se comparat patri, filios suos instituenti.*
221. Estius, *loc. cit.*, cites an impressive sequence of exegetical authorities, including Saints Ambrose and Thomas, who take this to be an ironic *dictum* of the Apostle.
222. Estius *in Epistolam ad Hebraeos, Prolegomena.*
223. Estius, *loc. cit.*, had a rather dense explanation of *fratres eos vocare* in which he entered upon discussion of Person, Nature, and Grace, in order to avoid the inference that all human beings are *cohaeredes* with Christ.
224. *In omnes Psalmos Explanatio,* 1611. Fevre ed. Paris, 1874, vol. X and XI, was derived, as Robert Bellarmine himself remarked, "more from my own meditations than from the study of many books," but it served Alphonsus' purpose

to treat this *Explanatio* as authoritative at many controverted places in his own Commentary. There is an English trans. *Commentary on the Book of Psalms,* O'Sullivan, J., Dublin, 1866.

225. *Traduzioni de' Salmi,* 1774, dedicated, without permission, to Pope Clement XIV, published with an Apology of the Author defending himself against recent critics of his moral system, *Dichiarazione del sistema;* English trans. by Livius, T., *Explanation of the Psalms and Canticles in the Divine Office,* London, 1887.
226. Alphonsus' comments on individual psalms are arranged according to their sequence in the Breviary rather than in biblical order and have the Vulgate numbering, so Psalm 21, "My God, my God, why have you forsaken me?" is now more usually Psalm 22.
227. Estius' commentary at Hebrews 2:12, *"per eosdem Apostolos"* and Alphonsus' commentary at Psalm 21:22.
228. Estius at 2 Corinthians 2:13, Romans 16:23, and Philemon 1.
229. *Glorie di Maria, Pte* II, *Opere ascetiche,* VII, p 250; Dolors of Mary, VI, the Deposition, citing Bernardine, *Sermones,* Brixen, 1558, III, *Mariale, pars.* X, *Sermo.* 3 ; *Glories of Mary,* p 529.
230. Alphonsus to Fathers and Brothers, August 8, 1754 and June 27, 1773.
231. Notebook entry, August 30, 1732, cited by Jones, F., *op. cit.*, p 100 with reference AGHR VI 10 63, 64 (Mozzicarelli 31).
232. *Via della Saluta e opuscoli, Opere ascetiche* X, p 342; Fifth of *Seven Days of Meditation* in honor of Saint Joseph.
233. Alphonsus to Fathers and Brothers, August 8, 1754. He was equally insistent that he loved them "more than my own sisters," Alphonsus to Maria di Gesu, December 1751, January 27, 1752, to Caione, August 31, 1754.
234. Alphonsus to de Paola, January 29, 1781.
235. Alphonsus to Villani, March 21, 1766.
236. Alphonsus to Tannoia, June 5, 1773.
237. Alphonsus to Donato Melaccio, 1732–1764, Spring 1764.
238. Tellería, R., S.H., IV, 1956, *art. cit.,* p 10.
239. "*Fratelli della costa*" was later, from their harassing capacity to prolong an official's voyage, applied to those who managed a "filibuster" in the Italian Senate.
240. Andrea Giovene was so expert at such fraternal networking that he was promoted by both Bourbon and Hapsburg rulers in Naples until he reached a pinnacle membership of the Camera Real in 1725. His law firm was just the place for a young man to observe the uses of "brother" among his class.
241. Letter to the Governors of the Sodality S. Maria a Misericordia (*misericordiella),* March 23, 1726, *Analecta CSSR,* XI, January 1932, p 347. *Cf.* letters to the Bianchi Confraternity, February 3, March 1 and 18, 1725; *Sant' Alphonso* 3, Pagani, 1932, pp 23f.

Part 2: Brotherhoods

1. For *sedile* organization and activities, *vid.* Capasso, B., *Sulla circoscrizione civile ed ecclesiastica. Richerche e documenti,* Naples, 1882, and Luigi de Lutio di Castelguidone, *I Sedili di Napoli (Origini, Azione Politica e Decentramento Amministrativo),* Naples, 1973.
2. Along with these five aristocratic clubs, there was also, from the days of King Robert the Wise, 1279–1343, "*il seggio del Popolo.*"
3. The Angevin meeting hall of the *sedile* next to San Maria in Cosmedin, which dated from 1587, had been restored in 1673 and much enlarged in 1706–1708.
4. Tellería, R., *San Alphonsus,* vol. I, p 43, note 17, and Gregorio, O., *Contributi,* p 64.
5. Tellería, R., *ibid.* p 43 for Alphonsus' election as *mastro delle crocelle* in 1714, 1716, and 1717.
6. That year the *sedile* meeting hall was being totally redesigned by Giuseppe Lucchesi, 1698–1751, with frescoes by Nicola Malinconico, 1695–1742.
7. Alphonsus' address, vid. Tellería, R., *San Alphonso,* I, pp 44f.
8. Cafaro to Sportelli, July 19, 1742, *Epistolae,* No. 4.
9. Black, Christopher F., *Italian Confraternities in Sixteenth Century,* Cambridge, 1989, p 133.
10. Highwaymen are met at *Glories of Mary,* Pt. I, VI.l and 3 and VIII.1, and in Pt. II *Raccolta* 25, *Op. asc.,* VII, p 375. Prostitutes come out, *ibid.,* Pt I.I.l, example, I.II.2, and VIII.l, example.
11. Tannoia, *Gerardo,* p 60; *Companions,* pp 309f.
12. *Ibid.,* p 98; *Companions,* p 362.
13. Masaniello, *vid.* references at Swanston, H. F. G., S.H., XLV, 1997, pp 518f.
14. For the early history of such confraternities, Meersseman, G. C., and Pacini, G. P., "*Le confraternite laicali in Italia nel Quattrocento,*" in *Problemi di storia della Chiesa nei secoli XV–XVII,* Naples, 1979.
15. For the very large number of Confraternities in Naples in Alphonsus' time, *vid.* Tannoia, *Vita,* II, xliii, p 270 and lxiii, p 368, and Orlandi, G., "*S. Alphonso Maria de Liguori, i laici e la fondazione della Congregazione, dell' Addolorata (o "dei Rossi") di Procida, Lateranum* 53, pp 503–526, Volpe, F., *Confraternite e vita socio religiosa nel Settecento,* Salerno, 1988, and Lazzarini, A., *Confraternite napoletane,* 1995.
16. *Tractatus de miserabilium personarum privilegiis,* 1623; Alphonsus cited Novario's *Juris canonici decisivarum conclusionem,* 4 vols., Naples, 1628, at several places in his *Theologia Moralis.*
17. Though the structures of Confraternity government commonly provided yet another opportunity for squire and parish priest to exercise their joint influence as President and Chaplain. For a most competent review of the character and effectiveness of confraternity social work, *vid.* Rusconi, Roberto, "*Confraternite compagnie e devozioni,*" in *Storia d'Italia,* Annali, vol. 9, ed.

Chittolini, G., and Miccoli, G., *La Chiesa e il potere politico,* 1986, Rome, pp 469–506.

18. Tannoia, *Vita,* III, xx, pp 98f.
19. *Storia della Congregazione del Santissimo Redentore,* ed. Chiovaro, Francesco, I/l, *cap.* I, Orlandi, G., "*Il Regno di Napoli nel Settecento,*" pp 55ff; English trans. *History,* Liguori, 1996, pp 80ff. Professor Orlandi says that there were 13,300 in the Kingdom. There were confraternities composed from several classes, artisans and merchants and gentry together. But they were in the main more socially distinguishing. The Jesuits, who were energetic organizers of such sodalities, worked with a near-complete set of classifications, of age and occupation as well as social status, as they placed applicants in the separate sodalities for nobles, students, university graduates, medical men, boys, cobblers, sculptors, *et al. pl.*
20. There were consororities of good women in the city, the ladies Devote di Gesu, founded in the mid-sixteenth century, for instance, and less class-conscious Societies of the Rosary set up in many suburban parishes. Black, C., *op. cit.,* pp 34ff. See, for Alphonsus' interest in such lay sororities, his letters to Francesco di Filippo, Archpriest of Frasso, January 19, 22, and 29, 1763. There were societies, too, in which women and men worked together, the sodality at Boscotrecase, for example, which looked after condemned prisoners, and the San Sebastiano sodality at Resina which tended the sick, female and male, in the local Poor Hospital, *ibid.,* p 46.
21. *Instructions for the People,* Practical Introduction, 3.
22. Eighteenth century authors were often content to use "Congregation" and "Confraternity" interchangingly, but modern historians more strictly distinguish a Congregation from a Confraternity which, usually, is directed to a public cult with its own especial habit, from a Pious Union which performs a particular charitable service in the community, and from a Third Order necessarily dependent on a Religious Order.
23. Tarugi, nephew of Pope Julius III, Ciocchi del Monte, 1487–1555, was made cardinal in 1596. He was, with Alessandro Borla, 1537–1592, the cofounder of the Naples Oratory, despite some misgivings of Saint Philip Neri. Borla had been brought from Piacenza to Naples by the Theatine archbishop Bl. Paolo of Arezzo, on whose death in 1578 he worked as a chaplain at the Incurabili; *cf.* the *Vie,* Ponnelle, L., and Bordet, L; English trans., Kerr, R. F., *St. Philip Neri and the Roman Society of His Times,* London, 1932, p 443.
24. They were officially entitled "*nobiles iuniores oratorii philippensis S. Ioseph.*" There were confraternities for youths in other cities, especially where there was a Jesuit house, at Lecce, for instance. But they were not always thought respectable. The several youth associations in Florence had developed from schools of religious instruction, Confraternities of Christian Doctrine, first into rival gangs of street-footballers and then into political hooligans. In Bologna, their meetings had had to be suppressed and the youths recruited into

the novice ranks of the adult confraternities of San Maria della Vita and San Maria della Morte. Black, C., *op. cit.*, p 48. No such rowdyism is recorded of the Young Nobles.

25. Donna Andreana was first married to Enrico Mastrillo and then, in 1668, to Domenico Liguori.
26. *Libro dell' Oratorio di S. Giuseppe*, printed in Tellería, R., "*S Alfonsus adolescens Oratorio Philippensi S. Ioseph adscriptus*," *Analecta CSSR*, 31, 1959, pp 307–312.
27. Alphonsus and his four kinsmen were mixing with rather grander youngsters, Francesco Filomarino and his brother Marc' Antonio, Gerardo Brancaccio, and others who were later to distinguish themselves in Naples government, Tommaso Caracciolo, Giuseppe Cappola, prince d'Ischetella, and Pasquale Guevara, prince de Satriano, and the Genovese johnny-come-lately, Antonio Grimaldi, son of the prince of Gerace, who had settled in Naples at the close of the seventeenth century. *Cf.* Orlandi, G., S.H., XLIV, 1996, p 254, note 82.
28. Tellería, R., "*R. D. Caietanus de Liguoro, S. Alfonsi Frater*," S.H., XIII, 1965, p 328.
29. Tannoia, *Vita*, I, ii, p 6; *cf.* for the fame of these gardens, Parrino, D. A., *Compendio Istorico*, Naples, 1708, and *Nuova Guida di Napoli*, 1714.
30. Tannoia, *Vita*, I, iii, p 8.
31. Or maybe more. Tellería, R., *San Alphonso*, I, p 16, note 67, suggests that there may have been an oratorio version of one of the *Poesie Sacre* of Cardinal Pier Matteo Petrucci, 1636–1701, published Venice, 1680. But there is no demon in his verses.
32. The Landi-Rospigliosi libretto had been published in Rome, 1634.
33. Pasquini's *Alessio*, with libretto by Gianfranco Bernini, first produced at the Collegio Romano in 1690, was a continuing favorite among the Jesuits and their baroquish friends, the Naples Oratorians not backward among them. For Landi's modernist boast, *vid.* Prefaces to 1679 printing of "*Dov'e amore e pieta*" and 1687 Modena printing of the libretto made by Francesco Contini for his *Il Martirio dei SS Vito, Modesto, e Crescenzio*. He had also composed, a little earlier, an oratorio concerned with Saint Philip and his miracles.
34. Landi's score requires quite a large concert of instruments; three violins, one base viol, one harp, two lutes, one tiorbe (a sort of lengthened lute), and two gravicembali.
35. The Demon is by no means the largest part in the 1539 line libretto of Rospigliosi, but the Pasquini librettist's revisions made him more important, appearing to great effect in Act II in comic scenes with a hermit and a cheeky pageboy, and having a grand chance for overacting in Act III on the collapse of his evil design at line 1271:

I fly defeated, conquered quite,
Alessio rejoice,
For you alone defeat my grandest schemes.

36. Tannoia, *Vita,* I, iii, p 8.
37. *Vera Sposa,* XXIV.vii; *cf.* Swanston, H. F. G., *Celebrating Eternity Now,* pp 67f.
38. He would never cease to practice at the keyboard. And to provoke, as he expected, a pleased and admiring stir among his hearers. Even as an octogenarian, he could be persuaded to play for the Students at Pagani, at the end of a day. *Vid.* Jones, F., *op. cit.,* p 14.
39. "*Il trionfo della castita di S. Alessio.*" The libretto, published in Naples in 1713, was by Nicola Corvo. *Vid.* Pecorone, Bonifaccio, *Memorie,* Naples, 1729, for the recollections of a man who did sing at Turchini performances of this music.
40. Casting around, many years later, for an image of the horrors of being excluded from heaven, Alphonsus suggested his congregation contemplate the pain of a nobleman if he were excluded from such an entertainment. "How bitter would be his anguish and disappointment when, from without, he would hear the shouts of joy and applause within." Sermon XLVIII for the Nineteenth Sunday after Pentecost; *cf. Vera Sposa,* XVI.iii.3.
41. Swanston, H. F. G., S.H., XLV, 1997, *art. cit.,* pp 536ff.
42. Burney, Charles, *Memoirs of the Life and Writings of the Abate Metastasio,* London, 1796, and Gavazzeni, F., *Studi metastasiani,* Padua, 1964; for Alphonsus' enthusiasm for Metastasian poetics, *cf. Pious Reflections,* notes to VII and XVII, where it is clear that he has been reading Xavier Mattei's *Memorie per servire alla vita di Metastasio e di Jomelli.* That other Redemptorists shared this enthusiasm is evident in the telling of the life of Antonio Cafaro, 1766–1786, Dumortier, *Quelques scolastiques,* p 370: "I have the drama of the Passion of Our Lord by Pietro Metastasio" and "That book moved me greatly," and in the accounts of Gerard's song-singings between mission villages, Angelomichele De Spirito, "*Gerardo Maiella e La Religiosita Popolare del suo tempo,*" in *San Gerardo Tra Spiritualita e Storia,* p 81.
43. Walker, F., "A Chronology of the Life and Works of Nicola Porpora," in *Italian Studies,* 6, 1951, pp 29–62, and U. Prota-Giurleo, "*Per una esatta biografia di Nicola Porpora,*" in *La Scala,* 36, pp 21–29.
44. Carlo Broschi took his stage name in gratitude to the Farina brothers, his first Neapolitan patrons, *vid.* Sacchi, G., *Vita del Cavaliere Don Carlo Broschi,* Milan, 1784, and Bouvier, R., *Farinelli, le chanteur des Rois,* Paris, 1946.
45. *Dedicatio* to the printed libretto for *La Nitteti,* 1756, produced for the court performance at Madrid, Buen Retiro, September 23, 1756.
46. For Vico's early life, *vid. Opere,* ed. Battistini, A., Milan, 1990, vol. I, pp 5ff, and Verene, D. P., *The New Art of Autobiography,* Introduction, p 12.

47. Alphonsus' great-grandfather, Emilio Cavalieri, had been such a hopeful provincial. On coming from Roccagloriosa to try his luck among the city attorneys he managed to make a nice little career for himself, and to establish the base for the execution of a grander design for his son Federico, *vid. Notizie d'alcune famiglie populari della Citta e Regno di Napoli,* Bib. Nazionale, Naples, MS XIV E 36, f 6. Donna Anna's hard-working father had, before his death in 1702, made his way from the Law Courts into the Royal Secretariat, and thence into the ranks of the most senior civil servants in the Office of the President of the Regia Camera della Sommaria. The money-strapped Don Giuseppe had been able to make a trade of his city nobility with the rich, influential, and lineage-seeking Don Federico. They could all expect that Alphonsus, a nobleman within a family of legal brains, would make a not-too-difficult way onto the Tribunal bench.
48. Colletta, M. G., "*Il Collegio dei Dottori dal 1722 al 1744 attraverso le carte dell 'Archivio di Stato di Napoli,'*" in *Archiv., Storico per la Province Napoletane,* 3 series, XVIII, 1979, pp 217–241; *cf.* also Del Bagno, I., "*Lo studio napoletano agli inizi del Settecento: il privilegio giurisdizionale*" in *Studi Veneziani,* 28, 1994, pp 91–105.
49. Colletta, M. G., *art. cit.,* p 227 and note 36; Del Bagno, I., *Legum doctores, La Formazione del Ceto Giuridico a Napoli tra Cinque e Seicento,* Naples, 1933, p 175. There was a convention allowing naturalized Neapolitans, "*cives per fictionem et non per veritatem*" to graduate, but admission to the College was not granted to legitimized bastards, even of citizens, *ibid.,* p 185.
50. *Theologia Moralis, Lib.* III, *Tract.* II, *cap.* II *de Juramento, dub.* iv; Gaude, 166.
51. Colletta, M. G., *art. cit.,* p 227 and note 38.
52. These fees were sometimes grudged by other children in the family, *cf. Theologia Moralis, Lib.* III, *Tract.* V, *de Septimo praecepto Decalogi, cap.* iv, *dub.* v, Gaude 955. Alphonsus was not the youngest student to graduate at the College. In 1733 the Secretary, on receipt of the appropriate fee for dispensation, registered a sixteen-year-old doctor; Colletta, M. G., *art. cit.,* p 227 and note 40.
53. *Glorie di Maria, Pte* II.1; English trans. "The Immaculate Conception," conclusion, p 312.
54. There was no express linkage of College and Confraternity. Dr. Giuseppe Crostarosa and his sons, Dr. Francesco who graduated in 1700 and Dr. Giacomo who graduated in 1712, were all three members of the college, and they knew Provost Mastrillo's family well, but they joined other lay associations sponsored by the Jesuits; Tellería, R., "*Ven. Sororis Mariae Caelestis Crostarosa Experientia Prima Religiosa,*" S.H., XII, 1964, p 94. Sportelli, on graduating, joined the Confraternity of Doctors supervised by Falcoia's Pious Workers, *vid.* Landi, G., *Notizie della Vita del P Cesare Sportelli,* p 1. There were several other Confraternities for educated men, *egrr.* dei Bianchi dell' Oratorio di S. M. dell' Avvocata at San Giovanni a Mare, and dell' Immacolata Concezione dei Nobili at Montecalvano.

Nor were those interested in the hospital necessarily members of this Confraternity. In 1601, a group of noblemen, whose charity was centered at the Incurabili, had set up a People's Bank so that the families of the poor patients might take out cheap loans and avoid the clutches of professional money lenders. From tending to the sick and lending to the poor, which was now their particular service, these nobles found themselves extending their good offices first to those relatives of the hospital sick who were enduring the city's debtors prisons and then to a whole range of needy folk beyond the hospital. Some of their money had even been spent on ransoming Christian prisoners from the Turks. And they were by now discovering the "ashamed poor" among the nobility who needed help to keep up their pretenses to grandeur. Don Giuseppe, looking for someone who'd give him the money for his daughters' dowers at San Girolamo, and perhaps relying on his Oratory connections, applied to these hospital bankers. Successfully. By this time these good men had formed themselves into a separate Confraternity, the Pio Monte della Misericordia, with their own chapel, for which they commissioned, not evidently restrained by any lack of disposable cash, Caravaggio's great altarpiece of "The Seven Works of Mercy." Their painting was a grand reminder of what had first led them to put their energies at the service of the Incurabili. Black, C. F., *op. cit.*, pp 258–260. The Brothers had themselves painted into Fabrizio Santafede's "Saint Peter reviving Tabitha" as a proper set of spectators of this miracle. These chapel paintings and others were grand tourist attractions, bringing into the Confraternity coffers each year far more than the artists had been paid.

55. Among Alphonsus' acquaintances, Giuseppe Sersale, 1708–1758, was granted the degree in March 1757 with an eye to his being made archbishop of Sorrento within the year; his friend, Niccolo Borgia, 1700–1779, left things a little late, only graduating, June 2, 1751, before being consecrated bishop of Cava dei Tirreni, July 5, 1751, but just about the same gap intervened between the doctorates and bishoprics of Gerardo Antonio Volpi, 1692–1768, who was doctored November 12, 1744, and consecrated bishop of Nocera-Pagani on December 21 of that year, Tommaso Pacelli, 1715–1780, doctored October 26, 1752, bishop of Bovino, November 27, 1752, and Angelo Antonio Pallante, 1703–1765, doctored October 19, 1761, consecrated bishop of Sansevero, November 23, 1761.
56. Tannoia, *Vita,* I, iv, pp 13f with Note (a). Alphonsus' affection for Abdalla is reflected in his telling the Christocentric story, at the very start of his *Reflections on the Passion,* of the King's son who dies instead of his slave.
57. Swanston, H. F. G., S.H., XLV, *art. cit.,* p 538.
58. Tannoia, *Vita,* III, xlii, p 214 and lxvii, p 361.
59. Tannoia, *Gerardo,* p 100 *et al. pl.; Companions,* p 366.
60. Swanston, H. F. G., *art. cit.,* pp 546f.

61. Raponi, S., "*I Fratelli laici redentoristi al tempo di S. Gerardo,*" pp 23–76 in *San Gerardo Tra Spiritualita e Storia,* ed. de Rosa, Rome, 1993, pp. 32, 39, for the single remark about Santagata: "*Quasi una leggenda,*" and *ibid.*, pp 35 and 37.
62. Toppi, F. S., *Maria Longo, Donna della Napoli del '500,* Pompei, 1997, pp 89ff.
63. Together with Toppi, *vid.* three older but still very useful essays, Bianconi, A., *L'opera delle Compagnie del Divino Amore nella Riforma cattolica,* Citta di Castello, 1914, pp 28ff, Tecce, R., *Dell' ospidale Incurabili e di due scritti inediti,* Naples, n.d., p 11, and Langasco, C., *Gli ospedale deli Incurabili,* Genoa, 1938, pp 75ff.
64. *Troilus and Cressida,* II.3.17.
65. Whatever the origin of the infection, it had been spread through all Italy, hospitals for the incurables were being established not only in Naples but in every city of size. Pope Leo X, Medici, was very ready to bless the Longo project, tending those who are "offensive to sight and smell," as he observed. His cousin, Pope Clement VII, always a supporter of such ventures, granted further privileges in 1523 to workers and benefactors of the Naples hospital, adding "Incurabili" to the hospital's legal title so that none of the poor "however oppressed with the misery of sores and ulcers" should be turned away. Toppi, *op. cit.*, pp 64, 67f, 78, and 89f.
66. Arrizabalaga, A., *et al.*, *The Great Pox,* Yale, 1997, pp 155ff and 166ff.
67. Black, C., *op. cit.*, p 196.
68. Burnet, G., *Some letters containing an Account of what seemed remarkable in Switzerland, Italy, etc, Rotterdam,* 1686, reprinted, London, 1972, p 193.
69. Swanston, H. F. G., S.H., XLV, *art. cit.*, notes 132 and 133.
70. *Ibid.*, pp 551–564 for this vernacular opera.
71. *Ibid.*, note 135.
72. In 1671, according to Enrico Bacco's *Descrittione del regno di Napoli,* there were 1300 persons, skivvies, dispensers, nurses, doctors, patients in the Incurabili.
73. Alphonsus to Villani, July 15, 1770.
74. For a contemporary account of the disease, *vid.* Nicholson, J. F., *The Modern Siphylis (sic),* London, 1718. It was not yet understood that the application of mercury led inevitably to yet more intense physical distress as the poor patient's liver steadily enlarged. It was not understood, more happily, that while applying this ointment on the infected parts, the nurse with a recent scratch, the orderly with the chancroid on his face, was most likely being inoculated against the disease. But then again, as they very likely all knew, S. Gaetano's colleague, Bartolomeo Stella, had contracted the disease during his time as an orderly at the Incurabili; *cf.* Gaetano da Thiene to Laura Mignani, Letter 5, *Theatine Spirituality,* trans. W. V. Hudon, New York, 1996.
75. Leo X, Brief *Nuper pro parte vestra,* 1519, and Clement VII, *Ex supernae dispositionis arbitrio,* 1523; *cf. The Great Pox,* pp 155, 159, 160, and 208.

76. Whatever their grumbles, neither Francesco Tartaglione nor Francesco Margotta nor the ungrumbling Gerard Majella needed to be told twice to offer their services at the Incurabili when they were stationed in Naples, *cf.* e.g., Tannoia, Gerardo, *cap.* XXIV; *Companions,* p 357.
77. It was not within the Congregation only that Alphonsus divined the workings of this punishing order. That view of our life under God was important for the difficulties he had in talking with the parish clergy of Sant' Agata. They could never quite appreciate the immediate connection of their people's famine and their parish maladministrations. Alphonsus was perhaps a little too ready to dread that his own inadequacies as a bishop would result in divine punishment for all within the diocesan borders.
78. Tannoia, *Vita,* I, vi, p 22.
79. *Ibid.*, vii, p 25.
80. *Riposta apologetica,* 1764; *vid.* Alphonsus to Remondini, July 13, 1761, to Villani, May 25, 1767, and November 21, 1773, and to Pietro Paolo Blasucci, November 1768. With Francois Genet's *Theologie morale,* 2nd ed. 1705, Alphonsus read Gennaro Maiello's probabiliorist *Moralis mathematicum in morem adornata.*
81. *Theologia Moralis, Lib.* III, *Tract.* II, *cap* 1, Gaude, 130; *Tract.* VI, *cap.* 3, Gaude, 1027; *Lib.* VI *Tract.* III, *cap.* 2, *dub.* ii, *art.* 1, Gaude, 257.
82. *Glorie di Maria, Pte.* I, *cap.* 3.2. For Mary herself as a hospital orderly treating "nauseous and revolting ulcers" and "loathsome wounds," *vid. ibid., cap.* 4.1.
83. Tannoia, *Vita,* III, vi, p 24.
84. *Glorie di Maria, Pte.* I, *cap.* 5.2.
85. S Gaetano, the idealogue of the first Theatines, had himself been, for a short while, a member of the Oratory-like Company of San Girolamo in Vicenza, working in the general hospital of the city, the Misericordia di Pusterla, and had then, from 1522, served alongside Roman Oratorians in the San Giacomo hospital of the Company of Divine Love. All four Theatine founders, Gaetano, Gian Pietro Caraffa, 1476–1559, who became Pope Paul IV, Bonafacio de'Celli, d. 1558, and Paolo Consiglieri, d. 1557, had remained in Rome for three years after the establishment of their rather exclusive, determinedly reformist, group of "clerics regular" in 1524. They had assisted in Oratorian efforts to renew Christian living in the capital, but their connection with the Oratory had been, along with much else in the city's life, greatly disrupted by the sack of Rome by the troops of the Holy Roman Empire in May 1527.
86. Gaetano composed this prayer during the civil disturbances of 1547; English trans. in *Theatine Spirituality,* p 111. *Cf. Le Lettere di San Gaetano,* ed. Francesco Andreu, Vatican Press, 1954, pp 131ff. There are some obvious likenesses to the devotional tropes of Saint Bernard as well as the rhetoric of Daniel 9. Neapolitan printers and book-hawkers kept several Theatine works on the market during the seventeenth and eighteenth centuries, e.g., Francesco Maria del Monaco, d. 1651, *Exercises in honor of the most blessed Virgin;* Girolamo Coppola, d. 1656, *On the Privileges of Mary,* 1649; Gian Battista Caracciolo, d.

1656, *On the Passion*, 1652; Francesco Maria Maggio, d. 1686, *S. Gaetano at the feet of the Immaculate Lady*, 1672; Giuseppe Gaetano Anguissola, d. 1716, *Practices in memory of the Passion of Jesus and Mary*, 1716.

87. Gregorio, O., *Contributi*, VII, *Alla Misericordiella*, p 59.
88. Lorenzo Scupoli, *Il Combattimento spirituale*, ed. Carlo di Palma, Rome, 1657, revised by Bartolomeo Mas, Rome, 1992; English trans. anon. *The Spiritual Combat*, 1905, p 146, and in *Theatine Spirituality*, p 197.
89. Statutes, *cap.* XXIV and XVII; *Capituli et Ordinationi de la fraternita* in Toppi, *op. cit.*, pp 214ff. They had sensibly established that those pilgrim clergy should be given roof and food and laundry for a three-day maximum.
90. This was a most necessary service. Funerals, like marriages, were regarded as occasions of bonus payments by most parish clergy. Middle-class persons had their burial societies—the Confraternity of Santa Sofia, for example. But these did not always provide what the thoughtful dead had planned. Vico's funeral was turned into a black farce, and once the Cathedral Canons were involved, cost far more than his family could afford. Verene, P., *New Art of Autobiography*, p 34.
91. Statutes XXI; Gregorio, O., *Contributi*, p 61. Alphonsus was watchful enough beneath his hood to learn something of grave-digging, Jones, *op. cit.*, p 248. Early in 1735, there was a suggestion that a Redemptorist foundation might be financed from the revenues of an already established Congregazione della Buona Morte, if Alphonsus and his men would undertake the duties of the *Fratelli*, *vid.* Tommaso di Palma to Alphonsus, February 20 and 22, 1735, de Meulemeester, *Origines*, pp 279ff.
92. Tellería, R., S.H., V. *art. cit.*, p 272, for burial directions in Don Giuseppe's will. Don Domenico de Liguori was also buried in this cemetery in 1752, *vid.* Gregorio, O., *Contributi*, p 64.
93. Gregorio, O., *Contributi*, pp 58ff, especially p 62, note 58.
94. Statutes XVII.
95. Tannoia, *Vita*, III, viii, p 33.
96. 1806 Process, pp 293f, "opere stesse composte."
97. There's a likelihood that Bonaventura was adapting a similar *corona* of Bl. Jordan of Saxony, Dominican Master General, 1222; Sbaraleo, *Supplement*, p 149 and More, *Hymni latini medii aevi*, II, Nos. 454 and 460.
98. Vulgate numbering, Ps. 119, 118.17ff, 125, and 122.
99. Alphonsus attempted the same persuasion as bishop when visiting a cleric whom he himself had put into prison. For Alphonsus as imprisoner, *vid.* letters to Matteo Miglior, March 13, 1763, to Duke of Maddaloni, December 18, 1764, to Nicola Pisanti, September 30, 1766. He could also be a releaser; letter to the Marquis Granito, August 1, 1763.
100. For Alphonsus as prison visitor, *vid.* Jones, p 375.
101. *Corona*, I *hymnus*, II *Oratio*, III *Oratio:* "*ut nos resurrectionis suae participes in praesenti….*"

102. *Il Combattimento, cap.* LII; English trans., p 191.
103. Alphonsus to Governors of Ven. Cong. of Pilgrims of Misericordiella, March 23, 1726; Gregorio, *Contributi,* p 63 and *Analecta CSSR,* XI, January 1932, p 347.
104. Alphonsus, June 19, 1732, gave testimony to the Naples Curia of Ercole's freedom to marry; Tellería, R., "*Prima S. Alfonsi Palaestra Missionaria,*" S.H., VIII, 1960, p 435, note 57.
105. The royal warrant was an example of that general laicization of religious life in the Kingdom which Alphonsus, when a diocesan bishop, much deplored. Such royal approval gave confraternities notions of independence from episcopal control. "Upon occasion," he told the Roman Curia, "I have not hesitated to oppose them steadfastly"; to Congregazione del Concilio, July 8, 1765.
106. Berthe, A., *Saint Alphonse,* I, p 587 and II, p 92; English trans. I, p 557 and II, p 88; Tannoia, *Vita,* II, xlix, p 303.
107. Tannoia, *Vita,* III, xix, p 92: "He foresaw in the Spirit."
108. Mascia, G., *La Confraternita dei Bianchi della Giustizia a Napoli,* Naples, 1972, a fine study of many aspects of this Brotherhood, Pontieri, E., "*Sulle origini della Compagnia dei Bianchi della Giustizia in Napoli,*" *Campania Sacra* 3, pp 1–60. For a more general survey of like associations, *vid.* Prosperi, A., *Il sangue e l'anima. Ricerche sulle campagnie di giustizia in Italia, Quaderni Storici,* XVIII, 1983, pp 959–999, and Toppi, *op. cit.,* pp 58ff. Probably the Bianchi fell into disrepair along with so much else in Naples society during the wars of the Barons' oath, 1494.
109. Gonzaga, F., *De origine seraphicae Regionibus, libri tres,* Rome, 1587, cited by Toppi, p 59.
110. *Cap.* I–IX. These Constitutions derived from the *Regole della Compania,* 1519, and ultimately from those of the Oratory of Divine Love; Toppi, pp 61ff.
111. *Regola; cap.* XI; *cf.* Saladino, A., "*Una fonte di Storia Napoletana: l'Archivio dei Bianchi della Giustizia in Atti della Accademia Pontaniana,* New Series, VII, Naples, 1959, pp 226ff.
112. *Cap.* XXIII.
113. *Exortatione de observare la charita et unita;* Toppi, p 219.
114. *Cap.* III and IV, and XXX, "*dell' iuramento.*"
115. Examples of this secrecy occur in letters of Alphonsus to Luigi Sagliano, October 30, 1753, to Girolamo Ferrara, February 27, 1764, to Andrea Villani, January 14, 1765, to Angelo Maione, July 1, 1771…for telling secrets in strictest confidence, Alphonsus to Villani, August 14, 1769, October 8, 1774.
116. In Alphonsus' time, the Bianchi were not alone in professing this exercise of a ministry to Neapolitan prisoners. The Noble Confraternity of the Crucified, founded by the grandest of Theatine parishioners in 1533, had at first undertaken the care of prisoners in city jails and then expanded into the protection of those chained in the galleys, and further expanded into the provision of dowers for the daughters of such men. But from these noble enterprises there

was a sad decline in mid-seventeenth century into the presentation of an annual pageant which used up all the Brothers' energies and cash. Again, the Confraternity of the Cross had, since 1600, been active in collecting money to redeem men from the debtors prison. And the Pio Monte della Misericordia worked to obtain the release of prisoners from Turkish jails. There were also confraternities in towns of the Kingdom which turned to visiting the inmates of local prisons—the rosary confraternity at Boscotrecase, for example. But the Bianchi were recognized as having a care for the largest range of prisoners. So they had been able, far more successfully than most other contemporary confraternities, to keep up their subscription list of loyal notables, even of foreigners, for their work in the city. viceroy Raimondo de Cardona, for instance, had, October 29, 1519, allotted three ducats a month to their use. Then the government saw a danger. In the 1580s, Philip II had grown so nervous of political conspiracy that he issued orders expelling the lay Brothers from the Confraternity, all eighty-eight of them, lest they use their access to prisoners as a cover for further plots. Clergy were, the King assumed, quite reliable in their loyalty to the regime. The orders against the lay members were withdrawn on the death of the King in 1598, but by then quite a number had died without the comfort of the chaplain's prayers and had been buried without the confraternity's white robe about them. Black, C., *op. cit.* p 62.

117. *Avvertimenti a Sacerdoti che assistono ai Condannati a morte,* Naples, 1775, Partial English trans., Jones, F., *op. cit.*, pp 51f.

118. *Visits to the Most Blessed Sacrament,* XIX. The experience of being in the cell with the condemned man, walking with him through the street, climbing with him onto the platform of the marketplace gibbets, remained with Alphonsus all his life. Memories of these executions lie behind his vivid retelling, in *Glorie di Maria, Pte.* I, 1.4; *Glories of Mary,* p 71, of a story from Bovio's *esempi,* and the rescue of the Englishman Ernest. Alphonsus' capacity to bring a recalcitrant criminal to repentance seemed to Tannoia to outlive him. He has a smug note about Nicola Mazzola, a republican bookseller jailed in 1799 after Nelson had restored Ferdinando IV. Standing in the Bianchi chapel waiting his execution in January 1800, Mazzola remembered that Monsignore Liguori had once put his hand on his shoulder and prophesied, "My son, the life you lead will bring you to a lamentable death." The bookseller had been condemned along with seventy-nine others, including Michele Natale, 1751–1799, bishop of Vico Equense, Monsignore Vincenzo Troise, 1748–1799, Don Marcello Eusebio Scotti, 1750(?)–1799, the learned parish priest of San Michele on Procida and his assistant Michel'Angelo Ciccone, 1761–1799. But Tannoia had no sympathy for any republican. He was sure that the remembrance of Alphonsus' words prompted Mazzola to a radical rethink. "This man," he marveled, "who had till then been a hardened criminal, died full of penitence invoking the saint in heaven." Tannoia, *Vita,* III, lviii, p 299. For Tannoia's opinion of "Jacobins," *ibid.*, XXVI, p 125. For a more enlightened judgment of Mazzola and his com-

panions, *vid.* Luigi Conforti, *Napoli nel 1799,* 2nd ed., 1889, and Vincenzo Cuoco, *Saggio Storico sulla Rivoluzione Napoletana del 1799,* 2nd ed., 1806, ed. with notes by Nino Cortese, Florence, 1926.

119. *Considerazioni ed affetti,* X; *Reflections,* p 346.
120. It was a great thing with him that the Statutes required that "when the highest God calls one of our Brothers to Himself," all the others in the confraternity were to recite the Office of the Dead and the priests were to celebrate Mass for the departed Brother, whose estate was now to be held responsible for that month's payment of the subscription. So, in May 1783, Alphonsus was assuring the Brother Secretary that he had already arranged for the stipulated Masses to be said, and suggesting, a little previously as it turned out, that they would all soon have to be saying Masses for him. He made the poor prisoners' cry his own: "Help me by your prayers."
121. Alphonsus' mentor, Giuseppe de Iorio, 1698–1788, was the most distinguished member of this "Congregation of Clerics." In 1767, on the suppression of the Jesuits, the Brothers were received by the Girolamini before being renamed and rehoused by the archbishop as "the Academy and Conference of the Missions." Gregorio, O., *"Giuseppe Iorio amico e corrispondente di Sant'Alphonso," Campania Sacra* 4, 1973, pp 270–290.
122. Vulgarly called "the Giorgini," this sodality had been started in 1680 by Antonio Torres, 1636–1713, at the city headquarters of the Pious Workers, San Nicola a Toledo.
123. For Tannoia's use of the language of "Brothers" in his account of Alphonsus' Propaganda experience, *vid. Vita,* I, x, p 33 and xi, p 36; II, ii, pp 85 and iii, p 88.
124. Solimeno, G., *L'Ave Maria della Missione,* Naples, 1677, p 692. This enthusiasm for foreign languages had waned a little by the time Gennaro Maria Sarnelli joined Propaganda in 1728. He, like Alphonsus, thought to get by with French and Latin, a little Spanish and less Greek. Like Alphonsus, Sarnelli remained a member until his death. The Apostolic Missioners paid for the printing of Alphonsus' short *Life* of Sarnelli; Alphonsus to Sparano, July 17, 1744.
125. Tellería, R., S.H., VIII, *art. cit.,* pp 393ff. For later Redemptorist resistance, *vid.* Jones, pp 297ff.
126. Tellería, R., S.H., VIII, *art. cit.,* p 402.
127. *Ibid.*
128. *Ibid.,* p 407.
129. *Avvertimenti ai Predicatori,* 1778, I.1 and 3.
130. *Vid.* listing of Congregation officers, Tellería, R., S.H., VIII, *art. cit.,* p 406; Alphonsus to Fathers and Brothers, August 13, 1758, with a further reference to "secret inspectors." The usefulness of such inspectors' reports was obvious to him: "I remember and will remember what I learn," September 30, 1758.
131. Attendance lists for the weekly seminars 1724–1725 and 1726–1727 are printed in Tellería, R., S.H., VIII, pp 412 and 418.

132. "*Nemine discrepante,*" *Giornali,* September 17, 1725. In April 1729, two votes were cast against Sarnelli's being accepted.
133. "Let us husband our time, in order to spend it in prayer…also in study because this too is absolutely necessary," Alphonsus to Fathers and Brothers, August 8, 1754; *cf.* Alphonsus to a young Father, 1755: "I would ask that for the future you devote at least half an hour daily to the study of Moral Theology, when you are not occupied with missions." For the weekly seminars held in each Redemptorist house, *vid.* Founding Texts, pp 96ff.
134. *Regola,* 1777, p 11. By 1773 there were 248. They were consistent through the century in their use of "*Fratelli*"; *vid.* Tannoia, *Vita,* I, x, p 33; xi, p 36; xv, p 56; xix, p 69; II, ii, p 85, for Alphonsus' acknowledgments of "the Brothers of this illustrious Congregation."
135. In Alphonsus' time the Confraternity at San Giovanni in Porta, founded in 1568, was a proselytizing center for the practice of frequent Communion.
136. There is an intelligent piety manifest in each paragraph of this first homily. Frederick Jones was, in my judgment, rather too quick to say "there is nothing remarkable about the sermon," *op. cit.*, p 53, and "a typical first effort from a deacon." Not many among contemporary preachers, even cardinal deacons, could work so well within the complex of scriptural, liturgical, doctrinal, and ascetical ideas that Alphonsus sets up.
137. Tannoia, *Vita,* I, xi, p 36.
138. Tellería, R., S.H., VIII, *art. cit.*, p 424.
139. Alphonsus to Luigi Capuana, September 7, 1773.
140. Tannoia, *Vita,* xvii, p 63, refers anonymizingly to "*una Religiosa di santa vita.*"
141. Tellería, R., S.H., VIII, *art. cit.*, p 431.
142. Tannoia, *Vita,* I, xvi, pp 59ff.
143. *Ibid.*, p 61; the order was voiced in Iorio's sermon "*ad fratres,*" March 3, 1732, and again at the end of the weekly seminar, March 10.
144. Tellería, R., S.H., VIII, *art. cit.*, pp 433f.
145. Orlandi, G., *Lateranum* 55, *art. cit.* and Zazzera, S., "*La confraternite dell' Isola di Procida, profili Etico-Religiosi, Economici, Sociali,*" in *Archiv. Stor. per le Province Napoletane,* III, 1993, pp 447–473.
146. Though not, I discovered during a pilgrimage, lasting into our own time. An old wall-notice, however, showed that someone once had been happy to boast Alphonsus' presence.
147. Orlandi, G., *Lateranum* 55, *art. cit.*, p 2, note 4.
148. *Ibid.*, p 25.
149. *Ibid.*, p 7, note 17.
150. *Considerazioni,* X.
151. *Cf. Glorie di Maria,* V; *Glories of Mary,* p 523.
152. The Jesuit refounding is described by Parascandola, M., *Cenni storici intorno alla citta ed isola di Procida,* Naples, 1892, p 108. *Cf.* Zazzera, S., *art. cit.*, pp 461ff.

153. Orlandi, G., *Lateranum* 55, *art. cit.*, p 28.
154. *Ibid.*, p 34.
155. *Ibid.*, p 35. Perhaps these "water sports" were the nearest thing the islanders had to those "plays and worldly amusements" that were forbidden to members of mainland Confraternities. *Breve Istruzione,* VIII.2.
156. "*De Apostolatu SPN Alphonsi in isola Prochyta olim exercito,*" *Analecta CSSR* XI, January 1932, pp 41ff.
157. *Ibid.*, p 41.
158. *Breve Istruzione degli Exercizi di Missione,* 1760, VIII.2.
159. *Riflessioni devote,* 1773, VII.
160. Alphonsus once told Tannoia that any good he had done as a boy had been because of his mother. Tannoia had not caught the reference to Wisdom 7:11. In the Procida confraternity, they'd all have appreciated what he was saying about their Mother and how "all good things come to me with her." *Vita,* I, ii, p 7.
161. *Glorie di Maria,* Pte. I.l.2; *Glories of Mary,* p 48 with reference to Saint Gertrude's *Legatus divinae pietatis,* IV.3. Alphonsus, keeping an interest in the Procida confraternity made the welfare of these men a charge on all his people in the Congregation, *cf.* Falcoia to Alphonsus, January 24, 1734, *Lettere* No. 77.
162. *Analecta CSSR,* XI, p 44.
163. *Egr.* the Congregation of Nobles; Tannoia, *Vita,* II, lii, p 313; the Congregation of Gentlemen, *ibid.*, II, xii, p 127, III, xiv, p 66 and xviii, p 79; the Congregation of Artisans, *ibid.*, II, xxvii, p 187; the Congregation of Workers, *ibid.*, II, lii, p 313; the Congregations of Girls, *ibid.*, II, xii, p 127, III, xiv, p 66, and xvii, p 79. It became a regular feature of the Return Mission that the leader of the missioners should preach a sermon on keeping the Rule of the Confraternity which had been established on the previous visit, *ibid.*, II, ii, p 311.
164. Tannoia, *Vita,* III, xxiv, p 119. The Talia Confraternity was attached to another of Saint Francis of Assisi in Rome.
165. Tannoia, *Vita,* III, xvii, p 79.
166. Tannoia, *Vita,* III, xiv, pp 66f. *Vid.* Alphonsus to Francesco Filippo, Archpriest of Frasso, January 15, 19, 22, and 29, 1763.
167. *Cf.* Sarnelli on "Congregations of the Secret," in which the more fervent men, "eager to reach perfection" attend these holy meetings "not from any hope of worldly benefit" but simply to serve God, "and become saints." *Il Mondo Riformato,* III.
168. Alphonsus to Francesco Filippo, January 22, 1763.
169. *Esercizi di Missioni,* VIII.ll.
170. Propaganda enjoyed a wide use of "Brother" in correspondence and conversation between members, *cf.* Tannoia, Vita, I, x, p 33, xi, p 36; II, ii, pp 85 and 86, and iii, p 87, *et al. pl.*
171. *Ibid.*, I, xx, pp 74f.
172. *Ibid.*, II, iii, p 87.

173. *Ibid.*
174. Torno to Alphonsus, October 20 (or December?), 1732, Tannoia, *Vita,* II, ii, p 86.
175. The Apostolic Missioners expected Alphonsus to assist them with their mission work when they should have need of him. In May 1737, he was part of their team at Panecocolo. In November that year he was honored with the appointment to the Great Preaching in the city-wide mission, *vid.* Michele Menga to Alphonsus, August 16, 1736. Tellería, R., S.H., VIII, *art. cit.*, p 440.
176. Berthe, A., I, pp 319f; English trans. I, p 296. But at least one section of Alphonsus' 1748 *Annotations to Busenbaum* was not so well received. Dealing with sinful seminarians, Alphonsus' remarks were thought by Jorio to be laxist. Pope Benedict XIV had interested him in this churchwide problem and Alphonsus, on looking more closely, decided that Jorio had the right of the matter and retracted his opinion, thereby gaining a pleasant note in the Pope's own treatise *De synodo diocesana. Vid* Alphonsus, *Medulla Theologia Moralis,* I, *De Sacramentis in genere,* Jorio, *Catechista di Villa,* V, 2nd ed. Naples, 1762, pp 480–481, and Benedict XIV, *op. cit.*, 1755, XI, 1. para 17.
177. Berthe, II, p 233; English trans. II, p 223.
178. Jones, F., *op. cit.*, pp 256–259.
179. *Cf.* his recommending Gaetano de Bergamo's *L'uomo apostolico al pulpito* in *Istruzioni ai Predicatori,* 1.34 and *Selva,* III, and *Esercizi di Missione, VII.*
180. *Vid.* the praise of old Gizzio's preaching as "*all' apostolica e senza belletti,*" *Esercizi di Missione,* I.37.
181. Alphonsus to Sersale, June 18, 1754.
182. *Supplex libellus,* early 1748; *Founding Texts,* pp 240 ff. Alphonsus never surrendered his membership of the Propaganda brotherhood. After 1779, he was the longest registered Brother and was so listed on each year's kalendarium until his death.

Part 3: Seven Brothers

1. *Commentaria de vita D Alphonsi et de rebus Cong. SS.R. futuro ejusdem Congnis Annalium scriptori diligenter praeparata a P. Frederico Kuntz C.SS.R.*, in XXI Folio ledgers, hereinafter Kuntz, XII, 1788–1791, p 233.
2. Tannoia, *Vita,* II, iv, p 89, viii, pp 109 and 111, and ix, p 115; for officials' references to Alphonsus "*co' suoi compagni,*" *vid. ibid.*, II, xxvii, p 191, and xxxvii, pp 239 and 240.
3. Sposato, P., *Aspetti e figure della Riforma Cattolico-Tridentino in Calabria,* Naples, n.d., pp 59ff.
4. Tannoia, *Breve memoria del Padre D. Angelo Latessa,* p 80; *Companions,* pp 182f.
5. Alphonsus to Spinelli, April 1748, with petitions of Casimiro Rossi, archbishop of Salerno, November 5, 1748, and Innocenzo Sanseverino, 1723–1793(?), bishop of Montemarano, December 3, 1748; *Founding Texts,* pp 262ff and 266.

6. Alphonsus to Ercole, November 12, 1762, telling the recently widowered brother to "send away the young house-maids" since "the devil always remains the devil" and "with that proximate occasion and deprived of all surveillance, I myself would fear lest I should fall." For "Ciomma" and her inheritance, *vid.* Tellería, R., S.H., XIII, *art. cit.*, p 356.
7. For Alphonsus' coming to the defense of his "*servidore,*" Tannoia, *Vita,* I, iv, p 5.
8. Alphonsus to Castelli, October 24, 1774, treating of "*camerieri,*" "*servitori,*" "*cavalli,*" and other *gente di servizio.*"
9. *Theologia Moralis, Lib.* III, *Tract.* III, *cap.* ii, *dub.* iv, "On the Obligations of Masters and Servants, Gaude, 342ff.
10. Estius, *Commentarii,* "in Epistolam ad Philemon," 16–19 with the explanation that the Apostle is talking of a man "in better condition than that of servility, as, indeed, a most loved brother."
11. Estius, *ibid.*, at verse 11.
12. Alphonsus to Tannoia, July 10, 1771.
13. Estius, *Commentarii,* at Philemon 16.
14. Alphonsus to Gaspare Caione, May 30, 1758.
15. Alphonsus to Giuseppe Muscari, October 16, 1751.
16. Alphonsus to Fathers and Brothers, November 1751.
17. Estius, *ibid.*, at Philemon 17, leading "*si ergo habes me socium*" into "*filius et frater Pauli.*"
18. Estius, "*in Epistolam Philemon,*" *Summarium* 1. Timothy is there said to be "*frater honoris causa*" because he is "*socius*" in missionary preaching, though Paul usually calls him "*filius.*"
19. Tannoia, *Vita,* II, lxi, p 357.
20. Kuntz, XIII, p 233.
21. *Vid.* "*puer*" in Vulgate Mt 8:5 and 12:18, Lk 7:7, *et al. pl.* In a postscript to his 1773 circular, added in his own hand at the bottom of the copy sent to the Ciorani house, insisting on the restoration of charity between Fathers and Brothers, Alphonsus orders a penance for any Father who talks of Brothers as "*garzonagli,*" "waiters," "footmen," "errand boys": *vid.* reedited text of the copy of the circular addressed to "my most beloved Brother, the Brothers of the house of the Most Holy Redeemer at Ciorani; Sampers, A., "*32 Epistulae S. Alfonsi indeditae scriptae tempore sui episcopatus, ann. 1762–1775,* S.H., IX, 1961, pp 348–349. *Cf.* the autobiography of Antonio Lauro, Kuntz, VI, p 463, who, on his arrival in 1746 was given a month's trial as "*garzone*" by Rossi and then received among the Brothers, formally shaking hands with each on one coming into their "*compagno,*" *ibid.*, pp 465f. Cafaro at d'Iliceto in 1747 made an equally clear distinction between "*Fratelli*" and the "*Garzoni*" who ran errands between house and town; Cafaro to Alphonsus, July 9, 1747, *Epistolae,* No. 9.
22. Estius, *ibid.*, at Philemon 15.

23. The Vulgate did not assist him in making this distinction, *vid.*, e.g., Deuteronomy 12.12, "*servus et famula.*"
24. *Theologia Moralis, Lib.* III, *Tract.* III, *cap.* ii, *dub.* iv, *Resp.* I.2.l, Gaude, 342.
25. *Ibid., Tract.* V, *cap.* iii, *dub.* xl, Gaude, 864.
26. Tannoia, *Vita,* III, xli, p 210.
27. Only by belief in a Supreme Judge, Alphonsus assured the Princes in his *Fidelity of Vassals,* can "submission to the sovereign" and "peace in the family" be conserved. *Cap.* I.l.
28. Tannoia, *Vita,* IV, x, pp 46ff. The pamphlet was quickly translated into French, with copies on the Seine-bank bookstalls in 1778.
29. "How greatly do those vassals esteem themselves honored to whom the king assigns an abode in his own residence!" *Visits,* III. If Alphonsus were thinking of the courtiers brought from their estates to live at Versailles, there must be a touch of irony in this account of their delight.
30. *Theologia Moralis, Lib.* III, *Tract.* III, *cap.* ii, *dub.* iv, *Resp.* II: "*famuli*" owe masters their love, reverence, and obedience, in the same way as children to parents," "*filii parentibus.*" Aquinas, *Summa Th.,* 2.2., 103, 3 and 4; Valerie Raynauld, S.J., 1543–1623, *Praxis fori poenitentialis,* 1616, *Lib.* 20, n. 59.
31. *Nova Scientia,* 1744, II.552; English trans. Bergin, T. G., and Fisch, N. H., Cornell, 1984. *cf. ibid.*, 257.
32. *Ibid.*, 555.
33. "*Nam servitus omnis hac vita finitur, at fraternitas christiana manet in aeternum*"; Estius, *Comm.* at Philemon 15.
34. *Theologia Moralis, ibid,* Gaude, 342, even though Estius was lauded by Benedict XIV as "*Doctor fundatissimus,*" "the really solid teacher."
35. Estius, at Philemon 16.
36. Ripa, Matteo, *Storia della Fondazione della Congregazione e del Collegio del Cinesi sotto il titolo della Sagra Familia di G. C.,* Naples, 1832, I, pp 9ff and 15ff.
37. Vico, *Vita...da lui stesso descritta,* Pt. A, 1725; English trans. Fisch, M. H., and Bergin, T. G., 1944, p 157. *Cf.* Zoli, S., *La Cina e l'eta dell'Illuminismo in Italia,* Bologna, 1974, and Daffina, P., "*La Cina nel giudizio di G. B. Vico,*" in *La Cina,* Rome, 1958, III, pp 39–51.
38. Ripa, *Storia,* I, p 21. De Vincentus, Gherardo, *Documenti e titoli sul privato fondatore dell' attuale R. Istituto Matteo Ripa,* Naples, 1904, and Kuo, J. M., *Elenchus alumnorum,* Chang-hai, 1917.
39. Ripa, *ibid.*, pp 23–104. The pair of them had been quite unprovided for life in Rome, for neither had told their family of their departure. They would have been wandering the streets if Torres had not warned another Neapolitan of their coming. Antonio Sanfelice found them cheap bed and board at a church hostel. But even this cost more than they could afford. They had to be rescued from starvation by several good persons, including the Pope, clubbing together to pay their monthly rent.

The young men were eager for China. They tried to hurry the Curia along by going on a pilgrimage to Loreto. There was a sign of unhappy things to come when the weakened Amodei fell dangerously ill during this little journey. And on their return, most disappointingly, Ripa was informed that the Pope had decided they should go back to Naples and wait until he found a more convenient time to consider their proposal. Amodei went home to recover his health. But Ripa stayed and gained some good opinions in Rome by preaching a mission in a poor suburb.

On Amodei's return, in October 1707, they again pestered the Curia to license their mission. This was the convenient time. The Pope wished to signal approval for his legate in China, Tommaso de Tournan, 1662(?)–1710, and needed someone to carry the red berretta to his new cardinal. Since no one else wanted to go, the young Neapolitans would be commissioned as papal envoys. They would, having delivered the berretta, remain to convert the Chinese people. It was not considered a hindrance that they had so far received no training for this China mission.

40. Ripa, *Storia,* I, p 120.

41. The Neapolitans were graciously received at the tolerant court of K'ang Hi, and Ripa made himself as agreeable an expert on the curiosities of European art as he had been on Chinese art in Naples. But he could not find, as he tried the tastes of ananas and coconut and made further drawings of exotic fish, enough opportunities to talk convertingly of Christ. Even his identifying the large-leafed jaqua as the fig of Eden did not provoke a rush of inquiries about Original Sin. And any of the Chinese who had been persuaded to give some serious attention to Christian doctrine cannot have been much impressed when Ripa and Amodei got themselves caught up in that disedifying quarrel of Franciscans and Jesuits about "Chinese Rites." But it was this flailing controversy among the Europeans about right attitudes to Chinese culture that finally showed Ripa the personal shape his service should take in the Church.

The happy success of Matteo Ricci, the first Jesuit superior in China, in gaining converts to Christianity had been achieved by some civilized acceptance of Chinese social customs, particularly the familial respect they entertained towards their ancestors and the civil tradition of respect for Confucius, and by the Jesuits' equally delicate regard for the usual Chinese language for the things of Heaven. But an edict of the Holy Office in the early years of the eighteenth century censured such civility as profane accommodation with paganism. Legate Tournon had been especially sent to ensure that all China missionaries obeyed the new Roman law. Retaliatingly, the Chinese authorities expelled him, and on his being bundled unceremoniously into Macao, he was imprisoned by the Portuguese. Tournon died, June 8, 1710, without ever receiving that red berretta which Ripa had carried half way round the world.

Ibid. I, p 128, and *Matteo Ripa Giornale 1705–1724.* ed. Fatica, N., Inst. Univ. Orientale, *Collana Matteo Ripa,* IX, 1991, vol. II, 1705–1711.

42. Ripa, *Storia,* II, pp 198ff.
43. His College gained so good a reputation so quickly that the polyglot Cardinal Giuseppe Mezzofanti signed up for a course in 1732. The Hapsburgs, envious of Portuguese and English influences in the Orient, learning that the Duc de Richlieu was offering Ripa a house in Paris for his College, granted him imperial patronage. The Hapsburgs sudden departure from Naples and the arrival of the Bourbons so far from adversely affecting Ripa's fortunes was the occasion for a more generous support. Carlo III celebrated the College as "a jewel of our Christianity, which only the King of Naples possesses in his Royal City."
44. Ripa, *Storia,* III, p 7. The evidence for Alphonsus' being a *Convittore* at the College is given weight by Brother Leonardo Cicchetti's testimony at the 1806 Process, *super* 267, *ar. Proc.* f. 891. *Cf.* Tannoia, *Vita,* IV, xl, p 215.
45. *Lettera...sopra l'abuso di maledire i morti,* 1746; Tannoia, *Vita,* II, xxxviii, pp 247f. *Vid.* Sampers, A., "*Controversia quam S. Alphonsus sustinuit ann. 1746–48, 'De maledictione mortuorum,'*" S.H., XIV, 1966, pp 3–47.
46. Tannoia, *Vita,* IV, xxix, pp 147ff.
47. *Vid.* for Colleges at Arienzo, Alphonsus' triennium report to Pope Pius VI, April 1775, and Tannoia, *Vita,* III, xvii, p 79, at Avella, *Vita,* IV, xlii, p 228, at Frasso, Alphonsus to Francesco di Filippo, January 15, 1763, at d'Iliceto, *Vita,* IV, xl, p 216.
48. Sportelli to Alphonsus, August 6, 1739; Cafaro to Celestino de Robertis, October 17, 1752; Tannoia, *Notizie della Vita del S. D. Domenico Blasucci,* p 7.
49. Ripa, *Storia,* III, p 8; Tannoia, *Vita,* I, xv, p 53.
50. Ripa, *Storia,* III, p 6.
51. *Ibid.,* p 9.
52. In April 1734, Ripa, who was about to leave Naples for Rome to badger the Curia again, had given Brother Giuseppe permission to go to Procida. His family had a vineyard on the island, and he was to sell the wine to support his mother. Just as Ripa was setting out, he was handed a confused message that Giuseppe had been taken prisoner of war by the Spaniards and was about to be shipped off to Oran on the African coast. It turned out later that Giuseppe had not sold his wine on Procida but, in hopes of getting a better price, had sailed off with his barrels to the Papal States. Knowing that he was doing all this without Ripa's permission, Giuseppe had changed out of his habit, putting on seaman's clothes. The boat, most unhappily, had encountered a Spanish frigate and on the discovery that they were sailing under an Imperial passport, captain, crew, and Brother were all clapped in irons. The seaman-clad Brother's protests that he was a religious were ignored. "Thus he lost both wine and liberty." Still, Ripa observed, when he retold the story of Giuseppe's

adventure, the Lord wished to help this scapegrace Brother. A magistrate's sympathy had been engaged, the boat carrying Giuseppe to Africa was delayed by a contrary wind so that it might be overhauled, and, more dead than alive, on May 9, he was returned to the college. There, after some penance, he was reinvested with the Brother's habit, and Ripa could start for Rome. *Ibid.*, III, pp 10ff.

53. Alphonsus had never signed on as a full member of the College. It seemed to him that he could take his own time about packing. He left in November. "He remained," Ripa wrote generously, "as an example and a model to all, eager only to serve the Church as Preacher and Confessor, following this ministry with great zeal." *Storia,* III, p 14. Reciprocally, Alphonsus, thirty years after Ripa's death in 1746, described him as "a man chosen by God for a great design," whose labors "by the grace of God had brought about the multitude of conversions." Letter to Chinese Collegers, May 24, 1777.
54. Ripa, *Storia,* p 12. The Chinese College survived Falcoia's poachings. Through the century, the papacy authorized student numbers to be increased from 8 in 1747 to 20 in 1760 to 28 in 1764. Numbers fell off rather in the nineteenth century, from 1871 to 1888, when the College was suppressed, there were only 17 students in all, of whom the last, Simone Wang, died in 1943.
55. Ripa, *Storia,* III, 11.
56. Estius, *Comment., Epist. I ad Timotheum,* citing Ignatius, *Epistola ad Trallianos,* and *Epist. ad Philipenses* at 1.1.
57. *Complesso;* Founding Texts, pp 80 and 84.
58. The "deacon" language survived, probably, in the 1747 *Ristretto* and, certainly, in the 1748 transcription of Cassali, and into the discussions towards the 1749 Brief, *ad Pastoralis Dignitatis; Founding Texts,* pp 241, 282, 315.
59. Pontifical Rule, Pt. II, chapter l.l. ix; *Founding Texts,* p 304.
60. *Ibid.*

Vito Curzio

1. Tannoia, *Vita,* I, xxi, p 78. *Brevi notizie della Vita e Morte di Fr Vito Curzio,* 1752, as an appendage to Alphonsus' *Life* of Sarnelli; English trans. Grimm, *Miscellany,* p 278. *Cf.* testimony of Domenico Corsano, 1716–1801, at 1796 Positio hearings. Vito was a notorious local name, reminding the citizens of the late fifteenth century Vito de Utietta, "the well-known super-grass," Raffaele Colapietra, "*Abruzzo e Puglia nell'Orizzonte Feudale degli Acquaviva tra Quattro e Cinquecento,*" *Arch. Storico per le Province Napoletane,* CXI, 1993, pp 33–88.
2. Acquaviva was held as a feudal fief by the Baron del Balzo, Alphonsus' brother-in-law, another of the Orsini clan. The cathedral, begun in the twelfth century, had not had a resident bishop since the beginning of the seventeenth century. *Cf.* Chirulli, I, *Istoria cronologica della Franca Martina cogli avvenimenti*

piu notabili del Regno di Napoli, Naples, 1749, 1980 reprint, p 82, and Palma, N., *Storia ecclesiastica e civile della regione piu settentrionale del regno di Napoli*, 1891, II, p 195.

3. Kuntz, II, 1741–1745, p 382, and, for Sportelli's remembrance of the pistol-packer, *ibid.*, p 437.
4. Jones, F., *op. cit.*, p 112.
5. Gregorio, O., *Sulle orme di S. Gerardo*, Materdomini, 1948, p 20, and Angelomichele De Spirito, "*Maria Francesca Gallo, Alphonsus de Liguori e il 'gran mimero' di bizzoche*," *Campania Sacra* 22, 1991, pp 395–440; *vid.* also the notice of Cesare's mother, Kuntz, II, p 383.
6. Kuntz, *ibid.*
7. Tannoia, *Gerardo*, p 126; *Companions*, p 405. Landi, *Vita* of Sportelli, p 198. *Cf.* for other fellows of that sort, Tannoia, *Vita*, II, xxxiii, p 220, and xxxvii, p 239, and Tannoia's notes on de Meo, *Companions*, pp 20ff.
8. Kuntz, II, p 382; Tannoia, *Vita*, I, xx, p 78.
9. Tannoia, *Vita*, I, xxi, p 78, where Vito is said to be "*Vicemarchese*" for island affairs, and Alphonsus, *Brevi Notizie, Miscellany*, p 279, for Vito as "Erario del Sig. Marchese."
10. Tannoia, *Vita*, I, xxi, p 79.
11. Kuntz, II, p 383.
12. *Ibid.*
13. Vito must have told the story of his dream time and again in various community rooms, Alphonsus and Tannoia both retell it, in slightly varying versions: *Brevi notizie, Miscellany*, p 485, and *Vita*, I, xxi, p 78.
14. *Brevi notizie*, Miscellany, p 280.
15. Tannoia, *Vita*, I, xxi, p 79.
16. *Brevi notizie, Miscellany*, p 280.
17. For a lively recollection of Vito and his holiness, *vid.* anon. *Trattato del divino segreto*, Naples, 1759, p 384.
18. They were always on Christian name terms; Tannoia, *Vita*, I, xxi, p 78, Alphonsus, *Brevi notizie, Miscellany*, p 278, and Kuntz, II, p 9, where Vito is "*semper Falcoiae comes sanctus*," with all the knightly cavalcade resonances of "*comes*," the "squire."
19. Jones, F., *op. cit.*, between pp 52 and 53 for an illustration of Vito's scratched heraldry, August 27, 1738.
20. Tennyson, *Idylls of the King*, "Gareth and Lynette," lines 541ff.
21. The kind Curzio, in both the Landi and Rospigliosi and the Pasquini tellings of the story, brings Alessio, in his beggar-man disguise, back to his parents' home.
22. "*Fratello*" or "*servitore*"; Falcoia to Alphonsus, July 9, 1742, *Lettere*, No. 225.
23. Tannoia, *Vita*, II, lxii, p 365.
24. *Ibid.*, i, p 83.

25. *Ibid.*, II, v, pp 93f, vi, pp 96f, for Neapolitan "derisions"; *cf.* evidences of Corsano and Deodato Criscuoli, 1738–1804, 1706 Positio hearings, pp 113 and 116, for a Congregation tradition of "Vito alone."
26. Tannoia, *Vita,* II, vi, p 96.
27. *Complesso; Founding Texts,* pp 75ff, Constitution I, 2, p 84. Falcoia to Alphonsus, July 24, 1733, *Lettere,* No. 69.
28. *Complesso; Founding Texts,* p 90. Constitution VIII.2.
29. Montealegre Memorial; *Founding Texts,* pp 70ff.
30. *Brevi notizie, Miscellany,* p 281.
31. Falcoia to Vito, March 23, 1737, *Lettere,* No. 149.
32. *Ibid.*
33. *Brevi notizie, Miscellany,* p 281.
34. Vito to Alphonsus, January 29, 1741, *Lettere* No. 215.
35. *Brevi notizie, Miscellany,* p 282, and Joshua 9:21.
36. *Ibid.*, p 285.
37. *Ibid.*, p 282.
38. *Ibid.*, p 283. If that Father had, all unselfaware, reported the Brother's sharpness, there would seem to be an attractive wink to his reader in Alphonsus' presenting this reply as an instance of the Christian character of Vito's conversations. Or, maybe, Alphonsus was himself the inconsiderate priest and was, in recording the incident, acknowledging at least one justified occasion for Vito's quick bite.
39. *Ibid.*, p 284.
40. *Ibid.*
41. *Ibid.*
42. Alphonsus to Fathers and Brothers, July 27, 1752.
43. Alphonsus to Fathers and Brothers, August 27, 1765.
44. Alphonsus to Fathers and Brothers, June 14, 1773.
45. Alphonsus to Tannoia, January 13, 1756; the editors of *Op. asc.* have not been able to locate the source of this exclamation. Nor have I.
46. Tannoia, *Vita,* II, lxi, pp 350f and 357.
47. Alphonsus to Don Giuseppe, March 28, 1743(?). He may be recommending the bulky anonymous collection of miracle stories published at Naples in 1690 on the saint's canonization. It was rumored that the cardinal archbishop, on perusing these stories, had remarked, "I've never heard the like," "*non est auditum tale.*"
48. Tannoia, *Vita,* I, xiii, p 46 and xiv, p 47.
49. *Vera Sposa,* II. xxii; Grimm, II, p 650.
50. *Trattato del divino segreto,* p 385.
51. *Ibid.,* The Alcantarine friars held the same opinion of Paschal's eucharistic theology, thinking that in controversy with heretics "he easily rebutted their sophistries with strong and lucid answers by that infused knowledge he had

of theological matters"; Louis-Antoine de Porrentry, *Pascal Baylon, Patron des Oeuvres Eucharistiques,* Paris, 1899; English trans. Staniforth, O., *The Saint of the Eucharist,* 1908, p 111.

52. Falcoia to Vito, May 12, 1737, *Lettere,* No. 150.
53. Vito to Falcoia, in de Meulemeester, M., *Origines de la Cong. du T. S. Redempteur,* Louvain, 1953, vol. 1, pp 310f.
54. *Ibid.*
55. S Vito appears, with SS Modestus and Crescentia, in the *Hieronymianum, vid.* Delehaye, p 320; Thiele, K., *Die Reichsabtei Corvey,* 1928, and Kunstle, *Ikonographiae,* II, pp 469–472.
56. Bernardo Pasquini, 1637–1710, enjoyed the patronage of Cardinals Ottoboni and Pamphili and of Queen Christina in Rome, and with Corelli, Alessandro Scarlatti, and Handel, dominated curial musical entertainments in the early eighteenth century. Most of his vocal and theatrical compositions are lost, but the 1687 *Il Martirio dei Santi* seems from the evidence of the libretto of Francesco Contini, to have been his usual mix of comic and serious scenes.
57. Vito added a postscript to a letter from Falcoia to tell his friend that that fine convent poetess Maria Rosa Giannini had recently died in Sicily, "and is already enjoying eternity," *Lettere,* No. 416.
58. de Porrentry, *op. cit.,* English trans., p 71.
59. "God wills perhaps that a Brother should be sanctified like a S. Paschal, a Student like a S. Aloysius, a missioner like S. Francis Regis." Tannoia, *Vita,* II, lxi, p 357.
60. Sportelli to Maria Anna Josepha, July 17 and August 21, 1739, to Falcoia, July 24, 1740, to Rosa Ferraiolo, October 25, 1745, and February 27, 1746, to Barbara Buonincontro, October 20, 1747, to Andrea de Filippi, June 18, 1748; *Epistolae,* Nos. 15, 20, 23, 99, 114, 101, and 115.
61. Tannoia, *Gerardo; Companions,* p 239. He could take it for granted that "the lay Brothers of our Congregation" should be "uniting the activity of Martha to the contemplation of Mary."
62. In just the way that Domenico Blasucci, 1732–1752, was enjoying the freedom of a Student of God when he chose adult missioner saints to place alongside the Jesuit youngsters proposed for Student devotion by Alphonsus. *Vid. Posizioni e Articoli per i processi ordinarii su la fama di santita, delle virtu, e dei miracoli del Servo di Dio Domenico Blasucci,* Rome, 1893, presented by Claudio Benedetti, *art.* 44, *Carita.*
63. *Complesso; Founding Texts,* p 88. Constitution V.
64. Toscano, Isodoro, *Vita di S. Francesco di Paola,* Venice, 1691; Perimezzi, G. M., *Della Vita, virtu, miracoli...di S. Francesco di Paola,* Milan, 1712, and Naples, 1713; Misasi, N., *La mente e il cuore di san Francesco,* Lanciano, 1907; Roberti, G. M., *San Francesco di Paola, Storia della sua vita,* Rome, 1915 and 1963; Capooni, F., *S. Francesco di Paola,* 1953; *S. Francesco di Paola, Chiesa e Societa*

del Suo Tempo, Papers from Congress of *Studio Paola,* March 20–24, 1983, Rome, 1984.

65. *Regola* of the Minims, 1493, 1501, 1502, and 1506, especially *Reg.* 1501, *cap.* 5 and *Reg.* 1506, *cap.* 5.
66. Toscano, *Vita,* IV.3; Perrimezzi, *Vita,* V. 1; Alphonsus cites this cry at *Pratica di amar,* Intro. I.i; *Practice of Love,* p 269.
67. *Reg.* 1506, *cap.* 5.
68. Gertrude was not a typical Helfta nun since she appears, when first entering the convent as a five-year-old, to have been a poor orphan, not a girl from a grand local family like her friend Mechtild of Hackeborn, 1242–1299. Both had received the exceptional liberal education instituted by the Abbess Gertrude, Mechtild's elder sister, so they both were able to get their meditations into written, Latin, form. Gertrude wrote down the *Messenger of Divine Duty, Legatus divinae pietatis,* herself, and was most probably, one of the amanuenses who copied out Mechtild's *Book of This Grace, Liber specialis gratiae.* These Latin texts gave, as their encouraging sisters and confessors very well appreciated, Europe-wide availability to their words. Alphonsus cites Mechtild's *Liber* from the Italian trans., Giorgio Lanspergio, *Libro della spiritual grazia,* Venice, 1710, at *Vera Sposa, XVIII.*2, XXXIV.3, *Via della Salute,* Corp. Christi Med. VIII, *Apparecchio alla morte,* xxxiv.
69. Alphonsus cites *Legatus* from Lanspergio, *La Vita della B. Vergine Gertrude,* Venice, 1606, at *Vera Sposa,* XI.2, XIII.l, XIV.2 (thrice), XV.2; *L'Amore della Anima,* VII.vi; *Breve trattato sulla necessita della preghiera,* III; *Del gran mezzo della preghiera; Pratica di amar,* V; *Considerazioni sopra la Passione,* Intro.; *Riflessioni sulla Passione,* I.2; *Via della Salute,* Corp. Christi med. VIII. Since Sarnelli, *Il Mondo Santificato* has a different quotation again, it would seem that some Gertrude literature was not unreadily available. Vito would likely have had access to Lanspergio's translation.
70. "*Gesu Pastore ed Agnello nel Ssmo Sacramento,*" 1726; MS 050105 SAM 05 317; extracts presented by Gregorio, O., *Osservatore Romano,* January 1, 1960, and Jones, F., *op. cit.*, pp 52f.
71. Lanspergio's *Vita* was reprinted three times at Naples during the seventeenth century until supplanted by the *Vita* of Gasparo Campacci, Venice, 1745. *Legatus divinae pietatis,* ed. Tilman Bredenbach, Cologne, 1563, (reedited by Nicola Canteleu, Venice, 1662), was translated into Italian by Vincenzo Buondi, Venice, 1606. English trans. anon. Poor Clare, *Revelations of St. Gertrude,* London, 1865 and 1870, from which I have taken my quotations.
72. *Revelations,* IV.l, p 73.
73. *Ibid.*
74. *Ibid.,* III.27, p 207, IV.9, p 337, and IV.37, p 409.
75. *Ibid.,* V. 11, p 522.
76. *Ibid.,* V. 12, pp 523f.

77. *Ibid.*, V. 9, pp 518f.
78. *Ibid.*, III.36, p 223.
79. "*In certo modo*," *Breve trattato, Op. Ascet.*, II, p 186; *Del gran mezzo,* III.1.
80. Vito to Falcoia, May 14, 1737.
81. *Via della Salute;* Corpus Christi Meditation VIII.
82. *Brevi notizie; Miscellany,* p 283.
83. *Ibid.*, p 285.
84. *Ibid.*
85. Tannoia, *Vita,* II, xx, pp 162f and Gregorio, O., *Sulle orme di S. Gerardo,* p 23.
86. *Vera Sposa,* XII.4, where Alphonsus cites "*Vita, cap.* V," from Lanspergio's *Vita,* I, *cap.* 5 is very near this. So is *Legatus,* I, *Cap.* 4. He is evidently confident enough to be quoting from memory, as he would in a recreation room conversation, while Vito listened.
87. *Brevi notizie; Miscellany,* p 286.
88. *Ibid.*, p 282.
89. *Ibid.*, p 283.
90. *Ibid.*, p 286.
91. Was this the d'Iliceto priest who proposed bequeathing his whole property to Alphonsus? Tannoia, *Vita,* II, xxxvii, p 237, or was that Vito's dear invalid?
92. *Legatus,* III.liii, cited, *Vera Sposa* XIV.2: "Our Lord appeared one day to Saint Gertrude, who suffered great torture from a fever, and asked her if she wished for better health; she embraced His Heart and said, 'This is what I want; I desire nothing but Your Holy Will.'" *Cf. Brevi notizie, Miscellany,* p 286, and Gregorio, O., *Sulle orme di S. Gerardo,* p 23.
93. *Revelations,* III.26, p 206.
94. *Brevi notizie; Miscellany,* p 286.
95. Tannoia, *Vita,* II, xx, p 163.
96. *Revelations,* V.10, p 521.
97. Tannoia, *Vita,* II, xx, p 163. Tannoia says, *ibid.*, that the Brother's skull was returned to the Congregation on the death of Bishop Amato of Lacedogna, "and is now venerated in the choir of our house at d'Iliceto." However that may be, it seems to have, a second time, slipped out of Redemptorist hands, for a curiously boned skull, revered as the relic of Vito, has this century made a return to the Congregation's custody in two stages, its first being taken into care by Giuseppe Consenti, CSSR, 1834–1907, bishop of Nusco and Lucera, whose family regarded the skull as inheritable property, and then handed back to Provincial Antonio di Masi of Naples by the Vicar General of Otranto, Mons. Giunfrida, December 7, 1998. There is a plan to erect a shrine for the skull at Scala.
98. *Brevi Notizie, Miscellany,* p 284.

Gennaro Rendina

1. Colletta, M. G., *art. cit.*, p 227 and note 36; del Bagno, I., *Legum doctores, La Formazione del Ceto Giuridico a Napoli tra Cinque e Seicento,* Naples, 1933, p 175. There was a convention allowing naturalized Neapolitans, "*cives per fictionem et non per veritatem,*" to graduate, but admission to the College of Doctors was refused to legitimized bastards even of citizens, *ibid.*, p 185.
2. Kuntz, VI, 1757–1763, p 478.
3. Alphonsus to Sportelli, October 1746.
4. Gregorio and Sampers, *Documenti,* S.H., XVI, and "Early Formulations" in *Founding Texts,* p 66.
5. Kuntz, VII, 1763–1767, p 262. Amato was capable of composing a very decent autobiographical sketch, Kuntz, III, 1746–1749, pp 423ff.
6. Alphonsus to Caione, May 16, 1756, and to Villani, September 1, 1769.
7. Kuntz, XV, 1803–1805; Brother Gerardo at Materdomini was generous enough to spend an hour with me, explaining the craftsmanship of Stefano's vesting press in the sacristy, one of the few pieces from the original house to survive the latest earthquake.
8. Falcoia to Alphonsus, January 24, 1734, *Lettere,* No. 77.
9. Strozzi to Alphonsus, March 27, 1733, Kuntz, XII, 1788–1791, pp 115f, and Falcoia to Alphonsus, June 2, 1734, *Lettere,* No. 88.
10. Falcoia to Alphonsus, April 3 and May 8, 1734, *Lettere,* Nos. 83 and 85. Falcoia knew it was difficult enough to get a man ordained who had talent and desire and a little money set aside. Sportelli was kept waiting for years. Only on his friend's becoming a bishop was his case resolved. Falcoia wangled a curial dispensation on his *ad limina* visit to Rome in 1737.
11. Alphonsus to Francesco de Viva, June 7 and July 15, 1734, January 25, 1736.
12. Alphonsus to de Viva, June 7, 1734.
13. Falcoia to Alphonsus, May 8, 1734, *Lettere,* No. 85.
14. Falcoia to Alphonsus, May 22, 1734, *Lettere,* No. 87.
15. Constitutions of Pious Workers, Naples, 1735, No. 116.
16. Falcoia to Alphonsus, May 22, 1734, *Lettere,* No. 87, where this rule against literacy is said to be "indispensable," that is, both necessary and not to be dispensed.
17. Kuntz, II, 1741–1745, p 264.
18. *Lettere,* No. 90.
19. *Ibid.*
20. *Ibid.*
21. *Ibid.*, Falcoia to Alphonsus, June 2, 1734, *Lettere,* No. 88.
22. Meanwhile, Falcoia had forgotten his name, referring to Gennaro as "that young John," July 11, 1734, *Lettere,* No. 91, twice.
23. Falcoia to Sportelli, July 6, 1738, *Lettere,* No. 185; *cf.* Falcoia to Alphonsus, May 22, 1734, *Lettere,* No. 87, where the bishop makes what Gregorio terms "a

poetic allusion" to the Castellammare girls' school and the Scala convent as "the little and large Gardens of Flowers."

24. Falcoia to Alphonsus, June 29, 1736, *Lettere,* No. 134.
25. Francesc' Antonio Romito succeeded to this demanding post about the time that Alphonsus became bishop at Sant' Agata. Romualdo di Cristoforo found being Brother Secretary to Sportelli so tiring that he was much relieved by Sportelli's death in 1749; *cf.* Sportelli to Teodora de Filippi, September 16, 1749, and Kuntz, II, pp 8 and 18f and 334.
26. Alphonsus to Sarnelli, April 3, 1740; *cf. Op. Ascet.*, IX, lv.
27. Alphonsus to Margotta, February 7, 1750.
28. Postscript to letter from Cafaro to Alphonsus, May 1, 1749, *Epistolae,* No. 18.
29. Though he was sometimes sent to be the boiler of cabbages away from home on the mission team; Alphonsus to Margotta, November 19, 1749.
30. When Sportelli and Garzillo went with Brother Gasparo Corvino, 1722–1805, to Ciorani, their kitchen cutlery consisted of only three forks and a knife, and two of the forks had been whittled from a piece of wood by Garzillo. *Vid.* Garzillo *memoire* at Berthe, I, p 313; English trans. I, p 291. The nuns of Solofra kindly swapped blankets, knives, and forks, for that blessed wooden cutlery.
31. Tannoia, *Vita,* III, lvii, p 341 and viii, p 345; *vid.* Falcoia's preliminary Rule draft *Per L'Istituto* 17, in *Analecta CSSR* X, p 106, in which it is proposed that though the kitchen should be spacious and the pots have lids against the cat, everything should be "shining with holy Poverty."
32. Alphonsus to Fathers and Brothers, November 1751. It was found, by experiencing, that if any food were left on his plate, the cat would not eat it, *vid.* Alessio Pollio's testimony at 1806 Process, p 285.
33. Tannoia, *Vita,* II, liii, p 300.
34. *Ibid.*, lix, p 351, and Alphonsus to Margotta, March 7, 1751.
35. Sportelli to Alphonsus, July 20, 1739, *Epistolae,* No. 17.
36. Tannoia, *Vita,* II, lvii, p 342.
37. Sportelli to Mazzini, August 28, 1747, *Epistolae,* No. 144, and Alphonsus to Mazzini, June 25, 1767.
38. For the "perpetual cook" story, *cf.* Baronio's writing "*Caesar Baronius coquus perpetuus*" in smoke-dust over the chimney piece of the Chiesa Nuova kitchen, *vid.* Bacci, *Vita,* English trans. Antrobus, F. I., *Life of Saint Philip Neri,* London 1902, vol. 1, p 89.
39. Kuntz, II, p 264, cited by Raponi, S., in *San Gerardo Tra Spiritualita e Storia, art. cit.*, p 37. Professor Raponi is the best of modern commentators on matters concerning the early Brothers of the Congregation. I am grateful for his sympathetic encouragement in the course of preparing this work.
40. Alphonsus to Margotta, March 7, 1752. This letter is tentatively dated to 1751, but *vid. Analecta CSSR* XIX, pp 253f for a fuller text than in the *Collected Letters* which suggests the later date on account of a reference to Muscari.
41. *Ibid.*

42. *Ibid.*
43. Alphonsus to Caione, December 12, 1754.
44. *Ibid.*
45. Alphonsus to Caione, August 31, 1754.
46. Alphonsus to Caione, July 6(?), 1755(?).
47. Alphonsus to Caione, August 31, 1754.
48. Alphonsus to Caione, September 8, 1754.
49. Alphonsus to Caione, September 21, 1754.
50. Alphonsus to Caione, September 21, 1754.
51. Pietr'Angelo Picone had been a clever boy who got into all sorts of trouble when sent from Manicalzati to Naples university in 1747. His behavior, it had seemed to his elder brother, had not improved after a year back at home, so he brought the unbiddable boy with him in 1752 to make a "retreat" at Ciorani. There he fell in with some cheerfully pious novices, joined them in the novitiate, and proved his Redemptorist credentials by writing to tell his family that they should now "give to God your attachment to me." On his becoming consumptive, there was talk of his being sent home, but he appealed to Alphonsus, and on the Rector Major's authorizing his profession on June 14, 1753, he wrote to Alphonsus rejoicing that "now that I am your child," he could die happy. This he did.
52. Alphonsus to Caione, September 28, 1754, and October 2, 1754.
53. Tannoia, *Gerardo; Companions,* pp 375f.
54. Alphonsus to Caione, June 30, 1755.
55. Tannoia, *Breve memoria del P Angelo Latessa*; *Companions,* p 179.
56. Alphonsus to Caione, January 5, 1757.
57. Tannoia, *Vita,* IV, xxxvii, p 197; at Sant' Agata, Alphonsus employed the services of a lay professional, Constantino Silvio: Tannoia, *Vita,* III, lxxvii, p 417. *Vid.* also the evidence of Pietro Volpicelli at 1806 Process, p 244.
58. He had, as bishop, forbidden his clergy to wear their hair long, *allo nazareno,* Jones, F., *op. cit.*, p 383, and had delayed an ordination while a haircutter was summoned and the candidate's locks lopped, *ibid.*, p 384.
59. Alessio Pollio, testimony at 1806 Process, p 460.
60. *Vid.* for Crescenzio's illness, Sportelli to Falcoia, May 11, June 22, August 5, 1742, *Epistolae,* Nos. 40, 42, 47, and Falcoia to Alphonsus, June 29, 1742, *Lettere,* No. 223. The Brother was soon having to rub himself down.
61. Giovine, Raimondo, *Vita del Gran S. di Dio Gennaro Maria Sarnelli,* vol. II, p 154.
62. Tannoia, *Gerardo; Companions,* p 439.
63. Tannoia, *Vita,* III, xxvi, p 131.
64. *Ibid.*, IV, xxxvii, p 197.
65. *Ibid.*, p 195.
66. Tannoia, *Latessa; Companions,* p 188.
67. Giovine, R., *op. cit.*, II, p 164.

68. *Ibid.*, pp 161 and 164.
69. Alphonsus to Rector of Ciorani(?), June 25, 1753(?), with the curious directive that the doctor at Materdomini be responsible for Nicola's arriving at d'Iliceto.
70. Alphonsus to Caione, December 12, 1758.
71. Alphonsus to Caione, December 12, 1754.
72. *Ibid.*
73. Alphonsus to Caione, January 5, 1757.
74. *Ibid.*
75. Alphonsus to Caione, August 17, 1758.
76. Alphonsus to Caione, September 24, 1758. Matteo D'Ancora, 1735–1824, was later sent to Materdomini.
77. Alphonsus to Tannoia, July 10, 1771.
78. *Ibid.*
79. Kuntz, IX, 1775–1778, p 63 with reference to Landi.
80. Alphonsus to Tannoia, June 5, 1773.
81. *Ibid.*
82. *Ibid.*
83. *Ibid.*
84. Alphonsus to Francesco de Paola, June 14, 1773.
85. *Vid.* editorial note at Alphonsus' letter of June 14, 1773.
86. Alphonsus to Caione, November 6, 1777.
87. There is a niggling doubt concerning who was Rector where in 1777. In 1773, Bartolomeo Corrado, 1733–1797, was appointed Rector at Ciorani; Sampers, A., "*32 Epistolae S. Alfonsi ineditae*," S.H., IX, 1961, p 356, with text of similar letter to Rectors, September 1, 1773. Sampers said that Corrado was succeeded in 1776 by Adeodato Criscuolo, 1738–1804, *art. cit.* continued, S.H., XI, 1963, p 40, note 2, but his alleging Kuntz, X, p 22, must be an uncharacteristic slip, since Kuntz is referring there to 1779 appointments, and at letters of January 14, 1777, and February 3, 1777, the anon. editor says plainly that Criscuoli (sic) was then Rector at Scifelli, and the Act confirming appointments, June 26, 1780, names him Rector at Ciorani. It is possible that Criscuolo (Criscuoli) was appointed to succeed an ailing Corrado in midterm and was then kept on in 1779. It is also possible that, against ordinary use, Corrado remained Rector at Ciorani for another term in 1776; Caione had been reappointed to Materdomini twenty years before, Alphonsus to Caione, September 24, 1758.
88. Alphonsus to Caione, November 6, 1777.
89. *Ibid.*
90. Alphonsus to Caione, November 10, 1777.
91. *Ibid.*
92. *Ibid.*
93. Alphonsus to Caione, November 19, 1777.
94. Alphonsus to Caione, March 1, 1778.

95. Alphonsus to Francesco de Paola, November 24, 1777.
96. Alphonsus to Caione, November 19, 1777.
97. *Cf.* letters of Alphonsus to Caione, December 8, 1779, "I alone will decide whether the cupola shall be taken down," and March 16, 1780.
98. Alphonsus to Stefano Liguori, November 6, 1779.
99. Cimino was expelled in 1780 and became bishop of Oria in 1798; on retiring to Pagani he was accepted as an Oblate of the Congregation.
100. For Alphonsus as architect, *vid.* Marcelli, E., and Raponi, S., *Un Umanista,* ch. 3, "*Anche architetto?*" pp 69–76.
101. Alphonsus to the Fathers at Ciorani, October 1779.
102. Alphonsus to Rector at Ciorani, November 4, 1779.
103. Alphonsus to Stefano Liguori, November 6, 1779. For an echo of these loud debates, *vid.*, Alphonsus to Criscuolo, October 1(?), 1779, in Sampers, A, "*32 Epistolae,*" S.H., XI, pp 40ff.
104. Directive for the Brothers' Retreat and Triduum, *Codex regularum,* p 192, no. 418 and p 194, no. 419.
105. Falcoia to Alphonsus, February 7, 1736, *Lettere,* No. 128, and Kuntz obituary, XII, pp 115f.
106. Kuntz, *Ibid.*

Francesco Tartaglione

1. Falcoia to Alphonsus, July 9, *Lettere,* No. 225; *cf.* Alphonsus to Francesco de Paola, August 12, 1774, where he assumes that there must be "two subjects, a Father and a Brother," for any community to be recognized in the Congregation.
2. Falcoia to Alphonsus, July 9, 1742.
3. Tannoia, *Breve memoria del Fratello Francesco Tartaglione,* in *Vite dei Padri…e die Fratelli Laici,*" Naples, 1812, p 106 (hereinafter Tannoia, *Francesco*); *Companions,* p 495.
4. *Ibid.*
5. *Ibid.*, p 103; *Companions,* p 491.
6. *Ibid.*
7. *Ibid.*
8. *Ibid.*
9. *Ibid.*, pp 103f; *Companions,* p 492.
10. *Ibid.*, p 104; *Companions,* pp 492f.
11. *Ibid.*; *Companions,* p 493. Clearly Ferdinando and Aurelia Tartaglione get so little mention in Tannoia's narrative on account of his suspecting that they would not have given a blessing to their son's Redemptorist vocation. They were paradigm parents. Just the sort of father and mother for a paradigm son.
12. Tannoia, *Francesco,* p 104; *Companions,* p 494.
13. *Ibid.*
14. *Ibid.*, p 105; *Companions,* p 494.
15. *Storia della Congregazione,* I/1, *Cap.* 3; *History,* p 183.

16. *Ibid.*, p 193.
17. Sportelli to Fathers and Brothers, March 24, 1743, *Epistolae,* No 61.
18. Giovine, R., *Sarnelli,* vol. II, "*Gli ultimi quindici giorni,*" p 154.
19. *Storia della Congregazione, Pte. cit.; History,* p 184.
20. Tannoia, *Francesco; Companions,* p 497.
21. He was released from odd-jobbing and habit-making by the arrival of "the young tailor," Nicola Casoria, 1725–1765, the son of a druggist with some knowledge of herbal remedies. He, however, very quickly fell ill at Ciorani, Alphonsus to Rector, June 25, 1753, and got worse at Pagani, Alphonsus to Francesco Giovenale, August 21, 1753. He was the first Brother to die at Agrigento, *vid.* Landi, *Istoria* II.30, and Giammusso, S., "*Atti della Visita Canonica del 1776,*" S.H., V, 1957, pp 339f, note 37.
22. *Codex regularun,* p 321, no. 812.
23. Alphonsus to Sparano, July 17, 1744.
24. Alphonsus to Sparano, August 10, 1744.
25. *Delle Quattro Regole Principali dell' Aritmetica,* 1750(?), ed. Librandi, R., *Brevi Avvertimenti di Grammatica e Aritmetica,* Naples, 1984. Tannoia, *Vita,* II, xxxiv, p 225, and "*L'Aritmetico*" in Marcelli, E., and Raponi, S., *Un Umanista del'700 Italia,* Rome, 1992, pp 157–167.
26. Orlandi, G., *Il Regno di Napoli,* p 78; 5 percent at least, 10 percent perhaps, of the general population of the Two Kingdoms were literate and numerate, 40 percent in Naples itself. *Cf.* Delille, G., *Famille et propriete dans le Royaume de Naples,* Rome and Paris, 1985.
27. For Francesco's general service in the Naples house, *vid.* Kuntz, I, 1735–1741, p 210, and Tellería, R., "*Super Domibus Palatiatis Familiae S. Alfonsi,*" S.H., XIII, 1965, pp 98–147.
28. Villani to Alphonsus, November 15,1748; de Meulemeester, M., *op. cit.,* II, pp 279f.
29. Villani to Alphonsus, November 19, 1748; de Meulemeester, M., *ibid.*, p 281.
30. Berthe, I, p 373; English trans. I, p 349, for something of this sort. Villani to Alphonsus, December 10 and 17, 1748, de Meulemeester, *ibid.* , pp 287f and 289.
31. Villani to Alphonsus, November 19, 1748.
32. *Storia della Congegazione, Pte. cit.*; *History,* p 211. Villani to Alphonsus, November 15 and December 26, 1748, de Meulemeester, *ibid.*, pp 277f and 292. Giuseppe de Rosa was, from 1746 to 1761, parish priest of Nucera-Pagani, and on consulting Alphonsus about a little local difficulty had returned to his presbytery saying, "We have a saint living here"; Tannoia, *Vita,* IV, xlii, p 228. He became bishop of Policastro in 1775 and was one of three bishops to pronounce eulogies in their cathedrals at memorial services for Alphonsus, Tannoia, *ibid.*, xl, pp 216f.
33. Villani to Alphonsus, December 26, 1748. Muscari became a prolific commentator on ecclesiastical administration: *vid.* (i) *Due lettere dell'abate,* Pavia,

1787, to a Tuscan delegate to a national council of ecclesiastical reform and a Naples Canon Lawyer on the proper powers of bishops; (ii) *Lettera consolatoria al vescovo di Pistoia,* Rome, 1788; (iii) *La fede e il cristianismo,* Poleastro, 1790; (iv) *Avvisi prattici a vescovi eletti,* Rome, 1792. Kuntz, III, pp 347, 349, 374, 405; IV, 18 and 149-175, *passim.*

34. de Meulemeester, *op. cit.*, II, p 208.
35. Villani to Alphonsus, January 28, 1749. Alessandro Furietti, the Secretary of the Congregation of the Council, was more interested in Roman mosaics than curial bureaucracy, Tellería, R., *San Alphonso,* I, p 455. Villani may, however, have been referring to Muscari as "the Secretary."
36. Villani to Alphonsus, January 28, 1749, with new prefix. For Villani's view of Gentili, *vid.* letter to Alphonsus printed by de Meulemeester, *op. cit.*, II, pp 285–287. Besozzi had encouraged Villani from the start, *vid.* Villani to Alphonsus, December 6, 1748.
37. Francesco could always pretend to be even more deaf than he had actually become during their exhausting days in Rome; Villani to Alphonsus, December 31, 1748, de Meulemeester, *ibid.*, p 295.
38. The cheese story is kept in circulation by Berthe, I, English trans., p 360. Tannoia, *Vita,* II, xxxi, p 214. Muscari tagged along at this audience.
39. Villani to Alphonsus, December 31, 1748, and February 28, 1749.
40. *Storia della Congegazione, Pte. cit.* ; *History,* pp 218ff.
41. Villani to Alphonsus, February 25, 1749.
42. Alphonsus to Students, July 27, 1758, to Fathers and Brothers, June 27, 1773, and August 8, 1754. His feelings for them were just the feelings he had for any child, *cf.* his horror at the notion of Ercole's elder son's marrying, Alphonsus to Ercole, September 1, 1779.
43. His lasting interest in astronomy is evidenced in his designing an orrery for the d'Iliceto Students; Tannoia, *Vita,* I, iii, p 9.
44. Tannoia, *Vita,* II, xxxv, pp 225f.
45. This was a "*fraterna correzione*" which, in Alphonsus' view, undermined his position as the Father in whom all should confide and who should be possessed of all family information.
46. Tannoia, *Vita,* II, xxxv, p 227.
47. *Ibid.*
48. Falcoia to Alphonsus, July 20, 1734, "and would you abandon those who live in the rest of Africa, in Asia, in America....?" *Lettere,* No. 92.
49. Tannoia, *Vita,* II, xxxv, p 228. *Vid.* Mark 6:8 but also, contrariwise, Matthew 10:10 and Luke 9:3.
50. Tannoia, *Vita,* II, xxxv, p 229.
51. *Ibid.* For another paternal recourse to tears, *vid.* Falcoia to Scala nuns, March 1733(?), *Lettere,* No. 52.
52. Pasquale Caprioli, cited Kuntz, IV, 1749–1752, p 169.

53. Tannoia, *Vita,* II, i, p 82, and most especially, the narrative of Don Giuseppe's antics when Alphonsus announced his intention of getting ordained, *Storia della Congregazione, Pte cit.*; *History,* p 141: "My son," he sobbed, "why are you leaving me, why do you want to abandon me?"
54. Villani to Alphonsus, January 28, 1749.
55. Tannoia, *Vita,* II, xxxv, pp 228 and 229.
56. Alphonsus to Giuseppe Muscari, October 16, 1751.
57. Alphonsus to Fathers and Brothers, November 1751.
58. Alphonsus to Vicar General of Benevento, November 4, 1751. Nicodemo de Angelis' later life in the Congregation proved Alphonsus, this time, a good judge of character. *Vid.* Lorenzo Niro, *Vita d'Antonio Puzzo,* Naples, 1792, for an enthusiastic obituary of de Angelis, who had just died "the death of the just," after five years enduring the effect of a stroke.
59. Kuntz, III, pp 304, 379–384; IV, pp 24 and 172; V, p 85; VI, obituary by Landi, pp 438–441. Spera died of tuberculosis.
60. Kuntz, IV, pp 68f, 125, 172, 226; X, p 403; XIV, p 108.
61. Kuntz, III, pp 304 and 379; IV, pp 18, 24, 167ff, 172. Alphonsus to Tannoia, January 9, 1759.
62. Pasquale Caprioli's narrative, cited by Kuntz, IV, p 169; Kuntz, III, p 235 and IV, pp 17, 167ff, and 172.
63. Caprioli's narrative, Kuntz, IV, p 169.
64. *Breve memoria del Fratello Francesco; Companions,* p 499.
65. *Ibid.*, p 498; Alessandro de Risio, *Croniche della Congegazione del Santissimo Redentore,* I, Palermo, 1858, p 135.
66. Tannoia, *Francesco; Companions,* p 499.
67. *Ibid.*
68. *Ibid.*, "*non scuso il delitto ma compassionado la sorpresa,*" p 498, much elaborated in the Oratorian translation.
69. Alphonsus to Saveno Rossi, May 10, 1752.
70. *Ibid.*
71. *Ibid.*
72. Tannoia, *Francesco; Companions,* p 499.
73. *Ibid.*
74. "*Con ingenuita,*" *ibid.*
75. *Ibid.*, p 500. Paolo Cafaro, on a mission at Morra Irpino was torn in mind about this whole affair and the Fathers' conduct: "I understand the strictness you have used with Brother Francesco," he wrote to Alphonsus, January 16, 1753, "you don't need me to tell you what he should have got, but this time he's been lucky." They must not misunderstand him. "I approve of your Paternity's being strict, and of the others' strictness." But he couldn't be so fierce himself. "I'm so proud and harsh of heart that I frighten myself and lean over backwards with an excess of kindness." Cafaro is certainly not blaming the others who don't get frightened by their own harshness, but he doesn't

quite fit with them. He doesn't think severity a practical policy for a Rector. "Subordinates cannot act like the Rector Major, they must proceed carefully; poor Superiors must be circumspect so as not to upset Fathers and Brothers or there'll be murmurings." *Epistolae,* No. 16.

76. One of the Brothers, at least, was rumored to have taken quite the wrong example from Francesco and the glass-chucking. Had he really given the novice a cuff about the ears? It made Alphonsus tremble just to think of it. There was some relief in the intelligence that "he scarcely touched his head in a playful way." So he was not in Brother Francesco's case. He was not to be stripped of the habit. "But there is no doubt that he has committed a thousand faults." Though it must be supposed that this cuff was the worst of them. This Brother knew what to do next. He took the literate Francesco's example in humility. "The letter he has written to me has consoled me." Alphonsus again ensured that the offender be punished by his Rector. And again ensured that he'd know that it was to the Rector Major he owed his being so leniently punished. So he wrote a letter to the Rector about the punishment he was to administer and included another for the Brother. "Let him read it." Alphonsus to Caione, April 17, 1757.
77. Tannoia, *Francesco; Companions*, p 499.
78. Dumortier, F., *Quelgues Scolastiques de la Congregation du T. S. Redempteur,* Antony (Seine), 1902, p 240.
79. "*Protesta della morte*" printed in *Apparacchio alla morte,* 1758, but already in common Redemptorist use for more than a decade.
80. Tannoia, *Vita,* III, xxxvi, pp 183ff, xlxix, pp 259ff, and Alphonsus to King Ferdinando IV, end of July 1767, to the lawyer Gaetano Celano, August 1767, and to Maione, September 24, 1770, and July 1, 1771.
81. Tannoia, *Francesco; Companions,* p 501.
82. "*Era continuamente chia mato per nome,*" Landi quoted by Kuntz, I, p 212.
83. Tannoia, *Francesco; Companions*, p 496.
84. *Ibid.*, p 495.
85. Alphonsus to the Remondini, October 21, 1773, January 7, 1766, January 31, 1773, June 19, 1773.
86. Alphonsus to the Remondini, June 4, 1761.
87. Alphonsus to the Remondini, June 22, 1766, and April 2, 1768; he told the publisher to send "a large number of copies" to them at Naples, August 1, 1765. *Cf.* Alphonsus to Niccolo Savio, January 7, 1766.
88. Geronimo Ferrara had set up "that arrangement about books in exchange for Masses" which was "working admirably." Francesco had never been trusted to keep the books of this arrangement. *Vid.* Alphonsus to the Remondini, April 28, 1768, and January 31, 1773, and Alphonsus to Margotta, February 7, 1750: "the Masses in payment for these eight or nine books are to be celebrated during the month of February, for if they should be said in May, it would be necessary for you to swap Mass intentions with me, and then I would repay

you in May. It will not be necessary to have 100 Masses said on loan, 72 will be enough. Note well, 72 are enough. Remember: No more. Otherwise I shall find myself in a mess."

89. Alphonsus to the Remondini, November 26, 1769.
90. Alphonsus to the Remondini, beginning of August 1773.
91. Alphonsus to the Remondini, October 7 and November 14, 1773.
92. Tannoia, *Francesco; Companions,* p 496.
93. *Ibid.*
94. *Ibid.*, p 501.
95. *Ibid.*
96. Alphonsus to Ercole, November 26, 1772; *cf.* Tannoia, *Vita,* II, xxxvii, p 237 for Francesco's being recognized as "the Brother of D. Ercole Liguori."
97. Similarly, it was the Brother tailor's fault that Rector Cafaro did not organize winter smallclothes, another Brother seamster's that some Fathers had introduced "pointed caps," and probably Brother Giovanni Torchionne, 1719–1759, who was killed during building works at San Angelo a Cupolo, was at fault in consenting to walk along unsteady scaffolding, *cf.* Alphonsus' *memoire* of Cafaro and Tannoia, *Vita,* II, lix, p 352.
98. Alphonsus to Caione, November 16, 1755.
99. Alphonsus to Sportelli, August 13 and 18, 1742, to Caione, December 25, 1755, and to Ercole, November 23, 1755, "*Epistulae 24 S. Alfonsi Ineditae scriptae annis 1735–1759,*" ed. Sampers, A., S.H., XII, 1964, pp 223-253.
100. Alphonsus to Muscari, May 28, 1749, to the Remondini, June 4, 1761, to Villani, July 15, 1770, to Margotta, August 6, 1753, to Maione, April 23, 1771, to Villani, June 29, 1768, and July 15, 1770.
101. Alphonsus to Villani, June 29, 1768. This was his habitual ejaculation on hearing of another's ill health, *vid.* again, letter of August 22, 1771.
102. Alphonsus to Maione, August 22, 1771.
103. *Ibid.*
104. *Ibid.*
105. Tannoia, *Francesco; Companions,* p 501.
106. *Ibid.*, p 502.
107. *Ibid.* Ercole was perhaps expected to be the organizer of a decent local funeral from the family palazzo, burying Francesco at the Chinese College as he had buried Vincenzo Maria Buonapana, 1743–1764. This student had been sent to stay in the Liguori's Naples house in hopes that he might recover from a chill caught in a Ciorani drenching. Alphonsus to Buonapane, January 28, 1762, and Kuntz, VII, pp 326 and 347f,
108. Kuntz, I, p 214.
109. On his discovering that Francesco had died at his work, Alphonsus at once sent Michele to the Naples station. He was the only Brother available. And he had several times been Alphonsus' messenger to Francesco, so he did at least

know the street where the Brother had rented a lock-up warehouse for the stock of Alphonsus' books.

For a while, Alphonsus persisted in regarding this Brother as a mere stop-gap at Naples. He told Villani so. "As for Brother Michele," he said unpromisingly, "I have written to you, on the word of several of our Fathers, that he does not appear to be the right man to transact our business at Naples." Villani, who had been given responsibility for such administrative matters, did nothing to find a better suited Brother. Alphonsus had, after all no personal knowledge of Michele. Had, perhaps, never met him. He had sent him to do the Naples job on the same principle that he had been putting almost all Brothers into almost all jobs. Any could substitute for any other. But then the Rector Major just happened to be going through the morning packet of letters for the Community and had noticed a letter from Michele to Brother Francesc' Antonio, "his handwriting is better than that of Brother Francesco, that blessed soul of Paradise." Things may not be going so badly after all. "Father Corrado writes to tell me that Michele also knows how to keep accounts." Did Villani know this? "If things are truly so, no change need be made, and the Brother may remain."

The Remondini having been told that the new Brother was not as good at the business as Francesco, whose reputation was now, it seems, rather better than it had been in his lifetime, they might be persuaded to take all that bookselling off the Congregation's hands. Alphonsus thought it best to assume so. "I have again written to the Brother at Naples to make an inventory of all your books without delay. As soon as I receive the list, I shall transmit it to you. I am very glad that you have determined to get in touch with some tradesman in Naples about getting your books sold." This new Brother would be unreliable. He'd not keep their account straight. Michele might be safely accused of some incompetence. He had no reputation to lose. A different notion had to be given of the Fathers. They were just too busy to deal with the book sales. "My Fathers would give you a good report of them." Though it had to be admitted that "when it comes to selling, they would not do better than I." *Vid.* Alphonsus to Villani, April 8, 1774, and to the Remondini, June 30, 1774.

110. Alphonsus to the Remondini, May 22, 1774. It was soon clear that Michele was doing a better job than any Father, Alphonsus included, at selling and buying. He was, also, proving to be a man of more sensitivity than your ordinary shopkeeper's assistant. He recognized a necessity of letting Alphonsus seem to run the business for a while, even while the Rector Major was protesting that he had neither time nor energy for such an enterprise. Michele would do nothing without an instruction. Alphonsus let the Remondini know how satisfactorily things were arranged with this Brother. "Brother Michele has already informed me of his receipt of your letter directing him to send the

books to Signor Moschini. I am now writing to the Brother to tell him to execute this command without further delay." It was no part of the Rector Major's understanding of the chain of "inform," "direct," and "execute," that Brother Michele should mistake himself or be mistaken for an active agent. It was, therefore, a great surprise to him that the Remondini, who had recognized Michele as a hardworker during the changeover period, should want to give the Brother a present. They had written to Alphonsus asking what gift Michele would find agreeable. "Do not, I beseech you, think of making any present to the Brother, especially since he has done so little for you." He had done what he'd done under Alphonsus' orders. "In attending to your affairs, these Brothers have been serving me, for it was I who charged them to be diligent in the selling and preserving of your books." Then he thought of a knock-down argument to use against this present idea. "Our Brothers, being bound by a vow of poverty in the same manner as the Fathers cannot receive gifts." Alphonsus to the Remondini, August 3, 1774.

Gioacchino Gaudiello

1. Andrea was already a little unsettled about his future, *vid.* Falcoia to Sportelli, *Lettere,* Nos. 172 and 180 for Falcoia's first thinking that poor Andrea's hesitations were put into his mind by demons and that he was conquering these.
2. Sampers, A., "*Due Manoscritti di S. Alphonsus sulla Fondazione della Casa di Ciorani,*" S.H., XXI, 1973, pp 301–310 and *Storia, Pte. cit.,* pp 199f; *History,* pp 177f.
3. Tannoia, *Vita,* II, viii and x, pp 108–112 and 116–120.
4. On June 2, 1737, Andrea had been thoroughly frightened on opening the Villa church door for morning Mass to find an armed crowd demanding that the Community quit the property. They'd been set on, it seemed, by the local clergy. Falcoia instructed the Community to make a checklist of the contents of the house and give the keys to the bishop of Caiazzo. They left the night of June 10. Andrea was sent on to Scala. But he was not able to settle. So he was sent on again to regain his composure with the bishop at Castellammare. But Andrea, quite unsettled by these goings and goings, managed thoroughly to annoy Falcoia. He was soon letting Mazzini know that the Brother had to be expelled: "I have sent Brother Andrea home after keeping him locked in his room for a couple of days. I have told him that he is not to go anywhere near Scala. He went in the badly worn pair of trousers he stood up in, with a salami and a loaf of bread. I made him leave behind the habit, and I'll send on to him the other clothes you sent here.

   "I made him leave at night so that the people here know nothing about it. Perhaps Mazzini had come across the clothes Andrea had been wearing when he came to join them, and sent them to Castellammare when they were packing at Scala." Falcoia to Mazzini, August 6, 1738, *Lettere,* No. 190.

5. *Storia,* I/l, pp 205f; *History,* pp 183f.
6. Tannoia, *Breve memoria de Fratello Gioacchino Gaudiello, Laico della Congregazione del SS Redentore,* Naples, 1812, (hereinafter Tannoia, Gioacchino), p 86; *Companions,* p 457. Sportelli insisted, letters to Falcoia, May 16, 1740, and to Alphonsus, September 24, 1740, on spelling the Brother's name "Gioacchimo"; *Epistolae,* Nos. 21 and 26.
7. Tannoia, *Gioacchino,* p 87; *Companions,* p 458.
8. *Vid.* Rule of Celeste Crostarosa, in Transcription of Cava, III; *Founding Texts,* p 37.
9. *Regole Grandi,* XII, Constitution "On the Rule of Love of the Cross"; *Founding* Texts, p 149, and Gregorio, O., "*Sentimenti di Monsignore,*" S.H., IX, p 455, No. 60.
10. de Maio, R., *Societa e Vita Religiosa a Napoli nell'Eta Moderna* (1656–1799), *Cap.* 4, *Il Comportamento Religioso,* pp 156ff, *Scritti agiografici* for the popular *Lives* of Maria Villani, Antonio de Torres, Gaetano, *et al. pl.*
11. Alphonsus suggested that his father buy *Lives* of Saint Aloysius, Saint Philip Neri, and Saint Pascal or Saint Peter Alcantara, Alphonsus to Don Giuseppe, March 28, 1743(?).
12. *Compendio,* Intro.; *Founding Texts,* p 156.
13. Cafaro to de Robertis, January 22, 1752; *Epistolae,* No. 39.
14. Tannoia, *Gioacchino,* p 90; omitted from English trans.
15. This was a quite usual, and revealing, title for Jesus in the devotional writing of Falcoia and, more especially, Sarnelli; *vid.,* Giovine, *Sarnelli,* II, p 173.
16. *Vid.* Gregorio and Sampers, "*Documenti,*" S.H., XVI, pp 37 and 236ff, and Gregorio, "*Frammenti di Mons Falcoia,*" S.H., X, 1962, p 339. The 1744 *Compendio* declares that "the purpose of this new and least Institute of the Disciples of the Most Holy Savior is none other than to imitate, as much as possible with divine grace, this divine Master and model." In the *Regole Grandi,* which Falcoia, working on these papers to his death in 1743, designated "the spiritual rules of the Institute," the Lord requires them to "show yourselves my followers by keeping me impressed as a seal on your hearts," "you who are striving to follow in my footsteps which I have left imprinted on the world," "follow me as closely as you can in all the virtues." Alphonsus was, equally, capable of putting the two languages together. His Memorial to the Marquis Montealegre of January 1736 tells this prospective patron first that "their chief aim is to imitate closely the life and virtues of our Lord Jesus Christ" and then that "they are striving with the help of divine grace to walk in the footsteps of our Redeemer." *Founding Texts,* pp 156, 126, 71. For a through review of the various early Redemptorist uses of "imitating" and "following," *vid.* Raponi, S., "*La Spiritualita Redentorista delle Origini,*" S.H., XLIV, 1996, pp 419–497.
17. Francesco Tartaglione to Alphonsus, Tannoia, *Francesco,* pp 109f; *Companions,* pp 499ff.

18. Tannoia, *Gioacchino,* p 87; *Companions,* p 458.
19. *Ibid.*, pp 91f; *Companions,* p 464.
20. *Ibid.*
21. *Vera Sposa,* VIII.ii.2; *True Bride,* p 231.
22. Tannoia, *Gioacchino,* p 88; *Companions,* p 459.
23. *Ibid.*, p 88; *Companions,* p 460.
24. *Ibid.*
25. *Ibid.*, p 90; *Companions,* p 462.
26. *Ibid.*, p 96; *Companions,* p 470.
27. *Ibid.*, p 90; omitted from English trans.
28. *Ibid.*, p 87; *Companions,* p 458.
29. Kuntz, I, p 206.
30. Alphonsus, *Notizie* for *Life* of Vito; *Miscellany,* p 289.
31. Falcoia to Mazzini, August 25, 1738, *Lettere,* No. 192.
32. Tannoia, *Gioacchino,* p 87; *Companions,* p 458.
33. *Ibid.*, p 88; *Companions,* p 459.
34. Villani deposition, *Summarium super virtutibus,* 1806, p 35.
35. Alphonsus to Marocco, August 2, 1740.
36. Vow of Perseverance, July 21, 1740; English trans. with parallel 1743 text, *Founding Texts,* pp 323f. *Cf.* de Meulemeester, *Origines,* I, pp 251–264 and II, pp 39–50.
37. Sportelli to Falcoia, July 24, 1740, *Epistolae,* No. 23.
38. Falcoia to Sportelli, *et al.*, July 29(?), 1740; *Analecta CSSR* I, 1922, p 46.
39. Tannoia, *Gioacchino,* "*Iddio mi ha chiamato a servire*"; curiously the Oratorian translator, *Companions,* p 463, has inserted adjectives here: "a stupid Brother or a learned Father."
40. *Ibid.*, *Companions,* pp 463f.
41. Sportelli to Falcoia, May 16, 1740, *Epistolae,* No. 21.
42. Tannoia, *Gioacchino,* p 90; *Companions,* p 461.
43. *Ibid.*, p 90; *Companions,* p 462.
44. *Ibid.*, p 91; *Companions,* p 462.
45. *Ibid.*, p 91; *Companions,* p 463.
46. *Ibid.*, p 92; *Companions,* p 464.
47. *Ibid.*
48. *Ibid.*, p 97; *Companions,* p 471.
49. Falcoia to Sportelli, December 1740, *Lettere,* No. 213.
50. Tannoia, *Gioacchino,* p 93; *Companions,* p 466.
51. *Ibid.*, p 94; *Companions,* p 466.
52. *Ibid.*, p 96; *Companions,* p 469.
53. *Ibid.*, p 94; *Companions,* p 467.
54. *Ibid.*, "*Mi rimiro nello specchio mio,*" p 95; *Companions,* p 467.
55. *Regole Grandi,* VI, Purity of Heart; *Founding Texts,* p 130.

56. *Compendio,* XII; *Founding Texts,* p 173. Celeste Crostarosa, seeing herself in Christ "as in a clear mirror," had written a verse for the reflective Lord:

> I am the looking glass
> Of all that is beautiful,
> Whoever looks in me
> The form shall take
> Of deity

As the Lord had taken the form of a Servant, the servant by His grace may take the form of the Lord "in whom there is no beauty." This was, as he lay dying, the climactic wonder of Gioacchino's Christian living. *Vid.* Crostarosa's song "Renouncing Self," Swanston, H. F. G., *Singing a New Song,* p 131, and comments on the use of this mirror language in her *Dialogues* and *Exercise of Love, ibid.,* pp 125ff.

57. Tannoia, *Gioacchino,* p 95; *Companions,* p 467.
58. *Ibid.,* p 95. This strong line was too much for the Oratorian who cut it from the English translation.
59. *Regole Grandi,* I, Faith; *Founding Texts,* p 112.
60. *Ibid.*; *Founding Texts,* p 115.
61. *Ibid.,* XII, Abnegation of Self and Love of the Cross; *Founding Texts,* p 147.
62. Tannoia, *Gioacchino,* p 95; *Companions,* p 468.
63. *Ibid.,* "*questo letto e croce per voi,*" p 96; *Companions,* p 469.
64. *Regole Grandi; Founding Texts,* p 148.
65. *Ibid.,* XII; *Founding Texts,* p 148.
66. *Singing a New Song,* pp 152ff.
67. Conza text, twelfth Rule; *Founding Texts,* p 212. For Alphonsus' imaging the Cross of Jesus as his bed of love and death, *vid. egrr., Reflections and Affections* XII; *Considerations* IV.2; *Meditations for the Last Fifteen Days of Lent,* XV.2.
68. Tannoia, *Gioacchino,* p 100; *Companions,* p 473.
69. *Ibid.,* p 101; *Companions,* p 476.
70. "*Non in ligno crucis sed cum crucis desiderio et crucifixi amplexu primus omnium praeriputt caelestis gloriae coronam.*" *Cf.* another, anonymous, obituary cited by Tannoia at the close of his "brief *memoire*": "*ardenti desiderio se conformandi Christo crucifixo admirabilis.*"
71. Tannoia, *Gioacchino,* p 100; *Companions,* p 474.

Gerard Majella

1. Caione, Gaspare, *Notizie della vita del F. laico Gerardo Maiella,* ed. Majorano, S., *Gerardo Maiella, Appunti biografici,* Naples, 1988 (*Contributi gerardini* 4), (hereinafter Caione), p 24. Tannoia, *Gerardo, Companions,* 245. Caione, p 23, speaks of a lightness of heart that set Gerard laughing with his whole body.
2. Tannoia, *Gerardo,* pp 366, 373, 411, and 262. The flautist was playing the great Metastasian verse "I wish for Thee, my God, alone," and Gerard sang the chorus-line as he danced, "Thy will, O God, and not mine own." Gerard always had a better taste in musical matters than most Fathers and Brothers, and more modern taste than Alphonsus. The Rector Major did not care for any dancing: "If you wish to sing, sing spiritual songs, but take care never on any account to dance; the very fact of taking your companion by the hand may cause bad thoughts and temptations"; *Vera Sposa,* XXIV.vi; *True Bride,* p 708. *Cf.* Alphonsus' *obiter dictum:* "Our life must be far from that of seculars, no enterprise, no game, among us, no writing even, like that of the world"; Gregorio, O.,"*Sentimenti di Monsignore,*" S.H., IX, 1961, pp 439–475, No. 29 on p 453.
3. Tannoia, *Gerardo; Companions,* p 372.
4. Caione, p 79.
5. Gerard to Maria of Jesus, May 1753, *Lettere di S. Gerardo,* ed. Capone, D., and Majorano, S., 1980, No. 11.
6. Gerard to Maria of Jesus, August 28, 1754, *Lettere di S. Gerardo,* No. 30.
7. Gerard to Maria of Jesus, August 23, 1755, *Lettere di S. Gerardo,* No 43.
8. Tannoia, *Gerardo; Companions,* p 331.
9. Ibid., p 357. Tannoia records, *Companions,* p 245, another story of Gerard's being "ravished into an ecstasy" when serving his apprenticeship in the Muro tailor's shop and how, ecstatic still, he hid under the cutting table, whence he was drawn by the angry foreman. "Gerard was so far from losing patience that he only replied with a sweet smile" which the foreman naturally took for an impertinence, and hit him again.
10. Tannoia, *Gerardo; Companions,* p 246. There were three friaries in the Muro area, the Conventuals at San Antonio, the Capuchins at San Francesco, and Eustachio's community at Santomenna, where fourteen friars lived under the Guardianship of Father Bonaventura.
11. *Ibid.*, p 250 and Caione, p 24. Luca Malpiede, the San Fele schoolmaster, seems to have been no more able than Gerard to control the boys. He returned to Muro after enduring their raggings for a month, convinced, wrongly, that teaching was not for him. Ferrante, N., *Storia Meravigliosa di San Gerardo Maiella,* Rome, 1955, (hereinafter Ferrante), pp 54f.
12. Tannoia, *Gerardo; Companions,* p 242.
13. *Companions,* p 248 and Caione, p 23.
14. *Companions,* p 243 and Caione, p 20.

15. Caione, p 20. Birgitta was not more understanding of this incident than Tannoia, *vid.* Gerardo, *cap.* I.
16. *Companions,* p 251 and Caione, p 21. There was another demon dog waiting for Gerard in the kitchen at d'Iliceto, Caione, p 42.
17. Caione, pp 24f. Claudio Albini had been Vicar General of Caserta, of Salerno, and of Urbino, and, having been handed on by these bishops, had been sent to serve Bishop Manfredi at Muro. They had soon come to fisticuffs. So, as a way out of this difficulty in curial relations, on May 25, 1736, Pope Clement XII had made Albini bishop of Lacedognia. More rows followed, with the cathedral Canons, the university Regents at Rochetta, the Orsini feudal landlords. Albini died suddenly, June 25, 1744, while visiting archbishop Giuseppe Nicolai at San Andrea di Conza and was buried in the church of the Reformed Franciscans.
18. Caione, p 30.
19. *Ibid.*, p 29.
20. Tannoia, *Gerardo; Companions,* p 241.
21. *Ibid.*, p 249.
22. *Ibid.*, p 258. Gerard never surrendered that family sense of the relation of play to reality, of what a play could mean for one's appreciation of reality. He was quickly affected by any performance. Some years later, watching a similar Passion play arranged by Canon Giove for Abbess Capano and her Benedictine nuns, *Companions,* p 312, he was so affected that "he was raised to a considerable height from the floor."
23. *Companions,* p 258.
24. *Ibid.*
25. Caione, pp 30f.
26. Ferrante, p 128, with the suggestion that the assistant was a "desperado" whom Gerard had met on the road.
27. Tannoia, *Gerardo; Companions,* p 266.
28. *Ibid.* Tannoia alleges eyewitness testimony of both Andrea Longarello and Francesco Giovenale, 1719–1782.
29. Alphonsus to Caione, May 19, 1755; for the tradition of the useless Gerard, *vid.* Ferrante, p 10.
30. Caione, p 147: "*Un soggetto inutile alla Congregazione.*"
31. Caione, p 34.
32. Stories of obedience to unuttered command occur at *Companions,* pp 292, 315, and 415. Stories of his leading parties of Students and of reprobates, Caione, pp 10 and 15.
33. Gerard's birth and baptism are discussed by Ferrante, "*Il nome e cognome di S. Gerardo,*" S.H., II, 1954, pp 461 and 462, and "*Quando e nato S. Gerardo?*" S.H., III, 1955, pp 456f.
34. Caione, pp 43ff.
35. *Ibid.*, p 41.

36. Tannoia, *Gerardo; Companions,* pp 360f.
37. *Companions,* p 311.
38. *Ibid.,* p 402.
39. *Ibid.,* p 322.
40. *Ibid.,* pp 329f.
41. *Ibid.,* p 381.
42. *Ibid.,* p 361.
43. Caione, p 71.
44. The grand Sicilian nun's life and work had been made more widely known by Girolamo Turano's two recent publications, *Vita e virtu della V. S. Maria Crocifissa,* Agrigento, 1704, Venice, 1711, and *Scelta di Lettere Spirituali* Agrigento, 1704. *Vid.* Bernardo Apice, 1728–1769, to Maria Arcangela Lipp, May 26, 1762, in Giammusso, *Lettere dalla Sicilia,* No. 28, and Alphonsus' remarks, Gregorio, O., *Sentimenti,* S.H., IX, p 464.
45. Tannoia, *Gerardo; Companions,* p 382.
46. Caione, pp 99f. A less confident priest came asking Gerard to help him understand *Il Pastore della buona notte* by Juan de Palafox y Mendoza, 1600–1659, the prolific bishop of Los Angeles, and being signed "in the name of the Trinity," found he could very well get the sense of what he had before thought quite impenetrable.
47. Caione, p 101. Perhaps they were all seeing for the first time the work method of an honest tailor who had not, at the end of the cutting, a length of cloth which he could devote to his own purposes. *Cf.* Alphonsus, *Theologia Moralis, Lib.* IV, *cap.* iii, on the state and duties of seculars, *dub.* X, the obligations of merchants, iv.2, Gaude, 292.
48. Tannoia, *Gerardo; Companions,* pp 302 and 303.
49. *Ibid., Companions,* pp 304, 312, and 316.
50. *Ibid.,* p 361.
51. Caione, p 54.
52. Tannoia, *Gerardo; Companions,* pp 330 and 396.
53. *Companions,* p 421.
54. *Ibid.,* p 431.
55. *Ibid.,* p 299.
56. *Posizioni e Articoli Per i Processi Ordinarii,* for beatification of Domenico Blasucci, Rome, 1893, p 50; Blasucci was born at Muro, March 3, 1732.
57. Tannoia, *Gerardo; Companions,* pp 294 and 382; *Murana seu Compsana Beatificationis Ven. S. di D. Fr. Gerardi Majella, Summarium,* Rome, 1871, p 284. The song was well known:

    Fiori felici voi, che notte e giorno
    vicino al mio Gesu sempre ne state
    ne vi partite mai, finche d'intorno
    tutta la vita alfin no vi lasciate

58. Cafaro to Alphonsus, July 9, 1747, *Epistolae,* No. 9, and Cafaro "*ad Fratrem laicum ignotum,*" June 30 (1753?), *ibid.*, No. 62.
59. Tannoia, *Gerardo; Companions,* p 385 and Alphonsus' *memoire* of Cafaro, *Miscellany,* pp 226f, with reference to 2 Corinthians 12:7.
60. *Vid. Posizioni* for Blasucci beatification, 55, with Tannoia's *Vita* of Blasucci, *Companions,* p 212, where the Brother Infirmarian says that Gerard's heart was "so dried up within him that he felt driven almost to despair," with the parenthetical comment, "these are his very words." This is the experience which informs his letter to Prioress Maria Michele di Francesco, late summer 1753. He knew what it was to live "in a house where the Superior does not show affection for those who are tempted," and what it is for them to feel "neglected, despised, driven to despair," *Lettere,* No. 18, *cf.* Nos. 5 and 24 to Maria of Jesus, April 16, 1752 and 1753.
61. Gerard's personal Rule of Life, *Regolamento di vita, Scritti Spirituali,* ed. Majorano, S., *Contributi Gerardini* 8, Materdomini, 1992, pp 144–156, *Ricordi,* No. 33. There are four transcriptions of this Rule, Caione, I and II, Tannoia, *Gerardo,* cap. XI, and *Summarium,* pp 311–318.
62. Tannoia, *Gerardo; Companions,* p 415.
63. *Ibid.*, p 299.
64. Caione, pp 73f.
65. Tannoia, *Gerardo; Companions,* p 333.
66. *Ibid.*
67. Caione, p 74.
68. Tannoia, *Gerardo; Companions,* pp 417f; The "Constitution on the Missions," 1747, had insisted on the missioners' being self-protective in this matter: "They shall never go alone" even if they have to be accompanied "by some priest or cleric when there are few of their own Brothers," *vid. Analecta CSSR,* I, 1922, pp 172ff, and *Founding Texts,* p 348; Alphonsus to Fathers, 1744, where the first sentence of "Rules to be observed during the Missions" declares, "They shall never go alone," regulating for "at least two Fathers, or one Father with a lay Brother, or in case of necessity some secular priest."
69. Tannoia, *Gerardo; Companions,* p 317.
70. *Ibid.*
71. *Ibid.*, pp 328f.
72. *Ibid.*, p 348. Caione, p 91, refers to Nerea's involving the Capucci girl. He thought that Nerea had left the Foggia convent as much because she was "homesick" as for "love of her confessor." There is a review of these complexities in Felipe, Dionisio, *San Gerardo Mayela,* Madrid, 1954, *cap.* XXXI, pp 373–387.
73. Ferrante, p 502.
74. Tannoia, *Vita,* II, ix, p 115. For a prefiguring of Gerard's imitation of Christ, *ibid.*, I, xvi, p 61: "Alphonsus did not open his mouth in his own defense and did not make any excuse; on the contrary it cheered him to see himself so abused and humiliated."

75. Constitution on Missions; *Founding Texts*, pp 348f.
76. Tannoia, *Gerardo; Companions*, p 405.
77. *Ibid.*, p 349.
78. *Vera Sposa*, XI.4, citing a Torres letter from Sabbatini's *Vita* of the famous Jesuit, vol. II, *cap.* ix.
79. Caione, p 79.
80. *Ibid.*
81. Tannoia, *Gerardo; Companions*, p 351.
82. Caione, p 81.
83. Tannoia, *Gerardo; Companions*, p 354.
84. *Founding Texts*, p 168.
85. *Ibid.*, pp 202f.
86. *Ibid*, p 305. *Cf.* Alphonsus' instructions issued after the Canonical Visitation of the Student House, Ciorani, in 1761. Declaring that his instructions are "taken for the most part from our Rules and from the Constitutions," he applies what is said of Fathers to "our young men" who are going to be Fathers. The first instruction is concerned with times when they are in hot water: "They shall show all possible respect, veneration, and obedience, as well to the Prefect as to be Lecturer; they shall neither defend nor excuse themselves in their presence."
87. Gerard's *Rule of Life*, "Maxims dearest to my heart," Nos. 5, 2, 3, and 6.
88. Tannoia, *Gerardo; Companions*, p 354.
89. *Ibid.*, p 274.
90. *Ibid.*, p 358.
91. *Ibid.*, p 329.
92. *Ibid.*
93. *Ibid.*, p 358.
94. For Melfi as a "theater," Tannoia, *Gerardo*, XVIII, p 68.
95. Tannoia, *Gerardo; Companions*, pp 363f.
96. *Ibid.*, p 360; *vid.* Gerard to Celeste Crostarosa, March 8, 1755, *Lettere di S. Gerardo*, No. 37. For the Jesuits' convent foundation, *vid.* Tannoia, *Gerardo; Companions*, p 339.
97. Tannoia, *Gerardo; Companions*, p 405.
98. Alphonsus to Caione, September 21 and 28, 1754, and during October 1754, with justified forebodings that Manfredonia was about to cause trouble; he ran away on November 21, returned May 30, 1755, and was dismissed as incorrigible, 1756.
99. Angelo Latessa died, October 5, the Student, Pietr'Angelo Picone, b. 1733, died on November 9, 1754.
100. Tannoia, *Gerardo; Companions*, p 378. When Margotta was sad and silent at recreation, Alphonsus sang him a song:

How grand and sweet, my Mother dear,
Is your name, O Mary

Margotta did not cheer up.

101. Tannoia, *Gerardo; Companions,* p 425.
102. *Ibid.*, p 424.
103. Gerard to Celeste Crostarosa, March 8, 1755, *Lettere di San Gerardo,* No. 37.
104. *Ibid.*
105. Caione, pp 117–120.
106. Gerard to Caione, August 23, 1755, *Lettere,* No. 43.
107. Tannoia, *Gerardo; Companions,* p 434; *vid.* Swanston, H. F. G., *Singing a New Song,* p 171 with note 161.
108. Tannoia, *Gerardo; Companions,* p 439; *vid.* for Carminiello's ringing a cheerful bell at Gerard's death, *Caione,* p 153. Tannoia says, *ibid.*, p 440, that there was another Brother looking after Gerard with Carminiello; Caione, pp 147–153 mentions Brothers Andrea, Saverio, Stefano, and Gennaro.
109. Caione, pp 153f.
110. Tannoia, *Gerardo; Companions,* p 441.
111. Caione, p 153.
112. *Ibid.*, p 154, Tannoia, *Gerardo;* Companions, pp 442f, and *Vita,* IV, xxxvi, p 193; Alphonsus sent a death-card to Ripacandida, *vid.* Alphonsus to Maria of Jesus, July 22, 1757.
113. The engagement of the missioners with the Buono Murante family, especially with "Mamma Vittoria" is evident at Gerard to Maria Michela, *Lettere di San Gerardo,* No. 16; *vid* also Ferrante, pp 176ff. Mauro, whom Alphonsus called, affectionately, "Mauriccio," proved an inconstant member of the Congregation, coming, going, coming, and at last returning to mamma to die. In January 1756, he was still the white-headed boy, "I am expecting you, my dear," Alphonsus wrote on January 7, 1756, "and hours appear to me ages."
114. Alphonsus to Murante, January 7, 1756.
115. Alphonsus to Caione, January 11, 1756.
116. For the "journey-structure," *vid.* Caione, pp 117–135 and Angelomichele de Spirito, "*La presenza redentorista in Irpina,*" *Richerche di Storia Sociale e Religiosa,* XXVI, 1951, pp 169–197. For miracles, *vid.* Tannoia, *Gerardo; Companions,* pp 420ff, and the testimony of Dr. Gaetano Federici at the beatification process, pp 69f.
117. Tannoia, *Gerardo; Companions,* p 255.
118. Caione, p 137.
119. *Ibid.*, p 144.
120. Gerard to Maria of Jesus, January 7, 1754, *Lettere di San Gerardo,* No. 31. *Cf.* Caione's record of Gerard's confiding to Brother Gennaro his wish to die of tuberculosis on account of the Community's leaving such patients so much alone, Caione, p 142.

121. Caione, p 144.
122. *Ibid.*, p 151. *Cf.* Gerard to Maria of Jesus, January 7, 1754, where he himself seems to be making a pun between "*aceto*," vinegar, and "*accetto*," "I accept"; *Lettere di San Gerardo,* No. 31.
123. *Lettere di San Gerardo,* No. 31.
124. Caione, p 136.
125. Caione, post-word, p 151.
126. Tannoia, *Gerardo; Companions,* pp 361 and 381.
127. Gerard to Santorelli, *Lettere di San Gerardo,* No. 27.
128. *Lettere di San Gerardo,* p. 330. The exclamation is not in the *Summarium* text, nor Caione II nor Tannoia, *Gerardo, cap.* IX. The editors of *Lettere* comment, note 17, that "the omission from these other sources derives perhaps from a difficulty in comprehending."
129. Gerard was very aware of the sorts of wrong-headed questions that fascinate a dull theologian. The Jesuit, Paolo Giunta, had plagued Maria Crocifissa about "the freedom of God in creating the world," and she had had to answer distinguishingly in terms of "act of divine Production," "effusion of divine essence," and "transfusion *ab extra,*" *vid.* Cabbibo, S., and Marilena, M., *La Santa dei Tomasi,* Turin, 1989, pp 162f and 174, note 24, all while protesting that the Lord had assured her that "from the Chair of my Cross, I do not propose scholastic treatises but things mysterious and divine," Ms 4920 f 267 v, cited by Locatelli, S., *La Ven. Maria Crocifissa Tomasi e il Seicento mistico Italiano,* p 71, in *Regnum Dei,* XIII, 1957.
130. *Letter e di San Gerardo,* No. 41.
131. Gerard to Celeste Crostarosa, March 8, 1755; *Lettere,* No. 37.
132. He began to sign himself not only with "*G. M. G. T*" (Jesus, Mary, Joseph, Teresa) but also with "*Pazza mia dei Pazzi*" ("My madwoman among the mad" or "my madwoman [Maddalena] dei Pazzi").
133. Gerard, *Rule of Life; Lettere di San Gerardo,* p 332.
134. *Lettere di San Gerardo,* No. 44.
135. *Ibid.*, Nos. 35 and 44; *cf.* also "My most Holy Trinity" and "My and your Most Holy Trinity," *ibid.*, Nos. 32 and 27.
136. "*Nella cattedra della mia croce*"; Locatelli, *art. cit.*, p 71. *Cf.* Her hints to her brother, San Giuseppe Maria Tomasi, 1649–1713, of "*li profondi arcani della scuola del Crocifisso,*" *Lettera* LXXXXVIII, cited, *ibid.*, p 72.
137. To Maria di Gesu, *Lettere di San Gerardo,* No 24.
138. Alphonsus to Tannoia, March 6, 1756, and to Maria di Gesu, April 22, 1756. As Raponi, Gerardini, 10, *art. cit.*, had noted, p 75, several Redemptorist writers have suggested that Brother Antonio Lauro was "a worthy imitator of Saint Gerard." *Cf.* Berthe, II, p 158, Gregorio, *Sulle orme,* p 61, and Kuntz VI, VI, pp 475–479.
139. Falcoia to Sportelli, July 1738, *Lettere,* No. 188.

140. *Cf. La Fedelta dei Vasalli,* 1777, for Alphonsus' understanding of social virtue in a well-ordered Kingdom.
141. Alphonsus to Tannoia, January 13, 1756.
142. *Ibid.*
143. *Ibid.*
144. Alphonsus to Caione, January 16, 1756.
145. Alphonsus to Ferrara, January 18, 1756.
146. *Ibid.*
147. Alphonsus to Brothers at d'Iliceto.
148. *Ibid.*
149. *Meditazioni per tutti i giorni dell'Avvento sino all'Ottava dell' Epifania,* 1758, *Opere ascet.,* IV, p 47; *Discourses for Novena of Christmas,* III.ii, p 56.
150. Alphonsus to Tannoia, January 20, 1756; Alphonsus to Ferrara, end of January 1756.
151. Pietro Paolo Blasucci to Tannoia, January 21, 1756, printed in Sampers, A., "*Epistulae 24 S. Alfonsi ineditae, 1735–1759,*" S.H., IX, 1964, p 249.
152. Ferrara had written to Alphonsus supporting Bartolomeo's protest, *cf.* Alphonsus to Ferrara, end of January 1766. Bartolomeo took his time, at least five years more, to leave the Congregation, Kuntz, VIII, pp 304 and 305. Giacomo was by then long gone.
153. Alphonsus to Tannoia, end of January 1756.
154. Journal of Pasquale Caprioli, 1728–1813, *vid.* Kuntz, V, 1752–1757, pp 4, 30, 51, and 72. Perhaps there was in all this simply, as in the convents of the Kingdom, "a general revolt against the despotism of Superiors." The Redemptorist Constitutions of 1764 explicitly forbade "the use of prisons in the Congregation," and the Rector Major was warned not to employ some self-justifying equivocation to subvent this ruling. *Codex Regularum,* p 237, n. 537, cited in *Storia della Congregazione,* p. 321, n. 178; *History,* p 293, n. 179.
155. Alphonsus to Tannoia, January 20, 1756.
156. Tannoia, *Vita,* II, lviii, p 348.
157. *Ibid.,* II, lxii, p 366.
158. Alphonsus to Tannoia, January 20, 1756.
159. Tannoia, *Vita,* II, xlii, p 266. Alphonsus arrived in Naples, February 24, 1756, and being disappointed of his hopes of conducting Congregation business with the King's minister, he fell in with Archbishop Sersale's suggestion of his giving the diocesan clergy retreat.
160. Tannoia, *Vita,* II, lxvii, p 267.
161. Tannoia, *Gerardo; Companions,* pp 278ff.

Francesco' Antonio Romito

1. Alphonsus to Tannoia, January 21, 1756.
2. Tannoia, *Domenico Blasucci; Companions,* p 211.
3. Alphonsus to Tannoia, January 21, 1756.

4. Alphonsus to Tannoia, February 1756.
5. Caione, p 150. Tannoia, however, tells this story with Carminiello as the demon-chaser, *Companions*, p 439.
6. Alphonsus to Tannoia, February 22, 1760.
7. Kuntz, XI, pp 451f.
8. *Ibid.*, pp 292f. This Brother was dispensed from vows and allowed to drink himself to death outside the Congregation.
9. Tannoia, *Vita*, II, xxxiii, p 221.
10. Kuntz, XII, p 117.
11. Alphonsus' *memoire* of Sarnelli, in Sarnelli, *Opere Complete*, Naples, 1888, vol. I, p 29; *Miscellany*, p 275.
12. *Ibid.*, *Miscellany*, p 276.
13. Kuntz, II, p 417.
14. Berthe, I, p 99; English trans. I, p 90.
15. Sportelli to Villani, December 22, 1747, *Epistolae*, No. 168.
16. Tannoia, *Gerardo*, *Companions*, p 260.
17. Cicchetti testimony, 1806 Process, *Summarium* 9, "*de fundatione Congregationis*," super 38, p 101.
18. *Ibid.*, super 31, p 101.
19. Romito testimony, *ibid.*, *Summarium* 9, *super* 25, p 100.
20. Flumeri testimony at Nocera-Pagani hearings, September 14 and 15, 1797, collated for 1806 Process, *Summarium* 9, Juxta 16, fol. 2149, p 109.
21. Tannoia, *Vita*, III, lxvi, p 355.
22. Cicchetii testimony, at 1796 hearings, *Summarium* 14, Juxta 18, fol. 796, p 190; *cf.* Pollio testimony, *ibid.*, super 163, fol. 1220.
23. Tannoia, *Vita*, IV, xxxiii, p 173.
24. *Ibid.*, III, ix, p 38; *vid.* the story Alphonsus tells of the endurance of Saint Joseph of Leonessa under a like operation, *L'Amore dell' Anime*, *Opere ascet.*, V, p 12; *Reflections and Affections*, Intro., p 18.
25. Tannoia, *Vita*, III, lxxi, pp 379f.
26. Vertucci testimony, collated for 1806 Auditors, *Summarium* 31, Juxta 29, fol. 1812.
27. Berthe, II, pp 474f; English trans., II, p 473.
28. Vertucci testimony, *ibid.*, pp 690f.
29. *Ibid.*, p 691.
30. Alphonsus to Villani, April 8, 1774.
31. Romito testimony, 1806 Process, *Summarium* 33, Juxta 32, fol. 1541, p 709, with the happy boast of Alphonsus' ascetical works reaching "*Paesi della Germania abitati dagli Eretici Luterani e Calvinisti, come mi ricordo bene.*"
32. Tannoia, *Vita*, III, lxvi, p 355, and lxviii, pp 368f.
33. Romito testimony, *ibid.* Alphonsus' triennial report to Sac. Cong. of the Council, July 8, 1765.

34. *Ibid.*
35. Alphonsus to Giovanni Maria Puoti, December 24, 1764, and to Primicerio Petti, Christmastide, 1764, Tannoia, *Vita,* III, xxvii, p 135.
36. Romito testimony, 1797, fol. 1281.
37. Alphonsus to Villani, February 1, 1765. *Cf.* his remarking to an aged lady who had expected to have a private moment but found the Brother standing next the bishop's chair, "He is prudent, you may depend on it." Tannoia, *Vita,* III, viii, p 32.
38. Tannoia, *Vita,* III, xxvii, p 135.
39. Alphonsus to "Chinese College" Superiors, May 24, 1777.
40. Alphonsus to Villani, November 1774, in Sampers, A., "*32 Epistulae S. Alfonsi ineditae, 1762–1775,*" S.H., IX, pp 296–365, No. 62 on p 361.
41. Alphonsus to Corrado, July 15, 1777.
42. *Egr.* appendage to Alphonsus' letter to Ciorani Fathers, October 1779.
43. Romito testimony, 1806 Process, pp 188f.
44. Tannoia, *Vita,* III, viii, p 34.
45. Jones, F., *op. cit.*, p 427.
46. Tannoia, *Vita,* IV, xxxii, p 156.
47. Romito testimony, collated for 1806 Process, *Summarium* 12, p 241 and *Summarium* 20, super 226, fol. 1537, p 488.
48. Sampers, A., "*Notizie R. D. Felicis Verzella,*" (collected by Tannoia for *Vita*), S.H., IX, pp 371–438, *Esercizi giornali(eri),* p 393, note 65. Alphonsus certainly did not value all Brothers equally, "This Brother, as you know, often talks nonsense," Alphonsus to Caione, July 15, 1757, and, of another Brother complainant, "I do not believe him," Alphonsus to Villani, June 29, 1767.
49. "*Focoso*" and "*bilioso*" and "*irascibile*"*;* Romito testimony 1796, *Summarium* 18, super 139, fol. 1326 and Verzella testimony, *ibid.*, fol. 761.
50. Romito testimony, 1796, *ibid.*
51. Jones, F., *op. cit.,* p 405, but Alphonsus had written a pleasant reference for Rubini to be made a bishop; Alphonsus to Francesco Gaetani, Duke of Sermoneta, January 4, 1768.
52. Jones, F., *op. cit., ibid.*
53. Alphonsus to Villani, March 28, 1763: "I do not wish to keep anyone here by force and against his will" and "I see that this whole affair was simply a temptation to disturb him and me."
54. Jones, F., *op. cit.,* p 398.
55. Romito testimony, 1806 Process, *Summarium* 30, super 304, fol. 545, p 647; Alphonsus had always recognized his need for someone to do the household chores.
56. "*E che io forse sono migliore di te?*"; this novice was totally confused as to the proper mode of treating the Rector Major. Romito testimony, *ibid., Summarium* 30, *super* 301, *art.*, p 652.

Alessio Pollio

1. Alphonsus to Ercole, August, 1762; Tannoia, *Vita,* III, viii, p 35. Domenico Antonio Janella lived long enough to testify at the November 1788 local hearings at the start of the beatification process. *Cf. Proces. S. Agathae* IV, fol. 1551ff.
2. Pollio testimony, Nucera-Pagani hearings towards the 1796 *Positio super Introductione Causae,* conducted by Decio Nola, the Under-Promoter and the "devil's advocate," Nicola Jozzo, Under-Promoter of the Faith, who finished their work, April 27, 1797; fol. 1007 "*io con tutto piacere corrisposi.*"
3. Tannoia, *Vita,* III, viii, pp 35–36.
4. *Ibid.*, III, viii, p 36.
5. "*Casualmente,*" Pollio testimony, *ibid.*, *cf.* Alphonsus to Clement XIII, end of 1776.
6. Alphonsus to the clergy of Sant' Agata diocese, July 30, 1762; June 8, 1764; December 1764; July 11, 1767; December 1768; December 29, 1770; Tannoia, *Vita,* II, lxii, p 365; Villani to Rectors, October 10, 1762.
7. Pietro Paolo Blasucci to Villani, October 10, 1766; *Lettere dalla Sicilia,* pp 146–147.
8. Report of Blasucci, Visitatore ordinario, and Sebastiano de Jacobis, Secretario della S. Visita, October 12, 1766, VII, printed by Giammusso, "*Atti della Visita Canonica del 1766 alla Casa di Agrigento,*" S.H., V, 1957, pp 312–349.
9. Francesc' Antonio testified that at Pagani the priest assisting at Alphonsus' Mass "always wore the cotta"; 1806 Process "*De fide ex ss Sacr. devotione,*" *Summarium* 12, *super* 57 *art.*, fol. 1561, p 241.
10. Pollio testimony, collated and printed in 1796 *Positio, Summarium* 18, *super* 143, p 220; *vid.* Tannoia, *Vita,* III, viii, p 34, for a story of the crisis on Alphonsus' sipping a drop of water after midnight.
11. Pollio testimony, 1796 Process, *ibid.*
12. Tannoia, *Vita,* III, vii, p 34.
13. Pollio testimony, 1796, fol. 1225.
14. Pollio testimony, collated in 1806 *Summarium super Virtutibus* by the Auditors appointed by Cardinal Diego Innico Caracciolo, 1754–1820, the Promoter at the S. Cong. of Rites; *Summarium* 19, *super* 207, fol. 496, p 455.
15. *Ibid., Summarium* 23, *super* 325, fol. 560, p 536.
16. *Ibid., Summarium* 19, *super* 225, fol. 509, p 460.
17. Ercole sometimes sent him a box of fruit, *vid.* Alphonsus to Ercole, December 13, 1763, and the fruit was sometimes a temptation to the servants, *vid.* the fury of Vicar General Rubino at the theft of some apples, and the fury of Alphonsus when he learnt of the culprit's being jailed, Pollio testimony; *ibid.*
18. Pollio testimony in 1806 Summaria, *Summarium* 19, *super* 218, fol. 506, p 459; Tannoia, *Vita,* III, lxix, p 373.
19. *Ibid.*
20. Tannoia, *Vita,* III, lxix, p 373.
21. Pollio testimony, 1796, V, *Summarium* 11, *super* 139 *art.*, fol. 463.

22. *Ibid., Summarium* 14, *super* 157 *art.*, fol. 1332.
23. *Ibid., super* 190 *art.*, fol. 1219.
24. *Ibid.*
25. Jones, F., *op. cit.*, p 397.
26. Pollio testimony, 1796 *Positio*, Summarium 18, *super* 139, fol. 1203, p 218.
27. *Ibid.*
28. Pollio testimony, 1796, *Summarium* 18, *super* 304, fol. 1203, p 219.
29. *Ibid.*
30. *Ibid.*, *cf.* testimony of Francesc' Antonio, *ibid., Summarium* 20, *super* 150, fol. 1330.
31. Greco, G., *Fra disciplina e sacardozio,* in *Clero e societa nell' Italia moderna,* ed. Rosa, M., 1992, pp 82, 90, and 97, and Orlandi, G., *Il Regno di Napoli,* pp 124ff for "*abati di mezza sottana.*"
32. Alphonsus received and read this letter in early August 1773, probably.
33. Alphonsus to Brothers, August 1773.
34. *Ibid.*
35. *Complesso,* Constitution II, "On clothing," Nos. 1 and 4; *Founding Texts,* pp 85 and 86.
36. Falcoia to Alphonsus, July 11, 1734, *Lettere,* No. 91.
37. "*Alia per Falcoiam decisa,*" *Cose dette da Monsignore,* III, in *Documenta coaeva de nostris Regulis et Constitutionibus primaevis,* XIV, *Analecta CSSR* IX, 1930, pp 107ff, "*In riguardo alle Vesti.*"
38. Conza text, Constitution on Poverty; *Founding Texts,* p 192.
39. Decrees of General Congregation, 1747, IV; *Founding Texts,* p 335. *Cf. Acta Integra* 15 for renewal of this Decree at 1749 Chapter.
40. *Ibid., Founding Texts,* p 336. *Cf. Acta Integra* 50.
41. Alphonsus to Brothers, summer 1773.
42. *Ibid.*
43. *Ibid.*
44. Alphonsus to Clergy of Sant' Agata diocese, July 30, 1762.
45. Falcoia to Mazzini, August 6, 1738, *Lettere,* No. 191.
46. Dumortier, F., *Neufs scolastiques,* Paris, 1902, III, Pierre Picone, p 272.
47. Tannoia, *Gerardo; Companions,* p 495.
48. *Ibid.*
49. Alphonsus to Tannoia, August 12, 1773.
50. *Ibid.*
51. Alphonsus to Rectors and Heads of Mission Teams, September 1773.
52. Tannoia, *Francesco; Companions,* p 311.
53. Alphonsus to Brothers, summer 1773.
54. *Ibid.*
55. Tannoia, *Gerardo; Companions,* p 311.
56. *Ibid.*, p 358.
57. *Ibid.*, p 362.

58. *Ibid.*, p 329. *Cf.* Gerard's disciples, "penitents, if I may so call them," at Castelgrande and Caposele, *Companions*, pp 319 and 387.
59. Kuntz, VIII, 1768–1774, p 207.
60. Tellería, R., "*Alexius Pollio S. Alfonsi Episcopi servus mox in eiusdem Congregatione Frater ac Filius,*" S.H., X, 1962, pp 256–268, note 12.
61. Tannoia, *Vita,* III, lxix, p 374 and 380.
62. Kuntz, IX, p 73; the draft was drawn, January 2, 1775, and the will witnessed October 20, 1775.
63. Desiderio testimony, *Process, S. Agathae,* f. 1850, repeated at 1806 Process, p 785.
64. *Evidenza della Fede, cap.* VI.
65. Alphonsus to Marc' Antonio d'Ambrosio, September 20, 1779. If Alessio thought fit to interfere in his master's business, Alphonsus, reciprocally, interfered in his servant's business. Alessio, his in-laws not paying the arranged dower, had taken the dangerous step of consulting a lawyer. Fabrizio d'Ambrosio got the papers stamped in the registrar's office and then, since there could be little profit for him in such a small piece of litigation, let the matter drop. The file grew dusty. In September 1779, Alphonsus determined to do something about the missing dower. He wrote to the head of the d'Ambrosio family, a respectable parish priest who would not at all care for any of his kin to be gaining a reputation for shoddy practice. Alphonsus begins by referring to the likelihood of there being some small-town gossip:

    > My dear Marc Antonio,
    > Alessio tells me that your brother, Signor Fabrizzio, has in his possession certain acts passed last year in the chancery of Arienzo: these acts refer to the dowry of Alessio's wife, a dowry that Ludovico di Addio has owed him for some time.

    He then suggests what Don Marco might do to get this nuisance out of his way:

    > You will afford me pleasure, if you draw the attention of your brother to this matter; let him try to do what he can to recover this dowry, for Alessio is in want, his wife having been bedridden for a long time.

    This last remark may have hinted to Don Marco that he should himself be doing something for the Pollio family. He might, as the well-esteemed amateur medical man of the parish, take a look at Fortunata. To this appeal for the priest to make some show of caring for the poor and the sick, Alphonsus added a sentence emphasizing his episcopal interest in the matter and suggesting that he still has an ability to assist Don Marco, even as a merely retired bishop, in the *quid pro quo* of diocesan business:

> Please render me this service, and I shall feel greatly obliged to you.

Alphonsus cannot conclude, of course, without his usual blackmail:

> Think of me in your prayers, that the Lord may grant me the grace of a good death, for I am approaching my end.

It may be assumed that Don Marco did what was required and that Don Fabrizio took some action in the local courts. At any rate, the priest was soon promoted to a vacant Canonry at the cathedral.

66. Alphonsus to Maria Angelica, OSSR, October 4, 1780.
67. *Ibid.*
68. Alphonsus to Villani, October, 1746. *Cf.* the shortening of the novitiate of Giambattista Ansalone, 1734–1818, Alphonsus to Tannoia, December 31, 1755.
69. Jones, F., *op. cit.*, p 359.
70. Alphonsus to Don Giuseppe, August 5, 1736.
71. Alphonsus to Ercole, March 21, 1762.
72. Jones, F., *op. cit.*, p 403.
73. *Ibid.*, p 359. Alphonsus to Villani, July 4, 1764.
74. *Ibid.*, p 361.
75. Alphonsus to Villani, November 9, 1774.
76. Alphonsus to Villani, mid November 1774.
77. "Villani was made of sterner stuff," Jones, *op. cit.*, p 446.
78. Alphonsus to Fathers and Brothers, November 1775.
79. Alphonsus to Fathers and Brothers, November 1776.
80. Alphonsus to Francesc' Antonio de Paola, January 1777.
81. Alphonsus to de Paola, March 21, 1777.
82. Alphonsus to de Paola, February 21, 1777.
83. Alphonsus to de Paola, September 19, 1777.
84. Alphonsus to de Paola, March 27, 1777.
85. Alphonsus to de Paola, July 7, 1777, March 7, 1777, and November 1777.
86. Alphonsus to the Rector at Ciorani, November 4, 1779.
87. *Ibid.*
88. Alphonsus to Maione, January 26, 1776, and to Stefano Liguori, November 6, 1779.
89. Alphonsus to Ercole, September 1, 1779.
90. Gregorio, *Sentimenti,* No 100, S.H., IX, p 474.
91. There was nothing exceptional in this. "It was his custom." Giammusso, *Lettere dalla Sicilia,* p 30.
92. Villani to Alphonsus, December 17, 1748.
93. Alphonsus to Corrado, March 10, 1780.
94. Alphonsus to Caione, April 7, 1780.
95. 1749 Pontifical Rule, Pt. III, *Cap.* 1; *Founding Texts,* p 310.

96. Alphonsus to a Father of the Congregation, April 12, 1780. Jones, F., *op. cit.*, p 521, note 11, remarks this power shift but does not enlarge on the topic.
97. Alphonsus to Margotta, February 1, 1750.
98. How much did Villani know about the Christmas 1774 discussions between Alphonsus and Blasucci to persuade the royal ministers to appoint "an assistant to the Rector Major"? Kuntz, VIII, p 476, Tellería, R., *San Alphonso,* II, p 513, note 18, and Jones, F., *op. cit.*, p 445.
99. Alphonsus to Corrado, March 10, 1780.
100. "Tannoia was irrationally opposed to the *Regolamento* and to its two principal instigators, Cimino and Maione," Jones, F., *op. cit.*, p 459.
101. For Tannoia's memorial to the Congregation of Bishops and Regulars, and his part in the *Regolamento* mess, *vid.* Kuntz, X, 1779–1783, pp 102ff, and Capone, Domenico, *Mendacia Tannoiana.* For the increasing importance of the distinction between oath and vow, *vid.* Alphonsus to Cardinal Tommaso Ghilini, April 14, 1781, to the Pope, June 1781, and to Fathers and Brothers, August 30, 1783.
102. Alphonsus to Amelio Ficocelli, 1743–after leaving in 1781, April 16, 1780.
103. Alphonsus to a Father of the Congregation, April 12, 1780.
104. *Ibid.* For the Scylla and Charybdis image, *vid.* Alphonsus to de Paola, January 10, 1781.
105. Alphonsus to Pius VI, December 15, 1780.
106. Alphonsus to de Paola, October 18, 1780.
107. Alphonsus to Blasucci, August 19, 1780.
108. Redemptorists of Agrigento to Villani, October 26, 1785; *Lettere dalla Sicilia,* No. 144.
109. Giammusso, S., *Lettere dalla Sicilia,* pp 291 and 146.
110. Alphonsus to de Paola, February 8, 1781.
111. Alphonsus to Corrado, March 13, 1780.
112. Alphonsus to de Paolo, January 4, 1781.
113. AGHR SAM V 10, *Instrumentum publicum de deceptione S. A. quoad Regulamentum,* 1789, p. 12, the two Brothers made this statement on oath as "of our own knowledge and experience."
114. Alphonsus to Maione, September 2, 1777.
115. Alphonsus to a young Christian woman (Grimm, "to a pious maiden"), 1781(?) "I can neither read nor write on account of my great age and infirmities. I am therefore obliged to have the letters that I receive read to me and to dictate my answers."
116. Alphonsus to Ercole, September 1, 1779. The negotiations with the Vespoli collapsed very soon after this, but the State Counsellor agreed to be nominated in Ercole's will as a guardian of both boys.
117. Alphonsus to Giuseppe and Alfonsino de Liguori, April 4, 1780.
118. Alphonsus to Criscuolo, March 28, 1780.
119. Tannoia, *Vita,* IV, xv, p 72.

120. Alphonsus to Gavotti, September 14, 1780. This letter is not quoted at Berthe, II, but is inserted at an appropriate place in the Eng. trans., II, p 459.

121. Years before, Alphonsus had persuaded Ercole to place Teresina as a boarder at San Marcellino along with her elder cousin Maria Anna de Liguoro, daughter of the Presicce prince. The girls were to advance under the eye of Antonia, who was now one of the senior members of the community. In 1776, Maria Anna had, gratifyingly, elected to become herself a nun at San Marcellino. Alphonsus determined to fix Teresina in the convent, too. He had old personal ties as well as these family connections with the convent. In 1759, while giving the nuns a Retreat, he had encountered Donna Brianna Carafa, and immediately discerned the distinction of this nun. He had so far distinguished her from the rest that, quite against the community's wishes, he had encouraged her in a plan to cut herself off from them as an anchoress. The design foundered when it proved impossible to renegotiate the Carafa dowry. She was now, Alphonsus instructed, to join her persuasions with those of Antonia to keep Teresina in the convent for life. So was Gavotti. Alphonsus wrote to him that his niece was a source of great affliction to him on account of the terrible suspicion that she was wishing to get married, "which is as much as to say that she will likely lose her soul." So, he wrote to the discomforted lawyer, "be so kind as to do your part in this matter." There were dangers everywhere. He could sniff out something rotten in the convent itself. Teresina seemed now not as enthusiastic about becoming a nun as he remembered her being before she ever went to the convent. "I fear," he wrote to Antonia, "that she has found some girl in the convent who is worldly minded." Still, Alphonsus himself was not without some worldly wisdom himself. "I know that your father has left you some fortune," he advised Teresina, "but yours is not a grand dowry, and if you go back to the world you'll never get yourself engaged to any but a poor cavalier."

Despite Teresina's undecidedness, and the doubts of Vespoli and Gavotti, who both recalled Don Ercole's injunction that his daughter should be twenty years old before deciding on such a step, Alphonsus was entirely confident in his own good judgment. He secured every exit. He wrote, as bishop, to Teresina's confessor telling him to "direct her most especially that she may embrace the religious life." He wrote then to Teresina advising her to "consult your confessor" and "act according to his advice." He wrote to Abbess Brianna, in whom the girl was confiding, commanding that she keep up her effort to persuade her. He wrote, as head of the family, to Antonia, fixing with her that those four months which ecclesiastical law required Teresina to spend out of the convent, so that she might discover what the world was like, should be spent at the home of his old friend, the Duchess of Bovino. This good dowager was to keep Teresina from balls and theaters and evening parties and all such frivolous assemblies. Tannoia was told that during this dangerous time in the world, the only outing the old lady allowed Teresina was a short visit to her uncle. Just long enough to obtain his blessing. Still, Teresina was worldly enough to wish for a memento of this excursion. She asked for a picture of the Lady which she saw on Alphonsus' desk. He gave her, instead, a copy of his *Preparation for Death.*

Even Alphonsus' planning could not be wholly accident proof. There was a last minute hitch when Gavotti thought he detected a sign, during the preparations for her clothing, that Teresina had changed her mind. The guardian told the bishop. Alphonsus wrote Teresina a short note. She went where she was directed. But after this crisis had been resolved, Alphonsus found that his design was being more strangely hindered. Once in the novitiate, Teresina developed an ulcer on her leg which, resisting the physician's efforts, threatened her profession. The nuns might have to send her home. Alphonsus now sent her the holy picture of the Lady of Sorrows. Teresina was to apply it to the wound. It cleared up nicely. But again, after her first profession, there was another cause for worry. Teresina found that her voice was reduced to a hoarse whisper. This trouble in her throat must prevent her taking part in the choir recitation of the Office, the chief occupation of the community. Again, a holy picture was sent. With instructions this time that it should be torn into small pieces, one to be taken with a little water, once a day. Teresina got her voice back. She went on singing to her death. Born probably in 1764, Teresina lived to hear accounts of her uncle's canonization, May 26, 1839, and died in 1850. *Vid. Notice sur la vie et les vertus du R. P. Celestin Berruti,* in *Les exercises de sainte Gertrude,* Naples, 1877, p lv. Teresina had by then migrated with other nuns to the convent of San Gregorio Armeno when the French government closed San Marcellino.

122. Gregorio, O., S.H., XX, *art. cit.*, p 31.
123. Kuntz, I, p 204.
124. *Epistolae Circulares Andreae Villani,* I, October 10, 1762, *Documenta Misc.*, pp 159f.
125. Kuntz, V, 1752–1757, p 326 and IX, p 256.
126. Kuntz, X, p 22.
127. Tannoia, *Vita,* lix, p 349 and Kuntz, X, p 22.
128. Alphonsus to Fathers at d'Iliceto, December 24, 1779, as his Christmas greeting.
129. Gregorio, O., "*Sentimenti,*" S.H., IX, p 468, note 91.
130. Blasucci to de Paola, July 30, 1780; Kuntz, X, pp 141f.
131. Alphonsus to his nephew Giuseppe, December 28, 1780.
132. Alphonsus to Fathers and Brothers, January 4, 1781.
133. Tannoia, *Vita,* IV, xxvii, p 138.
134. Kuntz, X, p 415. The Petition is preserved in Archiv. Gen., II A, 45c.
135. "*Lectum et ut Superiores utantur jure suo,*" September 5, 1782.

136. The middle-aged Agostino Salvadore, *"l'asiniello della casa,"* born Nocera dei Pagani, June 2, 1719, came to work at d'Iliceto in 1759. He remained "one of our *famuli*" to his death, May 24, 1789; Kuntz, XII, p 117. That same year at Ciorani died Brother Giuseppe Sereno, aged sixty-five. "Of this Brother we know nothing," *ibid.*
137. Kuntz, XII, pp 117ff.
138. Kuntz, VI, p 398.
139. Vertucci himself gave evidence of his former naughtiness, *cf.* 1806 Process, *Summarium* 31 with extracts from earlier local hearings, *Juxta* 29, fol. 1812, p 688.
140. *Egrr.* 1796, *Positio, Summarium* 8, *Ex Proc. Apost. Nucerino,* Juxta 10, fol. 375, p 74, and 1806 Process, *Catalogus Testium,* p 4. Alessio was not the first houseman to be translated into a Brother. In June 1767, Nicolo Rocca who "has been a servant of the Congregation for six years" was allowed by Villani to receive the habit; Alphonsus to Villani, June 1767. It would seem that he then went on doing just those jobs about the house that he had been doing those six years. And being treated by the Fathers, doubtless, in just the way they had been treating him.
141. Francesc' Antonio Romito's testimony, 1806 Process, *Summarium* 34, "*De obitu,*" *super* 357 *art.*, fol. 1654, p 738.
142. Kuntz, VI, p 412: "*in famulum sibi elegit optimum adolescentem annorum circiter vinginti. Ipse remansit semper ejus famulatus adelictus.*"
143. Kuntz, V, p 387.
144. Savastano also survived to testify; "*Io entrai a servire, come dissi, in qualita di Garzone di Cucina,*" 1806 Process, *Summarium* 31, Juxta 29, fol. 1805, p 690.
145. *Theologia Moralis, Lib* .II, *cap.* iii, *art.* iii, Gaude, 63, 64, 66, 68 and 78, and *Lib.* IV, *cap.* iii, *dub.* vi, Gaude 256.
146. Tannoia, *Vita,* III, viii, p 36.
147. Pollio testimony, 1806 Process, *Summarium* 11, *super* 41 *art.*, fol. 427, p 172, and *super* 169, p 201.
148. Tannoia, *Vita,* II, vi, p 96.
149. Pollio testimony, 1806 Process, *Summarium* 30, *super* 309 *art.*, fol. 550, p 647; Tannoia, IV, xxxi, p 163 and xxxiii, p 172.
150. Pollio testimony, *ibid.*, *Summarium* 25, *super* 267 *art.*, fol 524, p 571.
151. *Meditazioni per otto giorni nell'ottava del SS Sacramento,* Med. I, *Opere ascet.*, IV, p 437; Meditations for the Octave of Corpus Christi, I, in *Holy Eucharist,* Grimm, p 212.
152. Pollio testimony, 1806 Process, *Summarium* 16, *super* 122 *art.*, fol. 457, p 343, Pollio testimony, *ibid.*, *Summarium* 22, p 523; *ibid.*, *Summarium* 16, p 342.
153. *Visite al SS Sacramento,* 1745(?), VI; *Visits,* p 140.
154. *Visits to the Blessed Sacrament,* Intro. I.
155. *Preparation for Death,* xxxiv, 3; *Practice of the Love of God,* Intro. ll.ii. Alphonsus is probably the first person in Europe to be writing down the story in any

vernacular language, though Sarnelli may have pointed him towards the narrative in HRE Karl IV's *Vita* of Saint Wenceslas, *vid. Il Mondo Riformato, Pte.* II, para. 4, *Opere,* Naples, vol II, p 49.

156. *Visits,* Intro., Grimm, p 116.

Persevering to Good Deaths

1. Kuntz, I, p 49. Falcoia to Alphonsus, July 11 and August 15, 1735, *Lettere,* Nos. 120 and 122.
2. Falcoia, *Lettere,* no. 122.
3. Kuntz, II, 1741–1745, pp 8, 18f, and 334; VIII, 1768–1774, pp 304f.
4. *Compendio della Vita del Servo di Dio P. Gennaro Maria Sarnelli,* with *Brevi Notizie della Vita di Fr. Vito Curzio,* 1752, and *Brevi notizie della vita del Rev. P. D. Paolo Cafaro,* 1766.
5. Alphonsus to Fathers and Brothers, July 29, 1774.
6. Alphonsus to d'Iliceto novices, January 28, 1762; *cf.* to Fathers and Brothers, August 8, 1754, August 13, 1758, and July 29, 1774, and to Pope Pius VI, June 1781.
7. Alphonsus to Fathers and Brothers, August 13, 1758.
8. *Ibid.*
9. Califano died immediately after being readmitted by Villani; *cf.* De Risio, A., *Cronache della Cong. SS Redentore,* Palermo, 1858, pp 365f.
10. Alphonsus to Fathers and Brothers, July 1774.
11. Kuntz, II, p 247, *cf.* Raponi, S., "*I Fratelli laici,*" p 48.
12. Kuntz, II, p 246.
13. Kuntz, III, p 66.
14. *Atti del Capitolo Generale dell'Anno 1785, Pte.* II, *cap.* I, *para.* I, No. 162.
15. *Ibid.,* Nos. 159 and 160.
16. Pollio testimony at Nucera-Pagani preliminary hearings, Juxta 33, fol. 406, in 1806 Process, *Summarium* 34, p 727.
17. Romito testimony, 1806, *Summarium* 34, *super* 361 *art.,* fol 1656, p 739.
18. Pollio testimony, 1806 Process, *Summarium,* 34, Juxta 33, fol. 406, p 729.
19. *Ibid.* Everything seems to have been nicely arranged by this time. The Consultor, Nicol Mansione, thought it proper to speak only of "a most placid agony worthy of one of the just"; 1806 Process, *Summarium* 34, Juxta 33, fol. 1780, p 740.
20. Tannoia, *Vita,* IV, xxxvi, p 191.
21. *Ibid.,* p 193.
22. *Ibid.,* p 187.
23. Pollio testimony, 1806 Process, *Summarium* 34, *Juxta* 33, fol. 406, p 727; Tannoia, *Vita,* IV, xxxvi, p 197.
24. Tannoia, *Vita,* IV, xxxii, p 167.
25. Pollio testimony, 1806 Process, *Summarium* 34, *super* 357, fol. 1654, p 738. Alessio is particular in noting that Alphonsus "used the form in the *Pontificale* that Bishops use."

26. Tannoia, *Vita,* xxxviii, p 204.
27. Tellería, R., *San Alphonso,* vol. II, p 714.
28. Alphonsus to Giuseppe Melchionna, 1733–1803, nephew of Girolamo Ferrara, March 31, 1765.
29. *Vid. L'Amore delle Anime;* Reflections and Affections on the Passion, p 136.
30. Alphonsus to Fathers and Brothers, August 13, 1758.
31. XV *Visit to the Blessed Sacrament; Holy Eucharist,* p 161.
32. *IV Cap. Gen. 1793, Constituzioni, Pte. Seconda, cap.* III.6.
33. *Atti,* IV Cap. Gen., 277. The others were Leonardo Cicchetti, Rafaele Daniele, Teodosio Flumeri, Michele Guarrasio, 1723?–1798, Saverio D'Auria, 1734(?)–1824, and Matteo D'Ancora, 1735–1824.
34. Kuntz, XVI, pp 260f.
35. *Ibid.*, p 259.
36. *Ibid.*, p 262.
37. *Ibid.*, p 259.
38. *Ibid.*, p 262.
39. *Ibid.*, XVII, p 262.
40. While Alessio refers consistently to "our Congregation" and "the Fathers of my Congregation," *egrr.*, 1796 *Positio, Summarium* 14, *super* 157, fol 1218, p 191, and *et al. pl.,* this is not a usage which is wholly reciprocated, egrr., at the testimony givings of Fathers Giovan Battista de Costanzo and Vincenzo Magaldi, 1749—after 1797 when he left the Congregation.
41. *Theologia Moralis, Lib.* VI, *Tract. V, cap.* ii, "On the Sacrament of Orders," *dub.* i, Gaude, 771 and 780.
42. Opening statement to the Auditors at the preliminary *Positio* hearings, on May 27, 1797. Kuntz, XVI, p 263 records his making the same statement at the Pagani Process, June 20, 1788.
43. *Cf.* the consistent account of Francesc' Antonio, 1806 Process, *Summarium* 34, p 738.
44. At the 1796 hearings, Francesc' Antonio usually figured in the Fathers' testimonies as "*suo compagno,*" in 1806, he was generally "*VSD Socius*"; In both 1796 and 1806, Alessio is either "*suo Servitore*" or "*famulus VSD.*"
45. Pollio testimony, e.g., 1806 Process, *Summarium* 34, *super* 357, fol. 1654, p 738.
46. *Novena del Santo Natale,* discorso III, p 42; *Christmas Novena,* III.l, p 50.
47. *Ibid., discorso* V, *Opere ascet.* IV, p 150; *Festival of Christmas,* Meditation XII, January 5, p 266.
48. Pollio testimony, 1806 Process, *Summarium* 23, "*de Heroica VSD Paupertate,*" *super* 319, fol. 1643, p 539; *Summarium* 15, Juxta 26: "*una vita poverta e laboriosa,*" "*rinunciando...a richezze, onori, e commodi,*" "*vesti l'abito ecclesiastico,*" "*in perfetta rassegnazione.*"
49. Tannoia, *Vita,* III, xv, p 69.

50. Cardinal Giovanni Archinto was appointed *Ponens* of the beatification cause in 1794, six years after the Fathers had started collecting their evidences, but still before the canonical ten-year interval from death to the start of any investigative process had elapsed. On September 20, 1797, he was able to report that no cult was being given to the Venerable *famulus* of God.
51. Tannoia, *Vita,* IV, ii, p 11.
52. Kuntz, XVI, p 262.
53. *Ibid.*
54. *Visits* XX, p 174.
55. There was general agreement that, on death, Alphonsus had exhibited "*un certo giocundo riso,*" that he had become "*riboconde*" and that, as Francesc' Antonio put it, it seemed that there was a new liveliness in his countenance, "*colle faccia rubiconda,*" 1806 Process, *Summarium* 34, para. 47, "he was smiling to the picture of most holy Mary."
56. "*Cirasiello*" is a Neapolitan dialect version of "*ciliegiuolo,*" cherry-colored; Tellería, R., "*Alexius Pollio S. Alfonsi Episcopi Servus mox in Eiusdem Congregatione Frater ac Filius,*" S.H., X, 1962, pp 256–268, guesses that "*Cirasiello*" is a dialect form used of one to whom petitions are addressed, note 38. They would have to be rather informal petitions. That would be possible at Alessio's dying moment. But I rather suppose that Neapolitans generally are employing a usage of romantic love related to that parodied by Shakespeare in *A Mid-Summer Night's Dream*, III.2.139f, and V.l.317f:

    O how ripe in show
    Thy lips, those kissing cherries, tempting grow.

Index